STATE AND CULTURE IN POSTCOLONIAL AFRICA

AFRICAN EXPRESSIVE CULTURES

STATE AND CULTURE IN POSTCOLONIAL AFRICA

Enchantings

Edited by Tejumola Olaniyan

Indiana University Press

This book is a publication of

Indiana University Press
Office of Scholarly Publishing
Herman B Wells Library 350
1320 East 10th Street
Bloomington, Indiana 47405 USA

iupress.indiana.edu

The paper used in this publication meets the minimum requirements of the American National Standard for Information Sciences—Permanence of Paper for Printed Library Materials, ANSI Z39.48-1992.

Manufactured in the United States of America

Library of Congress Cataloging-in-Publication Data

Names: Olaniyan, Tejumola, editor, author.
Title: State and culture in postcolonial Africa : enchantings / edited by Tejumola Olaniyan.
Description: Bloomington : Indiana University Press, 2017. | Includes bibliographical references and index.
Identifiers: LCCN 2017022483 (print) | LCCN 2017022916 (ebook) | ISBN 9780253030177 (e-book) | ISBN 9780253029713 (cloth : alk. paper) | ISBN 9780253029980 (pbk. : alk. paper)
Subjects: LCSH: Art and state—Africa. | Africa—Cultural policy. | Africa—Civilization—21st century. | Africa—Social conditions—21st century.
Classification: LCC DT14 (ebook) | LCC DT14 .S73 2017 (print) | DDC 960.33—dc23
LC record available at https://lccn.loc.gov/2017022483

1 2 3 4 5 22 21 20 19 18 17

Contents

Acknowledgments

State and culture in Postcolonial Africa: Enchantings emerged from my time as senior fellow in the Institute for Research in the Humanities (IRH) at the University of Wisconsin, Madison. My deep gratitude to the Institute and its director, Susan S. Friedman, for providing an ideal context for imagining and executing high-level and innovative cross-disciplinary research in the humanities. Scholars across disciplines, and practicing professionals too, responded enthusiastically to my Burdick-Vary symposium call to subject one key institution—the state in postcolonial Africa—to a robust critical examination. We were all richly rewarded. My thanks to them, as well as to the dedicated staff who ran the event so well: Ann W. Harris, Spring Sherrod, Scott A. Carter, Heather DuBois Bourenane, and Valerie McLaurin. Support also came from other units such as African Studies Program, International Institute, Global Studies, Music-Race-Empire Research Circle, African Diaspora and the Atlantic World Research Circle, School of Journalism, Department of African Languages and Literature (now African Cultural Studies), Department of English, and the Louise Durham Mead professorship fund. Finally, my gratitude to Dee Mortensen, my editor at Indiana University Press, and her band of dedicated staff.

STATE AND CULTURE IN POSTCOLONIAL AFRICA

Introduction

State and Culture in Africa: The Possibilities of Strangeness

Tejumola Olaniyan

This book examines the broad and multisided interactions of contemporary African cultural forms and practices, and the postcolonial African state that is their generative canvas. Given the distinctive worldliness and immersive political references embodied in these cultural forms and practices, scholars have long felt the need to study them in the light of state structures and processes.[1] This is a classic instance in which thinking across conventional disciplinary divides is more obviously and meaningfully demanded by the reality on the ground than by fanciful academic debates on campus. There is no comparable demand, however, on the study of politics in Africa to understand the cultural forms and practices that constitute the foundation of political meanings and negotiations—in short, of legitimacy.[2] Overall, the bonds and rewards of disciplinary work are still overly tight and alluring, even if this has meant less than robust attention to our objects of study. According to the logic of our structures of training, accomplished political scientists and philosophers are not expected to be so skilled in cultural criticism, while expert cultural critics can get by with the obvious basic gestures to the political domain. This is not a condemnation of disciplinary training and work—they are and should still be foundational, given the increasing volume of information and complexity of forms, structures, and processes that we study. Very clearly, disciplinary mastery is a solid basis for meaningful interdisciplinary work.

For now, the more pragmatic and achievable plea is for a reasonable effort beyond the normative disciplinary call of duty toward the admittedly harder work of broadminded listening and unassuming but focused analytical *curiosity*.[3] Charged with this ethics of attention, the contributors to this book, from across disciplines in the humanities and social sciences, critically examine large and small consequential conjunctures of the postcolonial state and culture in Africa and their compound effects.

The rhetoric of "crisis" of the state in Africa that dominated the last four decades has lowered a few notches in decibel.[4] That, however, does not seem to be because the crisis has abated but because it has become normative and complex, and has overwhelmed the rhetoric beyond its explanatory capacity. "Crisis" seems to have been replaced of recent by a less declaratively pessimistic but only more ominously hopeful term, "fragility," as seen in the enormous influence in social science circles of *The Fragile States Index* published by the research organization Fund for Peace (FFP).[5] The *Index* annually ranks countries based on how stable they are and the key political, social, and economic pressures they face. Each country is then gorgeously color-coded on a world map on a scale from "sustainable" green to "moderate" yellow, "warning" orange to "alert" red. In a color scale refinement for the 2015 edition, the *Index* adds blue to the most desirable "sustainable" end of the spectrum, while demoting green to a middling "stable"; the "warning" spectrum is now yellow to orange, and red, in all its shades, is still for "alert." Not a single state in Africa is blue or green; the majority is red, and only South Africa is demonstrably yellow. In the ten years of the *Index*, from 2006 to 2015, not a single African state has been colored green; virtually all range from orange to red. Like "crisis," "fragility" is obviously rapidly becoming the norm and normative too.

From crisis to fragility, it is clear that the problematic of the postcolonial state in Africa is not just sociopolitical and economic, measurable in statistical figures of free and fair elections and growth in gross domestic product, but also epistemological, reckonable in the quality of knowledge about the structure of rule by state actors, scholars, professionals, and the general public, and the degree to which that knowledge engenders flexible and responsive state-citizen relations, policy recommendations and actions, and reasonable management oversight of competing interests. This epistemological realm is not one of data alone but foundationally of the vaster context of what constitutes data, what is its purpose, its many meanings, and its many possible paths from gathering, interpretation, and analysis to application and by whom and under which structure. This is the realm of culture writ large. This book is conceived in part as a contribution to the advancement of the much-needed epistemological task.[6]

The Productive State

The state, as a set of institutions comprising a supreme corporate entity and holding a monopoly in the exercise of coercion within a sovereign, geographically bounded territory, is no more than half a century old in Africa. It emerged in the 1950s with the wave of independence from colonial rule that swept the continent. The states vary in operational micro-details from one region or country to another and over stretches of time but they nonetheless all share a fundamental compound nature: an ancestry in the colonial state rather than in any autonomous evolution of indigenous histories; an inverted development in which the state structure and authority—coercively imposed by foreigners—preceded the nation conceived as an imagined community with more than less shared cultural traditions and worldview; official languages of governance and bureaucracy that are alien and alienating to a majority of the population; and formal institutions—political, juridical, economic, bureaucratic—with an unyielding extraverted mentality.[7] These, then, are the distinguishing features of postcolonial African states. They are the sources of much of its public image in the world today: authoritarian, corrupt, and unstable; and master fabricator of epochal and especially gendered inequalities, imponderable bureaucracy, endless awakenings or transitions to democracy, civil wars and antistate rebellions, recurrent refugee crises, and an epidemic of reverse expectations.[8] It is for the reason of this public image that, half a century after, the rhetorical bandwidth of the African state in discourse is no wider than the narrow orbit between crisis and fragility. In the reality of most people's experience of the state, those are two words for the same thing: the unproductive character of the postcolonial state. Though rarely remembered as such, the earliest and most profound articulation of that unproductivity is by the Martinican psychiatrist and theorist of the anticolonial revolution, Frantz Fanon.

In *The Wretched of the Earth*, published in the heat of the anticolonial struggle in the late 1950s, Fanon warns of a yawning gap of reverse expectations in the emerging new nations, given the dubious practical and ideological character of the nationalist leaders, the managers of the new kind of state. He mercilessly excoriates them as fake "bourgeoisie" characterized by "intellectual laziness," "spiritual penury," an "absence of . . . ambition," and a gross "incapacity" to "fulfill [the] historic role of the bourgeoisie."[9] In this class, Fanon argues, "the dynamic, pioneer aspect, the characteristics of the inventor and of the discoverer of new worlds" that are found in any bourgeoisie worthy of that name are "lamentably absent." The African bourgeoisie is an unoriginal class that is "not engaged in production, nor in invention, nor building, nor labor; [but] is completely canalyzed into activities of the intermediary type."[10] It is "bankrupt," lacks initiative, and its "mission has nothing to do with transforming the nation" but to be "content with the role of the Western bourgeoisie's business agent."[11]

The larger historical background of Fanon's critique is, of course, Karl Marx's lyrical articulation in *The Communist Manifesto* of that distinctive character of the European bourgeoisie: its productivity. To reread Marx alongside Fanon on this matter is to have a special appreciation of the fury and venom in Fanon's language. Just compare Fanon's plaintive lament with Marx's loquacious panegyric to the manifold accomplishments of the historical European bourgeoisie in imagining a different world and boldly bridging the gap to its realization.

The historical European bourgeoisie, Marx writes, "has been the first to show what man's activity can bring about. It has accomplished wonders far surpassing Egyptian pyramids, Roman aqueducts, and Gothic cathedrals; it has conducted expeditions that put in the shade all former Exoduses of nations and crusades. . . . [It] has created more massive and more colossal productive forces than have all preceding generations together. Subjection of Nature's forces to man, machinery, application of chemistry to industry and agriculture, steam-navigation, railways, electric telegraphs, clearing of whole continents for cultivation, canalization of rivers, whole populations conjured out of the ground." In a justified grandiose rhetorical flourish, Marx asks, "What earlier century had even a presentiment that such productive forces slumber in the lap of social labour?"[12] And I think we can only answer, None, Mr. Marx, none.

Fanon fixates on the unproductivity of the African bourgeoisie, but there is a related side that he overlooks: the gaudy consumption of that class. The accomplished Senegalese filmmaker and novelist Sembène Ousmane would later dramatize this squarely in *Xala*, both the novel and the film, released in the early 1970s. The African bourgeoisie is not just unproductive (i.e., stricken with impotence—*xala* in Sembène's Wolof language), but is an unproductive consumer. Sembène adroitly uses heterosexual impotence to symbolically figure the political, economic, social, and moral vapidity of the class, and in the process opens up a powerful feminist critique. After all, that African bourgeois class, though it is not unique in this, is male-dominated and masculinist, and the group of people who suffer the most from its unproductive consumerism is women. The apogee of this line of cogent extension of Fanon in African social and cultural criticism is, without question, the classic novel *Devil on the Cross* (1980) by Ngũgĩ wa Thiong'o.

Adversarial Contexts and Productive Creativity

The foregoing are truly prohibitive circumstances. But the state's unproductivity is a tad overstated. Its tenor is primarily socioeconomic and socioscientific. It overlooks how the socioeconomic failings are experienced, made sense of, resourcefully articulated, and mass disseminated in a variety of small and big, fleeting and settled, and quotidian and extraordinary social and cultural forms and practices. This is productivity, too, and it is substantive. The repressive character of African states has produced thriving literary and performance forms such as antidictatorship literature, theater for development, and writers' prison diaries. In the other arts, we find engaged cartooning, militant music, and guerilla journalism. There are also practices such as voluntary community and civic associations and microcredit unions, and urban garrison architecture, just to name a few. These all arose in response to the peculiarities of unresponsive postcolonial states and their failed promises of rapid modernization made on independence.

Take African literature, for instance. Its pervasive macropolitical content is world famous. Independence from colonial rule was barely achieved when powerful literary representations of systemic disjunctions between the people and the new states began to emerge: Tawfik al-Hakim's *Maze of Justice: Diary of a Country Prosecutor* (1937), Peter Abrahams's *A Wreath for Udomo* (1956), Chinua Achebe's *A Man of the People* (1966), Wole Soyinka's *Kongi's Harvest* (1967), and Ayi Kwei Armah's *The Beautyful Ones Are Not Yet Born* (1968)—the list is too long. The disjunctions raised several questions, especially formal and epistemological, about the nature of the new postcolonial state: the strangeness of its structure, the systemic ease with which its rules are disregarded with impunity especially by those who rule, its alien and alienating language, its overtly vulgar class character, its enthronement of money as the solvent of all values (in newly and unevenly monetized societies), its imponderable bureaucracy, its radically different codes of access to personal fulfillment and participation in the public realm—not with hard work and integrity but simply money, some smattering of Western education and, later on, possession of weapons of coercion. The literature, in short, proclaims the illegitimacy of the new state and its authority. While the new states were fashioning grandiose five- and ten-year development plans, African writers were insisting that the mighty feet of the elephant of independence were mere clay. And many of the writers were handsomely rewarded for their clairvoyance—with exile, imprisonment with or without torture and solitary confinement, and even death. Ruth First, Soyinka, Assia Djebar, Ngũgĩ, Breyten Breytenbach, Alex La Guma, Ken Saro Wiwa, Abdilatif Abdalla, Abdellatif Laâbi, Dennis Brutus, Nawal El Saadawi, Tahar Djaout—these writers cover all regions of the continent. This is the origin of that uniquely postcolonial African literary genre known as the writer's prison diary—not literally a diary, but an account of imprisonment by writers jailed because of their writings or related activist work. A few lucky writers such as Léopold Sédar Senghor of Senegal and Agostinho Neto of Angola actually got to the palace of political power and took over presidential thrones.

I acknowledge here just one strand of the other side of the postcolonial state: its immense productivity as catalyst of the creative imagination.[13] *That* productivity demands integrated consideration with the socioeconomic and political failures as a prerequisite both for a fuller understanding of the state as such, and for effective mobilization of reformative energies. This is not an instance of the common saying, necessity is the mother of invention. No one, after all, pleads for adverse necessities so as to enjoy the joy of inventions. The productivity of the African state is to be understood in the more chastening intertwined sense of (a) what low quality of inventions the state expects of its citizens by the fact of the primal, basic-level quality of challenges it imposed, and (b) what high quality of inventions could and would have been possible with much higher, more complex, and metalevel challenges that only a functioning state can engender. No one can give both descriptive and conceptual language to this complicated, very capacious picture of the productivity of the postcolonial state in Africa better than Soyinka:

> In a statement I made last year I referred to my generation as the wasted generation and I was thinking in terms of all fields, not just the literary: the technological talents that we have which are not being used; but I also had in mind our writers of course, the fact that a lot of our energy has really been devoted to coping with the oppressive political situation in which we find ourselves. A lot of our energies go into fighting unacceptable situations as they arise while at the same time trying to pursue a long-term approach to politics such as, for instance, joining progressive-looking political parties, but of course each step is always one step forwards and about ten backwards. I find the political situation very, very frustrating, personally frustrating. I mean, forget even the amount of let us say personal work one could have done, writing and so on, and just think in terms of the amount of time one could have spent on training, in theatre for instance, would-be actors, or devoting more time to would-be writers, many of whom are constantly inundating one with cries for help; the qualitatively different kind of creative community atmosphere, structures that one would really love to give more time to . . . I know, very definitely, that I feel a great sense of deprivation in terms of what I could have contributed to the general productive atmosphere of the country in literary terms and I'm sure a lot of other writers feel the same. That is one of the penalties of the political situation we've been undergoing since independence and which has got progressively worse, progressively more lethal. The penalties for the wrong kind of political action in this situation have become far more depressing.[14]

Agency is always at the junction of constraints and possibilities—we make the world after all, but never under the conditions of our choosing. Soyinka here simultaneously affirms and laments the yield, but also the constraints that are constitutively degraded—"unacceptable situations" of "one step forwards and about ten backwards"—in their catalytic power to challenge the polity's productive imagination at a higher level.

Soyinka's reading of the productivity of the postcolonial African state here is pragmatist in emphasis. I identify two more or less dominant conceptual reading orientations out there across the social sciences and the humanities: the pragmatist and the foundationalist. The pragmatist critique affirms the legality and authenticity of where the African state is here and now and insists that it could do much better by learning from its mistakes as well as from successful examples worldwide, and by bringing uncorrupted reason and commitment to bear on the business of government. It foregrounds the necessity for managers of people and resources to be of unimpeachable character, and avows that the soul of any institution is people of integrity. For the pragmatist, there is no human institution, no matter its wayward origins, that is untamable in a direction deemed proper after reasonable and critical analysis. Behind this claim is a fierce belief in the endless capacity of individuals to make a difference in society; after all, the only truly dynamic factor in politics is the individual person. This mode of critique is the pervasive dominant among African writers and intellectuals, and also scholars of Africa. In addition to Soyinka, other leading writers whose works express the pragmatist view include Achebe, Nurrudin Farah, Abrahams, Athol Fugard, and Tsitsi Dangarembga, to cite only a few examples. This is also the reigning position in the social sciences, and has been so since the wave of independence in the 1960s.[15]

The foundationalist critique argues that the origin of the contemporary African state in the dictatorial colonial state compromises it so much that without a thorough-going decolonization of the instruments and procedures of rule, the African state would not be able to resolve its crisis of legitimacy. For the foundationalist, the problem is at the foundations; in other words, the problem is structural or systemic. While conscientious individuals are certainly needed to run institutions, the foundationalist holds that no amount of moral suasion would keep large numbers of people upright when placed within circumstances that sneer at or even punish uprightness. Bad management of human and material resources, says the foundationalist, is not the root of the problem, but a mere symptom. What can the best and most honest of men and women do running a bureaucracy that speaks a language that a majority of the population it is managing cannot understand? Some of the writers for whom only a foundationalist critique of the state would suffice include Sembène, Ngũgĩ, and Armah. Also, significant social science literature on the state in the last few decades has been focusing on foundations, after what Patrick Chabal laments as "paradigms lost."[16]

There is a stimulating lesson to be learned in doing here what is rarely done: substantively engage the same thematic concern across disciplines. For that purpose, we can hardly do better than stage a comparison between Soyinka's classic pragmatist critique in his important book *The Open Sore of a Continent: A Personal Narrative of the Nigerian Crisis*, published in 1996, and Mahmood Mamdani's foundationalist emphasis in his equally significant book *Citizen and Subject: Contemporary Africa and the Legacy of Late Colonialism*, published in the same year.[17]

There is a critical supplementary relationship between the two books. While Soyinka analytically dissects a contemporary instance of the "crisis" of an African state, Mamdani's wide-ranging historicization shows how that crisis came about, how it could not have been otherwise. With perspicacious insight, Soyinka shows how the evil genie of tyranny, once unbottled, perpetuates itself and is perpetuated remorselessly even under different circumstances. Mamdani gives us a persuasive account of the historical—specifically colonial—origins of the evil specter; an account of "where the rain began to beat us," as Achebe once evocatively put it.[18] There is even a similar supplementarity in the respective prose styles of the two writers: Mamdani's is the clinical, sedate prose of the scholarly social scientist; his sentences are rarely more than four lines long. What we get from the irrepressible dramatist and novelist Soyinka is a near-average of seven lines per sentence, with not a few sentences running to twelve lines: a cascading, torrential prose of the embattled humanist and activist right in the thick and thin of the struggle at the moment.

To say that a logic of supplementarity connects the two books is also to say that the books are different in substantive ways. Effectively two of the three chapters of Soyinka's book are devoted to meticulous interrogations of the nation-state form. Nigeria provides the specific point of departure, interspersed with theoretical reflections on general issues such as "nationhood" and "nation-making," the nation and its boundaries, the nation and its constituent human groups, the nation and the state and their relations, national belonging and its modes, and the national will—the modes of its determination and elaboration, and consequences of its conservation or subversion by which groups and to what purpose. In all the observations and analyses, Soyinka is the clear-eyed pragmatist, keenly aware of the weak foundational structures of the nation called Nigeria, whether of awkward boundaries, unseemly mixture of different ethnicities, or a score of other forms of colonial gerrymandering, but at the same time deeply affirmative that those weaknesses are not—and ought not to automatically be—enough unmanageable reasons for the edifice to collapse. With patriotic vision, the type that transparently promotes the mutual interests of all the constituent groups within the nation space, Soyinka suggests, it is actually possible to survive the affliction of rickety foundations. This is the polemical pragmatism that subtends the title Soyinka gives to chapter 1: "A Flawed Origin—But No Worse Than Others," meaning that though the origin of the entity called Nigeria is defective, it is not thereby irredeemable.

Mamdani would certainly agree with that, though from a different perspective, for he is more interested in the contours of that form of rule specifically programmed to, among other things, engender endless animosities among the constituent groups within the nation space. This difference is quite significant. For Mamdani, the major legacy of colonial rule that has continued to impede democratic initiatives in Africa is the entrenchment of what he calls the "bifurcated state." By this he means colonial rule through ethnically organized Native Authorities (NAs) enforcing "customary law" in the rural areas; and through a racially based supervisory central state in the urban centers. The NAs speak the language of custom as defined and enforced by the colonizers, while the central state speaks the language of civil society. Africans under the NAs were "subjects" under oppressive local "overseer" states, while their entrance into civil society where they could be "citizens" was jealously guarded by colonial racialism and racism. At independence, the major reform carried out by the victorious nationalists was the Africanization or deracialization of the central state, while there was very little corresponding dismantling or "detribalization" of the NAs, much less the establishment of a noncoercive way of linking the rural and the urban. This, argues Mamdani, was ultimately the result, whether we are talking of "mainstream nationalists" who came to power through multiparty elections, or "radical nationalists" who adopted the single-party in order to detribalize the NAs.[19] The result was "decentralized despotism" in one and "centralized despotism" in the other.

In his book, Soyinka rails against what he calls the "spoils of office," which is transitory and position-based, and the "spoils of power," which is permanent and group- or ethnic-based.[20] Mamdani's submission is that the entrenchment of these spoils could hardly have been otherwise for two reasons: (1) because "civil society politics where the rural is governed through customary authority is necessarily patrimonial: urban politicians harness rural constituencies through patron-client relations"; and (2) because the tribalized and undemocratized NAs, through the economy of the patron-client relations, can only infect the deracialized civil society in the urban with its tribalism, which is why the nationalist deracialization of the central state on independence, in nearly all cases, wore an ethnic face.[21]

The lesson of all this is, of course, that a system of electoral politics alone does not guarantee democracy. In fact, it had in many cases been what the late distinguished Nigerian political scientist Claude Ake called it: the "democratization of disempowerment."[22] And specifically within the context of unreformed bifurcated power structure, electoral politics can only produce interethnic, interreligious, and other kinds of factional struggles and terrorisms that provide the ideal thriving ground for the politics of clientelism. Soyinka's book is a passionate attack on the venal and ethnic and religious character of this clientelism, while Mamdani's attention is on the embedded structures of the postcolonial state—and their historical origins—that by commission or omission were designed to produce none other than clientelism. This returns us, then, to Soyinka's polemical title: "a flawed origin—but no worse than others." Mamdani's foundationalist answer would be that a flawed origin cannot be so easily dismissed; that the implied meaning that Nigeria could do better even with flawed origins may be somewhat far-fetched; that other African countries that share similarly flawed origins are not necessarily doing better in democratic governance; that the question may be not so much being worse off than others as the historic challenge today of being better; and finally, that there may be no real movement forward in democratization, no matter who wins elections, without our returning to revise that primal origin of colonially implanted impediments to democratization.

Friend, Enemy, *Stranger*

The differences and similarities between the pragmatist and foundationalist critiques of the African state are meaningful. They carry consequential policy implications, though they are more of contingent emphases than absolute directions. For my purposes here, their significance is not to be sought in what we might judge to be their comparative strengths or limitations, tempting as that might seem. Their significance is to be located elsewhere: their equally moving heroic effort aimed at no less than taming Africa's one particular share of modernity, that historical aggressive Western imposition on Africa through the main organ of its rule, the modern state.[23] If the history of the state in Africa makes the state so unusually peculiar to those over which it rules, to tame it is to calm it, to master it, to make amenable the unusually peculiar. To tame successfully demands that what is to be tamed is readable within the hermeneutic horizon of the tamer. What is to be tamed must be known and digestible within that most elementary but fundamental form of understanding—friend or enemy, good or evil, and similar oppositions. The significance of these simple oppositions in ordering relationships, knowledge, and action is underscored by the distinguished sociologist Zygmunt Bauman, when he theorizes that "we may say that friendship and enmity, and only they, are forms of sociation; indeed the archetypal forms of all sociation," and that between them, "they make the frame within which sociation is possible, they make for the possibility of 'being with others.'"[24]

The distance between friend and enemy is not as important as their mutual self-recognition, which is comforting, paradoxical as that might sound. They may be in hierarchical relationship but are also bonded by their mutual self-(re)production. "Being a friend, and being an enemy," Bauman writes, "are the two forms in which the other may be recognized as another subject, construed as a subject 'like the self,' admitted into the self's life world, be counted, become and stay relevant."[25] So, friends and enemies are on the same terrain of the known and decidable, but how do modernity and the state form it generated in Africa fit into this framework of sociation? At a most oddly acute angle, I must say. The oddness holds certain immense possibilities but within a deep, circuitous thicket of incapacitating equivocations and ambiguities. I have elsewhere characterized this multifaced, simultaneously threatening and promising undecidable nature of modernity and the state in Africa as *enchanting*: an aporetic situation in which a modernity, forcefully imposed and inevitable, is railed at as an alien, oppressive, and bewitching illusion (a *dis*enchantment), and simultaneously hailed as a desirable and a catalyst for further striving (a *re*enchantment). Bauman's term for this enchanter is the "stranger," a figure that short-circuits the (discord-ridden, tension-soaked, yes, yes, but also fundamentally psychically comforting) friend-enemy economy, and disperses the protocols of recognition that sustain their opposition and coherent meaning-generation capacity. I quote Bauman:

> Against this cosy antagonism, this conflict-torn collusion of friends and enemies, the stranger rebels. The threat he carries is more awesome than that which one can fear from the enemy. . . . And all this because the stranger is neither friend nor enemy; and because he may be both. And because we do not know, and have no way of knowing, which is the case.[26]

The stranger thus poses the greatest challenge to taming. Attempts to tame the stranger will have to be prepared to accommodate inadequacies, wobbly edges, and bursting seams that inevitably result. Taming a stranger, a stranger that may be friend or foe, is thus bound to leave a trail of paradoxes, contradictions, and, more precisely, antinomies. But it is nevertheless what we do and must do continuously, the endless horizon of humanity's inescapable task in self-civilizing.

The postcolonial state in Africa is not a friend. It is not considered so by the majority of those it rules over, given its history and apparent unproductivity so far. Even the minority that has corruptly benefited from it is not saved the high anxiety of the state's instability and inconstancy. So, what is the state in Africa if not a friend? I insist that the state is not an enemy and it is not to be conceived as such. In postcolonial Africa, the idea of the state as enemy is more self-defeating in the illusion it sells of a possible permanent nonengagement with the state. There is no going out of the state today; only academicists, themselves safely ensconced in functioning states, still argue against this reality in talking about states elsewhere. In many ways, the state in Africa is very familiar. It is familiar in tangled inchoate different ways to different groups, from those who benefit plenty from it, to the deprived many whose benefit is having mastered an arsenal of stratagems to fitfully dodge the state. This is a key problem; whether they know it or not, both groups are losers, just unequally.

Aligning disparate understandings of the state, achievable only by measurable coherent and impartial state performance across the board, is the urgent task today. Toward realizing that goal, I propose a neutral, unprejudiced starting ground. The postcolonial state is a stranger and it is more usefully conceived and related to as such. Just consider again a few of its constitutive features. It is not foundational in the sense of arising out of the autonomous evolution of indigenous histories, but it is inevitable and indispensable. It is dominant in the sense that (all the wobbliness and fragmentation considered) it is the largest source of coercive authority, but it is nonetheless also the most nonhegemonic authority structure on the continent in its commanding so little affect or moral authority. Even so, its potential to be a most skillful and intensive articulator of vast resources, differences, and interests over vast territories—beyond what any ancient polity ever achieved—is so clearly evident, so indubitable, and still so much sought after. No other authority structure comes even close in potential. If Africans today seemed to be concerned more about matters of state than of nation or nationality/ethnicity—many scholars are still very deaf to this shift, still clutching to their old rusty but comforting tool of ethnicity, or worse, "tribalism"—it is for the clear reason of the evident potential of the state form. In any case, the nationality question was, in emergence, evolution, and constitution, a bargaining chip for state resource distribution; its narrow and anthropological horizon has become passé even if not dead.[27]

It is time to come to terms with the stranger, the postcolonial state in Africa. The stranger is seen and known, but is neither friend nor enemy. Such an attitude takes state estrangement as neutral normative, and procedurally demands a valiant suspension of our admittedly justified—because experienced—prior assumptions of state enmity or friendliness in the fulfillment of its obligations and in the staking of claims by citizens. Over the last half-century, such a priori assumptions have burdened our understanding of the postcolonial state and therefore also our efforts to effectively engage and productively reshape it. They have beclouded our efforts to think what freedom, the all-pervasive rallying cry of anticolonial nationalism, might really mean in the postcolonial dispensation. Freedom was once freedom from colonial rule; then it was freedom from neocolonial rule, imperialism, and global capitalism. All the goals are outer-directed, and the postcolonial state automatically assumed guardianship of the goals, more concerned about protecting itself in the name of territorial sovereignty than instituting and expanding citizenship rights.[28] Whether as citizen, scholar, politician, or state agent, to approach the state as a stranger is to foreground and make possible open and equal possibilities for everyone in dealing with the state, on the basis of citizenship as level ground. It is also to expect and make possible equal and appropriate sanction under the law, on the basis of citizenship as level ground. The state ought not to be anybody's enemy or friend, but a stranger—a stranger is structurally and substantively composed, in a chastening way, of the possibilities of both. The state is supposed to be and remain an undomesticatable stranger to all—never mind that the goal of practical politics will always be contentious struggles of diverse groups to exercise state domestication in their own interests—and therefore not easily capturable or monopolizable in an unchallengeable way for any stretch of time by any constituent group. This is the only kind of state that can manage Africa's constitutive diversity and complexity of needs today. And to begin to imagine that new kind of state is to begin to rethink how we study the state.

The state in Africa needs a new wave of scholarly attention, and from all disciplinary perspectives. Surely a key aspect of that project is a far more disciplinarily composite and integrated approach than currently exists. Rather than an either/or, this is a call for interdisciplinary work as well as much closer collaborations among disciplinary specialists. There is an immediate low-hanging fruit and it should be much easier to pick: a reconception of culture that discards its impulsive or tutored separation from politics. Culture is not the realm of literature, art, language, music, religion, and the expressive symbolic generally. It is that and also, simultaneously, the realm of politics—that process by which competing interest groups mobilize, organize, and share resources. The common understanding of culture as a people's more or less distinctive way of life, of the values and practices that organize them and help them make sense of that life, is actually more meaningful than its simplicity has been given credit for. Culture is the entirety of the vast context in which a society produces and reproduces itself. The processes of that are sutured differently and each domain may be identified for heuristic purposes and studied, but the way each is more or less an intimate part of the whole is more significant than its difference. This is more so when the issue under consideration is the very structure of authority or rule whose primary task is to oversee the orderliness of social production and reproduction itself. Culture is the art of making settled, normative, and credible the entire social process as composite, even while contingency and constitutive relentless adaptive change, chosen or coerced, are its key principles of operation.[29] The crisis or fragility of the postcolonial state in Africa has no precedent in the entire precolonial history of Africa. This means that the path to look to for direction is not just the past but also the changed and changing present and conjectured futures. If the state has been so unusually problematic for the past half-century, we can say as interpretive shorthand that it is in large part because it has not become cultural, or cultural enough. Culture is both tool and agent in the management of the strange compromise called society.

The essays gathered here speak to this larger vision of culture and of the postcolonial state itself as a genre of culture. This allows a perspective on the state that is fully aware of its uniquely contingent history but also affirms its invested African agency. This is neither pessimistic nor optimistic—labels are cheap.[30] On the contrary, it enables a conceptually rich accounting of the true dimensions of the living structure of constraints and possibilities here and now in the postcolonial state. The resulting book is simultaneously a fine-tuned cultural criticism that is alert to the social and political underpinnings of contemporary African cultural forms and practices, and a revelatory outline of a cultural biography of the modern state in Africa—that is, the emergence, evolution, and analytical accounts of constitutive strands of the state from its birth in the colonial state through its tumultuous postcolonial life so far, as *seen* or represented by the cultural forms and practices it engendered. The multidirectional exploration affirms the capability of sociocultural forms and practices to yield useful explanatory and analytical categories for understanding sociopolitical processes. It also demonstrates that studying the forms and practices this way contributes substantially to our understanding of the state—after all, to productively understand the state is to understand how the people over whom it rules, across all divides, conceive it. And how the people conceive it is deeply inscribed in their affective productions:

the symbolic cultural forms and social practices they produce, exchange, and consume within and outside the immediate bounds of the state.

I have divided the essays into three broad categories, but that is just one suggestive handle to begin engaging the state-culture problematics they explore. Though the arrangement proceeds from large explorations to specific forms and practices, neither the categories nor the chapters are in any inviolable order. They will reward entrance from any point; forward or backward or from the middle, there are mutually insightful overlaps between and among them. The area coverage is broadly continental, and the disciplinary and topical range are vast, from literature, politics, and philosophy to music, religion, theater, film, television, sports, journalism, city planning, and architecture. The contributors are all accomplished senior and junior scholars as well as practitioners.

The first group of chapters explores foundational intersections of culture and governance and their study. The essays also provide, from the vantage points of different disciplines, usefully overlapping archaeologies of the state. Patrick Chabal, in chapter 1, addresses the contentious issue of culture and politics, assessing dominant conventional approaches and laying out their limitations. "Culture is not merely an additional dimension of politics that requires attention," he argues, but "quite simply one of the fundaments of social life, the matrix within which what we understand as political agency takes place." The field of politics itself, he insists, "has to be examined within its appropriate cultural milieu, as it were." The consummate literary-cultural history of African politics that Niyi Osundare provides in chapter 2 buttresses Chabal's point. Writers are not political scientists or politicians but somehow, knowing African literature alone has been enough to warn anyone of the unwise separation of culture and politics on the continent. "Joined at the hip" is how Osundare describes the intimacy of African literature and the state. Thinking of a systemically healthier affair, though, he wishes they had been joined at the "head," for that would have "made their medical problem more critical and more intimidating, [which] would have ensured the possibility of a common think tank, so to speak, a unified intelligence, a mutual insemination and, possibly, a common purpose." The problematic of "common purpose" is of particularly great importance to philosophy, and Olúfẹ́mi Táíwò, in chapter 3, wonders why the discipline has not figured much in the Africanist discourse on the state, for "the philosophical idea of the state is crucial to the constitution and operation of the state in postindependence Africa." He masterfully redresses that absence, cogently exploring the philosophical assumptions of the idea of the state in modernity, and underscoring the agency of African thinkers in engagement with state discourse as well as the institution of the state.

Needless to say, governance is not all about formally articulated visions and institutional structures of politics. It is also about the governed large masses and the popular realm in which their expressive labors, in work or play, are most immediately manifested. Sport is one such labor, and there is no nitpicking the popular suggestion that soccer is the number one cultivator of national feelings in much of Africa. Surely this is not just a pastime, outside of the state and its many serious businesses. Michael G. Schatzberg sees a "moral structure" in soccer that is largely unstated but "relates to the cultural and political logics of daily life" in many parts of the continent. People value and are invested in the sport and its moral structure, he argues in chapter 4, because of the regularity of rules and fair predictability. There is a meaningful lesson here applicable to the official world outside the soccer pitch, especially on "understanding what is or is not legitimate or thinkable—whether in sport or political life." But content apart, what of the means by which soccer and its moral structure is most widely broadcast to the largest number of people? This is the television, and it plays a most fascinating role in the development of the modern state in Africa. It was the means through which the rituals and protocols of the new state, its symbols, and authority—indeed, its authoritativeness—were and continue to be visualized, shown, to millions as fact, lesson, and vision. The enchantment that moving pictures brought to the colonies is matched only by the showy appurtenances of the new state form itself. Matthew H. Brown studies the Nigerian state television network, the oldest and largest in Africa, mapping its origins from the colonial era to the present, and—just like the state—the many continuities and disjunctions in its structure and function. In chapter 5 he meticulously accounts for the trajectories of an institution and a medium that complicatedly did what it was supposed to do—"[supersede] the colonial broadcasting machine"—but also never strayed much from the function of that machine.

The second group of chapters focuses on the expressive arts. It offers a wide spectrum of the catalytic impact of the state as experienced and creatively transmuted, as well as of the impact of the arts on the state—what the state has become in public consciousness, courtesy of the ways it is named and imaged in the circulated imaginative expressions. The chapters foreground the especially polemical arts such as literature, drama, and theater—they, as related composites, constitute the single most consistent and most sophisticated opposition to the postcolonial state beginning right from its conception in the womb of the colonial state. No other cultural form better exposes postcolonial Africa's "social vulnerability," to use Luís Madureira's haunting phrase as he examines the intricate connections between and among theater, nationalism, state, and citizenship in Mozambique in chapter 6. The explosive September 2010 uprising of the poor in Maputo he evocatively describes left many dead and injured. That was no theater, but it was also not metaphorically far from what theatrical expressions in the country had long imagined, all the contradictoriness of those expressions considered. In that imagination and in the real social uprising itself, we are allowed the hard hope of seeing two locations of social vulnerability in the postcolony:

in the slums teeming with the dominated poor, but so also in the gaudy palace of the unsteady state, as the uprising surprised officialdom and "lay bare the ruling class's vulnerability." An illuminating similar logic is to be found in Névine El Nossery's wide-ranging account of the changing fortunes of women's gendered position in North Africa from pre-Islam to the present. Her particular attention in chapter 7 is on Algeria and Morocco, where gendered social vulnerability is especially harrowing and poignant since anticolonial nationalism's "political instrumentalization of Islam" in the first half of the twentieth century. In the fight against imperialism, that nationalism's strategic resort to orthodox Islam and the seclusion of women became righteous duties, and when independence came, those duties found a good target goal: affirmation of national identity and securing of national sovereignty. Arab women's narratives and actions refused to let this official gendered ruse have any legitimacy; they are fissures of trespass against the narratives of the state. It is not just that the modern state as such is patriarchal and gendered; it is also that there is the additional postcolonial state's burdensome weight of draping vulgar unequal social relations in the garb of divine, religious sanction.

In Sofia Samatar's chapter on the Sudan, the unequally and inchoately integrated fragment of the new state is not primarily class or gender as explored by Madureira or El Nossery, respectively, but ethnic and religious. Tayeb Salih (1929–2009), the accomplished Sudanese author, devoted much of his writerly life to examining the challenges and prospects of the Sudan state creating a nation out of diverse fragments—most especially the north, predominantly Muslim and self-identifying as Arab, and the south, mostly Christian and practitioners of indigenous African religions and self-identified as African. *Bandarshah*, originally published in two volumes in Arabic in 1971 and 1976, is Salih's last work of long fiction exploring the nation's search for community (*bandar*) and a fitting authority (*shāh*). Decades later, after a lengthy civil war and two years after Salih died, Sudan broke up into two nations in 2011, Sudan and South Sudan. By 2013, South Sudan had erupted into a civil war that is still ongoing; is there another state on the horizon? To read Samatar's meticulous literary archaeology of the Sudan through Salih's work is to have a full appreciation for a perceptive writer and "the revenge of the present" he identifies as an Achilles heel of the postcolonial state. Another instance of that revenge is the literary cultural form known as African writers' prison literature thoughtfully examined by Ken Walibora Waliaula in chapter 9. That cultural form—writers' prison literature—could be argued as almost a uniquely African one, thanks to the nature of the postcolonial state, the kinds of political oppositional responses it has elicited and continues to elicit from certain professional groups, and the treatments it typically metes out to offending individuals in such groups. Writers' prison literature is an affirmation of life against the insistence of the state in presenting itself only and generically as killjoy. Writing, for incarcerated writers, is the struggle of "becoming human" again, to damn the state that dehumanizes them for their creative self-expression. The thriving of different cultural forms in society is generally considered a sign of cultural health, but should we consider prison writing as part of that sign? One can almost indulge the embellishment that only postcolonial modernity can produce such an aporia.

What is not an embellishment, though, are the plentiful examples of such taxing contradictions and their unyielding character. They are in the area of popular culture especially, which, revealingly, does not often share the same self-critical or oppositional consciousness toward the state that defines elite literary forms. Just witness the recalcitrant spectrum of ideological contradictions in Nollywood, the raucous Nigerian film industry, which, without question, has become the most productive African cultural form of the last two decades, spawning related industries in regions and countries across the continent. Another is the explosive growth of Pentecostal churches all over the continent, too eager to provide ersatz succor in place of the social hope that only a functioning and fair state can provide. Reading the two popular forms and practices—Pentecostalism and Nollywood—alongside the state, Akin Adesokan, in chapter 10, illuminates that critical synapse often missed by political analyses alone—the "process by which the dramatic idioms characteristic of salesmanship are deployed in the service of parapolitical authority to substitute or supplement the failing bureaucratic state." If there is no Pentecostalism and its promise of easy victories and accessible culturally resonant idioms for making those promises, and if there is no mass accessible medium for its promotion such as Nollywood, the postcolonial state, in its effeteness in the face of an impatient populace, would have had to invent both of them. And it did.

It is important to note that in all these creative endeavors, local and individual agency comes out clearly, even if needlessly circumscribed and compromised by the only institution that could provide a wide enabling context, the state. The fine-grained ethnographic study of Shirimani Studios by Louise Meintjes is at once a celebration of new forms of empowerment in the postapartheid music industry for African entrepreneurs, musicians, and studio personnel in South Africa, and at the same time a chastening look at the marginalization of small-scale home-grown enterprises "pushed further into the precarious zone of post-apartheid's neoliberal economy." Meintjes's patient attention, in chapter 11, to the intimate processes of a Shirimani recording session is a staunch affirmation of creative labor slowed but undeterred by constraints. The session itself, in the interactive play among the musicians, reveals something else: "the affective dimensions entailed in working toward a future at the turn of the millennium" in South Africa under an "increasingly rationalized state shaped by the racialized history of colonialism and apartheid."

The chapters in the third group address problematic social practices that are more than less unique to the conjunction of the state and the city. The city is always everywhere the most intensely governed, largely because the state and its institutions are resident more in the city than elsewhere. That residence is itself both a response to and a sweller of city size. In the postcolonial African city, intensive state governance is more often an aspiration than actuality. Many city rules and ordinances hardly keep up with the explosive city growth, while many of those rules are of colonial origin and therefore outdated, impractical, or still to be domesticated. Many cultural or religious practices, kinship relations, and aspects of a befuddled cultural nationalism are often at odds with contemporary city expectations and social relations, zoning laws, or even law enforcement. Enforcement mechanisms and personnel are pitifully inadequate and technically unsophisticated. The bulk of the impoverished underclass in the cities claims no citizenship rights, even if it is aware of what those truly mean. The small percentage of the aware elite middle class still appears to think less of the class-group and more of the individual getting on in the city. This attitude serves the state well too—it allows it to muddle along until the next momentous conjuncture of events panel beats it into shape momentarily. The obverse: the attitude does not serve the state well at all in that many individuals in the city are able too frequently to escape the blurry sights of the state, leeching on it at the edges, draining it of its potential. But now and then the state descends, with violence that is more often than not disproportionate, because the purpose is more punitive than preventive. Put all of this together and one sometimes forgets the scores of other things that work in the African city. But then, it is condescension to remind people who demand more—or who deserve more even if they do not so explicitly ask—that not everything is bad in the city. They know. I have sketched here the large context for the inhuman trafficking in young male Koranic students called *talibés* in Senegal that Lark Porter, in chapter 12, so thoroughly accounts for. An affirmative custom of old has become a tool for exploiting the most vulnerable, and a state uncertain about its contemporary responsibilities and vague about its sense of cultural tradition, equivocates.

The resonance of Kunle Ajibade's riveting examination in chapter 13 of improvisational journalistic practice under authoritarianism in big-city Lagos, Nigeria, could not be more troubling. We all know what nightmare the Arab Spring of just a few years ago in North Africa has turned to and yet to emerge from. Egypt continues to roll out supposedly antiterrorism laws, part of which makes it illegal for journalists to contradict official accounts of terror attacks.[31] This would sound eerily familiar to Ajibade, accomplished journalist, once jailed for life by the late General Sani Abacha, for alleged violation of a similar prohibition.

Ato Quayson, Anne-Maria Makhulu, and Tejumola Olaniyan examine space use and living conditions by different segments of city residents as made possible or impossible by their own ingenuity as well as by the structures of authority. In chapter 14, Quayson's detailed ethnographic study of a fragment of Oxford Street in Accra does three things at once. It registers the vivacity and agency of the denizens of Oxford Street's "performative streetscape," underscores the decrepit public services they have to contend with as "the inefficiencies of the state sector are immediately translated into spatial effects," and also provides a useful way for studying how neighborhoods relate and acquire certain characteristics and image over time. The informal settlement situation in Cape Town that Makhulu expertly maps out in chapter 15 is harsher and starker. For some, that may make it a category difference. The tautly racially segregated apartheid city of old—of "old"—still bears more than the traces of its past. Its razor-sharp dividing walls are less susceptible to the inventive scratches of the excluded because the historical evolution of the state in South Africa and its control of space have given it relatively more effective oversight power. No, there is no Accra's Oxford Street in Cape Town. Even so, the connections and similarities are clear between the condition of the squatters of Cape Town and the lowly who imprint so much of their performative selves on Oxford Street. The stories behind them are similar. They stick out like sore thumbs and put paid to the aspiration of the postcolonial state to seamlessly account for all desires though within grave structural inequality. And they both reference a hideousness out of sight: a gross rural-urban divide and rural impoverishment—indeed, gendered rural impoverishment—that has no lengthier a history in Africa than the time of the modern state beginning from colonial rule. A critical odd question seems apt at this point: who is really benefiting from state, city, and space relations in the city? Certainly not that boisterous lot down on Oxford Street, and certainly not the oft-beleaguered squatters of Cape Town. How about the rich and the well-heeled who ride their Mercedes Benzes up to the front entrances of cavernous homes while the security gates slowly shut behind them? Any member of this group, too, is likely to answer "who, me?" in an accusatory manner. From my own research on what I call "garrison architecture," it is clear the stressful, alienating, and dehumanizing length the middle class and rich in the city must go to protect themselves and their property. Not even a well-armed postcolonial African state, not even overflowing bank accounts, as I show in chapter 16, could secure for them a blissful living amid the bountiful want of the majority in the postcolonial city. It is easy not to sympathize with the middle class and the rich, of course, but it is to be noted that state-system self-subversion is the name of what happens when a state cannot guarantee a modicum of safety and security for those who do the bulk of its high-level thinking and doing in all areas private or public. All will lose: the lowly, the elite, and the state. Our care needs to be multisided.

In recognition of the need for a renewed attention to the state in Africa today, the African Studies Association (ASA) of the United States, the largest umbrella association in the world for the study of Africa, chose for its 2015 annual conference the theme, "The State and the Study of Africa." The theme description acknowledged the dramatically contingent and unusual way the state in Africa was put together in different countries at independence in the 1960s, and the big and small challenges it has faced since then. Partly because of the recalcitrance of those challenges and partly in affirmation of the tight dependence of the study of Africa on the state—"It is the state and its institutions that generate our data. The temporal and geographic coordinates of the state are hard-coded into our research methods"—the theme statement called for new, bolder, less conventional, and more innovative scholarly approaches to studying the African state and the continent.[32] "We need a scholarship of idiosyncrasy, anachronism, and the out-of-place," the statement said:

> We need histories that explore the paths not taken, utopias, and visions of community foreclosed by national independence. We need a political science that takes seriously the arenas of life—borderlands, informalities, refugees and migrant populations—that lie outside the standard deviation. We need an economics that reaches outside government data sets and explores the generation of value as a subject of research. We need new ways of thinking about archives management, museology and other infrastructures of cultural preservation. We need a scholarship of development and public health that is not beholden to the encompassing demands of consultancy work. We need a humanities that re-engages the African state.[33]

The ASA's call is a welcome one indeed, and I am happy to say that this book should help in some way in the advancement of the agenda. Inspired by a similar realization as ASA's three years earlier, I organized a symposium, "Enchantings: Modernity, Culture, and the State in Postcolonial Africa," at the University of Wisconsin, Madison, in April 2012. The research gathered in this book had its first hearing in that forum. My gratitude to the contributors for sharing my vision, and I hereby invite readers to share in the wealth of their insights.

TEJUMOLA OLANIYAN is Louise Durham Mead Professor of English and African Cultural Studies at the University of Wisconsin, Madison. He is author of *Arrest the Music! Fela and His Rebel Art and Politics* and *Scars of Conquest*.

Notes

1. See, for a few examples, Wole Soyinka, "The Writer in a Modern African State," in *Art, Dialogue and Outrage: Essays on Literature and Culture*, ed. Biodun Jeyifo (Ibadan: New Horn, 1988), 15–20; Gideon-Cyrus Makau Mutiso, *Socio-political Thought in African Literature: Weusi?* (New York: Harper and Row, 1974); Kofi Ermeleh Agovi, *The African Writer and*

the Phenomenon of the Nation State in Africa (Pretoria: Unit for Development Analysis, 1990); Lillian Trager, *Yoruba Hometowns: Community, Identity, and Development in Nigeria* (Boulder, CO: Lynne Rienner, 2001); James McDougall, *Nation, Culture and Society in North Africa* (London: Frank Cass, 2003); Achille Mbembe, *On The Postcolony*, trans. A. M. Barrett, Murray Last, Steven Rendall, and Janet Roitman (Berkeley: University of California Press, 2001); Tejumola Olaniyan, *Arrest the Music! Fela Kuti and His Rebel Art and Politics* (Bloomington: Indiana University Press, 2004); and Tejumola Olaniyan, "Chinua Achebe and an Archaeology of the Postcolonial African State," *Research in African Literatures* 32, no. 3 (2001): 22–28.

2. See Patrick Chabal, *Power in Africa: An Essay in Political Interpretation* (New York: St. Martin's, 1992), and Patrick Chabal and Jean-Pascal Daloz, *Culture Troubles: Politics and the Interpretation of Meaning* (Chicago: University of Chicago Press, 2006). See also Michael G. Schatzberg, *Political Legitimacy in Middle Africa: Father, Family, Food* (Bloomington: Indiana University Press, 2001). This is one structural reason why there are more contributions to this volume from scholars in the humanities than in political science. I hope the book, in this uneven distribution, serves as a meaningful invitation and challenge to political scientists.

3. I borrow here some resonances of curiosity from Michel Foucault, social theorist and philosopher. Curiosity, he notes, "evokes 'care'; it evokes the care one takes of what exists and what might exist; a sharpened sense of reality, but one that is never immobilized before it; a readiness to find what surrounds us strange and odd; a certain determination to throw off familiar ways of thought and to look at the same things in a different way; a passion for seizing what is happening now and what is disappearing; a lack of respect for the traditional hierarchies of what is important and fundamental. I dream of a new age of curiosity. We have the technical means; the desire is there; there is an infinity of things to know; the people capable of doing such work exist. So what is our problem? Too little: channels of communication that are too narrow, almost monopolistic, inadequate." *Politics, Philosophy, Culture: Interviews and Other Writings, 1977–1984*, ed. Lawrence Kritzman (New York: Routledge, 1990), 325–326.

4. For sample expressions and critical reviews of the crisis literature, see Robert H. Jackson and Carl G. Rosberg, *Personal Rule in Black Africa: Prince, Autocrat, Prophet, Tyrant* (Berkeley: University of California Press, 1982); Samuel Decalo, *Coups and Army Rule in Africa: Motivations and Constraints*, 2nd ed. (New Haven: Yale University Press, 1990); George B. N. Ayittey, *Africa in Chaos: A Comparative History* (New York: Palgrave, 1997); Richard A. Joseph, "Africa: States in Crisis," *Journal of Democracy* 14, no. 3 (2003): 159–170; Jean-François Bayart, *The State in Africa: The Politics of the Belly*, trans. M. Harper, C. Harrison, and E. Harrison (London: Longman, 1993); Paul M. Lubeck, "The Crisis of African Development: Conflicting Interpretations and Resolutions," *Annual Review of Sociology* 18 (1992): 519–540; Abiola Irele, "The Crisis of Legitimacy in Africa: A Time of Change and Despair," *Dissent* 39, no. 3 (1992): 296–302; Robert Fatton, *Predatory Rule: State and Civil Society in Africa* (Boulder, CO: Lynne Rienner, 1992); Jonathan H. Frimpong-Ansah, *The Vampire State in Africa: The Political Economy of Decline* (Trenton, NJ: Africa World Press, 1992); Robert H. Bates, *When Things Fell Apart: State Failure in Late Century Africa* (New York: Cambridge University Press, 2008); George Klay Kieh, Jr., ed., *Beyond State Failure and Collapse: Making the State Relevant in Africa* (Lanham, MD: Lexington Books, 2007); and Korwa G. Adar, Monica K. Juma, and Katabaro N. Miti, eds., *The State of Africa, 2010/11: Parameters and Legacies of Governance and Issue Areas* (Pretoria: Africa Institute of South Africa, 2010). For a masterly summative account, see Crawford M. Young, *The Postcolonial State in Africa: Fifty Years of Independence, 1960–2010* (Madison, WI: University of Wisconsin Press, 2012), especially "Part Two. Itineraries: Three Cycles of Hope and Disappointment." The literature is replete with fanciful descriptive adjectives for the state—praetorian, hard, soft, vampire, personalist, prebendal, and so many

more that "adjectival state" could be another not unreasonable label, as Michael G. Schatzberg usefully pointed out to me. Sure, the rhetoric of "crisis" could be used to pathologize a social condition and affirm an unjust status quo. Janet Roitman's *Anti-Crisis* (Durham, NC: Duke University Press, 2013), a fine critique of the rhetoric of crisis, is well argued in this regard. The real task, though, is not to be overly academicist and miss the social pain in the scholarly debate over its naming; language will never completely capture its object without an arguable excess. I apply the same answer to the far less debated issue of whether "failure," in its implicit assumption of an ideal that needs to be met and is unmet, is an appropriate term to describe the postcolonial state in Africa and its evident limitations.

5. The FFP describes itself as "an independent, nonpartisan, 501(c)(3) non-profit research and educational organization that works to prevent violent conflict and promote sustainable security." It goes on to say, "We promote sustainable security through research, training and education, engagement of civil society, building bridges across diverse sectors, and developing innovative technologies and tools for policy makers. A leader in the conflict assessment and early warning field, The Fund for Peace focuses on the problems of weak and failing states. Our objective is to create practical tools and approaches for conflict mitigation that are useful to decision-makers." "The Fragile State Index 2015," *Fund for Peace*, July 2015, http://fsi.fundforpeace.org/rankings-2015.

6. I am reminded here of a statement by Achille Mbembe in an interview: "But economic growth alone will not be enough. It should be accompanied by a serious shift in the terms of cultural rendition of contemporary African experiences. People, images and commodities have to circulate. A continental public sphere has to be nurtured through the development of mass media and new technologies.... Bridges have to be built between a new social science and the various domains of the humanities, including philosophy, the arts, music, architecture, film and design." Christian Höller, "Africa in Motion: An Interview with the Post-colonialism Theoretician Achille Mbembe," *Springerin* 3, no. 2 (2002): http://springerin.at/dyn/heft.php?id=32&pos=1&textid=1195&lang=en. In their book *The State as Cultural Practice* (Oxford: Oxford University Press, 2010), Mark Bevir and R. A. W. Rhodes argue persuasively that "political scientists should think of the state as a series of contingent and unstable cultural practices, which in turn consist of the political activity of specific human agents." They "also argue that political scientists should explain these cultural practices by reference to the meanings embedded in them, where these meanings arise against the background of contingent historical traditions and dilemmas" (1). The conceptual plea is very apt, but the Westphalian state is always already taken as cultural—a product of Western culture—by Westerners and others. A more than passing reference to Africa—five references of which four are from book titles—would have proven a more challenging testing ground and therefore enriched their argument immensely. See also David Lloyd and Paul Thomas, eds., *Culture and the State* (New York: Routledge, 1998).

7. For the structural conception of the postcolonial state in Africa I advance here, I have benefited from Claude Ake, *Revolutionary Pressures in Africa* (London: Zed, 1978); Betrand Badie and Pierre Birnbaum, *The Sociology of the State*, trans. A. Goldhammer (Chicago: University of Chicago Press, 1983); Basil Davidson, *The Black Man's Burden: Africa and the Curse of the Nation State* (New York: Random, 1992); Pierre Bourdieu, *On the State* (Malden, MA: Polity, 2015); Ngũgĩ wa Thiong'o, *Penpoints, Gunpoint, and Dreams: Towards a Critical Theory of the Arts and the State in Africa* (New York: Oxford University Press, 1988); and Chabal, *Power in Africa*. The current challenges of the state in Africa are many; on maintaining sustainable ecosystems, see Carl Death, *The Green State in Africa* (New Haven, CT: Yale University Press, 2016).

8. See Marwan Muasher, *The Second Arab Awakening and the Battle for Pluralism* (New Haven, CT: Yale University Press, 2014); Sokari Ekine and Firoze Manji, eds., *African Awakening: The Emerging Revolutions* (Cape Town: Pambazuka, 2011); and Jason Brownlee, Tarek Masoud, and Andrew Reynolds, *The Arab Spring: Pathways of Repression and Reform* (New York: Oxford University Press, 2015). On the notion of reverse expectations, see Tejumola Olaniyan, "Contingencies of Performance: The Gap as Venue," *Theatre Survey* 50 (2009): 23–34.

9. Frantz Fanon, *The Wretched of the Earth*, 1961, trans. Constance Farrington (New York: Grove Weidenfeld, 1963), 149, 153.

10. Ibid., 153, 150.

11. Ibid., 163, 152–153.

12. Karl Marx and Friedrich Engels, *The Communist Manifesto*, trans. Samuel Moore (London: Penguin, 1967), 83, 85.

13. The productivity is the classic paradoxical relationship that structure adversarial contexts and creativity. The Guyanese Wilson Harris is quite evocative, though writing of different but similar context: "I speak . . . of fiction that seeks through complex rehearsal to consume its own biases. The difficulty in accepting the force of the intuitive imagination lies, I think, in uncertainty over validating the discoveries a writer makes through interior guides that appear within his or her fiction. This is a task for scholarship and criticism. The fabric and texture of the work needs to be scanned closely. The detection of parallels woven into the evolving weave and cycle of fiction can be exciting in its illumination of profoundest unity of the human spirit." "Adversarial Contexts and Creativity," *New Left Review* 1, no. 154 (1985): 127.

14. Jane Wilkinson, ed., *Talking with African Writers: Interviews with African Poets, Playwrights, and Novelists* (London: Heinemann, 1992), 92–93.

15. For reviews, see Chabal on "paradigms lost" in *Power in Africa*, 11–34; and Mahmood Mamdani on "history by analogy" in *Citizen and Subject: Contemporary Africa and the Legacy of Late Colonialism* (Princeton, NJ: Princeton University Press, 1996), 3–34.

16. See also Davidson, *Black Man's Burden*; Crawford Young, *The African Colonial State in Comparative Perspective* (New Haven, CT: Yale University Press, 1997); and Mbembe, *On the Postcolony*.

17. Wole Soyinka, *The Open Sore of a Continent: A Personal Narrative of the Nigerian Crisis* (New York: Oxford University Press, 1996).

18. Chinua Achebe, *Morning Yet on Creation Day: Essays* (New York: Anchor, 1975), 44.

19. Mamdani, *Citizen and Subject*, 289–290, 290–291.

20. Soyinka, *Open Sore*, 62.

21. Mamdani, *Citizen and Subject*, 289. It is possible to argue that there is no inevitability in this, even if things eventually happened that way. In southern Nigeria, for instance, it was Lord Lugard's 1906 court reforms that forcefully racialized the dispensation of justice, consigning Africans to provincial courts where legal representation was restricted. Thanks to Olúfẹ́mi Táíwò for bringing this to my attention.

22. Claude Ake, *Democratization of Disempowerment in Africa* (Lagos: Malthouse, 1994).

23. For an introduction to my conception of modernity, see Aimé Césaire, *Discourse on Colonialism*, 1955, trans. Joan Pinkham (New York: Monthly Review, 2001); Walter Rodney, *How Europe Underdeveloped Africa* (Washington, DC: Howard University Press, 1981); Olúfẹ́mi Táíwò, *How Colonialism Preempted Modernity in Africa* (Bloomington: Indiana University Press, 2010); and Zygmunt Bauman, *Liquid Modernity* (Malden, MA: Polity, 2000).

24. Zygmunt Bauman, "Modernity and Ambivalence," in *Global Culture: Nationalism, Globalization and Modernity*, ed. Mike Featherstone (London: Sage, 1990), 144.

25. Ibid.

26. Ibid., 145.

27. Pierre Englebert usefully wonders about the "unusual territorial resilience of Africa's weak states" in *Africa: Unity, Sovereignty, and Sorrow* (Boulder, CO: Lynne Rienner, 2009), 9. I say it is in part because of a deeper, even if unspoken—or unheard—preference of Africans for that authority form over alternatives. Perhaps sovereignty is not so much the problem as its particular African powerlessness in relation to the world. It seems to me that that powerlessness—and the unscholarly or condescending casualness with which some scholars address it—is no more evident than in one of the "policy fantasies" that Englebert proposes: "revoke the unconditional international recognition of Africa's postcolonies and promote the conditions for the rise of domestic sovereignty or empirical statehood in Africa" (10). How is this not a call for recolonization?

28. For informative entrance into this subject, see Ayo Langley, ed., *Ideologies of Black Liberation, 1850–1970. Documents on Modern African Political Thought from Colonial Times to the Present* (London: Rex Collings, 1979); and Obafemi Awolowo, *Path to Nigerian Freedom* (London: Faber and Faber, 1947). See also, as a useful general historical and theoretical background, S. I. Benn, *A Theory of Freedom* (Cambridge: Cambridge University Press, 1988); Orlando Patterson, *Freedom: Volume 1: Freedom in the Making of Western Culture* (New York: Basic Books, 1991); and J. E. E. Dalberg-Acton, *The Theory of Freedom and Other Essays* (London: Macmillan, 1907).

29. Some of the texts I have benefited from in the conception of culture elaborated here are Wole Soyinka, *Myth, Literature and the African World* (Cambridge: Cambridge University Press, 1976); Amilcar Cabral, *Unity and Struggle: Speeches and Writings*, trans. M. Wolfers (London: Heinemann, 1980); Terry Eagleton, *The Idea of Culture* (Oxford, UK: Blackwell, 2000); Nawal El Saadawi, *The Hidden Face of Eve: Women in the Arab World* (London: Zed, 1980); Paulin J. Hountondji, *African Philosophy: Myth and Reality*, 2nd ed. (Bloomington: Indiana University Press, 1996); Pierre Bourdieu, *The Logic of Practice*, trans. Richard Nice (Stanford, CT: Stanford University Press, 1992); and Zygmunt Bauman, *Culture in a Liquid Modern World* (Cambridge, MA: Polity, 2011).

30. For a portable summative account of Afropessimism and its opposite, see Ebere Onwudiwe, "Afropessimism," *New Dictionary of the History of Ideas*, http://www.encyclopedia.com/doc/1G2-3424300021.html.

31. Brian Rohan, "Egypt President Approves Sweeping Anti-Terrorism Law," *Associated Press*, August 17, 2015, http://m.washingtontimes.com/news/2015/aug/17/egypt-president-signs-new-anti-terrorism-law-into-/.

32. Dismas A. Masolo and Derek R. Peterson, "The State and the Study of Africa," theme statement for the 58th Annual Meeting of the African Studies Association, San Diego, CA, November 19–22, 2015, http://www.africanstudies.org/publications/asa-news/winter-2015/462-call-for-proposals.

33. Ibid.

PART I

Culture and Governance: Conceptual and Practical Explorations

1 Culture and the Study of Politics in Postcolonial Africa

Patrick Chabal

What do political scientists make of culture, particularly when they study postcolonial Africa? Why is it that the mere mention of "culture" should provoke what can only be described as a lively debate in Africanist circles? Can we ever hope to overcome the academic and political hurdles that make the study of culture so contentious?[1]

For the past ten years, I have been working on two broad themes. One turns around the use of culture in political science analysis. The aim here is to suggest ways of conceptualizing culture that would make it possible to compare Africa with other parts of the world, including contemporary Europe. The other is a more wide-ranging study of Western social sciences. Here I try to go beyond postcolonial analysis by grappling with the ways in which what I call the non-West (or what is often dubbed the South) has challenged Western rationality—that is, the instruments we use to understand and act on the world in which we live. This involves a wholesale reassessment of Western social sciences. In my last book I explain how the West is now finding it increasingly difficult to understand the social and political dilemmas it faces at home and abroad.[2] I show how the conceptual and theoretical instruments the West deploys no longer manage to make sense of these challenges. I conclude that Western social sciences have now reached their limits, which will only be overcome when we refashion theory to include the postcolonial realities in which we all live.

However, I want here to focus on the question of culture in political science, which led me a few years ago to rethink the ends and means of comparative politics. I felt compelled to do so because it became obvious to me that the standard political science we are taught in the academy (especially in the United States) has failed miserably to come to terms with the cultural realities political scientists face when coming into contact with the cultures of Africa. Indeed, I reached the conclusion that African cultures have exposed Western social science for what it is: an ill-conceived attempt to apply to the continent the theories that have been developed to explain the West's social and political development. In other words, the study of Africa made plain to me that social sciences as taught and practiced in the West are but a way to force the non-West into the Western experience. Or, to put it another way, social sciences are built on the assumption that modernization means Westernization.

It is tempting, but ultimately futile, for students of the comparative politics of Africa to attempt to conceptualize culture by searching for a comprehensive definition, identifying in the process all its politically significant constituent parts. The very method that consists in seeking to list the attributes of human life that could be classified as cultural is itself the outcome of the vain quest to endow political science with the quality of a hard science. It is indeed precisely because such a quest has more often than not frustrated political scientists that they have been induced to look on culture as a residual category, fit only to reclaim those areas of politics for which there is no good conceptual home. It is also for this reason that a good number of cultural analyses as practiced by political scientists have appeared to be constructed on weak theoretical grounds, placing them immediately on the defensive within a discipline with aspirations to the highest scientific ideals.

My approach starts from an opposite premise. Culture is not to be defined exhaustively, by reference to all the possible elements that might come to represent what it is at a particular (and inevitably frozen) point in time. It is best understood as an environment, a constantly evolving setting, within which human behavior follows a number of particular courses—many of which may be contradictory. Culture is not merely an additional dimension of politics that requires attention. It is quite simply one of the fundaments of social life, the matrix within which what we understand as political agency takes place. In other words, the field of politics itself has to be examined within its appropriate cultural milieu, as it were. Far from being a residual category, culture is that which constitutes the coordinates, the mapping, the language, or the very blueprint of politics.[3]

The key here is an analysis of culture as a system of meanings and not as values. To look at culture in terms of values, on the one hand, is to approach the question from a normative and, frequently, ethnocentric perspective—making it difficult, for instance, to explain "cultural" differences within a single society. To look at it in terms of meanings, on the other hand, is to attempt to reveal the language in which people who may disagree about values or political ends can do so within a shared perspective. In this way, an explanation of the cultural context no longer requires an explicit definition of culture in terms of norms and beliefs—or even an analysis of how these differ from our own, in the West. My work, therefore, offers a study of politics that is different from the standard political science approach in terms of political culture. It also provides an analytical framework that is radically at variance with that adopted in a volume like *Culture Matters*, in which, typically, culture is equated with values.[4]

My approach is not just an effort to explain how culture is germane to comparative analysis; it is an attempt to show how the very business of political science needs theoretically to be grounded in a proper cultural perspective. This does not mean that culture necessarily explains, even less determines, the outcome of political action. Rather, it implies that the elucidation of such action calls for proper recourse to theories that allow relevant consideration of the appropriate cultural environment(s).[5] Thus, culture is not simply useful to comparative politics. Comparative politics can only be meaningful insofar as it succeeds in making sense of the cultural setting within which local politics take place.

When conceptualizing culture for the political analysis of contemporary Africa, I, like many, am stimulated by the work of Clifford Geertz; his work itself is a reflection on comparative analysis deeply informed by the historical legacy of a number of social scientists. Therefore, I develop my views from three of his best-known arguments. The first tackles the question of definition:

> The culture concept to which I adhere has neither multiple referents nor, so far as I can see, any unusual ambiguity: it denotes an historically transmitted pattern of meanings embodied in symbols, a system of inherited conceptions expressed in symbolic forms by means of which men communicate, perpetuate, and develop their knowledge about and attitudes towards life.[6]

What does this characterization imply for political analysis? The key notion here is that culture is a "system of inherited conceptions expressed in symbolic forms." This makes it plain, first, that what may appear merely as a conglomeration of discrete values is in fact an interrelated and structured whole. Second, it highlights the historical dimension of culture, which is to be understood not as being simply the current language of norms and habits (synchronically) but as the living environment, evolved in the *longue durée* (diachronically). Finally, the emphasis is clearly placed on the fact that culture is expressed in symbolic form, and not, as is sometimes believed, only in factual statements. Comparative analysis, therefore, must concern itself with all three aspects of culture, and not just with those that may appear to be more directly applicable to the business of politics.

Further, Geertz writes:

> The concept of culture I espouse . . . is essentially a semiotic one. Believing, with Max Weber, that man is an animal suspended in webs of significance he himself has spun, I take culture to be those webs, and the analysis of it to be therefore not an experimental science in search of law but an interpretive one in search of meaning. It is explication I am after, construing social expressions on their surface enigmatical.[7]

The second key element of Geertz's proposition is thus that the concept of culture is first and foremost semiotic, in the sense in which it is defined above—that is, having to do with signs as modes of communication.[8] This is critical and needs reasserting forcefully, not only because it is an aspect of the question that is habitually elided in political science but also because it informs the method I have used in the analysis of politics in Africa. The reason this notion of culture is unpalatable to political scientists is twofold. First, because it touches on what appear to be subjective characteristics of human agency—the words and symbols by which people recognize and express themselves. And second, because an acceptance of such a conception of culture would imply a research agenda with which most political scientists are uncomfortable, since it puts a premium on the study of meanings as they matter to the individuals and communities they try to understand. This is admittedly a demanding requirement, but I believe it is imperative to place it at the heart of comparative analysis if we are to advance the analytical value of the discipline.

Indeed, Geertz's reminder of Weber's understanding of culture should be a timely prompt to comparative analysts for, whatever our view of the German social scientist, it cannot be disputed that he was the pioneer of comparative historical sociology, and there is much to be gained by reexamining his methods.

Finally, addressing specifically the issue of culture and politics, Geertz comments, "Culture, here, is not cults and customs, but the structures of meaning through which men give shape to their experience; and politics is not coups and constitutions, but one of the principal arenas in which such structures publicly unfold."[9] This statement is useful in that it focuses attention both on the object of political analysis and on the method most relevantly used to study politics. By suggesting that politics is an arena, rather than a black box, Geertz goes right to the heart of the question.[10] From this point of view, what is consequential is not so much the study of functional equivalents within the body politic but the translation of the meanings, the symbols, of what is political in a particular society into a language that lends itself to comparative analysis.

It may be thought that my discussion of the concept of culture is all too Geertz-centered, or at the very least excessively dependent on an anthropological approach. Are none of the definitions used in political science of any use?[11] The question is not purely rhetorical because the answer is important to our approach. For reasons developed at length elsewhere, I believe that political theory as it is commonly understood today propounds a concept of culture that is inimical to the type of analysis I propose. Not only does it seek to narrow down the scope of culture to variously operational common denominators, often dubbed variables, but it fails to take seriously the question of the "webs of significance," which Weber quite rightly considers critical for comparative analysis. However, the current resurgence of interest in Weber's work is proof that his method is once again attractive to social scientists dissatisfied with the state of their disciplines.[12]

I make no apology for taking as my starting point a conceptual perspective best expounded by an anthropologist. Nor do I feel it incumbent on me to defend Geertz's position on the subject, even if I recognize that it has been contested by his professional colleagues.[13] Mine is not a quest for a definitive characterization of culture but for an approach that manages to respond to the dilemmas faced by practitioners of comparative politics as they grapple with the contextual and historical complexities of their very diverse case studies. In my work on Africa, I find it immensely rewarding to integrate some of the most illuminating insights derived from anthropology.[14] And I believe firmly that the most convincing comparative accounts of political processes are those that have combined solid historical and anthropological research with the use of concepts from other appropriate, relevant social sciences.

My advocacy of a cultural approach to the comparative study of politics does not simply derive from an a priori bias. It stems from the conviction that the discipline as it now stands is in danger of reducing the scope of its activities to what is easily quantifiable. It is in this way liable to forget that the only justification for what we do, other than to construct models in the air, is to further the understanding of politics across the world. Comparison is warranted if it provides a more plausible account of what is happening politically in various settings. The so-called science of politics can only aim at explaining political events and processes more credibly than mere common sense when its theoretical framework enables a new, and more meaningful, elucidation of the facts.[15]

Of course, theory in the social sciences provides a simplified model of how human beings behave and form social relations over time, but the litmus test of theory, here as in the natural sciences, is how it facilitates the explanation of observable events—or to put it differently, how it allows us meaningfully to unpack the complexities of real life. Comparative analysts should explain, not simply paraphrase, actual politics. And they can scarcely hope to do that unless they begin to develop methods that allow them to integrate a cultural approach—that is, not just pay lip service to a few self-evidently important cultural factors, like ethnicity or language, but to disentangle the relevant webs of significance that impinge on political agency. Why is this? Let me explain by reference to Africa.

It is generally argued by comparative analysts in the field that there is in sub-Saharan Africa, as elsewhere, a trend toward democracy. On the face of it the evidence is strong, since in the last two decades most countries have held (single or repeated) multiparty elections.[16] Furthermore, recent comparative research appears to confirm, by means of large-scale surveys, that there is increasing support among the population at large for democracy.[17] Based on such work, then, it would seem legitimate to conclude that Africa is indeed moving in the same direction as other regions of the globe. This would not be an inaccurate inference, given the limited procedural definition that is usually given of democracy—meaning simply the holding of regular, more or less free and fair, multiparty elections—but it would be a highly misleading one, for several important reasons.

First, it would convey the impression that the direction in which politics is evolving in Africa is, in some meaningful way, taking the continent toward a model akin to that found in the West.[18] In fact, the opposite is the case, since whatever the effects of multiparty elections, they have emphatically not led to political behavior that resembles substantively those to be found in Europe, North America, or even Southeast Asia. Second, it would imply that the characterization of present-day African polities as democracies is an insightful manner of conceptualizing the exercise of power in those countries. Again, not only is the reality totally at odds with this conclusion, but the emphasis on the democratic nature of current African governments tends to obscure the actual complexities of the present situation. What we find south of the Sahara are, with few exceptions, (functioning or collapsed) clientelistic and/or patrimonial regimes that have, more or less reluctantly, adopted the procedures of multiparty elections.

This example is not intended simply to demonstrate the limits of the current comparative work on Africa, although it is, of course, impossible to ignore them, but to illustrate why the failure to integrate a cultural approach into a study of the continent has vitiated our understanding of its present predicament. This is not to imply that a stress on contemporary political transitions is irrelevant. Multiparty elections in Africa have brought about important changes, such as much greater freedom of expression, which bear examination. It is, rather, that the incorporation of African politics within the broader field of comparative democratic studies has led to the adoption of what I would call an acultural (and, incidentally, ahistorical) theoretical framework, generating a highly misleading account of politics on the continent. Therefore, such a model does not in my eyes meet the basic scientific criterion of plausibility.[19]

My work on Africa has shown how a cultural approach makes it possible to understand the extent to which the exercise of power south of the Sahara is predicated on a personalized concept of politics. This explains, first, why relations of legitimacy, representation, and accountability are primarily vertical, between patrons and clients. Second, it provides clear reasons why, on the continent, there has been so little political institutionalization—in the sense in which Weber defines it—and that whatever institutionalization had taken place by independence was undermined by the logic of informal politics that prevailed afterward. It makes plain why such a pattern induces the political elite to seek to accumulate wealth—both to display their political substance and to have the means to redistribute to those on whose support they depend. Finally, it reveals why present transitions are unable to change the nature of politics in Africa. The holding of regular multiparty elections, which is usually equated with democratization, has come about largely because of outside pressure from the international community. But the realities on the ground in Africa are that, more often than not, it is democracy that has been adapted to the logic and rigors of clientelism and not, as is so often proclaimed, the reverse.

What lessons can we draw from this African example? Three remarks are relevant to the claim that a cultural approach helps to explain the complexities of real-life politics. The first is that it is clearly necessary to build into any account of sub-Saharan politics a method for conveying what the notion of power means for the local actors, from the top to the bottom of society. This entails an ability to explain what makes sense to them and it implies research into areas of social, cultural, and religious life—such as, for instance, the occult—that may be less relevant to other regions of the world.[20] Second, it means that we must go beyond the surface of formal political processes—such as, here, multiparty elections—to probe deeper into the significance of political change. Most people in Africa conceive of democracy in terms of personalized politics and not in terms of institutionalization. Finally, it shows that the best way to compare African political systems with those found elsewhere is not to focus primarily on their procedural complexion but to attempt to contrast how political forms of exchange like accountability or representation actually take place.[21]

Making progress in the use of culture in comparative analysis entails developing the means to understand such webs of significance as are relevant to the questions we ask. This, as suggested earlier, rests on the issue of translation, or as I would put it, the art of interpretation. For an elegant elaboration of what is meant by translation in this context, I turn, yet again, to Geertz: "'Translation' . . . is not a simple recasting of others' ways of putting things in terms of our own ways of putting them (that is the kind in which things get lost), but displaying the logic of their ways of putting them in the locutions of ours; a conception which again brings it rather closer to what a critic does to illumine a poem than what an astronomer does to account for a star."[22]

Such a view of translation is evidently not a mode of interpretation to which social scientists would readily adhere, and it is certainly one from which the practitioners of rational choice would recoil. Can one really base analysis on such a very personal vision of what webs of significance might mean in different settings? Is this not a far too ethnological approach, useful for in-depth case studies but unsuited to the broad comparative canvas? These objections are legitimate and go straight to the tension that lies at the heart of the discipline of comparative politics: How to reconcile specific local knowledge with the general sweep of trends and processes? There is no easy answer to that question, but there is a price to pay for ignoring it.

Geertz's contrast between the calling of the astronomer and that of the critic points to the key issue at stake. The choice between the one and the other is not arbitrary, or whimsical, but derives from the nature of the problem to be solved. There is room for both; it is simply that each does a different job. Of course, a poet could account for a star (many have) and an astronomer could explain a poem (rather fewer have), but what they would be doing would be distinct. Stars, after all, are poetic; and poems are metric. There is merit in recounting the particular sentiment a star may unleash in one single soul. Equally, the algebraic patterns of rhymes can be scientifically elegant. But this is not the issue. The point of a poem is how it says what it says, not whether a computer can identify its architecture. The interest of a star usually resides in the data it provides about the motion of celestial bodies or the creation of the universe. More generally, therefore, my argument is that the method employed ought to derive from the problem at hand, not from a priori theoretical or ideological choices.

Therefore, the claim that analysis rests on the art of interpretation comes from the recognition that comparisons demand the ability to display the logic of others' ways of putting things in our locutions. This can only be done if we take seriously the job of trying to reveal what that logic might be—that is, to make sense of the behavior of political actors in their own, specific and local, settings. Interpretation, therefore, is far from arbitrary. It is, I would argue, scientific, in that it requires a systematic and consistent approach—that is, the disciplined use of theories and concepts as instruments for the translation of the material to hand. Hence the art of interpretation is based on clearly identifiable methods that can be explained and, more importantly, replicated. The ways in which those methods are applied ought to be determined by the contextual factors most relevant to the case studies under examination.

I take as example the comparative study of what is all too blandly called corruption, which is far from being a straightforward issue.[23] The standard comparative approach consists in providing a definition of the phenomenon, commonly based on juridical terms; putting forward a number of hypotheses about what factors may most usefully correlate with corruption; and setting out to gather the data to test such suppositions. My approach would differ in every respect. I would not attempt to offer a tight, or closed, definition of corruption other than to say that the phenomenon touches on the tension, in every society, between what is deemed to be financially profitable and what is seen to be locally permissible. I would then develop concepts about the best way to approach that question and emphasize that what is at stake is essentially the way in which different societies consider and sanction illicit transactions. I would then explain why there may well be significant differences in the meanings of "licit" and "legal," why in any event such notions might differ significantly from those current in the West, and whether the concept itself made sense in context. Finally, I would study the "moral and political economy of corruption" in various countries with a view to disclosing the nature of that tension within each society.[24] Only then would I hazard a comparison between different cases.

Therefore, my concern would not be to compare corruption per se, but to contrast the varying logics of illicit acts in the different case studies. Comparing corruption in different societies consists in being able to explain to ourselves, and to those who read our books, why avoiding tax in Italy, making corporate donations to political parties in South Korea, pilfering funds from the state in Nigeria, pocketing a commission on a commercial transaction in Kuwait, or giving a job to a poorly qualified acquaintance who went to the same public school in Great Britain are all illicit but widely perceived as "culturally legitimate" acts within each one of those countries.[25] The point here is not to establish a hierarchy of illegal acts and cast a comparative moral judgment so as to identify which is worse, or even to see which form of corruption is more detrimental to, say, economic growth. It is, rather, to understand how in every society individuals and groups exploit the tensions between the desirable and the permissible, seeking at every opportunity to make use of the loopholes, or interstices, through which such "corruption" can be achieved.

However, the art of interpretation is not just about a scientific method. It is also about the narrative of comparative analysis, that which Geertz calls the work of the critic. Explaining what makes sense to others, the logic of what they do, depends on our ability to find the right locutions in our own analytical language. Here, too, present trends in political science are adverse, for they tend to narrow down comparative discourse to jargon-like utterances that merely attend to the lowest common denominator. In the case of corruption, what is comparatively least interesting is a statement such as, for instance, "there is more corruption in societies where economic growth is low." The banality of the conclusion, true as it may well be, is made worse by the fact that the formulation lacks any real critical insight. What is interesting about corruption is not so much why it exists, but what it signifies. To give texture to that question is to try to articulate the complexities of what corruption actually means in these different settings. How do the Italians, South Koreans, Nigerians, Kuwaitis, or British express their form of corruption, and how do they use language both to justify and condemn such activities?

What is needed is to write about the phenomena we attempt to compare by means of a language that is attuned to the terrain in which we are working. We cannot, of course, merely translate the words that are used by the actors themselves, but we can find more original ways of reflecting what those words mean if we allow ourselves to stray far beyond the constraints of social science terminology. There is, clearly, a thin line between language that sheds light on what is happening in any given society and facile metaphors with implicit meanings that may distort what is being discussed. It is, for example, debatable whether the expression "the politics of the belly," as employed by a French political scientist to conjure the complex links between politics and economics in Africa, evokes in the Western reader the image that is most illuminating.[26] This is because, in this case, "the politics of the belly" immediately points to corruption whereas what is interesting in the book in question is the extent to which modern political practices are anchored in the cultural and historical roots of African polities—or, to put it differently, how the state is historicized.

The point here is less to focus attention on the (admittedly) intricate question of corruption than to illustrate the extent to which both interpretation and enunciation can be made meaningfully scientific. What is at stake is not just the right language but the critical method best suited to comparative politics. Although there are no obvious standard means of understanding and accounting for different political arenas, there are approaches that are more attuned to the job of listening, interpreting, and rendering in the appropriate language the realities we study.

The cultural methodology I advocate is not one beholden to any particular theory, either in political science, anthropology, or literature. I seek to use a notion of culture that is enabling, and not restrictive; open ended, and not constraining; enlightening, and not obscuring. This is the measure of the undertaking. The validity of the analysis does not lie in the accuracy or pedigree of a definition of culture, but only in the extent to which it helps explain political acts, events, and processes within a comparative perspective. I have found Geertz's approach helpful both in the manner in which it conceptualizes culture and in the framework it proposes for looking at politics as an arena. However, mine is not a Geertzian model—insofar as that exists—but, as I argue in my book *Culture Troubles*, a call for an eclectic methodology.

PATRICK CHABAL was a leading scholar on African history, politics, and literature. He taught at King's College London for over thirty years. His books include *The End of Conceit: Western Rationality After Postcolonialism* and *Power in Africa: An Essay in Political Interpretation.*

Notes

An earlier version of this argument appeared in Patrick Chabal and Jean-Pascal Daloz, *Culture Troubles: Politics and the Interpretation of Meaning* (Chicago: Chicago University Press, 2006).

1. On this debate, see Patrick Chabel, "Who Speaks for Africa?" *Cahiers d'Études africaines* 204 (2011): 979–988.

2. Patrick Chabal, *The End of Conceit: Western Rationality After Postcolonialism* (London: Zed, 2012).

3. As Clifford Geertz writes: "As interworked systems of construable signs (what, ignoring provincial usages, I would call symbols), culture is not a power, something to which social events, behaviors, institutions or processes can be causally attributed; it is a context, something within which they can be intelligibly—that is, thickly—described." "Thick Description: Toward an Interpretive Theory of Culture," in *The Interpretation of Cultures* (New York: Basic Books, 1973), 14.

4. See Lawrence Harrison and Samuel Huntington, eds., *Culture Matters: How Values Shape Human Progress* (New York: Basic Books, 2000).

5. On this issue, M. H. Ross writes: "I argue that two distinct, but not unrelated, features of culture are relevant to comparative politics. First, culture is a system of meaning that people use to manage their daily worlds, large and small; second, culture is the basis of the social and political identity that affects how people line up and how they act on a wide range of matters." "Culture and Identity in Comparative Political Analysis," in *Comparative Politics: Rationality, Culture and Structure*, ed. Mark Lichbach and Alan Zuckerman (Cambridge: Cambridge University Press, 1997), 42.

6. Geertz, *Interpretation of Cultures*, 89.

7. Ibid., 5.

8. Whether Geertz would today be unhappy with the use of the concept of "semiotic," which he would see as being aligned with the structural approaches he disliked, is an open question. I, for my part, am in agreement with his original formulation and do not follow the structuralists on this point. I am concerned with meanings and not merely signs. For a more general discussion, see Kenneth Rice, *Geertz and Culture* (Ann Arbor: University of Michigan Press, 1980); and, more particularly, Sherry Ortner, *The Fate of "Culture": Geertz and Beyond* (Berkeley: University of California Press, 1997).

9. Geertz, *Interpretation of Cultures*, 312.

10. As it is in much American classical political science since the days of Karl Deutsch. See *The Nerves of Government* (New York: Free Press, 1963).

11. There is, of course, a body of work that defines culture in terms of the symbolic and, along with this, an approach to politics that takes symbolism seriously. See, for instance, Murray Edelman, *Politics as Symbolic Action* (Chicago: Markham, 1971), although for me, however, this author takes an excessively instrumental view of culture.

12. Of course, Weber was influenced by nineteenth-century evolutionary theories and believed, for instance, in the gradual rationalization of politics over time. However, one can find rich conceptual insights without subscribing to such teleology.

13. For a discussion of Geertz's work in context, see Fred Inglis, *Clifford Geertz: Culture, Custom and Ethics* (Cambridge: Polity, 2000).

14. See here Patrick Chabel, *Africa: The Politics of Suffering and Smiling* (London: Zed, 2009).

15. On common sense, Geertz again provides us with a pithy comment: "Common sense [is] a cultural system; a loosely connected body of belief and judgement, rather than just what anybody properly put together cannot help but think. . . . Common sense is not a fortunate faculty, like perfect pitch; it is a special frame of mind, like piety or legalism. And like piety or legalism (or ethics or cosmology) it both differs from one place to the next and takes, nevertheless, a characteristic form." *Local Knowledge* (New York: Basic Books, 1983), 10–11.

16. A comprehensive analysis of democratization is to be found in Michael Bratton and Nicholas van de Walle, *Democratic Experiments in Africa: Regime Transitions in Comparative Perspective* (Cambridge: Cambridge University Press, 1997).

17. See University of Michigan's ongoing Afrobarometer Series (www.afrobarometer.org), conducting surveys on key political issues, many of which are related to democratization, in a number of African countries.

18. The following argument is drawn from Patrick Chabal and Jean-Pascal Daloz, *Africa Works* (Oxford: James Currey, 1999); and Patrick Chabal, "The Quest for Good Government and Development in Africa: Is NEPAD the Answer?" *International Affairs* 78, no. 3 (2002): 447–462.

19. For a discussion of plausibility in social sciences, see Chabal, *End of Conceit.*

20. See here Chabal, *Africa.*

21. For a comparative discussion of the state and political representation in Sweden, France, and Nigeria, see Chabal and Daloz, *Culture Troubles*, chapters 9 and 10.

22. Geertz, *Local Knowledge*, 10.

23. See here how corruption is understood by the influential nongovernmental organization Transparency International, which publishes a yearly *Global Corruption Report*: https://www.transparency.org/research/gcr/.

24. For an enlightening analysis of the African situation, see J. P. Oliver de Sardan, "A Moral Economy of Corruption," *Journal of Modern African Studies* 37, no. 1 (1999): 25–52.

25. I do not mean to imply here either that all members of a particular society agree or that they all behave in the same ways, or that there are not significant differences between groups within a given society.

26. Jean-François Bayart, *The State in Africa: The Politics of the Belly* (London: Longman, 1993).

2 Joined at the Hip

African Literature and Africa's Body Politic

Niyi Osundare

We may as well begin by pressing the gynecological metaphor in the title of this chapter into fuller service since a major part of our deliberation focuses on the birthing of two vital and closely related phenomena and their respective and/or collective roles in the bewildering conundrum called African modernity. African literature as we know it today and African nation-states (if "nation-state" is, indeed, not an ambitious, even unreal designation in our present circumstances) are offspring of the same body politic. More intimately, more specifically, they are like Siamese twins, joined at the hip, troubled and agitated, fraternal but not identical, facing different directions but bound by a common destiny, longing for a common destination. They are parallel lines that meet at certain junctures before veering once again onto different pathways. Quite often, I wish they had been joined at the head, a condition that, no doubt, would have made their medical problem more critical and more intimidating, but that would have ensured the possibility of a common think tank, so to speak, a unified intelligence, a mutual insemination, and, possibly, a common purpose.

However, a second thought on the peculiarities and demonstrated dispositions of these two phenomena compels a reconsideration of my former wish. Maybe it is just as well that these two are not joined at the head. Maybe it is to the eternal benefit of Africa that the brain that runs its politics is separate from the one that controls its mind, though the danger in this situation is that the separation that leads to the prevention of mutual pollution also frustrates the possibility of reciprocal regeneration. For we are dealing with two crucial institutions here: Africa's republic of politics and Africa's republic of letters, the former the province dominated by politicians and public functionaries, the latter the domain of writers, public intellectuals, and other generators and purveyors of dreams and visions, ideals and ideas.

For a time these two parallel lines did indeed meet—when the two republics coincided in vision, purpose, and practice; when the same fire for a free, just, and sane polity burned in their breasts, and their definition of humanism came from the same dictionary. The arsenal of words and ideas from literary and liberal arts reinforced those forged from the metal and iron of *realpolitik*, assailing the bastions of imperialism, with a clear and urgent call for FREEDOM NOW. Poets, pundits, pamphleteers, and politicians joined forces and became prophets of a new dawn.

The nineteenth and early twentieth centuries constituted a period prodigiously famous for the birth of African nationalism especially in the West African region. Towering writers and intellectuals such as Edward Wilmot Blyden, Alexander Crummell, James "Holy" Johnson, James Africanus Beale Horton, and Samuel Ajayi Crowther laid a solid foundation for the promotion and development of the idea of this nationalism and the generation and dissemination of the discourse that imprinted that idea in the public mind. Mostly recaptive African slaves, immigrants from the United States and the West Indies, these soundly educated men made it their historic duty to spread the gift of enlightenment to fellow Africans, to provide the kind of education without which political and cultural liberation would simply have remained a distant dream. The trail they blazed was soon followed by the likes of J. E. Casely Hayford, S. R. B. Attoh Ahuma, J. M. Sarbah, Kobina Sekyi, Mojola Agbebi, and Reverend Samuel Johnson, author of the perennially relevant *History of the Yorubas*.[1] Without a doubt, these are the real fathers (yes, fathers—they were all chronically male!) of Africa's political and cultural independence. Fortified by their education and intimate knowledge of the sources of Western power, they understood the complex dynamics of imperialism and its methods of operation. More importantly, they understood the twists of history; that the thrasonically imperial Europe of the late nineteenth century also crawled before it walked. Here, Horton reminds imperial Europe about an unflattering bit of its own history:

> "Rome was not built in a day"; the proudest kingdom in Europe was once in a state of barbarism perhaps worse than now exists amongst the tribes chiefly inhabiting the West Coast of Africa, and it is an incontrovertible axiom that what has been done can again be done. If Europe, therefore, has been raised to her present pitch of civilization by progressive advancement, Africa, too, with a guarantee of the civilization of the north, will rise into equal importance. . . . We may well say that the present state of Western Africa is, in fact, the history of the world repeating itself.[2]

There is, no doubt, a lot in Horton's statement that would make the contemporary African reader uncomfortable: his ascription of barbarism to the African "tribes"; his arrogation of "progressive advancement" to Europe; his confident belief in the "civilizing mission" by the "north." We may want to quarrel with Horton's attempt to use the past to enlighten and humanize the present through his appropriation of the recursive trajectory of history ("what has been done can again be done") to make a case for the possibility of Africa's advancement. We may cringe at the fact that his vocabulary, much like his thinking, sprang straight out of the colonial lexicon, thereby forcing us to wonder what kind of civilization he had in mind, and the complexion of the future he envisaged for Africa. But we must not forget that Horton was very much a man of his time—and that is no idle cliché—a roundly Victorian intellectual with solid Creole credentials, who saw no contradiction between his status as an enlightened citizen of the empire and his role as an African nationalist. But there is an important lesson that must not be missed in Horton's statement: in his appeal to historical antecedents, Horton sought to teach Europe a lesson in humility and so-called barbarous Africa a lesson in history-derived fortitude and the possibility of hope.

Horton, Blyden, and others were the public intellectuals of their day. But they were philosophers who never became kings because their contemporary domain was occupied and ruled by kings from other lands. So, to reiterate our core metaphor, they were predominantly denizens of the republic of letters, not commanders-in-chief in the republic of politics. To them and their tremendous initiatives must be traced the achievements of later figures such as Kwame Nkrumah, Nnamdi Azikiwe, Julius Nyerere, and Léopold Sédar Senghor, who utilized the vital inspiration and impetus from the pioneers in the struggle for political independence. These and other independence-era leaders stood tall on the shoulders of the pioneers, plunged themselves into the robust anticolonial discourse that suffused the world in the wake of World War II, fueled this discourse into ardent agitation, which drew additional sustenance from the Pan-Africanist philosophy of titanic diasporic Africans such as W. E. B. Du Bois, Aimé Césaire, Léon Damas, C. L. R. James, and so on, and wrested independence from the jaws of the colonial behemoth. Parallel lines still found a way to meet: the republic of letters and the republic of politics did not only coincide; in a number of cases, they did so in the same individual.

In the few instances where that happened, we had a felicitous meeting of dream and daring, ideal and idea; a happy correspondence between the hand that pushed the pen and the one that held the scepter. Nkrumah, acute political theorist and writer, philosophized his way into supreme power, becoming the founding president of the new state of Ghana. Senghor, prodigious poet and noted theoretician of negritude, rhapsodized his way to the presidency of a new Senegal. Nyerere, teacher, thinker, and literary translator, reasoned his way into the state house in Tanzania. These examples were followed by the likes of Agostinho Neto, the poet of tender heart and sacred hope who became the first president of Angola after a long and bloody war against a rapacious Portuguese colonialism.

These statesmen progressed from theory to practice, from the idea of state to the complex reality of statecraft. Like former Czech president Václav Havel, the playwright and political thinker who was literally drafted from the theater of painted masks and fleeting phantoms to the bristling theater of political leadership in a period of chronic national crises, the new African statesmen were confronted with enormous challenges involved in birthing new nations and nurturing them into steady health, sustainable growth, and meaningful development. Of course, I am not unmindful of the fact that the African statesmen mentioned previously faced problems more fundamental and more daunting than those faced by their Czech counterpart. And, as is evident in the contemporary African situation, their achievements are anything but even, their legacies hardly without a certain measure of controversy.

But their examples have shown that there was a time in Africa when the republic of letters and the republic of politics coincided in the same figure/actor; when the mind that thought wielded a strong influence on the hand that wrought. Noticeably, though not surprisingly, this also occurred at a time when both republics had a common enemy in the colonial system, a time when the fight for independence provided a rallying platform and a common vision. Unfortunately, that common cause concealed the cracks in the commonweal. The intent of the freedom fighters was the same; the plan of battle was without contention, but the resultant dividends opened up the gap between loyalty and betrayal, opportunity and opportunism. Seek ye first the political kingdom, the legendary Nkrumah is reputed to have counseled; and all other things shall be added unto thee. But when that kingdom arrived after bloody battles and enervating delays, it came with kings with golden crowns and slippers made of human skin, palanquined by a populace ravaged by hunger and humiliating poverty. Alas, the sun of independence, as the Ivorian novelist Ahmadou Kourouma reminds us, has been stifled by clouds of regret and disillusionment.

All over Africa, the gap between the euphoria of independence and the angst wrought by dispiriting disappointment was tragically short. African tyrants maneuvered themselves onto thrones vacated by erstwhile colonial masters. New orders now came from the same old colonial castle on the hill, the accent this time native and tellingly fàmiliar, the message hollow and laced with deceit. The people looked at the old white oppressors and then at their new black successors, and what confronted their gaze was an aching similarity. Colonialism is dead; long live neocolonialism! Welcome to Africa's era of turbulent modernity.

With postindependence disillusionment came a historic rupture between the two republics. The republic of letters looked at the unfolding situation in Africa and distilled its agony into a rhetorical question: Is it for this we drove away the invaders/usurpers? Ayi Kwei Armah took one long cynical look at the rot and chaos of postindependence Ghana and summarized his verdict in a memorably declarative sentence: *The Beautyful Ones Are Not Yet Born* (1968), a title that came, symbolically enough, from the legend on a public transportation vehicle.

The scorching veracity and alarming candor in Armah's title is a signature tune for the drastic change in the relationship between the two republics. This is just as well. For the republic of letters, which took Africa's politics to task in the aftermath of independence, is populated by well-educated and articulate young men and women old enough to witness the struggle for independence, mature enough to behold its attainment, and wise enough to assess its aftermath. Time and its chronological/genealogical imperatives also play a role in the relationship between the two republics, as revealed by the following long list. At Ghana's independence in 1957, Efua Sutherland was 33, Kofi Awoonor was 32, Armah was 18, and Ama Ata Aidoo was 15. When Nigeria became independent in 1960, Chinua Achebe and Mabel Segun were 30, Christopher Okigbo was 28, Wole Soyinka was 26, and J. P. Clark-Bekederemo was 25. Raymond Sarif Easmon and Syl Cheney-Coker were 48 and 16, respectively, at Sierra Leone's independence in 1961. Ngũgĩ wa Thiong'o was 25 years old when Kenya became independent in 1963, while Okot p'Bitek was already 31 by the time the Union Jack was lowered in Uganda in 1962. At Senegal's independence in 1960, Sembène Ousmane was 37. And to cite the most curious of them all, when South Africa attained its own independence in 1994, its major early writers were old enough to be its great-grandparents: Es'kia Mphahlele was 76, Nadine Gordimer was 71, Daniel Kunene was 71, Dennis Brutus was 70, Athol Fugard was 62, and Mazisi Kunene was 60.

In a manner of speaking, we are dealing with writers who are older than their countries, and whose developments in every sphere are intimately tied up with the growth of those countries. Thus, these writers had thrust on them the heavy responsibility of helping their countries through their birth pangs, nurturing them into a healthy adulthood, and guiding them along the path of enlightenment and sound, enduring development. Every aspect of their youthful talents, including their art, became a veritable brick in the nation-building process. And from the very outset, these writers saw the fault lines in the new national terrain and assumed the somewhat shamanic role of proffering visions against the cataclysmic quakes that loomed in a cloudy horizon. For example, Soyinka was barely 25 when he wrote *A Dance of the Forests*, a play commissioned for Nigeria's independence celebrations in 1960. This prodigiously precocious play (arguably the playwright's most complex, most thronged, and least unstageable to date), confronted the new nation with a stark, disturbingly embarrassing image of itself. The young writer looked beyond the orgy of revelry and jollification arising from the independence euphoria, beyond the syrupy optimism and naïve, self-serving nationalism in the air; and what he saw was not a nation but "a gathering of the tribes," custom-bound, incoherent, riotous; tormented by unexpiated crimes of the past, incapable of the daunting challenges of the present, too dense, too myopic to think about the future. His verdict? Independence, Nigeria's darling trophy, was nothing more than Half-Child, pulled in different directions by mindless oligarchs, a veritable corpse-in-waiting. There goes the tale: the nation asks for a song of celebration of itself; the writer gives it instead an elegy coupled with a warning. Today, over fifty years since independence, Nigeria's nationhood is still a contentious issue; the atmosphere is still rent with discordant antagonisms of the gathered and gathering tribes. Soyinka's prophetic pessimism in this play serves as a chilling antecedent to the morbid nihilism in *Madmen and Specialists* (1971), a play strongly influenced by the murderous barbarism of the Nigerian civil war—a war that ensued when, brutalized by blood-curdling pogrom, one of the tribes made a desperate attempt to secede from the gathering, while the gathering did everything it could to bomb it back into the fold.

Very early in his literary career, Soyinka had made known his preference for divination over postmortem, *Moniran* (I-saw-it-coming) as against *Abamo* (Had-I-known). This credo was already clear in his works and utterances even before it was neatly and memorably coded in his 1968 Stockholm declaration in which he saw the writer as "the voice of vision in his own time"; a voice that must begin "by exposing the future in a clear and truthful exposition of the present."[3] In this declaration, Soyinka was at one with virtually every member of the first generation of modern African writers. The similarity in the symptoms of postindependence malaise in nearly all African countries strengthened the commonality of the writers' resolve. The yawning gap between promise and fulfillment, between lofty expectations and sordid actualities, threw Africa's young literature into a paroxysm of protest and revolt. There seemed to be no solution to the parting of ways between the republic of politics and the republic of letters.

Differential visions. Clashing dreams. Competing apprehensions. Divergent pathways. The republic of letters holds up the mirror; the republic of politics looks away. One plays Country-Hide; the other responds with Country-Seek. To my mind, no African writer, except perhaps Ngũgĩ, has been clearer, more insistent, and more consistent than Achebe in the articulation of the necessity of social and moral accountability of African literature and the inevitability of the writer's role in the shaping of the destiny of the continent. In his justifiably famous essay "The Novelist as Teacher," published pretty early in his career, the author of *Things Fall Apart* left no one in doubt as to the imperative of the task of "re-education and regeneration that must be done" by the writer who, he agrees with Mphahlele, is the sensitive point of his community.[4] In this his cogitations are not far from Abiola Irele's reflections on "the immediate correlation in African literature between life and expression," since literature is a unique communicator of a "structure of feeling" as well as a reflector of "a climate of thought."[5] In these and similar instances, African literary practitioners were, to borrow the words of Olakunle George, nothing short of vociferous "theorists of agency."[6]

Now, let us pause for a moment and consider the definitive, even baptismal audacity in the very title of Achebe's essay. "The Novelist as Teacher"? What transgressive impudence, what tendentious rebelliousness, what bullish chutzpah could have led a (then) little-known African writer just emerging from the overwhelming clutches of colonialism to toy so irreverently with the sacrosanct tenets of one of the empire's received literary genres? Achebe even scoffed at the art-for-art's-sake, the-text-is-the-thing doctrine and its ancillary pure art credo in an era when the shadows of New Criticism still loomed awesomely large with all its formalist strictures, and the literary text was regarded as an autotelic, self-contained, self referential entity disengaged from social answerability and external considerations no matter how relevant. At a time when unelected legislators of literary taste privileged form over content, and the likes of I. A. Richards and William Empson pointed the way to microscopic psychologizing of the text, Achebe opted for a holistic sociological embrace manifested by a literary community in which the writer is aware of his duty and the audience never loses sight of its expectations. Achebe was advocating an art that was meaningful, useful, and socially accountable.

To some, Achebe's position here may sound overly defensive, indirectly proactive, or even preemptive, but one thing is sure: he set the tone for the criticism, evaluation, and reception of an emerging African literature by focusing the world's attention on the peculiar circumstances of that literature and the historic responsibilities imposed on its creators. In other words, Achebe was making a case for differential aesthetics, a reconceptualization of principles and standards that allows the new literature a reasonable degree of autonomy of theory and practice consistent with its own provenance, ontology, and imperative, different from existing standards, but no less viable, no less engaging. From the very beginning, African writers were not only possessed by the urge to write, they also felt the need to show to the world the historical and pragmatic factors that informed and drove the theory behind their practice. They had to do this because they were inserting themselves and their art into a tradition that was already formed and set in its cultural, epistemological, and social certitude, one that had no place for them, and was therefore likely to treat them with the kind of misrecognition and misnaming that had been the lot of other aspects of the African universe. They were dealing with a tradition for which Achebe's idea of "applied art" was nothing short of insufferable blasphemy.

Enlarge the reading list, "un-can" the canon, broaden the theoretical and critical criteria, humanize the imperative of form with the necessity of content, Achebe seems to be saying to the empire's guardians of literary taste. Thoughtful admonitions, no doubt, for without these, the dialogue between Africa's republic of letters and its republic of politics would not have been possible. The form of Africa's art cannot avoid the pull of its content. Achebe's 1965 essay could not have been far from Ngũgĩ's mind when, sixteen years later, and just out of incarceration without charge in his native Kenya, he made that clear, defiant declaration: "Every writer is a writer in politics. The only question is what and whose politics?"[7]

This clamorous politicality, this bold confidence in the didactic, regenerative power of literature, is something like an article of faith among second-generation African poets, many of whose works are prefaced with memorable manifestoes. Hear, for example, Odia Ofeimun, a prominent member of that group:

> I have come down
> to tell my story
> by the same fireside
> around which
> my people are gathered
> . . .
> And I must tell my story
> to nudge and awaken them
> that sleep
> among my people[8]

Not quite done with this declaration in the prologue, the poet blares forth his mission that is chilling in its putrescent specificity:

> I cannot blind myself
> to putrefying carcasses in the marketplace
> pulling giant vultures
> from the sky[9]

In a diction and tone that evoke powerful intimations of the Guyanese poet Martin Carter, Ofeimun sweeps to an assertive coda: "A garland of subversive litanies / should answer these morbid landscapes."[10]

Those "subversive litanies" rally to song and credo in Frank Chipasula. In his appositely titled, eminently quotable poem, "Manifesto On *Ars Poetica*," the poet tells the world:

> My poem is exacting a confession
> From me: I will not keep the truth
> From my song . . .
> . . .
> I will not wash the blood off the image
> . . .
> I will not clean the poem to impress the tyrant
> I will not bend my verses into the bow of a praise song
> I will put the symbols of murder hidden in high places

in the center of my crude lines of accusations.
I will undress our raped land and expose her wounds.
I will pierce the silence around our land with sharp metaphors
And I will point the light of my poems into the dark
nooks where our people are pounded to pulp.[11]

The war against collaborative silence; the poet's burning desire to put the light in the dark(ened) tunnel of his country; conflation of patriotic love and romantic love (or the idealization of the country as woman); images that walk the thin line between reactionary violence and revolutionary violence: these are constant tropes in African poetry from Tanure Ojaide's gnomic admonitions to the diasporic sweep of Kofi Anyidoho and Kwadwo Opoku-Agyemang; from the wry, satiric witticisms of Jack Mapanje to the fiery antiapartheid, solidly pro-human songs of Dennis Brutus; from the urgent, carefully crafted battle songs of Ogaga Ifowodo to the gender-powered verses of Omolara Ogundipe-Lesie and Toyin Adewale. Like Cheney-Coker, poet of Sierra Leone, poet of the world, I can hear each of these poets saying:

I practice the art of poetry
Because all my country's misery rises up
From my belly[12]

These are all instances of the poet as town crier, visionary, gadfly, and patriot—the poet as a griot with a pen in his or her hand.[13]

For Soyinka, Fugard, Ola Rotimi, Femi Osofisan, Bode Sowande, Bole Butake, and Bate Besong, "the play is the thing" with which the republic of letters has been trying to catch the conscience (whatever is left of it) of the republic of politics. Virtually every African tyrant of notable notoriety has been a guest on Soyinka's stage—from the fictive Mata Kharibu to the murderously real Idi "Kamini" Amin, Emperor "Boky" Bokassa, and General Sani "Baabu" Abacha. If apartheid had any sense of shame, it would have wept to death in the theater of Fugard. Ngũgĩ and Micere Mugo resurrected the soul and spirit of Dedan Kimathi, the legendary Kenyan liberation warrior, holding up his struggles and dreams to a gaggle of rapacious neocolonial inheritors whose warped values and mimic grotesqueries are displayed before the audience in *Ngaahika Ndeenda* (*I Will Marry When I Want*; 1977). In play after play, Osofisan has confronted us with the corrupting nature of power, the deficit of Africa's political leadership, the dangers inherent in gullible, lethargic followership, while the theaters of Butake and Besong ripple with parables that excoriate the antics of their country's despotic democracy. In nuanced and carefully orchestrated dramaturgy, Penina Mlama Muhando tells the story of contemporary Tanzania, reminding her compatriots that no incense can completely mask the foul smell of rot.

The African writer's transgressive and combative interventions have not come without cost. The emperor's sword has frequently come down hard on the poet's pen. The walls of Africa's prisons are littered with graffiti left behind by political prisoners whose paths to incarceration were paved by the nibs of their pens: Brutus, Soyinka, Ahmed Fouad Negm, Ngũgĩ, Nawal El Saadawi, Abdellatif Laâbi, Awoonor, Arthur Nortje, Mapanje, Felix Mnthali, Chipasula, Besong, Kunle Ajibade, Ifowodo, Akin Adesokan—the list is long. Some have been thrown into a painful, prolonged exile (Nuruddin Farah and Chenjerai Hove). Some have been made to pay the supreme price: Christopher Okigbo, one of Africa's finest poets, perished in the Nigerian civil war; while Ken Saro-Wiwa was hanged by the Nigerian state under the murderous grip of General Abacha. Ruth First, second to none in the enlightened and courageous fight for human freedom, was assassinated by a letter bomb by South Africa's apartheid government. The republic of politics is blissfully aware of the irresponsible and apparently unlimited power of the ruler in the modern African state, his or her monopoly of the weapons of coercion and control, and the alarming frequency of the deployment of those weapons. The republic of letters presses ahead all the same, empowered by a combination of idealism and stubborn hope, the justness of its cause and the apparent imperishability of its vision, believing against all odds, as Keorapetse Kgositsile did in the height of the apartheid barbarism, that "Change is gonna come!"[14]

Alas, the purposive conviction, committed intelligence, moral energy, and visionary acumen that have driven African literary discourse in the last half-century or so seem to have waned in recent times. The "truth" that the fiction of our letters spoke to the "fact" of our politics now lies choked up in the verbiage of crass, indulgent academicism and servile genuflections at the altar of High Theory (to borrow Biodun Jeyifo's apt designation).[15] Time was when African literature was deemed undertheorized, and many of us saw that flaw as one of the sure signs of our underdevelopment, even intellectual inadequacy. No longer, thank goodness. Now we labor to out-Derrida Jacques Derrida; out-trope Jacques Lacan; and over-transgress Michel Foucault with the "interrogative" head of his subversive arrow pointed in the wrong direction. We jumped on the "post-" bandwagon without a thorough, insightful probing of our own "pre-"existing conditions; without a long and deep consideration of the politics of the provenance of these theories—the historical, social, cultural, and epistemological imperatives that mothered their birth, and which, therefore, necessitated a critical and selective application of their paradigms to the African situation. We became postcolonial (or we were baptized so) all of a sudden, at the instance of trendy theory and theorists, at the expense of our peculiar reality and experience.

Yes, a masquerade called postcolonialism (and allied "posts") entered with a flourish, and many of us responded with an apparently literal, even fallacious interpretation of the term and an almost superstitious belief in its denotative import. Some of our finest scholars even played typographical and grammatical games with the hyphen between the prefix "post-" and its complex morpheme "colonialism."[16] The more the trendier "postcolonial" rides the wind, the less we hear of its older, truer alternative, "neocolonial." Thus, a couple of years ago, the very postcolonial nation of Côte d'Ivoire, or Ivory Coast, a very postcolonial country once called the Eden of West Africa, was ravaged by a series of interethnic and religious pogroms that were primordial in their logic and medieval in their barbarism. After a long period of bloody conflict resulting in a virtual political meltdown of this postcolonial country, it was gendarmes from France, the mother country, that came to the rescue. And now a gratefully postcolonial Ivory Coast totters on, on scar-ravaged feet. Not quite half a decade later, Mali, another West African country, had nearly half of its territory occupied by Islamic fundamentalists who immediately declared war on ancient sites and monuments, including the world-famous treasures of the City of Timbuktu. A helpless Mali had to look beyond its borders for assistance in the de-Talibanization offensive, from fellow African countries—equipped and prodded by mother countries from the West. At the economic level, the central banks of most African countries are under virtual receivership by the World Bank, the International Monetary Fund (IMF), or both. With postcolonial begging bowls in hand as they crawl for loans and handouts in Paris or London or New York, the most astringent, most dehumanizing conditionalities are imposed on these countries, resulting in sudden, irrational currency devaluation, massive poverty and disease, closedown of firms and factories engendering a drastic reduction in the productive capacity of the people, loss of national confidence, political instability, and recursive postcolonial anomie. I ask: Is Africa's situation, then, that of colonial postcoloniality or postcolonial colonialist?

And what is the fate of African culture in our fiercely postcolonial discourse? With the vernacularization of indigenous languages in the educational system, their progressive loss of function and significance in public affairs, and their overall devaluation in the national psyche, more and more Africans are trying to get by without being able to spell their indigenous names. There are talks now about "the dying languages of Africa," "Africa's disappearing languages," "Africa's threatened languages," "languages in perils," and so on. And those among us not too postcolonial to notice our progressive deracination should proclaim in loud and clear voices that a language does not die alone. Since the advent of colonialism, Africa has fallen into a state of abysmal silence. That silence is becoming more chilling, more dangerous as most Africans sink into alingualism, a terrible state of disarticulation in which one has sacrificed his mother tongue in pursuit of a foreign language that he is not in a position to master to any appreciative degree. Have any of our postcolonial theorists ever wondered why African literature is a discipline in which you can become an expert, even a professor, without ever knowing any African language? Or are there any weapons in the postcolonial arsenal to justify or rationalize this baffling and significant anomaly? African languages are going the way of indigenous African *orishas* (deities): abused, subjugated, subverted, and displaced. The effect of colonial Talibans on our articles of faith and our consequent loss of belief in the indigenous dispensation is closely allied to the psychological, social, and political chaos that is the lot of contemporary Africa. It is also one of the reasons Africa has come to the so-called modernity with missing values, as that "languageless monster" that Shakespeare saw in his Caliban four centuries ago.

And yet no sooner are these issues raised, no sooner are these losses and dispossessions identified for possible deliberation than the charges of nativism and essentialism are unleashed in the postcolonialist arena. How so dismissively, and at times, how so derisively, we deploy these epithets! Who can forget the fury with which they were hurled at Ngũgĩ some years ago for daring to declare his faith in Gikuyu as a fitting medium of literary expression? Would that have happened if his declaration had been: "From now on it is English all the way?" Hardly, for the curious logic of our reasoning goes this way: the choice of English is a sign of cosmopolitanism and internationalism; a vote for Africa's indigenous language is a symptom of nativism and localism. On many occasions I have met non-Africans that are much more protective, more positive, and more defensive of African languages than the very Africans themselves! Without any attempt at atavistic regression into neo-Tarzanism or the syrupy extremities of Senghorian negritudism, we need to apply a more sympathetic intelligence to our appraisal of African culture, particularly the genuine attempts at the retrieval of Africa's indigenous soul and the foregrounding of its peculiar circumstances. Also urgently needed: a drastic rethinking of our current theory of alienation, with the focus on the following questions: What exactly are we alienating ourselves from, or what is alienating itself from us; isn't it time we *dis*-alienated the concept of alienation itself in its apparent valorization of estrangement from the autochthonous self and rationalization of an abstract and reified exilic ideal?[17] How do we evaluate a rootless cosmopolitanism that plies the global sky but is completely empty of its African content? I see nothing postmodernly odd or postcolonially perverse in the effort to restore the African soul, especially at this time in our history when what the continent desperately needs is a second stage of decolonization. But to be able to do that, we need to first decolonize our discourse and find a cure for that pathological eccentricity that Olúfẹ́mi Táíwò has discussed with such insight and visionary engagement in a piece auspiciously entitled "Celebrating Yoruba Culture: An Open Letter to the Global Yoruba Elite."[18]

It is no exaggeration to aver that the misnaming of the African condition has resulted in a certain kind of misrecognition and false consciousness, which in turn have engendered a degree of false security. In many contemporary writings, "writers in politics" (à la Ngũgĩ) look very much like trespassers in a strange land, irksome interlopers in matters that are far from their legitimate concern. After all, colonialism has been "posted"; therefore, further preoccupation with it can only end up being an otiose indulgence, passé, even essentialist.

The fact on the African ground is so tragically far from the engagement of many of our contemporary scholars and their discursive practices (forgive that cliché; its chic and airy denomination makes its use unavoidably attractive!). There is too much idle theorizing in our current discourse; too much exogeneity; too much ventriloquism and chronic jargoneering; too much zealous genuflection at the altar of High Theory. There is a crying need to balance erudition with wisdom; reflection with relevance; a need to achieve sophistication devoid of sophistry.

I believe very strongly that our present exogeneist mentality is a child of many parents, one of them being the massive "migration, exile, and displacement" of African writers and scholars in the past two decades.[19] Whether we agree with Emmanuel Obiechina's passionate and well-argued reading of this situation as a major symptom of the African intellectual's "many-sided dilemma" as stated in his article "The Dilemma of the African Intellectual in the Modern World," or pitch our tent with Jeyifo's characteristically cerebral and rigorous riposte in "One Year in the First Instance," one fact remains: for many African writers, the relocation at issue here is nothing short of *dis*location, a profound, fundamental rupture with multiple consequences.[20]

The falcon is finding it more and more difficult to hear the falconer, to borrow from William B. Yeats. With a substantial portion of African literature coming from African writers living abroad, and the literature itself being published where the authors live, and frequently subject to the trends of current theoretical and critical pressures and demands in their new habitation, an aching gap threatens the bond between the writer and his or her home audience. We may hold up a few exemplars such as Helon Habila, Sefi Attah, Véronique Tadjo, Calixthe Beyala, Biyi Bandele-Thomas, and the wondrously gifted Chimamanda Adichie as significant exceptions to this rule, but we must not allow this to blind us to the profundity of the problem that arises when the native tongue is too far from the writer's ear, and the home is nothing more than a dimly remembered landscape. There is a hunger in the soul, a thirst in the heart that can hardly be assuaged by glamorously hyperbolic denominations such as "citizen of the world," "global intellectual," "universal verity," "traveling theory," "traveling texts," and suchlike purveyors of essentialist globalism. We must be honest and realistic enough to admit that something vital is lost when the writer no longer remembers the smell and sound of the source from which she claims to draw her idioms, when the yearning hands of the indigenous characters she purports to create can no longer touch the helm of her consciousness. But swept along by the tide of trendy theorizing, we become mimic men of the margin who hardly ever ask where, exactly, is Africa's place on a global map drawn by those who control the pencil as well as the paper?[21] How do we answer so eagerly to names invented for us by others while we forget and denounce our own? Why do we bend so obediently to the whiff of foreign winds?

I remember the years between 1960 and 1980 with palpable nostalgia: the sense of history, clarity of vision, and urgency of message that characterized the discourse of the Achebe generation; the way literary discourse broke through disciplinary boundaries, connecting cogently with disputations in the social sciences where the development theories of pacesetters such as Samir Amin, Walter Rodney, Claude Ake, Omafume Onoge, Segun Osoba, Bala Usman, Ola Oni, Bade Onimode, and Abdulrahman Mohamed Babu reverberated through classrooms and seminars before bouncing into the policy profiles of the likes of Nyerere's *Ujamaa* (familyhood, African socialism) and Nkrumah's discourses on sociopolitical engineering and Pan-Africanism. Those were days when words *meant*, not merely signified; a time when literary communication thrived on critical and evaluative explication, not obfuscated by jargon-choked theory; when African scholars stood for African culture, unafraid of strident charges of nativism. Our obscurantist, overprofessionalized monologues today can hardly rise to such a mission and are patently incapable of such purposive ambition. When African dictators and presidents-for-life deepen our millennial misery and push us further into medieval darkness, we respond with texts laden with triumphal "aporetic" peregrinations, "dialogic contestations," "metaphysics of presence," and the like—handed-down phraseology in discursive practice. Colonialism eats deeper into the fabric of our being while we argue valiantly, so sophistically over the "post" before its name. The republic of politics laughs self-congratulatorily at the vapid antics of the republic of letters, marveling at the hermetic insipidities of the modern, postmodern, postracial pugilists of contemporary Africa's academic arena.

To ensure that that laughter is feeble and short-lived, we need to do something to the current state of our discourse. For there is so much in our fiction that can set right the truth of our polity if we heed Gordimer's counsel about the need to put "morals" solidly in the middle ground between fiction and politics.[22] Moradewun Adejunmobi indisputably captures the kernel of my concern in this chapter when, in her advocacy for "a new ethics of locality for Africa," she tells fellow African scholars in no uncertain terms that "there is a sense in which we must regain a rigorous and balanced practice of public relevance that seems to have eluded us in recent years."[23]

Literature must have a "local habitation" before it can ever have a "name"—allow me to take liberties with the words of Shakespeare. Our local habitation is Africa, the site of some of the most gruesome tragedies in human history and one of the contemporary world's most beleaguered arenas. The legendary rot and chaos in its republic of politics is constantly challenged by the excoriative energy and moral vision of its republic of letters. Between these two, there is hardly a moment of truce. This antagonistic encounter is so euphemistically summed up by Tejumola Olaniyan when he avers as follows: "For those who are familiar with African literature, its uneasy relationship with African politics is legendary."[24] It is, indeed, the "uneasy relationship" between Siamese twins joined at the hip; parallel lines that meet at awkward and dangerous places. What Country-Hide conceals beneath the shrouds, Country-Seek has been trying to unravel with the tip of the pen. Africa's journey to modernity is lit by the sparks from the clash of these two momentous phenomena.

NIYI OSUNDARE, leading poet and essayist, is Distinguished Professor of English at the University of New Orleans. His books include *City Without People: The Katrina Poems* and *Thread in the Loom: Essays on African Literature and Culture.*

Notes

1. See Gareth Griffiths, *African Literatures in English East and West* (Essex, UK: Longman, 2000); and Stephanie Newell, *West African Literatures: Ways of Reading* (Oxford: Oxford University Press, 2006).
2. Quoted in Griffiths, *African Literatures*, 32.
3. Quoted in Bernth Lindfors, *Early Soyinka* (Trenton, NJ: Africa World Press, 2008), 164.
4. Chinua Achebe, *Hopes and Impediments: Selected Essays, 1965–1987* (New York: Anchor Books, 1990), 5.
5. Abiola Irele, *The African Imagination: Literature in Africa and the Black Diaspora* (Oxford: Oxford University Press, 2001), x, xviii.
6. Olakunle George, *Relocating Agency: Modernity and African Letters* (Albany: State University of New York, 2003), 104.
7. Ngũgĩ wa Thiong'o, *Writers in Politics* (Oxford, UK: Heinemann, 1981), xii.
8. Adewale Maja-Pearce, ed., *The Heinemann Book of African Poetry in English* (Oxford, UK: Heinemann, 1990), 185.
9. Ibid., 186.
10. Ibid.
11. Ibid., 182.
12. Syl Cheney-Coker, *The Graveyard Also Has Teeth* (Oxford, UK: Heinemann, 1983), 65.

13. Newell, *West African Literatures.*

14. Cosmo Pieterse, ed., *Seven South African Poets: Poems of Exile* (London: Heinemann, 1971), 95.

15. See Biodun Jeyifo, "Literary Theory and Theories of Decolonization," in *Literary Theory and African Literature*, ed. Josef Gugler, Hans-Jürgen Lusebrink, and Jürgen Martini (Munster/Hamburg, Literature Verlag, 1994), 17–30.

16. Newell, *West African Literatures*, 172–181.

17. For a discussion of alienation, see Abiola Irele, "In Praise of Alienation," in *The Surreptitious Speech: Presence Africaine and the Politics of Otherness, 1947–1987*, ed. V. Y. Mudimbe (Chicago: University of Chicago Press, 1992): 201–224; and Tejumola Olaniyan, "On Postcoloniality and Alienation: Abiola Irele's 'In Praise of Alienation' Reconsidered," in *Africa in the World and the World in Africa: Essays in Honor of Abiola Irele*, ed. Biodun Jeyifo (Trenton, NJ: Africa World Press, 2011), 99–110.

18. Olúfẹ́mi Táíwò, "Celebrating Yoruba Culture: An Open Letter to the Global Yoruba Elite," unpublished manuscript.

19. Newell, *West African Literatures*, 186.

20. Emmanuel Obiechina, "The Dilemma of the African Intellectual in the Modern World," *Liberal Education* 78, no. 2 (1992): 3; Biodun Jeyifo, "One Year in the First Instance," in *Meditations on African Literature*, ed. Dubem Okafor (Westport, CT: Greenwood, 2000), 199.

21. Niyi Osundare, *Thread in the Loom: Essays on African Literature and Culture* (Trenton, NJ: Africa World Press, 2002), 2.

22. Nadine Gordimer, "Three in a Bed: Fiction, Morals, and Politics," in *African Literature: An Anthology of Criticism and Theory*, ed. Tejumola Olaniyan and Ato Quayson (Oxford, UK: Blackwell, 2007), 115–121.

23. Moradewun Adejunmobi, "The Humanities and a New Ethics of Locality in Africa," in Jeyifo, *Africa in the World*, 131.

24. Tejumola Olaniyan, "African Writers, Exile, and the Politics of a Global Diaspora," *West Africa Review* 4, no. 1 (2003): 3.

3 Philosophy and the State in Postcolonial Africa

Olúfẹ́mi Táíwò

PHILOSOPHY RARELY, if ever, features in the discourse of the state in postcolonial Africa. In this chapter, I argue that the philosophical idea of the state is crucial to the constitution and operation of the state in postindependence Africa. The chapter is divided into three sections.

The first section unpacks the philosophical idea of the state.[1] It argues that the character, evolution, performance, and significance of the state in Africa cannot be separated from the ongoing struggle by Africans to have redeemed for them the benefits of modernity. Only if we take this pedigree and its genealogy seriously are we in a position to realize why, in spite of the failures—and the preponderant percentage of the discourse is devoted to disseminating these failures—of the state in the postindependence period, abridging the distance between this philosophical idea of the state and its empirical realization in different African countries may be the key to more salubrious living conditions in Africa in the future.

In the second section, I contend that African contributions to the discourse, both before and while colonialism lasted, have not been given the pride of place that they deserve. This is, in part, due to the fact that the state's particular meanings to the people it rules, the cultural dimensions, going back to the colonial period and even before, have not been taken seriously. What did Africans make of the state form that colonialism foisted on them? What were their expectations of it? How did they expect it to impact their lives? These are questions that one does not come across often in the dominant literature on the state. We put these questions in focus.

The third section insists that we are not likely to come up with an adequate understanding of the vicissitudes of the state in Africa if we do not reengage with philosophy and the philosophical contributions of African thinkers, postindependence, to the discourse.

The Modern State

We begin by unpacking the type of state that we are concerned to explain.[2] In its earliest incarnations, if we were to believe Quentin Skinner's account, there was no distinction made between the state and the rulers' "'estate royal,' *estat du roi*, or *status regis*."[3] According to Skinner: "Underlying the suggestion that a distinctive quality of stateliness 'belongs' to Kings was the prevailing belief that sovereignty is intimately connected with display, that the presence of majesty serves in itself as an ordering force. . . . As late as the end of the seventeenth century, it is still common to find political writers using the word 'state' to point to a conceptual connection between the stateliness of rulers and the efficacy of their rule."[4]

That was the era of majesty, of spectacle, of the unification and embodiment of the state in a ruler whose status was absolute and whose word was law. To insult the person of the ruler was at the same time to transgress the state. It was a time when the quip "L'état, c'est moi," attributed to Louis XIV, was indeed a truism, not the delusion of a mercurial ruler that it has seemed to us since the eighteenth century. The metaphysics of separation that now characterizes our understanding of the relationship between the state and the government through which it operates, the state and the ruler or rulers who happen to have control of it at any given time, among the many components that make up the state, or between the state and the diverse forms of life abroad in any society (e.g., religion), was not a part of the understanding back then. This general idea of the state could be found worldwide.

There is no doubt that African instantiations of these forms of state exist. In exploring them we can see how they were incorporated into the colonial state with, in some cases, disastrous results. I think here of Northern Nigeria, Western Nigeria, the Asante Empire, the Buganda Kingdom, Zululand, Morocco, and Libya. It is fair to say that monarchies in these polities were all based on ascription and their monarchs embodied the state. The relationship of the colonial state to these ascription-based hierarchies might, indeed, better enable us to see a principal subversion of the transition to modernity in the sphere of political philosophy enacted by colonial authorities in various parts of Africa.

Examples abound. In Nigeria, the *sarauta* system emplaced by the Fulani jihadists became the lynchpin of the indirect rule that characterized the colonial state in Northern Nigeria. Its expansion to the rest of the country, including areas without traditions of monarchical or quasi-monarchical rule in the Middle Belt and Eastern Nigeria, helps explain a significant part of the distortion under which the modern state still labors. The stout resistance to the system, in the western parts of the country, by those who had embraced the modern way of life, including a preference for the modern legal system, speaks precisely to the kind of nuance that I insist is required in the discourse on the state in Africa. The British administrators may have had their way, but their African antagonists left them in no doubt that they thought the British were perpetrating a fraud. In another instance, the determination of British colonialists to turn the postindependence Ugandan state into the indigenous Buganda-state writ large planted an instability time bomb that eventually detonated a few years into independence.

Let us get back to Skinner. By the time we come to Thomas Hobbes in the mid-seventeenth century, a sea change was afoot in Europe in both the idea of the state and that of the relationship between the individual and the state, the society and the state, and among the individuals who make up the society and on whom the state holds sway. The metaphysics of diremption was being constructed, and Hobbes would become its founding exponent in political philosophy. This is why Hobbes claimed to have invented "the discipline of political science. His suggestion that the duties of subjects are owed to the state, rather than to the person of a ruler, was still a relatively new and highly contentious one. . . . So, above all, was his use of the term 'state' to denote this highest form of authority in matters of civil government."[5]

We can now state the peculiar characteristics of the state in its modern acceptation.[6]

1. (a) It is the institution armed with the monopoly of legitimate violence. This is one of the less realized but often remarked features of the modern state. One would think that the absolute monarchs of old would have had more of a monopoly of violence than the diffuse sovereignty of the modern state, but this is not the case. The absolute monarch could not always make good on this monopoly. Challenges could come from other legitimate contenders to the throne. Under feudalism, the authority of lesser potentates to administer their own fiefs with all means at their disposal was recognized as long as they paid obeisance to the monarch. The right of self-help among the subjects, the occurrence of feuds, and so on, meant that the right to deploy violence was diffuse throughout premodern societies. Indeed, the need to abrogate parallel loci of sovereign power and concentrate it all in the one sovereign designated as the Leviathan was what led Hobbes to insist that no one could opt out of the social contract to create the commonwealth once it was chartered. From then on, anyone who would deploy violence legitimately must be authorized by the state, and one who appeals to self-help in the use of violence against another must convince the state that such an act falls under the exceptions legitimated by it.

   (b) The state is empaneled as the ultimate arbiter of disputes among citizens, guarantor of the public good, and the protector of each individual citizen from the designs of both the state and their fellow citizens on their body and all that pertains to it. There is a reason that the modern state is required to be impartial between the parties that it governs. If the embodied state of monarchs and other potentates exemplified a direct relationship with their subjects, the modern state is utterly disembodied; it is an abstraction. The relationships among citizens and between citizens and those who run the state at any given time are indirect: they are always routed through the state. That is why in criminal law, the state files charges on behalf of the aggrieved citizen in the name of the collective. And the state is supposed to tend only to the common good. But given that it cannot but be run by humans—there are bodies within the state and there are state bodies—the institution needs to be inoculated from the disease of faction and the play of desire in those who run it on behalf of the polity. As much as possible, in adjudicating disputes among citizens, and between citizens and itself, the state must be seen not to have any favorites. It is also limited to the political sphere as opposed to what is usually called "civil society" in which individuals regulate their own relations, mostly through contract, but without interference by the state. The state is banished from civil society because such is the new metaphysical template at work that the state had become an abstraction from both those who direct and those whom they direct. As such, the state is not supposed to have its own goals beyond the broad one of creating the conditions for citizens to run their lives as individuals and in groups.

2. Unlike the metaphysics of connection that typified earlier state forms, the modern state is founded on a metaphysics of diremptions: separation of the state from the government that happens to dominate it at any given time; separation of the state from those who work in it, hence, the distinction between the state and government; and the separation of those who work in it from their own interests as individuals and citizens. With this new form of state came a new foundation of political legitimacy and the obligation that is attendant upon it: the doctrine of governance by consent under which no one should be bound by a government in the constitution of which she has had no hand. It will take us too far afield to spell out the enabling philosophical principles at stake in this formulation. But the idea that governance derives its legitimacy from the consent of the governed is connected to the next feature of the modern state that we identify here.
3. At the base of the foregoing is one of the core tenets of modernity: the principle of subjectivity on which is founded the idea of the sovereignty of the subject. This sovereign subject, the individual whose welfare and protection is the object of solicitation in the modern state, is the one whose dignity is held inviolate, whose freedom may not be restricted without cause, and who may not be interfered with by others, especially the state and its functionaries.[7] It is almost as if the modern state is set up primarily to protect the subject in her or his solitude and to ensure that neither their safety nor freedom is jeopardized by the state or their fellows.

In light of what I have just said, the relationship between the modern state and the citizens whose lives it coordinates, governs, directs, secures, and on occasion, sanctions, is the product of an elaborate, delicate choreography that is the preoccupation of political philosophers. At the bottom of this drama is a philosophical anthropology under which the individual is held to be free by nature. African thinkers have made this philosophical heritage their own and have striven in word and action to realize some version of it in their countries.

Bringing Africans Back In: The Discourse of the State in the Colonial Period

First, we consider the discourse of the state in Africa before and during colonialism. At the beginning of the first chapter of *How Colonialism Preempted Modernity in Africa*, I asked a framing question: "What do Canada, the United States, South Korea, Australia, Nigeria, and South Africa have in common? The answer: they are all ex-colonies."[8] There are different varieties of colonialism. The colonialism that is of moment here is that denominated by modernity. Modern colonialism, I argued, was not uniformly realized across Africa. But the peculiar brand of colonialism that prevailed in much of Africa, "exploitation colonialism," constituted a bulwark against the successful implantation of modernity in the continent. It was a kind of colonialism that did not even pretend, till close to the end of its tenure, to be concerned with anything but the extraction of wealth from the colonies. The question of the well-being of the colonized was never on the table.[9]

Different types led to different outcomes for states that emerged at the conclusion of colonial rule. The contours of the state that emerged from settler colonialism in Algeria that provoked armed struggle for liberation cannot be assimilated to the negotiated disengagement that marked the other French colonies in Africa, save Guinea-Conakry. And the colonial state that was preferred by the *Colons* was much less modern than the state favored by the settler minority in South Africa that eventually transformed into full-blown apartheid from 1948 onward. Certainly, toward the end of its life, as the armed struggle became more intense, and black "cooperation" with apartheid's state apparatuses waned after the 1976 Soweto Uprising, the South African state began to mimic, for its own community of settlers, the repressive character of the dominant colonial state form. The same can be said of the state in Liberia founded on the same philosophical principle—the love of freedom—as that of its model—the United States—dominated by settler Americo-Liberians—in its relationship with the native elements of its population.

The successors to the colonial states would also vary in their character. If it is the case that a specific form of state commensurate with the type of colonialism that dominated the African landscape obtained in much of the continent, it is reasonable to suggest that a corresponding successor state form may have taken root in the relevant areas of postindependence Africa. Simultaneously, if, as we suggest, the African experience of this dominant colonialism was not monolithic, it stands to reason that neither the operation of the state in postindependence Africa nor the people's experience of it could be characterized by uniformity. That is, the dominant form was not realized in the same way in all areas of Africa. However we cash this out, one thing seems clear. The colonial state and its postindependence successors are approximations of a concept: the idea of the state, described in the first section. In the African case, the state at issue is the colonialism-inflected modern state. Thanks to this realization, the metric with which we identify and/or evaluate the state in Africa is how well or ill it mirrors the characteristics of the modern state and to what extent its empirical embodiment approximates or departs from the modern state.[10]

What would the state in Africa look like that worked the way that its ideal type—the modern state—is meant to work? And would we prefer it to what we have now? If the empirically realized state in Africa falls short of its ideal, why is this so and how might we explain the disjuncture?

The state that we are talking about was originated in and bequeathed by colonialism. I argue that the state was not just a politico-pragmatic instrument. It was that and more. It was preeminently philosophical. This philosophical pedigree has received short shrift in the literature.[11] The philosophical idea of the state was what Africans first fell in love with in their embrace of the philosophical discourse of modernity in the nineteenth century before formal colonialism was imposed on much of the continent. In their enthusiasm for this new way of being human and organizing life and thought, African thinkers sought to remake their societies, including their states, in modern fashion. The Fante Confederacy was a brilliant example. Its relationship to the modern state soured on its realization of the chasm between the philosophical idea it embraced and the empirical analogue of it embodied in the abandonment of this idea by the colonial state.[12]

I cannot stress this enough. Colonialists could not stop Africans from constructing the practices, institutions, processes, and ideas of the colonialists in their own way. This capacity for agency, enhanced by the spread of literacy in European-derived languages, and education in the ways of their conquerors, meant that Africans could make of the colonial institutions and their enabling ideological foundations what they would. In West Africa, Africans had been crafting their reaction to modernity and its institutions, of which the state we are talking about is an instance, long before they became colonial subjects. Their relationship with colonialism throughout its career was shaped in very profound ways by this engagement with the philosophical foundations of modernity. As the colonial state, motivated by racism, betrayed the promise of moving Africans to modernity, Africans reviewed their relationship with it. Some retained, others abandoned the dream. For the most part, most sought to realize the best of the modern state, conditioned by their specific histories, but designed to procure the best life possible for African humans.

The absence of this discourse in the dominant accounts of the state in Africa may, in part, be due to the fact that the discourse is dominated by social scientists.[13] Simultaneously, refraining from taking a position on what the state in postcolonial Africa ought to be must not be conflated with a critical engagement with what African thinkers say the state ought to be and assessing how those among them who were at the helm did when they had charge of the state. For the latter, disciplinary considerations do not avail. The philosophical dimensions get lost in the gale of empirical descriptions of how badly the state performs. I argue that the African response to the idea of the modern state must form a significant element of the discourse of the state in postindependence Africa if it is to meet the criterion of adequacy, if not completeness. Philosophy is one place to look for the response to colonialism by its victims.

Many colonized Africans accepted colonialism's initial justification. Having accepted that modernity promised a better way of being human, this group of Africans studied and obtained myriad modern qualifications. Among other things, they sought to modify or transform indigenous modes of governance in line with modern forms of governance based on principles undergirding the modern state. When formal colonialism came, they expected it to install modern institutions at the running of which they would have the requisite practice to enable them to redeem the promise of modernity for Africans in the aftermath of colonial rule. They were acutely aware of the philosophical foundations of the modern state and of its genealogy. In fact, their approbatory attitude toward colonialism at the beginning stemmed from their embrace of modernity and the modes of governance inherent in it. Their appraisal of the state was part of this orientation. They sought to make themselves worthy legatees of the modern institutions, specifically the state. Their exertions on behalf of the philosophical underpinnings of the state form one strand of our discussion. This is by no means limited to West Africa. The struggle to install the modern state was also a feature of the history of Egypt and the Maghreb. The struggle over how to relate Islam and modernity and what type of state should succeed Ottoman rule explains in part the divergent political fortunes of Tunisia and Libya. Those debates have continued.[14]

Although philosophy is crucial to explaining first, the constitution of the contemporary state and, later, its mixed fortunes in Africa, academic or professional philosophy is hardly a standard presence in public life and discourse in postindependence Africa. Despite writings by academic or professional philosophers on issues pertaining to the state and politics, paradoxically, we have not written with the frequency that one would expect given philosophy's centrality to the constitution and working of the modern state. Among the few who have ventured, mention must be made of Henry Odera Oruka, Kwame Gyekye, Kwasi

Wiredu, Kwame Anthony Appiah, Emmanuel Chukwudi Eze, Paulin Hountondji, Peter Bodunrin, D. A. Masolo, Jean-Godefroy Bidima, Olusegun Oladipo, Ifeanyi Menkiti, C. N. Siame, and me.[15] Nowhere is this paradox more poignantly illustrated than in the area of political life and discourse. The state in Africa, by its very colonial provenance and continuing postcolonial evolution, is supposed to be a modern phenomenon. I shall expound this shortly.

Few are the works that take seriously this defining attribute of the state in postcolonial Africa and its underlying, enabling philosophical presuppositions. The promise of independence is tied closely to the incontrovertibly modern genealogy of the dominant state form in Africa. A core tenet of modern political philosophy holds that governance must be based on consent. Colonialism claimed that it wanted to bring Africans to modernity.[16] If true, it must perforce include installing the principle of governance by consent. In its modern provenance lie the colonial state's worst defect and its greatest hope. Colonialism distorted it and its operators switched on Africans after having baited them. This is the basis of the belief by African philosophers who had embraced the promise of modernity and had fought to mold the state they would inherit after colonialism was to have ended to the contours of modernity; that the colonizers would allow them to have practice at running the state and at developing the requisite temperaments before independence was to be assumed. Examples of those thinkers go back to the mid-nineteenth century, when formal colonialism was in its nascent stages, and include James Africanus Horton, Joseph Casely Hayford, John Mensah Sarbah, S. R. B. Attoh Ahuma, the framers of the Fante Confederacy constitution, and the author and inspirer of the Egba United Board of Management, George M. Johnson.[17]

The colonizers, in the main, never meant to redeem the promise of modernity for the African colonized. There was no question of the colonial state being founded on the consent of the governed, in this case, the colonized. If we assume with the worst of the colonizers that Africans were permanent children, then it is okay to discount what Africans had to say about the modern legacy, including the state. But if we recognize the capacity of Africans for subjectivity—a core tenet of modernity—it stands to reason that Africans would have their own take on modernity and its later incarnation, colonialism. They did, and many fought colonialism and its operators on exactly this score: their wish to have the benefits of modernity redeemed for Africans.

Indeed, it was because in many areas, the colonialists were not convinced that Africans had imbibed enough of these temperaments and deep sympathies for the "intimations of the traditions" of the modern polity that they were reluctant to "rush" to hand over the levers of state to Africans.[18] At the same time, the Africans' suspicion that the colonizers were not implanting the correct form of the state in the colonies formed the basis for much of their hostility to the colonial regime and its subterfuges. This is the best way to understand Frantz Fanon's indictment of the colonial situation in his comparison of the colonial state and the metropolitan state.

Frantz Fanon was quite prescient in his analysis of the contradictions of colonialism as it unfolded in much of Africa. He was early in calling colonialists on their duplicity.[19] He realized that the peculiar nature of modern colonialism meant that it had to square the circle: recognizing agency while inflicting unconsented-to rule on the African colonies. This meant that the state could not count on the "educated consent" of the colonized; it had to coerce the latter's submission to its rule. This is the basis of Fanon's comparison of the different methods and models of the relationship between governor and governed in the metropolis and the colonies, respectively.

When Fanon talked of the division of the colonized world in two, the principle of division is only secondarily spatial or even social. It is primarily a political division and it turned on how the state operated in it.[20] This is clearly seen in the fact that Fanon did not compare, initially, the colonizers' quarters and those of the colonized. The primary contrast was between how the state was in what he called "capitalist societies"—the metropolis—and the colonies which, presumably, were not capitalist societies. The nature of the state is what set apart the two kinds of society. No one would suggest that the state in either society is to be differentiated by power or by its ubiquity in the lives of those it governed. In fact, it has always struck me as absurd how much is made of the power of the state in African countries for, as has been demonstrated repeatedly in recent history, that state has been shown to have only the power of bluster, for the most part. When its people have pushed back, it has been shown to have no lasting power to assert its will.

By contrast, the most powerful states in history have been in capitalist societies, and it is instructive that the description proffered by Fanon continues to hold true for our own time, too. The implication to be drawn here is that the *differentia specifica* of the state in capitalist societies and the state in the then colonies was that the capitalist instance knew that its might must be transformed into right; the colonial state was convinced that either its might was right, *ex definitione*, or its might was not in need of right. This is a centerpiece of the philosophical idea of the state, especially its modern variant.

Even in its most naked deployment, the state must find a way to wrap its nakedness in the glove of right or pretend that its power is self-justifying. It has to go out of its way to convince, or at least persuade, those whom it governs that it has acted according to right and on behalf of the interests of the governed. This is why it needs "a multitude of sermonizers, counselors, and 'confusion-mongers' [to] intervene between the exploited and the authorities."[21] The state in the colony was defined by "the barracks and the police station."[22] Power and its deployment were not mediated; there were no gloves of right to soften the blows of the state. "The agent does not alleviate oppression or mask domination. He displays and demonstrates them with the clear conscience of the law enforcer, and brings violence into the homes and minds of the colonized subject."[23]

Implicit in Fanon's critique is the assumption that whatever may be wrong with the state in the metropolis, especially in its relations with the lowliest segments of its population, it, at least, was committed to treating those it governed with the dignity attached to their sheer humanity, beginning with its acknowledgment that its legitimacy to govern derived from their consent. All other elements of the intricate dance between the state and the governed stem from this fundamental recognition of, and respect for, the subjectivity of the governed regardless of their station in life. It is in cashing out the defining characteristics of the metropolitan state that we can then locate our dissatisfaction with the career of the state on the morrow of independence. The state that was inherited from colonialism was the distorted, disfigured modern state.[24] The metropolitan state is what the state in Africa would be if we could realize the promise of independence.

The trajectory of the implantation of this distortion varied from one part of the continent to another. For instance, in North Africa, the struggle for modernity, which erupted with greater intensity in the Arab-African Spring beginning in 2010, is traceable to Emperor Napoleon's arrival in Egypt in 1798.[25] The history of the state in the Maghreb following the collapse of the Ottoman Empire is inseparable from the shenanigans of British and French colonialism, on the one hand, and the conflicted attitudes toward modernity on the part of the North African elite and ruling classes, on the other. That Libya and Morocco ended up with monarchies while Tunisia did not is a result of these struggles. The presence of settler colonialism represented a different path to the state in postcolonial Algeria comparable more to Kenya's experience than to, say, Senegal's.

Given the preceding, it should be clear that there was no historical inevitability to what transpired after independence all across the continent. That is, the day after independence came with several possibilities: (1) dismantle the state and go back to some model of state indigenous to different and specific areas of the continent; (2) keep what has been bequeathed but make it worse: one-party rule, pseudo-democracy with rigged elections, abridgment of freedom and denial of the rights of citizens to control their lives; (3) change it for the better by reducing the chasm generated under colonialism between the enabling philosophical idea of the state and its inadequate empirical realization.[26] The third option is what Mahmoud Mamdani canvassed in *Citizen and Subject*.[27] A modification of the same is found in the work of Gyekye in *Tradition and Modernity* and in Claude Ake's *Development and Democracy in Africa*, Kwame Nkrumah's *Consciencism*, and Léopold Sédar Senghor's *On African Socialism*.[28] In different ways, they all canvassed a modification of the modern state to reflect some indigenous African values, practices, and institutions.

The first possibility was the option of William Esuman-Gwira Sekyi, known as Kobina Sekyi, in some of his essays, as it was that of Julius Nyerere in his *Ujamaa*.[29] A variation on that theme is found in Wiredu's spirited defense of No-party, Consensus democracy in several publications.[30] Unfortunately, the second option has dominated the discourse of the postcolonial state in Africa. Even then, the near universal identification of the postcolonial state with nothing but pathologies—"the underdeveloped state," "the overdeveloped state," "Bula Matari," "the centralized state," "the marginalized state," "the weak state," "the strong state," "the rentier state," and so on—I dare say, is incorrect or, minimally speaking, problematic.

If, as is often touted, there is continuity between the colonial state and the postcolonial state, then it is almost illogical to talk of the postcolonial state or it is otiose to so speak of one. Almost without exception, all the characteristics predicated of the colonial state can, with little variation, be predicated of the postcolonial state. By the same token, unless we assume that the aborted modern state is the only possible outcome of the anticolonial struggle, or is coterminous with the modern state, it stands to reason that the challenge that independence brought in its wake was to realize that dream of a state that answers to those it governs and derives its legitimacy from their consent, that is, the true modern state.

African independence leaders and their peoples aspired to have polities, postindependence, that were more like the modern democratic states that colonialism subverted while it lasted. While we are right to raise questions about the sincerity of colonial authorities that waited till the eve of independence to introduce bills of rights into the political instruments of the newly minted states, we may not scoff at the desire and enthusiasm of Africans, leaders and followers alike, to make these aspirations a reality. We present evidence of this desire on the part of some of the important leaders of the independence struggle in Africa. Independence was meant to be the starting point for the realization of the promise of a modern state and its advantages. Nor was this aspiration ever limited to the small elite coterie that the colonialists always insisted was the case.

The desire for freedom, the demand for a state that is both responsive and responsible to those whom it governs, the insistence that right be substituted for might, that the people's dignity be recognized and respected, and so on, had become diffuse throughout all sectors of the African population. As a result, Africans came to independence with significant segments of the population insisting that they were citizens, not subjects; people deserving of the respect of their governors for their humanity and the dignity that attached to it. Indeed, it can be argued that the people became dissatisfied with the state, postindependence, in part because it showed itself to be too closely hewed to the monster that the colonial state was.[31]

I argue that the second option, above, the continuation of the colonial state in the postindependence period and all that it represents, is nowhere inevitable, and that the third option, the realization of a properly modern state, was a live option in postindependence Africa. Africans had always debated the state and its place in their polities. They had divided over the nature of the state; the grounds of political obligation and the nature of the good society to the realization of each of which the state is vital and what philosophical basis it is built on is crucial. Changing the state for the better and narrowing the gap between the ideal of the modern state and its ugly reality on the day after independence was the preference for Africa's major thinkers, many of whom led the struggle for freedom. They wanted to deliver on the promise of independence for their newly minted citizens and at the base of this aspiration was a fully functioning democratic state.

The State in Postindependence Africa: The Urgency of Philosophy

Much of the discourse on the state does not show any awareness of or respect for Africans' contributions to and appropriation of that discourse both during colonialism and after independence. It is why the record just described in the last section plays no role in the discourse of the state in Africa. Postindependence, the continuing engagement with and embrace of the idea of the modern state by African thinkers and significant segments of the populace remain a disturbing absence in the literature. This section completes the modest task of this chapter of remedying this lack. The core argument in this section is that only because we have ignored African participation in the politico-philosophical discourse of modernity does it appear that the second option—the degenerate state—was inevitable in the aftermath of independence, rather than engage the centrality of the idea of freedom and of its protection by the state in African discourse that predates formal colonialism. Like their forebears who embraced modernity before the imposition of colonialism, the state that Africans and their leaders expected to be at the apex of their polities after independence is the modern state. They knew too well what farce colonialism had perpetrated in their lands when it came to redeeming for them the benefits of the philosophical discourse of modernity. Regardless of the litany of failures at operating the modern state in the postindependence era, it may not be denied that Africans' aspiration was to have a modern state in place all across the continent. This is what is represented in what we have earlier identified as the third option.

Were we to adopt the third option—make the state optimally modern—much of what has characterized the experience of Africans at the hands of the state graphically and harrowingly spelled out by African writers and journalists routinely could have been avoided. That this was the expectation that Africans had of their state at independence and have even now can be seen in our excoriation of the state when it fails to act in consonance with its philosophical template—for example, when it wastes citizens' lives, when it turns itself into accuser and judge when its agents slap suspects before they are charged (routine occurrences across the continent), when it issues backdated laws to proscribe newspapers (Nigeria, Zimbabwe), and so on. Africans and their intellectuals regard all these as aberrations. Africans in their numbers do not accept that these are what they expected self-rule to bring them.

The evidence for our claim lies in the fact that the realization that they had not installed the modern state in Africa partly explains the rushed efforts at democratization of the various polities made by the colonialists on the eve of independence. Africans knew that the colonial state was a distortion of the state form they had cherished since their embrace of modernity, via Christianity, at the beginning of the nineteenth century. The promise of independence meant more than having full bellies. Nkrumah aptly put it: "We prefer self-government with danger to servitude in tranquility."[32] For Obafemi Awolowo and his Action Group party, freedom was lexically prior to abundance in their slogan for the elections in 1959 that ushered in independence for Nigeria: "Freedom for All, Life More Abundant."

This brings us back to the centrality of philosophy to the discussion of the state in postindependence Africa. When professional academic philosophers have joined the discussion, they, too, have not taken seriously the basic character of the modern state. They, too, have accepted the distortions as the rule. It explains why they think the modern state is the problem. At other times, unaware of the history of African engagements with the philosophical idea of the state, they have all too facilely succumbed to pedigree arguments regarding the unsuitability of modern state forms for African conditions.

Nonprofessional philosophers have not been absent from the discourse about the matters that we have highlighted in the preceding discussion. In their ruminations, African thinkers have divided over the role of the state and its nature in Africa and have instantiated all possible permutations of the state: as engine of economic development (Awolowo in Western Nigeria even before Nigeria's independence, Nkrumah's Ghana, Nyerere's Tanzania), as an enabler of economic initiative fueled by private property (Félix Houphouët-Boigny's Côte d'Ivoire, Jomo Kenyatta's Kenya), to the state as producer of economic goods, right down to the operation of corner stores (Samora Machel's Mozambique till 1985). But none of them, even when they did not mean it, ever dared to say that their state was for tyrannizing their citizens, denying them human rights, or failing to protect them from the predations of their fellows. They all knew that the state ought to embody the three characteristics that we have identified in the first section.

Although ordinary people do not dominate the debate about the nature of the state and its underlying presuppositions, ordinary people have a sense, sometimes a gut feeling, that things are not right with their societies where the nature or quality of their state or their relations with it are concerned. That is, they often apprehend some measure of misalignment between what their state is or what those who dominate it say it is and what they believe it ought to be. Ordinary Africans may not have sophisticated explanations for this gap. Yet, they gave their lives and suffered unspeakable brutalities to force the colonial state to reduce the chasm between the real state and its modern ideal. They never thought—even though they expected it—that the distance was abridged or eliminated by the mere fact of independence. The language of rights was an integral part of the struggle for independence and Africans laid down their lives for civil and political rights throughout the colonial period. They were insistent that the state recognize limits to its power and respect their dignity in its dealings with them. They fought land alienations, organized trade unions, funded political parties, and so on.

After independence, it took time for the cancer of one-party rule and military coups to infect and spread throughout the body politic across the continent. Even then, with a few exceptions, the state did not dare adopt the we-don't-owe-you-any-explanation attitude that was definitive of the colonial state. No state in Africa dismantled the judiciary; they may have weakened or compromised it. The legal system is an indispensable constituent of the modern state. And all ex-colonies inherited at independence some form of the modern judiciary or another. A cynic might think that African rulers after independence just went along without really setting any store by those institutions. But looking at countries like Nigeria and Ghana and the bevy of great jurists that they produced and, in the case of Nigeria, shared with other African countries—for example, Uganda, Gambia, and Botswana—to help the latter grow the quality of their own judiciaries, again the evidence is overwhelming that those who initially stewarded the state, postindependence, did strive to reduce the gap between what the state was and what it ought to be.[33] The judiciary, as the arm of the state that is charged with stepping in, through various writs, to safeguard the rights of the individual against or in conflict with the state, may not have a distinguished record in postindependence Africa. But it is wrong to treat it as if it has no record or that nothing is ever done according to procedure in African countries.

Even if those who directed the state sought to subvert it to their own ends or deny the people their rights, the people, both as individuals and as organized groups in civil society, never failed to inconvenience the power-wielders by their insistence that procedure be followed and the rule of law observed. More scandalous still is ignoring the sense of justice that the African masses demonstrate when they protest their state's actions when they feel that such actions violate the principles of natural justice and equity. Ordinary people who sue to have illegal takings by government reversed must have some faith in right in the face of government's might. Whether they meant it or not, most African rulers felt the need to appear to rule by right. That is why the military does not, for the most part, dismantle judiciaries on its accession to power after military coups. For example, the military dictatorship of Ibrahim Babangida in Nigeria ultimately foundered on account of its annulment of elections that had been adjudged to be the freest and fairest ever conducted in the land. The people of Benin, in another instance, removed a military regime through their political organizing in a sovereign national conference, the first of its kind in the continent.

What is more, the record of African philosophical engagement with what the modern state, properly conceived, is supposed to be is considerable. Nyerere did believe that indigenous modes of governance in Africa were democratic, though he admitted that, in that situation, "the African's mental conception of 'government' was personal—not institutional. When the word government was mentioned, the African thought of the chief; he did not, as does the Briton, think of a grand building in which a debate was taking place."[34] In other words, it was more reminiscent of the premodern state highlighted by Skinner in the first section. Under colonialism, "this 'personal' conception of government was unchanged, except that the average person hearing government mentioned now thought of the District Commissioner, the Provincial Commissioner, or the Governor."[35] The reference to colonialism indicates the transition in the African context, too, from the personalized state form, of which Skinner spoke earlier, to the modern state promised by those who colonized Africans, in part, to bring them to modernity. Nyerere counts himself among those Africans who accepted the promise of change and sought to hold the colonialists to their pledge:

> When, later, the idea of government as an institution began to take hold of some African "agitators" such as myself, who had been reading Abraham Lincoln and John Stuart Mill, and we began demanding institutional government for our own countries, it was the very people who had now come to symbolize "Government" in their persons who resisted our demands—the District Commissioners, the Provincial Commissioners, and the Governors. Not until the eleventh hour did they give way; and free elections have taken place in most of our countries almost on the eve of independence.[36]

Nyerere's embrace of Lincoln and Mill is neither gratuitous nor lightly taken by him. He was calling out colonialism directly on this score for its bait and switch. A new mode of governance had been advertised, but as soon as Africans showed an interest in buying into it, the colonial administrators substituted premodern modes of personal and personalized government. Protesting colonial rule, criticizing the administrators, or questioning the legitimacy of colonial rule was designated as sedition, a felony punishable by imprisonment.

Postindependence, there is no reason to believe that Nyerere and some others of his cohort of African philosophers did not wish to realize what colonialism had promised but failed to deliver: the modern state. We do have some evidence. After insisting that "the government of a nation must necessarily be government by 'representation,'" he goes on to argue:

> The two essentials for "representative" democracy are the *freedom of the individual,* and the *regular opportunity for him to join with his fellows in replacing, or reinstating, the government of his country by means of the ballot-box and without recourse to assassination.* An organized opposition is *not* an essential element, although a society which has no room and no time for the harmless eccentric can hardly be called "democratic." Where you have those two essentials, and the affairs of the country are conducted by free discussion, you have democracy. And organized opposition may arise, or it may not; but whether it does or it does not depends entirely upon the choice of the people themselves and makes little difference to free discussion and equality in freedom.[37]

This passage illustrates a centerpiece of modern political philosophy. Of course, it is plausible to dismiss Nyerere's stand here as mere lip service. To do so, however, would mean that (1) African thinkers can have no complexity or evolution in their thinking, and (2) Nyerere was pragmatically embracing liberal democracy to win independence but never intended to install a democratic regime in postindependence Tanzania.

Both thoughts are untenable. We should criticize African thinkers for their hypocrisies. But ignoring the contradictions in their thinking as evidenced by their writings is to present them as one-dimensional actors with no depth to their thinking. A better method is to explore Nyerere's writings and use his earlier embrace of liberal democracy to criticize his later preference for one-party rule. Even then, we have to acknowledge that he continued to struggle with the challenge of liberal democracy as he ran a one-party government. The provision for some kind of pluralism in the one-party system may have been his solution to the problem that an official opposition was designed to solve.

Kofi Busia was another thinker who spent considerable time on the requirements of democracy in Africa in his book *Africa in Search of Democracy.*[38] In chapter 6, "The Ingredients of Democracy," he contrasted the views of democracy held by Sékou Touré and Nnamdi Azikiwe, respectively. He did not think that Touré's preference for a one-party state could really be a democracy. He preferred instead Azikiwe's formulation:

> The domestic policy of Nigeria will be framed on the assumption that Nigeria shall continue to be a Parliamentary democracy. The Government of Nigeria shall exercise power so long as it retains the confidence of the legislature. It will express its belief in parliamentary democracy as government by discussion,

> based on *the consent of the governed*, whose will is collectively expressed by the duly accredited representatives of an electorate that is based on a universal adult suffrage and that votes by secret ballots at periodic elections.[39]

Busia proceeded to add his own take on the requirements of democracy. "Democracy is founded on respect for the human being—every human being."[40] He used the UN Declaration of Human Rights as a good summation of the "liberties befitting the dignity of man in democratic society."[41]

Finally, Nkrumah is celebrated as a foremost philosopher of African communalism in the early stage of his career and, later, as a Marxist-Leninist philosopher. But earlier in his career he was a stout defender of liberal democracy and a severe critic of aspects of indigenous modes of governance based on ascription. Nkrumah wrote that after independence:

> We introduced principles basic to the settled and established democracies of the world, such as the separation of powers, between the executive, the legislature and the judiciary. As the repository of the people's will, the legislature is supreme. It is sovereign and unlimited in its enactment of laws, which are binding upon the people and the government. Election to the legislature is by universal adult suffrage, and men and women enjoy equality of rights and duties. That all persons in the state are equal before the law is another principle well enshrined in our constitution.[42]

Nkrumah was alert to the problem of what kind of state should be installed in postindependence African states. He addressed a chapter of his book to "problems of government." "*In our struggle for freedom*," he averred, "*parliamentary democracy was as vital an aim as independence. The two were inseparable. It was not our purpose to rid the country of the colonial régime in order to substitute an African tyranny. We wanted to free our people from arbitrary rule, and to give them the freedom to choose the kind of government they felt would best serve their interests and enhance their welfare.*"[43]

The preceding is why I insist that regardless of what the colonialists thought they were doing or what they thought of Africans or what Africans deserved, African agency took hold of the modern inheritance and sought to use it as the yardstick with which to measure the nature, quality, and legitimacy of the state postindependence. I have left out the Marxists, but Abdel Khaliq Mahgoub, the Sudanese communist, stands in a class by himself in his plea before a Sudanese military court in 1959 in which he defended himself in the name of Marxism invoking many tenets of modernity as justification for his choice of struggle against the Sudanese state.[44] I have also not cited the evidence from North Africa. There again we find evidence of the embrace of the core tenets of modernity and a long history of struggle to realize the modern state.[45]

One is right to wonder why what African philosophers and other intellectuals have to say about the state, their experience of and reflections on it, do not rivet the attention of the authors of much of the scholarship on the state in postcolonial Africa. I argue that a serious consideration of the state in Africa, in whatever era, is intimately tied to philosophy. It is even more so in modern times. The state whose career we consider in postcolonial Africa is quintessentially modern. From the standpoint of philosophy, our identification and evaluation of the state in postcolonial Africa must focus on its modern and, by extension, philosophical provenance. The many failures of the empirical analogue of the philosophical state are better explained as products of the incongruence between its philosophical template and the distorted realization of it in much of the continent. To focus on this must include serious engagement with what African thinkers have made of this ideological inheritance at both theoretical and practical levels.

This is what I have tried to do thus far by reinserting the state in postcolonial Africa into the universal discourse of the modern state and showing how this offers us a better tool to unravel the failure that we talk about much in the literature. No thanks to the neglect of the modern provenance of the state in postcolonial Africa by philosophers and nonphilosophers alike, the field has been abandoned to the aficionados of witchcraft and myriad other forms of obscurantism, the theorists of all manner of orifices and purveyors of African exceptionalism whose charter membership of the cult of difference would not allow them to see beyond the accursed boundaries of an undifferentiated, sui generis, Africa.[46]

It is time for us to get back to philosophy. We must acknowledge the fact that the state in postcolonial Africa is more or less the realization of an ideal type and that the key to unraveling its many conundrums is philosophy. This return to and reengagement with philosophy must mean the recognition of the relevance to Africa and African institutions, policies, practices, and processes, of the classic formulations of modern philosophy, especially in social and political philosophy. It must mean respect for and willingness to argue with African appropriations and adaptations of those formulations, especially where the latter have been modulated by the peculiar history of various peoples on the continent and the many cultural formations found therein. The importance of this philosophical turn cannot be overemphasized at the present when Africa looks best placed to redeem the benefits of modernity for its peoples. Issues of constitutionalism, human rights, citizenship, rule of law, and the like are center stage again. Philosophy must be in the forefront of enabling Africans to obtain the best in political life for humans. Africa cannot wait.

OLÚFẸ́MI TÁÍWÒ is Professor of African Political Thought at the Africana Studies and Research Center at Cornell University. He is author of *Africa Must Be Modern: A Manifesto* and *How Colonialism Preempted Modernity in Africa.*

Notes

I would like to thank Ebenezer Obadare, Wale Adebanwi, and Tejumola Olaniyan for comments and interventions that have helped to improve this chapter vastly through its many iterations.

1. Harold J. Laski, *The State in Theory and Practice* (New Brunswick, NJ: Transaction, 2009), chapter 1.

2. The dominant form of the state in Africa at present has no organic roots in the continent. The exceptions are Morocco, Swaziland, and, in a very qualified sense, Egypt. What this means is that the philosophical idea of the modern state is at once the foundation of the state in Africa and the end toward which it is striving.

3. Quentin Skinner, "The State," *Contemporary Political Philosophy: An Anthology*, 2nd ed., ed. Robert E. Goodin and Philip Pettit (Malden, MA: Blackwell, 2006), 4.

4. Ibid.

5. Ibid., 3.

6. For a different account, see Crawford Young, *The African Colonial State in Comparative Perspective* (New Haven, CT: Yale University Press, 1994), chapter 1.

7. I have omitted talk of territory. I assume that the idea of a modern state and a specific geopolitical space over which it presides does not require any argument.

8. Olúfẹ́mi Táíwò, *How Colonialism Preempted Modernity in Africa* (Bloomington: Indiana University Press, 2012), chapter 1.

9. Ibid.

10. This is not an overreach. Both Ethiopia and Egypt, the states that may not be traced to colonialism, are also now striving to reduce the distance between the state that is in them and the ideal of the modern state.

11. For an extensive theoretical analysis of the state, see Young, *African Colonial State*; and Crawford Young, *The Postcolonial State in Africa: Fifty Years of Independence, 1960–2010* (Madison: University of Wisconsin Press, 2012).

12. See Táíwò, *How Colonialism Preempted Modernity*, chapter 3.

13. To those who may want to make light of this absence, I would like to point out that this is all too reflective of the treatment of African intellectual contributions. However sensitive they otherwise are or claim to be to African agency, Africanist scholars, be they African or non-African, seem to think that what Africans have to say regarding the intellectual bequeathal from their engagement with Euro-America is not worthy of serious engagement. This point was crystallized for me by the respective contributions to Robert H. Taylor, ed., *The Idea of Freedom in Asia and Africa* (Stanford: Stanford University Press, 2002) by Crawford Young, "Itineraries of Ideas of Freedom in Africa: Precolonial to Postcolonial," 9–39; William J. Foltz, "African States and the Search for Freedom," 40–61; and Sudipta Kaviraj, "Ideas of Freedom in Modern India," 97–142. The reader of the two articles on Africa cannot but think that the idea of freedom has not exercised African thinkers at anything that approaches the levels of theoretical or philosophical expostulations that could rivet the attention of serious political scientists or philosophers. In Young's article, some of those thinkers only merited cameo appearances with not a sliver of material from their perorations on the matter of freedom. Contrast that with the robust exposition of the ideas of Ram Mohan Roy regarding the evolution of the modern idea of freedom in India. I have inscribed these ideas in this chapter and in other works cited throughout this discussion.

14. For the history, see Jamil Abun-Nasr, *A History of the Maghrib in the Islamic Period* (Cambridge: Cambridge University Press, 1971); John Cooper, Ronald L. Nettler, and Mohamed Mahmoud, eds., *Islam and Modernity: Muslim Intellectuals Respond* (London: I. B. Tauris, 1998); and Eugene Rogan, *The Arabs: A History* (New York: Basic Books, 2011).

15. Here is a representative sample: Henry Odera Oruka, *Practical Philosophy: In Search of an Ethical Minimum* (Nairobi: East African Educational, 1997); Kwame Gyekye, *Tradition and Modernity* (New York: Oxford University Press, 1997); Kwasi Wiredu, *Cultural Universals and Particulars: An African Perspective* (Bloomington: Indiana University Press, 1996); Kwame Anthony Appiah, *In My Father's House* (New York: Oxford University Press, 1992); Emmanuel Chukwudi Eze, "Democracy or Consensus: Response to Wiredu," in *Postcolonial African Philosophy: A Critical Reader*, ed. Emmanuel Chukwudi Eze (Oxford: Blackwell, 1997), 313–323; Paulin Hountondji, *The Struggle for Meaning: Reflections on Philosophy, Culture, and Democracy in Africa*, trans. John Conteh-Morgan (Athens: Ohio University Center for International Studies, 2002); Peter Bodunrin, "Federal Character and Social Justice," in *Federal Character and Federalism in Nigeria*, ed. P. P. Ekeh and E. E. Osaghae (Ibadan: Heinemann, 1989); D. A. Masolo, *Self and Community in a Changing World* (Bloomington: Indiana University Press, 2010); Jean-Godefroy Bidima, *La Palabre: Une jurisdiction de la parole* (Paris: Éditions Michalon, 1997); Olusegun Oladipo, "Tradition and the Quest for Democracy in Africa," *polylog: Forum for Intercultural Philosophy* 2 (2000), https://them.polylog.org/2/foo-en.htm; Ifeanyi Menkiti, "Philosophy and the State in Africa: Some Rawlsian Considerations," *Philosophia Africana* 5, no. 2 (2002): 35–51; Chisanga N. Siame, "'Two Concepts of Liberty' Through African Eyes," *Journal of Political Philosophy* 8, no. 1 (2000): 53–67; Olúfẹmi Táíwò, "Post-Independence African Political Philosophy," in *A Companion to African Philosophy*, ed., Kwasi Wiredu (Malden, MA: Blackwell, 2004); Olúfẹmi Táíwò, "The Political Thought of Obafemi Awolowo," *Nigerian Journal of Philosophy* 6–7, nos. 1 and 2 (1986–1987): 11–33; and Olúfẹmi Táíwò, "'The Love of Freedom Brought Us Here': An Introduction to Modern African Political Philosophy," *South Atlantic Quarterly* 109, no. 2 (2010): 391–410.

16. At least, the arch-philosopher of British colonialism, Frederick Lugard, did so argue in *The Dual Mandate in Tropical Africa* (London: Frank Cass, 1965).

17. James Africanus Horton, *West African Countries and Peoples, British and Native* (1868; repr., Edinburgh: Edinburgh University Press, 1969); Joseph Casely Hayford, *Gold Coast Native Institutions, With Thoughts Upon a Healthy Imperial Policy for the Gold Coast* (1911; repr., London: Frank Cass, 1970); Magnus J. Sampson, ed., *West African Leadership: Public Speeches Delivered by J. E. Casely Hayford* (London: Frank Cass, 1969); John Mensah Sarbah, *Fanti Customary Laws*, 3rd ed. (London: Frank Cass, 1968), the constitution of the Fanti Confederacy is reproduced there as an appendix; and S. R. B. Attoh Ahuma, *The Gold Coast Nation and National Consciousness* (1911; repr., London: Frank Cass, 1971). See Táíwò, *How Colonialism Preempted Modernity*, chapter 6, for a full discussion of these constitutions.

18. See Michael Oakeshott, "Political Education," in *Rationalism in Politics and Other Essays* (New York: Basic Books, 1962), 111–136, for a full explication.

19. He was not alone. Aimé Césaire, too, in *Discourse on Colonialism* (New York: Monthly Review, 1972), indicted colonialism from an immanentist modern standpoint.

20. Frantz Fanon, *The Wretched of the Earth*, trans. Richard Philcox (New York: Grove, 2004), 3.

21. Ibid., 4.

22. Ibid.

23. Ibid.

24. For a contrary view, see Patrick Chabal, *Power in Africa: An Essay in Political Interpretation* (New York: St. Martin's, 1992), 87–91.

25. "The elements of liberalism helped usher in Western-type democracy first in Egypt, at the end of the 19th century, and then in a score of Arab countries from the early 1920s to the mid-1950s. The seeds of liberalism were sown in Egypt as early as the turn of the 18th century.

When Napoleon's ships anchored in Alexandria's harbor in July 1798, the West had its first significant encounter with the Arab Middle East since the last Crusade in the 13th century. . . . With Napoleon, the French Revolution arrived in full dress on the banks of the Nile.

"Among the things the French brought to Egypt were the printing press and a new vocabulary—words for liberty, fraternity, equality, human rights, and municipal councils. The Egyptians were intrigued, but soon revolted and pushed the French out with the help of the British and Ottomans. The French took with them their guns but left behind the printing press and revolutionary slogans. These would have a lasting impact on the emergence of a modern state and society in Egypt." Saad Eddin Ibrahim, "An Open Door," *Wilson Quarterly* 28, no. 2 (2004): 36–37. See also Rogan, *The Arabs*, 4–5, 62; Samir Amin, "An Arab Springtime?" *Monthly Review* 63, no. 5 (2011): 8–28; and Lisa Anderson, "Demystifying the Arab Spring," *Foreign Affairs* 90, no. 2 (2011): 1–7.

26. Regarding the first option, it is worth noting Swaziland still has an absolute monarchy while Lesotho's monarchy became constitutional.

27. Mahmoud Mamdani, *Citizen and Subject: Contemporary Africa and the Legacy of Late Colonialism* (Princeton, NJ: Princeton University Press, 1996).

28. Kwame Gyekye, *Tradition and Modernity: Philosophical Reflections on the African Experience* (New York: Oxford University Press, 1997); Claude Ake, *Development and Democracy in Africa* (Washington, DC; Brooking Institution, 1995); Kwame Nkrumah, *Consciencism* (London: Panaf, 1972); Léopold Sédar Senghor, *On African Socialism* (London: Pall Mall, 1964).

29. See William Esuman-Gwira Sekyi, "The Future of Subject Peoples," "Church or State," and "The Best Constitutions Are Born Not Made," in *Ideologies of Liberation in Black Africa 1856–1970*, ed. J. Ayo Langley (London: Rex Collings, 1979), 242–260, 440–446; Julius Nyerere, *Ujamaa: The Basis of African Socialism* (Dar es Salaam: Oxford University Press, 1968).

30. See note 15.

31. Reading the vast literature on the state is not likely to educate one on this score. It is as if the masses of Africans are dumb brutes who are quite happy to have full bellies but not freedoms. I must remark on the arrogance of some of the commentators when they make light of this aspiration and pronounce on their unattainability, especially in the current situation of Africans trying once again to develop a culture of freedom and democracy. I find the following particularly problematic in this respect: Patrick Chabal and Jean-Pascal Daloz, *Africa Works: Disorder as Political Instrument* (London: Oxford: James Currey, 1999); Jean-François Bayart, Stephen Ellis, and Béatrice Hibou, *The Criminalization of the State in Africa* (Oxford: James Currey, 1999); and Jean-François Bayart, *The State in Africa: The Politics of the Belly* (London: Longman, 1993).

32. Commonly known motto of Nkrumah's political party, the Convention People's Party, and newspaper, the *Accra Evening News*, founded in 1948. See Robert Andrews, *The Columbia Dictionary of Quotations* (New York: Columbia University Press, 1993), 75.

33. At one time or another, a Nigerian served as chief justice in the three countries mentioned.

34. Julius Nyerere, "The African and Democracy," in *Africa Speaks*, ed. James Duffy and Robert A. Manners (Princeton, NJ: D. Van Nostrand, 1961), 33.

35. Ibid.

36. Ibid.

37. Ibid., 34 (emphasis added).

38. Kofi Busia, *Africa in Search of Democracy* (New York: Praeger, 1967).

39. Ibid., 97–98 (emphasis added). For the full text, see Nnamdi Azikiwe, *ZIK: A Selection from the Speeches of Dr. Nnamdi Azikiwe* (Cambridge: Cambridge University Press, 1961).

40. Busia, *Africa in Search of Democracy*, 93.

41. Ibid., 94. See also Fatima Mernissi, *Islam and Democracy: The Fear of the Modern West*, trans. Mary Jo Lakeland (Reading, MA: Addison-Wesley, 1992); Abdullahi Ahmed An-Na'im, *Toward an Islamic Reformation: Civil Liberties, Human Rights and International Law* (Syracuse, NY: Syracuse University Press, 1990); and Abdullahi Ahmed An-Na'im, *Islam and the Secular State: Negotiating the Future of Shari'a* (Cambridge, MA: Harvard University Press, 2008).

42. Kwame Nkrumah, *Africa Must Unite* (New York: Praeger, 1963), 66.

43. Ibid. (emphasis added).

44. Abdel Khaliq Mahgoub, "By Virtue of Marxism, Your Honor," *South Atlantic Quarterly* 109, no. 1 (2009): 159–176. I would like to thank Salah Hassan for bringing this work to my attention in the first place.

45. For a selection, see Mernissi, *Islam and Democracy*; Ibrahim, "An Open Door"; and Saad Eddin Ibrahim, "Crises, Elites, and Democratization in the Arab World," *Middle East Journal* 47, no. 2 (1993): 292–305; as well as others cited in note 25.

46. Even Bayart, who criticized the literature on the postcolonial state on this score, does not escape the same problem despite his claim to eschew African exceptionalism.

4 Soccer and the State

The Politics and Morality of Daily Life

Michael G. Schatzberg

It has long seemed to me that among the major pillars of popular culture throughout much of Africa are nightlife (meaning music, dance, and drink); religion, especially of the charismatic and evangelical varieties; and sport, which usually means football, or soccer. These all are important subjects for reflection, yet space is limited, so this chapter focuses on soccer. First, I provisionally explore the largely unstated moral structure of sport, while examining how it relates to the cultural and political logics of daily life in various societies in different parts of Africa. I suggest that people value this moral structure because it provides both visual and ethical symmetry, as well as a certain, although quite variable, sense of predictability. In this manner it may reduce uncertainty by emphasizing regular rules and structures in a most uncertain and chaotic political world where, for the most part, the usually implicit moral structure of sport does not apply, however much people might wish that it did. Moreover, this disjuncture between a hypothesized and wished-for order and a frequently chaotic reality is a latent and continuing source of frustration for many that regularly appears in the world of African football. This moral structure, and especially the manner in which it is enforced, is often relevant to understanding what is or is not legitimate or thinkable—whether in sport or political life.

Second, and more specifically, in several African states I examine some of the interconnections between football, on the one hand, and the politics and morality of daily life on the other, by focusing on the political organization of football. Does the easily apparent lack of order often characteristic of the official, associational, and formally organized world of African football belie the moral structure of the sport? Does the visual symmetry and apparent equality of a football match provide a model of transparency, rules, and order that people might then apply to the political sphere? Can any society be truly democratic in its public sector if various segments of daily political life operate on the basis of implicit models of governance that are antidemocratic? Does it matter, especially in ostensibly democratizing societies, that the realm of sport is usually governed autocratically? Or, put differently, how a sport's moral structure is understood and enforced may speak directly to our implicit understanding of critical political concepts such as fairness, justice, and legitimacy. These are far-reaching questions, and in this chapter I make an initial attempt to provide certain tentative and preliminary replies to some of them.

In addition to being one of the main pillars of popular culture in Africa, football, or more properly what the sociologist of sport Richard Giulianotti has termed "the soccerscape," is simply a microcosm through which we may more sharply discern those political, cultural, and economic processes that are actually critical to peoples' lives. Giulianotti defines the soccerscape as "the geo-cultural circulation of football's constituent parts: players and coaches, fans and officials, goods and services, or information and artefacts."[1] Although he omits the ideational dimension, which is quite important, we may still take his notion of the soccerscape as a reasonable point of departure.[2] In other words, I assume that whatever occurs within the metaphoric touch lines of the soccerscape—the small, daily politics of football—will probably reflect the same, or quite similar, fault lines present in the politics of the wider society. I also assume that the quotidian, in this case as represented by the politics of football, is linked in a variety of ways to the society's larger political arenas. To start, however, let us address the moral structure of sport.

The Moral Structure of Sport: Premises and Assumptions

What are the premises and assumptions of this moral structure? If we reflect on this question, we can readily see that most of them fall under the rubric of common sense, or those implicit guides to daily life that are almost never stated because people simply take them for granted. We may enumerate them briefly.

First, we assume that in any sport there are two (or more) equal sides or teams of competitors. In other words, there must be a competition between numerically equal teams. The teams do not have to be relatively equal in ability, and often are not, but the number of competitors on each side needs to be the same. Depending on the sport in question, the teams may range in size from a single person (in the so-called individual sports such as singles in tennis, golf, track and field, and swimming) to eighty-five or more in US collegiate football. It should thus follow logically that each competing individual or group should have an equal and, therefore, fair chance of winning the contest. In real life, of course, and depending on the particular sport, the ability level of the competing teams may well vary enormously. But theoretically, both teams should begin the match with an equal chance of winning. In addition, there needs to be an agreed-on number of possible outcomes—usually win, lose, or draw.[3]

Second, there is an accepted set of rules that govern the conduct of the contest, and these are usually codified. That is to say, while the rules may change from time to time, they nevertheless must have some degree of stability and legibility. They are written and thus visible for all to see and may be consulted in case of dispute. In the evolution of both cricket and golf, for example, codification of the rules came about in 1744 because bookmakers and gamblers demanded it. They needed to have consistent rules with a governing body that would enforce them. How else could people be sure that the results of the contest were just and that they were not being cheated? The codified rules of the game thus came about because of the need for a regularized set of procedures to follow in case there were disputes over the outcome of the competition. In effect, odd as it may sound, codified rules were needed to ensure the integrity of the wagers that gamblers placed. Gambling, after all, depends on a certain perceived fairness and bettors had to be confident that the environment was one in which they could both win and know that mechanisms for the resolution of disputes were available and in place.[4]

Third, there is an umpire, judge, or referee responsible for enforcing the rules either by rewarding teams that comply or penalizing those teams or individuals who do not. The presence of a referee may be especially important because in many societies those realms in which arbiters or those who have either judicial or conflict management functions are present, legitimate, and respected are few and far between. In addition, the referees often wear clothing that distinguishes them from the players, thus increasing their visibility and legibility. Depending on the sport, and the particular culture, people will often refer to these figures by referring to the clothing they wear. "Zebras" and "men in blue" are but two examples.

In consequence, and fourth, in addition to the formally codified laws or rules of the game, there is usually an unwritten code of conduct governing the behavior of all the participants. These codes of conduct often regulate behavior in such a way as to prevent excesses and to preserve the integrity of the sport and the health and well-being of the players. Deliberately seeking to do bodily harm to an opposing player is usually frowned on, for example, even in violent sports such as American football. When the New Orleans Saints of the US National Football League (NFL) placed cash bounties on key players on opposing teams, hoping to encourage their players literally to knock their opponents out of the competition, an outcry ensued and the league penalized both the offending players and coaches.[5]

Fifth, there is an agreed-on arena where the contest occurs. The arena does not need to be a formal structure; it might well be an unpaved street in an urban slum or a cleared patch of ground in a suburb with rocks or shirts marking the touch lines. Interestingly, however, although baseball features arenas that are of different sizes and shapes that often have different dimensions and varying outfield configurations, the infields are invariably identical, and are always a geometrically symmetrical diamond. Nonetheless, because of the variability in the configurations of the outfields (e.g., the Green Monster in left field at Fenway Park in Boston), baseball is unusual in this regard. The dimensions of the arenas and playing surfaces in most sports are constant. In addition, because the dimensions do not vary much and are almost always symmetrical, there is a visual equality and balance that presents itself to both players and spectators. The boundaries of the playing field are thus clearly visible and legible for all who participate and attend as spectators. In soccer, for example, one side of the field will be exactly the same size as the other side, so the players on each team will have an identical distance to travel to the goal of the opposing team. The playing field, or arena, also has to be level so that neither team is placed at a competitive disadvantage by having to run uphill to score.

Sixth, although there are some exceptions in certain sports (e.g., gender, weight, age, size, disability), we generally assume that performance within a sport is irrelevant to ascriptive characteristics such as one's race, religion, or appearance. In fact, historian Allen Guttmann argues that one of the characteristics of modern sport is its secularism. He writes, "Whether or not one considers the passions, the rituals, and the myths of modern sports as secular religion, the fundamental contrast with primitive and ancient sport remains. The bond between the secular and the sacred has been broken, the attachment to the realm of the transcendent has been severed. Modern sports are partly pursued for their own sake, partly for other ends which are equally secular."[6] But while this is certainly true on one level, students of African soccer must nevertheless consider the substantial role of sorcery in the African game. Arnold Pannenborg's ethnographic study of a week in the life of two football teams in Buea, Cameroon, indicates clearly that sorcery and the realm of the supernatural have a great deal to do with what occurs both on and off the pitch in the daily lives of these sides.[7] Players have even been known to employ these spiritual forces on their own teammates so that they themselves could advance and receive more playing time. In addition, Oliver Becker's fascinating film documentary, *Kick the Lion*, explores the role of sorcery in African football, especially in Tanzania, Uganda, Ghana, and portions of southern Africa.[8] By no stretch of the imagination confined to Africa, the realm of the spiritual and supernatural dimensions of life also play a role in Brazilian football.[9]

The last observation pertaining to the moral structure of sport, in some ways perhaps the most important for this particular discussion, is that—sorcery notwithstanding because it is widely assumed that all sides engage in these occult practices—each of these premises requires a certain degree of visibility and transparency. Each premise, therefore, whether singly or in conjunction with others, may occasionally form the basis of an implicit cognitive comparison that individuals may make both to aspects of the formal organization of the sport and to analogous aspects of the larger world of politics and society. In addition, in all seven premises there is a tacit assumption of a certain orderliness and thus predictability that I suspect is quite important politically, especially in those societies that do not have a thick or well-articulated institutional matrix. Moreover, in many of these societies, the world of sport, at least in its more idealized constitutional and organizational forms, may provide a stark contrast to the opaque, murky, and occasionally menacing political world.

In this regard, the work of the Trinidadian historian C. L. R. James, *Beyond a Boundary*, has always been relevant to any discussion of the largely implicit moral structure of sport. In describing his days as a schoolboy, James writes of cricket and football, and is worth citing at length:

> And I had been brought up in the public school code.
>
> It came doctrinally from the masters, who for two generations, from the foundation of the school, had been Oxford and Cambridge men. The striking thing was that inside the classrooms the code had little success. Sneaking was taboo, but we lied and cheated without any sense of shame. I know I did. By common understanding the boys sitting for the valuable scholarships did not cheat. Otherwise we submitted, or did not submit, to moral discipline, according to upbringing and temperament.
>
> But as soon as we stepped on to the cricket or football field, all was changed. We were a motley crew. The children of some white officials and white businessmen, middle class blacks and mulattos, Chinese boys, some of whose parents still spoke broken English, Indian boys, some of whose parents could speak no English at all, and some poor black boys who had won exhibitions or whose parents had starved and toiled on plots of agricultural land and were spending their hard-earned money on giving the eldest boy an education. Yet rapidly we learned to obey the umpire's decision without question, however irrational it was. We learned to play with the team, which meant subordinating your personal inclinations, and even interests, to the good of the whole. We kept a stiff upper lip in that we did not complain about ill-fortune. We did not denounce failures, but "Well tried" or "Hard luck" came easily to our lips. We were generous to opponents and congratulated them on victories, even when we knew they did not deserve it. We lived in two worlds. Inside the classrooms the heterogeneous jumble of Trinidad was battered and jostled and shaken down into some sort of order. On the playing field we did what ought to be done. Every individual did not observe every rule. But the majority of the boys did. The best and most-respected boys were precisely the ones who always kept them. When a boy broke them he knew what he had done and, with the cruelty and intolerance of youth, from all sides our denunciations poured in on him. Eton or Harrow had nothing on us.
>
> Before very long I acquired a discipline for which the only name is Puritan. I never cheated, I never appealed for a decision unless I thought the batsman was out, I never argued with the umpire, I never jeered at a defeated opponent.[10]

Please note that here when we speak of the moral structure of sport we are not talking about the economic structure of sports or sports leagues. Similarly, we are not talking about labor-management relations or the possible exploitation of players or other workers in the various ancillary sports industries. Nor are we talking about the governance structure of individual sports or teams. To be sure, these subjects all have obvious moral dimensions, but it is not my task to explore them here because they themselves do not speak to the implicit moral structure of sport.

Except for the passage just cited, James does not really discuss this implicit moral structure in detail because for him morality was subsumed under the larger rubric of politics, and he saw cricket as a means of teaching both a political and moral lesson. Furthermore, for him the lesson was that skin color and social class did not matter in determining the outcome of the contest either on the pitch or, for that matter, in politics. This lesson may seem self-evident and obvious to all today, but it never is during anticolonial struggles because it is never especially apparent to colonial overlords. Nor was James especially concerned with cheating in sports, although he did mention at one point that he found it shocking.[11]

Throughout the remainder of this chapter, I assume three things. The first is that sports do have a moral structure. The second is that people value this moral structure because it fosters a sense of symmetry, as well as a certain predictability, thus reducing uncertainty by providing some regularity in a most uncertain and disorderly political world where, for the most part, the largely implicit moral structure of sport does not apply. To be sure, although the results of the sporting contests themselves are not predictable, the structure of the competitions is quite consistent. The matches will be held on certain days, at certain times, in certain venues having a level playing field, with two competing teams present, and with referees in charge of regulating the contest and enforcing the codified and well-known rules of the game. All this, moreover, will be visible, legible, and transparent. Even when sorcerers are employed to influence the outcome through the intervention of occult spiritual forces, the usual assumption is that both sides will engage in similar practices. The third assumption is that this moral structure and, especially the manner in which it is enforced, usually has something to do with a society and culture's manner of understanding what is acceptable and what is not, of understanding what is thinkable and what is not, and—therefore—almost certainly has something to do with our understanding of what is, or is not, "cricket."

Cases: FIFA and Nigeria, Cameroon, Uganda, and South Africa

FIFA and Nigeria

FIFA, an acronym commonly used for the Fédération Internationale de Football Association, is the worldwide governing body of the sport. An international nongovernmental organization (INGO) based in Zurich, FIFA is a membership organization composed of the world's national football associations. So although FIFA and thus world football is organized largely along national lines, at least in theory, nation-states and their respective governments are not supposed to have anything whatsoever to do with the game of soccer. Instead, it is the responsibility of each of FIFA's 211 national football associations, themselves nongovernmental organizations, to organize domestic sporting competitions and leagues; to ensure that its teams are represented in the relevant and important international competitions; to act in ways to promote, spread, and develop the sport; and to assure that the local sport is smoothly and competently run.[12] Indeed, one of FIFA's most important and most seriously enforced rules is that states may not intervene in the governance of football. Although as is often the case in a world filled with state institutions called ministries of sport and national sports councils, this particular FIFA statute is honored more in the breach than in practice.

In fact, it is quite common for states, particularly in Africa, to intervene in the affairs of soccer for three reasons. First, as we shall see when examining the case of Uganda, in parts of the economically disadvantaged world, FIFA may provide local football associations with substantial economic resources. The top management positions in the various African football associations are thus seen as political plums because the people fortunate enough to be either elected or appointed to them often find themselves in a position to regulate the flow of FIFA's economic resources. While in the cosmic scheme of things such resources and financial flows might not be all that large, in the local context they may still be quite impressive and thus worth a political struggle to control them.

Second, although most Americans could probably not name the head of the US Soccer Federation (Sunil Gulati), in Africa and other parts of the world where soccer is a hegemonic sport, the president or chief executive of the national football association is usually a major figure who is often in the news.[13] Moreover, other high-ranking officials and personalities in the world of soccer are more than occasionally able to translate their visibility and popularity into political office. For example, John Kufuor, president of Ghana from 2001 to 2009, had once been chairman of Asante Kotoko, a powerful and successful team in Kumasi with ties to the Asantehene and his court.[14] In like manner, even if an African politician has no ties with a popular football club, chances are good that sooner or later even an incumbent will seek to develop them. Malawi's Big Bullets Football Club is a case in point. Perhaps the most successful and popular club in Malawi's history, in 2003 the then president Bakili Muluzi offered the team his sponsorship and quickly renamed them the Bakili Bullets.[15]

Third, football is important to African states and especially to the politicians who run them because it is far and away the most popular sport on the continent. A successful campaign culminating in a trophy can bring outpourings of national joy. Politicians, of course, like nothing better than to bask in popular adulation. Even though the president of the republic did not score the winning goal, he or she is invariably overjoyed to take as much credit for the victorious campaign as possible. After all, regardless of who might have actually facilitated the favorable conditions under which the national side labored, regardless of who might have actually authorized the incentives and bonuses paid to the players and coaches, the president will surely take the lion's share of the credit for such a sporting success. A major victory will often be accompanied by a national holiday, a parade, and a reception at the state house or the presidential palace. Gifts of cars and cash for the coaches and players quickly follow. It is another example of the "feel-good factor" that politicians often seek by hosting major sporting events.[16] Politicians know that a victory in a serious international competition often produces the same effect.

There is a dark side, however, because the national team often loses, or is eliminated too early from the competition. Then politicians are often tempted to show that they are doing something about the deplorable condition of football in their country and will thus seek to intervene in the management of football by interfering with the policies and procedures of the national football association. When this occurs, FIFA will often react sharply so as to ensure its control over the international game.

Events in Nigeria after the 2010 World Cup in South Africa are a case in point and illustrate the larger trends involved. The Nigerian side, the Super Eagles, performed abysmally in South Africa, finishing without a single win and at the bottom of its group. (It drew with South Korea, but lost to Argentina and Greece.) Its failure to advance to the knockout round of the competition was a bitter disappointment for all of Nigeria's fans. In fact, the Nigerians had not won a World Cup match since 1998; they went out with two losses and a draw in 2002; and failed to qualify at all in 2006.

The reaction from President Goodluck Jonathan was immediate. Following the team's poor showing in South Africa, he personally suspended the national team from international competition for two years. The stated purpose of the ban was to reorganize Nigeria's football administration, even though the Nigerian Football Federation (NFF, the national football association) had earlier offered an apology to the government and to "all football loving Nigerians" for the early elimination from the competition.[17] In addition, the government announced that it planned a financial audit of all football operations, and a special presidential advisor announced that "If any financial misappropriation is discovered, all officials responsible will be held accountable."[18] Shortly after, FIFA issued a terse statement indicating that it had not yet been officially apprised of the matter and had no official information. The statement, however, did reiterate that FIFA's position in matters such as political interference in football was already well known:

"Our statutes do not allow for any political interference."[19] In consequence, if the situation was not rectified, Nigeria's national and club teams, in addition to its referees, ran the risk of being banned from all international events. Moreover, Nigerian football officials would themselves not be permitted to attend meetings or events, and Nigeria would no longer be the recipient of financial resources from FIFA. Such series of actions would have effectively banned Nigeria from world football.[20]

The crisis continued, and within the next few days the NFF announced the sacking of its president and vice president, as well as a member of its technical committee in an effort both to appease the Jonathan administration and to ward off possible sanctions from FIFA. And as a further sop to the administration, the NFF also promised "to take urgent steps to address the maladministration of football in the country."[21] Also fearing the imposition of serious sanctions, the country's House of Representatives passed a resolution asking Jonathan to withdraw his suspension order. FIFA held firm and imposed a deadline for compliance and the withdrawal of Jonathan's actions. Jonathan relented shortly before FIFA's deadline.[22]

Cameroon

One scholar of Cameroonian football, anthropologist Beata Vidacs, expresses the desire for order, consistency, and predictability this way:

> The structured nature of both a match and of a championship, the repetitiveness, despite the infinite variety of the actual game itself, lends an air of certainty and calculability which is otherwise lacking in Cameroonians' lives. If it is Wednesday during the championship season you know that you will be in the stadium, you know that there will be a match, you know that there are certain people you will find there, and you can also know what their reactions are going to be. Rituals of repetition in a world where there are no certainties are extremely comforting.[23]

She also notes that the owner-coach of the team she studied in Yaoundé possessed an optimistic vision of football. More to the point, in contradistinction to the rest of Cameroonian society, in football a certain form of meritocracy was at least thinkable, conceivable, and thus legitimate if not always probable. In this realm of life one could at least hope for clear-cut progress based on work, discipline, and achievement. There was, in other words, a tenacious illusion of order in a world that was largely disordered.[24] Football was thus a source of optimism and hope for it represented "'normalcy' in a world where 'things are not normal,' where everything is in disorder. Football is an ideal vehicle for the expression of such order, its rules and regulations, its rituals, the need to fill in forms before the match, its whole administrative structure creates a reality, a routine, a predictability which is lacking everywhere else."[25]

To this I would also add that the visual geometric order and symmetry of the pitch itself may be more important than we commonly realize. These symmetrical, structural features are readily visible, even quite transparent, whereas those of other institutions might not be. A bureaucracy, for example, may have a pyramidal and hierarchical structure in the mind's eye of an analyst, but citizens do not see this in their daily encounters with it, even in countries where such institutions operate reasonably efficiently and are generally taken for granted. For many, bureaucracies are opaque institutions where little light ever penetrates and from which even less light ever emerges. But people can see a football pitch with eleven Rwandans and eleven Ugandans competing under the gaze of an umpire who is supposed to enforce the rules to ensure a fair contest. As we shall see, the Ugandan football association's (Federation of Ugandan Football Associations, FUFA) bureaucracy and procedures under the reign of Denis Obua certainly defied description in any visible, legible, or geometric terms.[26]

The importance of, and emphasis on, visual geometric order, symmetry, and a level playing field would appear to be universal. As mentioned previously, most arenas in most sports display these characteristics. Even more telling, perhaps, is that cheating is often described as a violation of this geometric order and symmetry. The World Anti-Doping Agency's (WADA) mission is to prevent any athlete from seeking a chemical, performance-enhancing competitive advantage, and thus preserve the legitimacy and integrity of the particular contests in question. WADA's website features a two-minute video entitled "Level the Playing Field" that is part of the Agency's Play True campaign designed to eliminate doping in sport.

This particular video features visual images of a row of archery targets, one of which is tiny in comparison to the others; hurdles on a track oval, one of which is much higher than the others; a football pitch where the center line is far closer to one goal than the other; a tennis court where one side of the court slants downward and is actually below ground; a basketball court where one basket is very low while the other is excessively high; a swimming pool where one of the lanes narrows precipitously; and an ice hockey rink where one goal mouth is enormous and the other is tiny. As these distorted images are flashed on the screen, the narrators comment on the necessity of a "fair shot," the need to "play by the same rules," the importance of a "level playing field," the importance of "fair play," and the desire to "sanction those who cheat their sport." As the video progresses, the visual and geometric imbalances are slowly corrected restoring symmetry and thus fairness.[27]

Uganda

My experience in Uganda and my subsequent attention to the evolution of FUFA as a governing body further reinforces some of the points Vidacs raises in the

Cameroonian context. Most of my informants within the Ugandan football community lamented, in one way or another, Ugandan football's lack of progress and lack of success in international competitions. More specifically, when asked to relate what they felt were the major challenges facing Ugandan football, virtually all commented on various aspects of the prevailing lack of political and social order.

One, a former first division player and now a referee, noted in response to my query:

> The three big clubs [Villa, Express, Kampala City Council] are big only because of their fans and their resources. But the quality of their game is just as low as the bottom portion of the league. Did you go to the game on Saturday between Villa and Express? I wasn't there, but I heard about it. They couldn't play 20 minutes without there being "rugby" interruptions. For these teams training isn't really training. They don't do drills to work on the skills and fundamentals. Training for them is just 11 on a side games. [I ask why.] The fans demand that. They go to the practices and they don't want to see drills; they want to see the team playing a game. The coaches know that if they don't comply with the fans they will come under pressure and they will be gone. Training camp for a major match is one week, and that's all. Basic skills such as penalty kicks are not taught at all, are not coached and developed. Resources are also a problem here.[28]

He further noted that the coaches are insecure.

Another voice, a journalist who covers sports, bemoaned the fact that since 1995,

> one stopped being able to enumerate the national team. That's when things really got worse. People started [to] scramble for power at the expense of the game. Ever since then we lack a stable football administration. Unfortunately, the present administration [FUFA] is lacking. It has received unprecedented sponsorship, both in terms of corporate grants and grants from FIFA. They have received more or less billions of shillings. All of this money has been eaten up with nothing to show in terms of development.[29]

Finally, a former player and a current club official maintained that FUFA was far from transparent. As he put it:

> The problem is that the players are not committed because they are not treated as well as Cranes [Uganda's national men's team]. It's pathetic that we treat our national team so poorly. There is a lot of match fixing because of this. Players and referees are bribed to throw matches or to influence matches. The desire to improve skills is not there. The fans want to win at all costs. Fairness is something we are moving away from in football. If I train hard, and play hard, but lose it's okay because I can go back and train harder and try to do better. But the fans don't understand that. They don't accept that. The coaches go abroad

> for courses but none of them want to come back to train us. The coaches do not cooperate with each other because they come under pressure to win at any cost.
>
> Money comes from FIFA, but nothing goes to youth development. I even see many administrative lapses within [a club]. Individuals fund club activities. They, FUFA, have no moral authority to challenge the clubs. The clubs do not keep any books. FUFA has no books. No one wants to point a finger at the other, and everything is rotting away. Players chase referees around the field and attack them when there is a call they don't like. The government should intervene, but there really can't be any government interference because of the fear that FIFA will ban us if the government does intervene. But the government can come in and reverse the trend. People concerned about football need to get into FUFA. We need serious people there. If I were Minister for one day, the one thing I would do would be to appoint people of integrity. Rules have to be enforced as they were meant to be. Then we can affect clubs, players, referees, and coaches. Football is very partisan and many promote the club's interest above the general interest. They don't care how they win as long as they do.[30]

Running through these diagnoses and complaints is, I suspect, a yearning for a more ordered reality, as well as a sense of outrage that the larger moral structure of Ugandan football has been violated. Note, for example, this club official's insistence on enforcing the rules and his sympathy for the referees. In one sense, this desire for order, predictability, and understanding is also reflected in how people use three different causal modes of understanding to make sense of football. Briefly, outcomes and events on the pitch, and elsewhere in daily life, are explained either scientifically, in terms of demonstrable cause and effect (e.g., the team with the best players and most resources will win); on the basis of an understanding that a superior spiritual being has intervened in earthly processes (divine intervention); or through an understanding that certain individuals have the power to affect events and cause outcomes by precipitating the intervention of various spirits (sorcery). These are not only approaches to understanding causality, for the individuals involved they are also, and perhaps even primarily, ways of explaining and understanding the outcomes of daily life. They are also, therefore, ways of reducing uncertainty both on and off the pitch.[31]

South Africa

The quest for the certainty of a moral structure in a turbulent and unpredictable world, especially among the powerless, is evident in the story of football on Robben Island under apartheid. Historian Chuck Korr and dramatist Marvin Close relate how football was used to bring some unity, happiness, and predictability of control—especially democratic control—into the lives of the political prisoners on Robben Island during apartheid. The Makana Football Association (MFA) was formed to conduct league matches according to strict FIFA rules and regulations. The resulting prisoner-run bureaucracy gave the inmates a sense of control as well as structures that were regular, predictable, not arbitrary, and democratic. The emphasis on a correct and precise organizational structure was striking. "For the political prisoners, forming a football league was a chance to organize themselves, to practise the skills they would one day need when they had won the right to run their own country—and, if they were going to do it, they were going to do it right."[32] Doing it "right" in this context meant meticulous bureaucratic guidelines and procedures, democratic structures and organization, and oversight committees. The prisoners also organized a referees union because they knew it was critical to demonstrate to the prison guards that they were capable of regulating themselves and of controlling their passions. The existence of a formally structured and trained cadre of referees, therefore, was critical because the prisoners understood the existence of referees to be a metaphor for their ability to solve problems and arbitrate disputes within their own community.[33]

Korr and Close emphasize repeatedly the importance of both organization and structures, noting that these were the words that the prisoners themselves used to describe what they did:

> The constant emphasis on the need to organize and the respect for procedure stemmed in part from their political background, but there was much more involved. Putting together an organization with a written constitution and a set of committees, rules, and by-laws was a way to show both themselves and the warders that these prisoners were not common criminals. However, as well as these idealistic motives for organization, there were also pragmatic considerations. If sport could be maintained on Robben Island, the prisoners would have to overcome two opponents, the prison authorities and their own disunity. They needed a united front to negotiate guidelines with the authorities. They needed structures to govern the activities of various sports bodies to ensure that everyone had a chance to participate.[34]

In other words, as in Cameroon and Uganda, but this time within an extreme case of a total institution, the apartheid-era prison on Robben Island, football was used to create and maintain a sense of ordered regularity, political autonomy, and legitimacy in an environment where all these things were in very short supply.

Conclusion

The moral structure of sport consists of a series of interlinked premises and assumptions that speak to equality, visual symmetry and legibility, order and predictability, as well as legitimacy and fairness. Since the moral structure of sport is mostly implicit, it usually only becomes visible when it is violated in some serious way. Such violations, however, even if infrequent, instruct us about various dimensions of politics writ small—the small-scale world of daily politics that envelops our lives but of which we are usually only dimly aware. When articulated explicitly, they demonstrate to us that politics and basic political concepts such as fairness, legitimacy, and equality suffuse the realm of sport even though few of us are consciously aware of it. Moreover, the relationship is reciprocal in that it is through our socialization to the moral structure of sport that we often learn basic political concepts. This is illustrated in the views of two former African heads of state, Ahmed Ben Bella of Algeria and Nnamdi Azikiwe of Nigeria.

Ben Bella, the first president of independent Algeria, also found a moral structure in sport. Referring to the 1930s he wrote:

> I believe that what saved my morale at this time was sport. . . . Of course, I realize today that, at that time, football became a kind of compensation for me. The world of sport was one in which there were no restrictions and where my own ability set the only limitations. When I manoeuvred at speed against the enemy, nobody asked me whether I was European or Algerian—I either scored a goal or I didn't, and that was that. I was responsible only to myself for success and failure alike. . . . At Tlemcen as centre-half, I was the pivot of the team. That is to say, of the Algerian team. For at Tlemcen, unlike what happened at Marnia, segregation had even penetrated the world of sport. There were two teams, one of Algerians, and one of colons. And once a year the colons' team met ours at the Grand Bassin. To be truthful, I must admit that the colons nearly always won. I believe that we were very superior to them in tactics and technically; but they were heavier and more athletic than us. Let's face it, they were better fed. It was at this period that I made contact with Nationalist groups.[35]

In other words, for Ben Bella there was both an equality of opportunity and a transparency in the sport that he found refreshing because they stood in stark contrast to the harsh, daily reality of political life under French colonial rule.

Azikiwe, the first president of independent Nigeria and one of the giants of Nigerian nationalism, also found that there was a moral structure of sport although he phrased it in slightly different terms in his autobiography: "Athletes who are appointed or selected as captains of their teams are usually leaders of quality. I have found that, in general, politicians who have at some time participated in team sports like football, cricket and athletes [*sic*] tend, in their political roles, to be more fair and reasonable. . . . I was convinced that even in the realm of politics the ideals of sportsmanship were attainable."[36] Or, put another way, how a sport's subjacent moral structure is understood and enforced may speak directly to our implicit understanding of critical political concepts such as fairness, justice, and legitimacy.

And yet, this chapter demonstrates in the cases of FIFA and Nigeria, Cameroon, Uganda, and South Africa that chaos and disorder often characterize the official world of African football. Indeed, the daily operations of this world often seem murky, possessing neither light nor clarity. At times the events and interactions between FIFA, the state, and the football associations can resemble a comedy of errors. In consequence, there is often a disjuncture between the clarity, legibility, and transparency of the moral structure of sport and the real world of organized football, a point former Liberian footballer and former presidential candidate George Weah implicitly recognized in 2009 while promoting the World Cup:

> In Europe, people who played the game govern the game. . . . But in Africa, people who don't know anything or have passion for the game govern the game, so it kills the game in Africa. . . . We have to come together and show the world that we were good on the pitch and we can be great off the pitch as well. . . . Football being run as a comical circus needs to change—when we decide to do that, then we will restore respect to football and it will take a different trend in Africa. But if we don't fight for football's soul now, it's going to stay the same way and we'll watch the game lose its relevance and power. The people who have been on the pitch and played it like their lives depended on it should come on board because they know what the sport means to Africans. Together we should start taking responsibility to revive the game here, because football means life, freedom and power to the people of Africa.[37]

MICHAEL G. SCHATZBERG is Professor of Political Science and African Cultural Studies at the University of Wisconsin, Madison. He is author of *Political Legitimacy in Middle Africa: Father, Family, Food* and *The Dialectics of Oppression in Zaire*.

Notes

I am grateful to Tejumola Olaniyan and Elisabeth Karpov for their cogent critiques of this chapter. Of course, they are absolved of responsibility for any remaining deficiencies.

1. Richard Giulianotti, *Football: A Sociology of the Global Game* (Cambridge, UK: Polity, 1999), 24.

2. See Michael G. Schatzberg, "Soccer, Science, and Sorcery: Causation and African Football," *Afrika Spectrum* 41, no. 3 (2006): 351–369.

3. Guttmann sees this as equality. See Allen Guttmann, *From Ritual to Record: The Nature of Modern Sports* (New York: Columbia University Press, 2004), 26–27.

4. David Forrest and Robert Simmons, "Sport and Gambling," *Oxford Review of Economic Policy* 19, no. 4 (2003): 598–611, esp. 598.

5. Mark Maske, "NFL Bounty Penalties: Sean Payton, Gregg Williams, Mickey Loomis Suspended," *Washington Post*, March 21, 2012, https://www.washingtonpost.com/blogs/football-insider/post/nfl-bounty-penalties-sean-payton-gregg-williams-mickey-loomis-suspended/2012/03/21/gIQAJHdoRS_blog.html?utm_term=.6cd01ca55ca5.

6. Guttmann, *From Ritual to Record*, 26.

7. Arnold Pannenborg, *How to Win a Football Match in Cameroon: An Anthropological Study of Africa's Most Popular Sport* (Leiden, Netherlands: African Studies Centre, 2008).

8. *Kick the Lion: Witchcraft and Soccer in Africa*, directed by Oliver G. Becker (Occasione Documentaries, 2006). Also see Schatzberg, "Soccer, Science, and Sorcery."

9. Alex Bellos, *Futebol: The Brazilian Way of Life* (New York: Bloomsbury, 2002), 189, 196.

10. C. L. R. James, *Beyond a Boundary* (1963; repr., Durham, NC: Duke University Press, 1993), 25–26. Published by Yellow Jersey. Reprinted with the permission of The Random House Group Limited.

11. Ibid., 44.

12. For an overview of FIFA, and especially the politics of FIFA, see Paul Darby, *Africa, Football, and FIFA: Politics, Colonialism, and Resistance* (London: Frank Cass, 2002). For a journalistic account that emphasizes some of the problems and flaws of the organization, see Andrew Jennings, *Foul! The Secret World of FIFA* (London: HarperCollins, 2006).

13. On the notion of a hegemonic sport, one that dominates a nation's sporting imaginary, see Andrei S. Markovits and Steven L. Hellerman, *Soccer and American Exceptionalism* (Princeton, NJ: Princeton University Press, 2001).

14. Kevin S. Fridy and Victor Brobbey, "Win the Match and Vote for Me: The Politicisation of Ghana's Accra Hearts of Oak and Kumasi Asante Kotoko Football Clubs," *Journal of Modern African Studies* 47, no. 1 (2009): 19–39, esp. 27.

15. Aubrey Sumbuleta, "Muluzi's Bullets," *BBC*, June 2, 2003, http://news.bbc.co.uk/sport2/hi/football/africa/2956716.stm.

16. Georgios Kavetsos and Stefan Szymanski, "National Well-being and International Sports Events," *Journal of Economic Psychology* 31 (2010): 158–171.

17. "Nigerian Team Suspended for Poor Play," *ESPN*, June 30, 2010, http://www.espn.com/espnw/news-commentary/article/5342521/nigeria-president-suspends-team-two-years-poor-showing-world-cup.

18. "World Cup 2010: Nigeria President Suspends Team," *BBC*, June 30, 2010, http://news.bbc.co.uk/sport2/hi/football/world_cup_2010/8777118.stm.

19. Ibid.

20. "Nigerian Team Suspended for Poor Play"; "World Cup 2010: Nigerian President Lifts Ban on Team," *BBC*, July 5, 2010, http://news.bbc.co.uk/sport2/hi/football/world_cup_2010/8790094.stm.

21. "World Cup 2010: Nigeria Awaits FIFA Ban Deadline," *BBC*, July 5, 2010, http://news.bbc.co.uk/sport2/hi/football/world_cup_2010/8786834.stm.

22. "World Cup 2010: Nigerian President Lifts Ban on Team."

23. Beata Vidacs, "Visions of a Better World: Football in the Cameroonian Social Imagination" (PhD diss., City University of New York, 2002), 14.

24. Ibid., 78–88.

25. Ibid., 100. On Cameroonian football also see André Ntonfo, *Football et Politique du Football au Cameroun* (Yaoundé, Cameroon: Editions du CRAC, 1994).

26. On the Obua period in Ugandan football, see Michael G. Schatzberg, "Les Complexités de la 'Démocratie': La Fédération Ougandaise de Football en tant que 'Polity,'" *Politique Africaine* 118 (June 2010): 123–141.

27. See "Level the Playing Field," World Anti-Doping Agency, *YouTube*, November 12, 2009, http://www.youtube.com/watch?v=gZY-syOmqNQ&list=FLt8uUiDNlZuicZH1C-OI_4Q&index=1&feature=plpp. The video may also be found on WADA's website (https://www.wada-ama.org/en/resources/general-anti-doping-information/level-the-playing-field).

28. K-1, interview by the author, July 3, 2001, 3.

29. K-2, interview by the author, July 3, 2001, 1.

30. K-7, interview by the author, July 11, 2001, 1–2.

31. For a fuller version of the argument, see Michael G. Schatzberg, *Political Legitimacy in Middle Africa: Father, Family, Food* (Bloomington: Indiana University Press, 2001), 111–144; Schatzberg, "Soccer, Science, and Sorcery"; and Michael G. Schatzberg, "La Sorcellerie Comme Mode de Causalité Politique," *Politique Africaine* 79 (October 2000): 33–47.

32. Chuck Korr and Marvin Close, *More Than Just a Game: Football v Apartheid* (London: HarperCollins, 2008), 62–63. For an overview of football in South Africa, see Peter Alegi, *Laduma! Soccer, Politics and Society in South Africa* (Scottsville, South Africa: University of KwaZulu-Natal Press, 2004).

33. Korr and Close, *More Than Just a Game*, 76, 78.

34. Ibid., 286–287.

35. Quoted in Philip Dine, "France, Algeria and Sport: From Colonisation to Globalisation," *Modern and Contemporary France* 10, no. 4 (2002): 498.

36. Quoted in Wiebe Karl Boer, "Nation Building Exercise: Sporting Culture and the Rise of Football in Colonial Nigeria" (PhD diss., Yale University, 2003), 295.

37. Quoted in Oluwashina Okeleji, "Weah Calls for Players to Govern," *BBC*, July 28, 2009, http://news.bbc.co.uk/sport2/hi/football/africa/8172507.stm.

5 The Enchanted History of Nigerian State Television

Matthew H. Brown

> Il ne s'agit pas d'une vocation à transformer la nation, mais prosaïquement à servir de courroie de transmission à un capitalisme acculé au camouflage et qui se pare aujourd'hui du masque néo-colonialiste.
>
> It's [the bourgeoisie's] vocation not to transform the nation, but prosaically to serve as the transmission belt for a capitalism driven into camouflage and today hidden behind the mask of neocolonialism.
>
> —Frantz Fanon, *Les Damnés de la Terre* (my translation)

I HAVE CHOSEN to quote this chapter's epigraph from *Wretched of the Earth* (*Les Damnés de la Terre*) in French because neither of the two widely available English translations catches all of the significations that apply to my reading of state motion picture broadcasting in colonial and postcolonial Nigeria.[1] In the cited lines, Fanon makes the now commonplace argument that the postcolonial bourgeoisie is but a servant of global capitalism, which, in the absence of direct imperial political control, constitutes a subtler form of metropolitan, or *néo-colonialiste*, domination. Though Fanon characterizes his description of the bourgeoisie as prosaic (*prosaïquement*), he actually uses a remarkably poetic metaphor, *courroie de transmission*, to illustrate his point. I prefer the most literal translation of the metaphor, a "transmission belt," which best illustrates the tension between structure and agency at the heart of Fanon's critique.

A transmission belt is a mechanical device, a closed loop of flexible material that transmits the force of a powered gear to an unpowered gear. Probably the most common example of a transmission belt is the drive belt found in many automobiles. The drive belt harnesses the rotation of the crankshaft, which is powered by combustion, in order to turn the gears of multiple peripheral devices—such as the alternator, water pump, and air pump. While these devices have no power source of their own, they are able to produce mechanical action because of the force transmitted to them by the belt. Fanon's metaphor implies that, while capital may fuel a powerful mechanism of productivity in the metropole, postcolonial productive forces resemble free-spinning gears that depend on outside influence for motivation.

Regardless of the source from which they derive power, however, alternators and water pumps do necessary things that make the continued operation of the overall machine possible. The alternator provides the spark needed for combustion, while the water pump ensures that the machine does not melt under its own heat. As a result, the drive belt is more than a one-way transmitter; it links together different nodes of coordinated specialization. To use Fanon's metaphor analytically, therefore, we might take note of the ways in which postcolonial elites, and the institutions they have created, coordinate various specialties with the needs of a larger, global system. In classical macroeconomic terms, we might think of Fanon's bourgeoisie as a finely tuned instrument of the law of comparative advantage.

After more than five decades of independence, however, it is now quite obvious that economic overspecialization has been ultimately counterproductive for many postcolonial societies, but we would be overstating the case to argue that African states have not attempted to diversify their portfolios. Unfortunately, one of the key obstacles to unleashing the nation's productive imagination, whether deriving from internal corruption, external coercion, or structural defects—which are all really intertwined—is that the bourgeoisie, and the colonial state it inherited, has conceived of its position as the gatekeeper, rather than the enabler, of productive capacity. In the case of Nigeria, the bourgeoisie precociously and lavishly invested in state television precisely because elites wanted to institutionalize their role in voicing new ideas, promoting new ventures, and training the minds of the workforce. Nigeria's state television network is, in fact, the oldest on the continent, and during its long life it has become the largest as well. It has produced thousands of hours of content. And it has done all this with the sincere intention of developing the nation. Indeed, rather than a boorish propaganda mouthpiece (though it has been that at times), and rather than a cultivator of consumer desire (though it does a little of that, too), Nigerian television has positioned itself as an instructor in all things modern. But this position assumes that the audience of state television is both in need of, and will eventually benefit from, modernization.

Narratives of modernization and development tend to be chronotopic.[2] That is, they combine a temporal dimension—here the concept of change over time—with a spatial dimension—in this case, a discourse of socioeconomic convergence.[3] There is a future, they propose, when all economies will take all people to the same place. Fanon's transmission belt model calls this narrative into question on two fronts. It denies the inevitability, or even the possibility of convergence. A water pump cannot become the same as a crankshaft; in fact, the crankshaft's future depends on the water pump remaining a water pump. Fanon's model also denies the proposition that modernity lies in the future. By making the modern power of the crankshaft possible, the water pump is already implicated and entrenched in that modernity. From a perspective informed by Fanon, then, the concept of development is only ever ideological. It is the capacity to hold together two fundamentally competing concepts—mechanical specialization and economic convergence—within one frame that makes the discursive position of Nigerian state television so intriguing.

In this chapter, I return to the origins of the Nigerian state television network and link later developments in broadcasting with those origins. Like a transmission belt, state television, and the elite Western-educated men and women who staff it, has generated tangible, consequential results while simultaneously, and perhaps unavoidably, reproducing a relationship between metropolitan and local power that is essentially colonial in form—but maybe only superficially so. As connected parts in a rattletrap global machine, metropole and postcolony may depend on one another functioning precisely as they have been cobbled together to function.

Colonial Cinema and the Advent of Nigerian Television: 1953–1959

State motion picture exhibition was inaugurated in Nigeria by the British Colonial Film Unit (CFU), which was formally established in 1939 and remained active through the 1950s. The CFU most famously operated mobile cinema vans that roamed the countryside projecting short films, documentaries, and newsreels in order to, as the director of the unit, William Sellers, writes, "[help] to develop self-reliance and to break traditional ground so that the seeds of progress in health, industry and agriculture could be planted."[4] After 1950, the CFU began a long transition from producing its own films to training, encouraging, and assisting African bureaucrats to produce theirs. The process was meant to be slow and deliberate, since many CFU officials believed that, "some inventions have been thrust upon the African before he has been taught how to make use of them and the result has been confusing and bewildering to their very conservative minds."[5] However, events in southern Nigerian politics forced a precipitous shift from imperial to local control of mass-mediated motion pictures. The story of that shift has become mythic in the history of Nigerian mass media.[6]

As the story goes, Nigerian nationalists were forced to seek out means of mass communication that superseded the colonial broadcasting machine. In 1953, during a heated debate in the colonial parliament concerning provisions in the latest constitution, a major figure in Nigerian nationalism, Obafemi Awolowo, led his party, the Action Group, on a remonstrative walkout. The chief secretary of the house reacted by calling on the governor-general of the colony, Sir John Stuart Macpherson, to issue a public statement condemning Awolowo and his loyalists. Macpherson obliged, broadcasting his speech to the colony via radio, courtesy of the Ministry of Information's Nigerian Broadcasting Service (NBS). Awolowo requested NBS airtime to respond but was categorically denied. Members of his party realized, therefore, that in order to cultivate their image before the Nigerian public and rival parties, they would have to speak louder than Macpherson. For the next six years, they nurtured plans for a television station, which they formally launched in Ibadan on October 31, 1959. Western Nigeria Television (WNTV), as they called it, was the first television broadcasting facility south of the Sahara.

Because it was the first of its kind, the history of WNTV has attracted sustained, if scattered, scholarly attention over the years. Much of the literature argues that, although Awolowo was justified in seeking control of mass communication, radio would have been a viable option and, therefore, his foray into the relatively expensive medium of television was conspicuously bold. As Yemi Farounbi, one-time general manager of the station writes, "Ibadan Television was established as a missionary in a wilderness of unbelievers and critics. To many, it was a diversion of the scarce resources of the region to a prestigious project."[7] Awolowo assuaged his critics by making the developmentalist claim that "television will serve as teacher and entertainer, and as a stimulus to us all to transform Nigeria into a modern and prosperous nation."[8] His language is remarkably similar to that of the CFU, which claimed that it served as a source of "constant education and teaching of the Colonial people towards a higher standard of life and better knowledge of the world."[9] Of course, the similarity runs deeper than a particular use of words. It is both epistemic and structural. In fact, before the Action Group could afford television broadcasting facilities, its officials had already invested heavily in a method of mass communication modeled on the CFU—a fact that the dramatic story of Awolowo's walkout has, for many studies of Nigerian television, effectively obscured.

Between Awolowo's walkout and the launch of WNTV, the Western Region embarked on a "Government Free Cinema" scheme in which forty cinema vans and six cinema barges were sent to tour southwestern Nigeria.[10] Journalist Frank Aig-Imoukhuede characterizes the work of government cinema this way:

> The government mobile van penetrates deep into the heart of the country and brings not just entertainment to remote villagers but also educates them by showing them films of the new farming techniques, the advantages of co-operative societies and the importance of education. The success of the mobile cinema can be judged from the influx of commercial concerns into the game. In between films of boxing and football, companies could bring in advertising strips of their products.[11]

Here, not only does Aig-Imoukhuede reproduce the Conradian imagery of penetrating Africa's "heart," but he reproduces with great fidelity the developmentalist narrative of the CFU. Of particular interest, however, is the fact that government cinema screenings evolved a format similar to broadcast television, where short segments in various genres are separated by commercial advertisements. More than a structural retention of a colonial institution, then, Government Free Cinema continued the aesthetic and ideological tendencies of colonial cinema, while simultaneously acting as the crucible in which Nigerian television aesthetics would be cemented.

The flagship production of Awolowo's free cinema project was the 1958 newsreel *Self-Government for Western Nigeria.*[12] In his words, "the 85-minute film in colour which covers all aspects of our self-government celebrations and the visit of Her Royal Highness the Princess Royal," was one of his "outstanding achievements."[13] It presents, in encyclopedic style, every official event carried out by the British and Western Region governments to mark the transfer of certain powers from the colonial administration into the hands of Nigerian elites in November 1957. Some of these events include religious services (at a mosque and an Anglican church), the arrival of Princess Margaret, a variety of ceremonies in which she participates—including a procession in front of seventeen thousand school children at the Ibadan racecourse and the planting of a tree—a garden party, a visit to the legislature, a number of local dance troupes giving celebratory performances, an exhibition football match against Ghana, simultaneous celebrations taking place among the Nigerian community in London, and, finally, an elaborate state ball at which Awolowo dances with the governor's wife. The film is narrated by a British voice-over, which often carries the words and sentiments of figures like the princess, as well as Awolowo.

The film's significance derives as much from what is not said as from what is. At one point, the voice-over mentions that one of the planned events—a visit to University College, Ibadan—had to be canceled. The reason is not disclosed in the film, but it turns out that the visit was canceled because, following student protests, the university had been shut down. A segment of the student body had long been agitating about the school's racialized promotion and remuneration policies, a phenomenon that administrators staunchly denied, but which many third-party observers repeatedly noted.[14] The chief catalyst for the protests, however, was the installation of barbed-wire fences—or cages, as the students called them—around the campus's residence halls. These cages were built in response to the death of a female student, in a male dorm, resulting from an attempted abortion.[15]

Such a salacious event, of course, would have had no place in *Self-Government for Western Nigeria*, but choosing to omit references to racial and administrative conflict at the university exemplifies the kinds of political calculation that Nigeria's nationalists often had to make. Awolowo was pursuing an established timeline toward independence that hinged on multilateral cooperation, as well as regional prestige—a narrative that student protests would have undermined. One consequence of such a teleological focus, however, was that the ultimate determiner of the timeline, the British, indirectly controlled the ideological tone of a film that had oppositional origins. As Tom Rice writes, "The film was intended for African audiences, but avoids any references to nationalist demands, unrest or any anti-colonial rhetoric, instead presenting the events largely from a British perspective, as the camera follows the Princess Royal on her tour of the region."[16] He goes on to suggest that "in its focus on British dignitaries, in showing local popular support for the visiting Princess, and in the British voiceover and speeches, the film largely propagates an established colonial rhetoric."[17] The key tension here is between an oppositional orientation to the British and the projection of a celebratory, accommodationist attitude about decolonization to local audiences. This is the direct obverse of the depiction of elites as transmission belts that we are used to seeing in critical narratives of decolonization. In Ousmane Sembene's novel and film *Xala* (1975), for instance, the bourgeoisie privately colludes with, but publicly admonishes colonists.[18] Meanwhile, Awolowo's Action Group is in this instance publicly extolling the virtues of the late colonial agenda while working against it by less ceremonious means.

This tension has its roots in the contradictions I have already mentioned—namely, the developmentalist target of eventual economic convergence with Euro-America and the reality of expanding global inequality, or what Walter Rodney famously denounced as "underdevelopment."[19] Awolowo reproduces this tension during the speech he delivers at the self-government ceremonies—a speech that is not ventriloquized by the voice-over, but in this case delivered directly, in Awolowo's own voice:

> Time was when those of us that belong to the black race, in the British colonies, were considered or we considered ourselves, as distant relations of the members of the British family of nations, but that time is gone now, and gone forever. We have become members of the British family of nations.

Here, convergence is cast in racial and political, rather than economic terms. Of course, in 1957, none of these convergences had actually been achieved. Decolonization was moving forward, but the authorities in various Nigerian parliaments were members of the British political family only insofar as that family remained extremely hierarchical. That fact makes the racial basis of Awolowo's convergence narrative even more remarkable. After all, the hierarchy of the "British family" was constructed primarily on the concept of race. Awolowo's speech thus sets the stage for the moment, in the final scenes of the film, when he steps in and briefly dances with Macpherson's wife. In semiotic terms, that move is so laden with its own semantic weight that it hardly needs interpretation, but when we recall that the image was projected to the people of the region, it implies that there is a claim to political legitimacy embedded within it. As Crawford Young succinctly argues, the logic of racial substitution was central to the nationalist conception of power:

> The racial subtext of colonial administration—that European agents by their presumed innate superiority and role as natural bearers of "civilization" had an unquestioned right to rule—was transformed into a comparable prerogative of the youthful educated nationalist generation to exercise tutelage over an unlettered citizenry.[20]

Even circumspect interpretation of the film, therefore, indicates that it depicts less the broad social convergence of Nigeria with its erstwhile colonial masters, and more accurately the calculated convergence of the local bourgeoisie with colonial officers. In this light, the tension between convergence and inequality appears to loosen. A bourgeoisie that understands itself to have converged with Europe, but has achieved that status less by emergence from the social base and more by fiat, and then understands itself to be responsible for the "tutelage" of "an unlettered citizenry," engages in a post-fiat project of developing the citizenry to eventually become convergent with itself. In this formulation, the elite are always mediators between modernity and the people. They are both specialists and agents of convergence simultaneously. And it is this conception of development that Awolowo and his party brought to bear on the institution of state television when it was formally launched in 1959.

Television as Nationalism and as Regionalism: 1960–Present

Before independence, the Western Region government of Nigeria had little access to administrative funds, and certainly not enough to operate a fully functional television network. WNTV was therefore launched as a public-private, local-foreign partnership with the London-based company Overseas Rediffusion Limited. As part of the partnership, the station was to be a commercial venture and, as such, it rebroadcast relatively cheap foreign programming and sold advertising time to raise revenue. Even in bare structural terms, then, the station was little more than a transmitter of metropolitan audiovisual capital. However, the relationship with Overseas Rediffusion disintegrated quickly and, by the end of 1961, the Western Region government bought up all the shares in the station, making it a fully state-owned institution. This was an important step in Nigerian nationalism, as it put the new government on a path to defy the predictions of observers like Fanon.

Unfortunately, despite the ousting of its foreign partner, nearly 80 percent of WNTV's programming in the early days remained foreign in origin. Of course, there simply was no other choice at the time, since very little television content had been developed in Nigeria. In the early 1960s, the station's locally produced content consisted of those films developed by Government Free Cinema, such as *Self-Government for Western Nigeria*, and daily or weekly broadcasts of news and information. Foreign content consisted of serials like *The Cisco Kid* and *Hopalong Cassidy*, two US programs about extra-judicial vigilantes in the American West, and *The Adventures of Robin Hood*, a British program about a very similar kind of national outlaw.[21] These foreign examples are particularly interesting because, in combination with the news programming, they offer an inroad to thinking about the ways that Nigeria's development-oriented elites conceived of their role on the national stage. These programs also reveal how astute an observer Fanon was.

The Cisco Kid, *Hopalong Cassidy*, and *The Adventures of Robin Hood* each feature a social antihero who represents the central myths of their respective nation-states' modernity—either by taming the American West or by undermining the English monarchy. In their local contexts, these programs would also serve conservative ideological agendas by perpetuating the notion that moral economies consist of rugged individuals struggling against an overbearing and/or inept state. In Nigeria, however, rather than undermine state interference in the economy, rebroadcasting these programs—and breaking them up with news about local dignitaries—established a conceptual link between rugged individuals and state officials. Through broadcast after broadcast of news that consisted of little more than the various inaugurations, installations, and celebrations of the elite, state officials used television to position themselves as the heroes of a national agenda in which, like the modern outlaws of Euro-America, they courageously supplanted traditional forms of authority. Moreover, Brian Larkin observes that capturing these events on camera was yet another practice adapted from colonial cinema:

> The installation of royal leaders, the appointment of colonial officials, the comings and goings of important personages, and the marching bands that saluted them, the charging of natives that hailed them. All of these visual elements were endlessly repeated early on. . . . Having one's installation filmed became part of the symbolic repertoire of royal authority. By 1960, to not have one's installation filmed was almost an insult.[22]

Larkin continues:

> This imperial spectacle, it must be remembered, has prominently continued in postcolonial television, where it has often exhausted its power to evoke any response beyond boredom.[23]

Breaking from foreign outlaw programs to run boring newsreels about the appointment of a new minister or the opening of a new government house linked local progress with international norms. But, whereas the heroes of American and British programs were common men, contravening the traditions of a domineering elite, Nigeria's nationalists ended up depicting themselves as heroes precisely because they were not common men, because they were, as Young implies, "lettered" elites who had mastered the ways of the domineering, foreign elite. In the early years, this boring and self-absorbed programming constituted the station's only truly internally generated content. So, in order to excite local audiences, the station set about putting local popular culture on screen, though with very little adaptation and very little thought about the relationship between popular culture and the national project in which the station was involved.

Some of WNTV's most beloved programs were teleplays created by the biggest names in the Yoruba traveling theater movement, including Moses Olaiya ("Baba Sala"), Hubert Ogunde, and Duro Ladipo. They inaugurated a tradition of Yoruba motion pictures that, though beyond the scope of this chapter, would have an important effect on commercial Nigerian cinema.[24] Nevertheless, WNTV's focus on Yoruba language and culture would also be a double-edged sword. On the one hand, such programs engaged audiences in ways that more boring motion pictures were incapable of, and they similarly engaged and encouraged local cultural industries—two key missions of the new Nigerian state. On the other hand, WNTV's focus on the Yoruba constituency in the Western Region would amplify ethno-regionalist politics.

Ethnic and regionalist politics were inherent even to the mechanical structure of WNTV. Mike Egbon reports that when creation of WNTV was being debated in the Western Region parliament, legislators from non-Yoruba parts of the region questioned the proposed location of the station's transmitters.[25] Positioned in Ibadan and Ikeja, the transmitters reached no further than the core Yoruba-speaking areas of the region. Moreover, many of the legislators who were opposed to the transmitters' locations formed the opposition to Awolowo's Action Group, belonging instead to the National Council of Nigeria and the Cameroons (NCNC), which was headquartered in the Eastern Region. It is not by coincidence, then, that the Eastern Region launched its own television station on Independence Day in 1960, not quite a year after the launch of WNTV. While the motto of WNTV was "First in Africa," the dialogic motto of the new Eastern Region Television (ENTV) was "Second to None." The Northern Region was not far behind, establishing Radio Kaduna Television (RKTV) in 1962. Charles C. Umeh frames the early proliferation of television this way:

> The [NCNC] government of the Eastern Region and the Northern People's Congress (NPC) government of the Northern Region had to prove to their respective peoples that whatever the Action Group government of the West could do, they too could do for the people of their regions.[26]

This regional one-upmanship could be said to have resulted from Awolowo's bold foray into television, but the phenomenon is not limited to broadcasting. The contrast between serving local constituents—in their language and through their institutions—but at the cost of intra-ethnic cooperation, is one of the defining paradoxes of Nigerian, indeed African, modernity.

The history of Nigerian television is thus more than a history of the elites at the helm of the state, it is also coeval with the history of regionalist pressures, activated under colonial rule, with which elites had to reckon. Awolowo was one of Nigeria's most vocal federalists and a self-proclaimed enemy of tribalism, but in his autobiography he wrote that "Nigeria should have had as many provinces, zones, regions or states as there were linguistic or ethnic groups in the country and that each region should have a legislature and a government of its own."[27] To be more exact, then, Awolowo was one the country's first consociationalists. Consociationalism is a form of federalism in which regionalism is robustly fostered, but also offset by a strong central government. In such an arrangement, some amount of autonomy may devolve to ethnic or religious blocs, but certain macroeconomic considerations fall under the increasingly tightfisted control of the federal bureaucracy. Awolowo's consociational position was not adopted in the run-up to independence, but it would prevail almost immediately in postcolonial politics.

When a military government seized power from the civilian government in 1966, it divided Nigeria's three regions into twelve subnational states, many of which would establish their own broadcasting facilities. Umeh writes:

> The creation of the new states caused a new wave of sectional consciousness, referred to as "statism." Every state wanted its own facilities, a university, a polytechnic, a college of education, a teaching hospital, its own radio and television stations, and so on.[28]

In various stages since then, the Nigerian state has become only more consociational, today with thirty-six subnational states and a Federal Capital Territory in Abuja, each with its own television station. As the nation has splintered, however, the federal government has inevitably strengthened its grasp on certain forms of power. The most prominent power has come in the form of control over oil extraction and marketing, but the federal government has also found ways to mirror, and use, this kind of control in the broadcasting sector.

In 1973, Nigeria hosted the All-Africa Games, and instead of allowing each of Nigeria's broadcasting institutions to overrun the arena, the state established the Broadcasting Organization of Nigeria in order to pool and coordinate media resources. The result was so orderly—and so enchanting to authoritarian-minded policy makers—that the military government decided, a few years later, to establish one network, called the Nigerian Television Authority (NTA), under which all stations would be gathered. The NTA remains a federal institution in control of thirty-seven state stations today. Nevertheless, in 1979, when Nigeria returned briefly to civilian rule, many states exploited a loophole in the constitution that allowed them to reestablish their own state-operated television stations. The tension between the two is ongoing.

Despite the near monopoly that the state has on broadcasting, I should note that later developments also introduced some amount of private broadcasting into the Nigerian television landscape. In 1992, during the period of structural adjustment, Nigeria opened the door to broadcasting applications and, since then, fourteen nongovernmental television stations have sprung up, a few of which have thrived. Some private stations, such as Channels Television, focus on news reporting, and have been able to offer an alternative voice in Nigeria's news discourse (even though the network's chief executive, John Momoh, came out of the NTA). Others, such as African Independent Television (AIT) and Silverbird, focus on entertainment, although AIT's stated goal is to "project Africa from an African perspective."[29] Indeed, none of these stations can reach all corners of Nigeria, let alone the world, without satellite distribution. And though it is expanding, satellite television is primarily available to the middle and upper classes, as well as those living abroad. Thus, networks like AIT and Silverbird may be better positioned to "project Africa" to Nigerians who live in, or travel to Europe and America, than to those at home.

As a recent report on Nigerian broadcasting by the Open Society Initiative states, "Nigeria's liberalisation journey in the broadcasting sector has gone only half-way."[30] With so little coverage by private stations, it remains the prerogative of the NTA and the subnational state television networks to broadcast moving images to the vast population of the country. The report argues that this prerogative is not merely economic—in the sense that minimal media capital is available in Nigeria apart from the state—it is political:

> About 50 years after political independence, legislation constricting media freedom and freedom of expression which dates from colonial times remains on the statute books and new laws are being enacted which retain the culture of harshness. These legal instruments have been used extensively by government authorities throughout the period of post-independence governance under military and civilian rulers.[31]

This legal framework not only perpetuates colonial-style centralized control of motion picture production and distribution, it ensures that—as the next section illustrates—even in the realm of messages and aesthetics, the NTA has continued to operate as a transmission belt for the power of global capital.

National Network, International Agenda: The 1980s and *Cock Crow at Dawn*

While the consociational nature of Nigerian television may have further regionalized national politics, greater federal control has also translated into greater nationalization of the medium. For example, if WNTV sourced 80 percent of its programming from abroad, today only 10 percent of the NTA's programming is foreign in origin.[32] This is noteworthy because, by the mid-1980s, the NTA estimated that importing a foreign program would cost the equivalent of two thousand dollars, while producing a program locally would cost more than three times as much.[33] In other words, though more expensive, the NTA has dedicated itself to producing or acquiring local programming and therefore nationalizing its message. This is crucial work.

One of the most successful programs that the NTV produced in the 1980s was *Cock Crow at Dawn*. It first aired in April 1980 and lasted for 104 episodes, making it one the network's all-time longest running serials. It was written by Peter Igho, an NTA employee who eventually moved on to a string of high-level bureaucratic posts. It was underwritten by the United Bank for Africa, which is derived from the British and French Bank Limited, a colonial institution dating back to 1949. This coordination of the federal bureaucracy and global capital is precisely what Fanon had in mind, but the plot is even thicker.

Cock Crow at Dawn dramatizes the lives of farmers in northern Nigeria and their interaction with various agricultural technologies—some indigenous and some developed abroad. This concept was carefully crafted within the state bureaucracy to foster local support for what politicians and the international economic, political, and scientific community called the Green Revolution. Defined simply, the Green Revolution consisted of transferring agricultural technologies, developed in Europe and North America, to countries in Africa, Asia, and Latin America. The ostensible goal of the program was to dramatically increase grain outputs so that third-world countries could feed their exponentially growing populations. In its realization, however, the program paved the way for industrializing and converting the agricultural sectors of poor countries into nodes of the neoliberal economy. As Ebele N. E. Ume-Nwagbo writes, "The primary goal of [*Cock Crow at Dawn*] was to 'sell' through entertainment large-scale, mechanized farming, largely to the upper and higher classes of the working population and the business economy."[34] Significant here is the fact that the message, though seen by all, was directed less at rural audiences, who constituted the agricultural sector, than at other members of the urban bourgeoisie.[35]

The plot of the program pitted two men against each other—Uncle Gaga, who defended traditional farming practices, and Bello, who signified all that is modern and progressive. While Uncle Gaga spoke in a mixture of English and Nigerian Pidgin, Bello expertly deployed the kind of standard English that colonizers once promoted. Bello and what he stood for usually prevailed within the world of the program, but, in a genuine exercise in verisimilitude, Uncle Gaga frequently won arguments and the sympathy of the audience—though often to comic degree. As Ume-Nwagbo describes it:

> *Cock Crow at Dawn* graphically represents the daily life of a nation in search of a solution to nagging food problems. While only a few villagers regard Bello as insightful or progressive, to the majority of them he is an embodiment of antisocial forces, an upstart of the worst kind. Thus, his progressive and seemingly revolutionary ideas about farming are pitched against the arch conservatism and monolithic skepticism manifest in Uncle Gaga. To most villagers Uncle Gaga's opposition to Bello's apparent unpatriotic actions is justifiable. Uncle Gaga is the vivacious protector of the traditional, a microcosmic depiction of the anger, frustration, and helplessness of many Nigerians over the nation's perennial inability to deal effectively with the problem of self-insufficiency in food production.[36]

Despite Uncle Gaga's firm grounding in the social base, however, Bello was the better farmer. His successes were depicted as the triumph of optimism and persistence in the face of endemic traditionalism and retrogression. Beyond his personal accomplishments, Bello's village also became more dynamic and sophisticated because of his visionary resolve to bring large-scale farming to the area. Ume-Nwagbo's audience reception research suggests that Nigerians, across socioeconomic groups and regions, preferred Bello to Uncle Gaga—more than two to one—indicating that they were largely supportive of the Green Revolution message.[37]

More than selling capitalist farming to Nigerians, however, the most palpable and long-lasting local effect of the program may have been the way that it normalized the process of urbanization. This is despite the fact that both colonial and postcolonial governments fed rural populations messages about the value and dignity of agriculture. Modern agricultural practices, both in cultivation and in marketing, have instead decreased the value of rural labor while simultaneously serving urban expansion. Thus, people continually flood into cities like Lagos and Abuja in the hopes of accessing some of the wealth that has been siphoned from rural populations.

To illustrate this process, we can actually learn a great deal from colonial cinema, which was invested in modernizing agriculture long before *Cock Crow at Dawn*. The CFU production *Good Business* (1947), for example, was one of the first films made and distributed in Nigeria to promote farming practices that benefited urban centers more than rural target audiences. *Good Business* details the interactions that a Yoruba cocoa farmer, Lawani, has with institutions like marketing boards, cooperative societies, and trade unions. Lawani runs a large farm, but he can neither read nor write, so he must depend on his Western-educated son, Belo, for assistance with new institutions.[38] While the film depicts cooperative societies as safe, lucrative, globally oriented, and even socially relevant, the fact is that, through marketing boards, cooperative societies regularly exploited farmers. According to Basil Davidson, in Ghana (a comparable nearby cocoa-producing British colony) the process worked like this:

> [The British] paid cocoa farmers notably less than the value of cocoa when exported to the world market. This had been justified on the grounds that the difference between the price paid by the state marketing board to the farmer and the price received by the board from foreign buyers would be held in a "reserve" which could be drawn upon by the farmer whenever the world price fell in value. In practice, the "reserve" was simply added to Britain's sterling assets in London.[39]

What is worse, Davidson notes, is that Ghana's postcolonial government inherited this tradition, maintaining the "reserve" for so-called modernization and national development schemes that almost solely benefited urban centers, "continuing," he writes, "the costly triumph of the 'city' over the 'village.'"[40]

Part of the reason urbanization has been "costly" in Africa, according to Davidson, is that rural populations have turned their backs on the state. "They have contented themselves with growing food for purely local consumption," he writes, meaning that many nation-states have been forced to import food.[41] While importing food to a continent that had never before relied on that kind of assistance showed the breakdown of the bourgeoisie's transmission belt, *Cock Crow at Dawn* and the Green Revolution were meant to get the gears of the local economy spinning once again. But, more than that, argues Harry M. Cleaver, Jr., "The international team" responsible for promoting the Green Revolution

> has also been making an effort to teach personal gain and consumerism where it feels peasants lack sufficient motivation. In his handbook, ADC [Agricultural Development Council] president Arthur T. Mosher harps repeatedly on the theme of teaching peasants to want more for themselves, to abandon collective habits, and to get on with the "business" of farming. Mosher goes so far as to advocate extension educational programs for women and youth clubs to create more demand for store-bought goods. The "affection of husbands and fathers for their families" will make them responsive to these desires and drive them to work harder. These tactics of the ADC are more than efforts to bring development to rural areas. They are attempts to spread capitalism with all its business-based social relations and the markets such relations support.[42]

Here, turning the gears of local agriculture becomes but a pretext to cultivating consumer markets, so that *Cock Crow at Dawn* serves primarily to tap the local economy in order to keep the global machine running smoothly. The correlation between this postcolonial motion picture project and the CFU's *Good Business* exposes how little has changed since political independence.

Conclusion: The Recipients of Modernity

The concept of development, the way colonial and postcolonial elites have employed it, and their use of state institutions and television technology to do so, have all contributed to the strange and enchanted character of the Nigerian state. At the end of the colonial era, a well-educated and affluent class of Nigerians stepped in and took over the roles of departing colonists. And like colonists, they understood their position, relative to their populace, as primarily pedagogical. They also believed that the motion picture was indispensable for transmitting a particular form of modernity to the nation. The new nation, however, was of course fully implicated and entrenched in a more expansive conception of modernity. Indeed, contributions from Africa had made possible the very features of the modern world that colonists and their inheritors so enjoyed and extolled. To the contrary, then, what colonial Nigerian elites and the postcolonial Nigerian state have offered the nation, therefore, is not modernity as such, but a particular role to play in relation to modernity: the recipient. Nigerian state television has not simply constructed its audience as underdeveloped, but it has consistently addressed that audience as a contrivance indebted to developmental power transmitted from abroad. Whether in the form of praising the princess royal as she arrived to bestow political development, whether equating themselves with Euro-American outlaw heroes who steal from the rich to feed the poor, or whether extolling the virtues of neoliberal farming technologies invented, packaged, and delivered from abroad, Nigerian elites have used state television to position spectators as the beneficiaries of a modernity they had no hand in creating. To accept modernity in such a form, however, the nation is forced to reproduce its distance from the engines of the modern world, even while ensuring that those engines keep running.

The final deduction to be made from Fanon's transmission belt metaphor might be that, if the postcolonial bourgeoisie quit working, if they boarded up their institutions, if state television suddenly went off the air in Nigeria, the global economic system would grind to a halt. That hardly seems to be the case. But as many scholars, from radical historians like Rodney to contemporary anthropologists like James Ferguson, and even literary critics like Timothy Brennan have argued, there is a real economic benefit to be gleaned, on the part of the global machine, from the maintenance of large pockets of woefully underdeveloped productivity. These are the spaces, as Brennan puts it, of potential primitive accumulation.[43] It is precisely in this kind of space that something like a Green Revolution could be waged. And it is, therefore, not simply the case that Nigerian state television positions Nigerian citizens as capable only of receiving modernity—rather than making it—but it has evolved and thrived in an environment where such a discursive formulation is profitable. The contradictory set of notions whereby the nation is integral to modernity, but separate from the origins of modern power, all the while contributing to a power that then makes the nation move, can only hold together through the essential, almost magical role played by a transmission belt.

MATTHEW H. BROWN is Assistant Professor of African Cultural Studies at the University of Wisconsin, Madison.

Notes

1. Constance Farrington translates the metaphor as "transmission line," while Richard Philcox translates it as "conveyor belt." A transmission line is a specialized cable that carries high-frequency electromagnetic signals from a power source to a receiver, while a conveyor belt is a device consisting of a wide, flat belt that rotates around two pulleys and conveys material from one place to another. Both metaphors imply that the national bourgeoisie assists in transporting certain capitalist processes from the metropole to the postcolony, but both also fail to convey the sense that metropolitan capitalism has power unique to it, while postcolonial capitalism only runs on the power distributed by the national bourgeoisie, and all the while postcolonial capitalism makes metropolitan capitalism possible. See Frantz Fanon, *The Wretched of the Earth*, trans. Constance Farrington (New York: Grove, 1963), 152; and Frantz Fanon, *The Wretched of the Earth*, trans. Richard Philcox (New York: Grove, 2004), 100–101.

2. For a discussion of the concept of the "chronotope," see M. M. Bakhtin, *The Dialogic Imagination*, ed. Michael Holquist, trans. Caryl Emerson and Michael Holquist (Austin: University of Texas Press, 1981).

3. "Convergence" is a widely used term in the scholarship on economic development. For a critique, see James Ferguson, *Global Shadows: Africa in the Neoliberal World Order* (Durham, NC: Duke University Press, 2006), 182–185.

4. Quoted in Rosaleen Smyth, "The Post-War Career of the Colonial Film Unit in Africa: 1946–1955," *Historical Journal of Film, Radio, and Television* 12, no. 2 (1992): 166.

5. William Sellers, "The Production of Films for Primitive Peoples," *Oversea Education: A Journal of Education Experiment and Research in Tropical and Subtropical Areas* 13 (1941): 226.

6. Versions of the story appear in Mike Egbon, "Western Nigeria Television Service: Oldest in Tropical Africa," *Journalism Quarterly* 60, no. 2 (1983): 329–334; Luke Uka Uche, *Mass Media, Peoples and Politics in Nigeria* (New Delhi: Concept Publishing, 1989); and Charles C. Umeh, "The Advent and Growth of Television Broadcasting in Nigeria: Its Political and Educational Overtones," *African Media Review* 3, no. 2 (1989): 54–66.

7. Yemi Farounbi, "Preface," in *Fotorama*, ed. Gbenga Awe (Ibadan, Nigeria: NTV Ibadan, 1979), ii.

8. Umeh, "Advent and Growth of Television Broadcasting in Nigeria," 57.

9. "The Colonial Film Unit," *Colonial Cinema* 5, no. 2 (1947): 31.

10. Obafemi Awolowo, *Awo: The Autobiography of Chief Obafemi Awolowo* (Cambridge: Cambridge University Press, 1960), 289.

11. Frank Aig-Imoukhuede, "The Film and Television in Nigeria," *Présence Africaine: Cultural Review of the Negro World*, English Edition 30, no. 2 (1966): 90.

12. *Self-Government for Western Nigeria*, dir. Cedric Williams (Western Nigeria Film Unit, 1958).

13. Awolowo, *Awo*, 289.

14. See George Z. F. Bereday, "Student Unrest on Four Continents: Montreal, Ibadan, Warsaw and Rangoon," *Comparative Education Review* 10, no. 2 (1966): 193.

15. Ibid., 193–194.

16. Tom Rice, "*Self Government for Western Nigeria*: Analysis," *Colonial Film: Moving Images of the British Empire*, April 2009, http://www.colonialfilm.org.uk/node/1819.

17. Ibid.
18. *Xala*, dir. Ousmane Sembene (New Yorker Films, 1975).
19. Walter Rodney, *How Europe Underdeveloped Africa* (1972; repr., Abuja, Nigeria: Panaf, 2009).
20. Crawford Young, "The End of the Post-Colonial State in Africa? Reflections on Changing African Political Dynamics," *African Affairs* 103 (2004): 29.
21. Some programming information is taken from Obaro Ikime, ed., *Twentieth Anniversary History of WNTV* (Ibadan, Nigeria: Heinemann, 1979), 7.
22. Brian Larkin, *Signal and Noise: Media, Infrastructure, and Urban Culture in Nigeria* (Durham, NC: Duke University Press, 2008), 104–105.
23. Ibid., 105.
24. Karin Barber, *The Generation of Plays: Yoruba Popular Life in Theater* (Bloomington: Indiana University Press, 2000).
25. Egbon, "Western Nigeria Television Service," 334.
26. Umeh, "Advent and Growth of Television Broadcasting in Nigeria," 57.
27. Awolowo, *Awo*, 153, 163.
28. Umeh, "Advent and Growth of Television Broadcasting in Nigeria," 58.
29. "About AIT," *Africa Independent Television*, http://www.aitonline.tv/page-about_ait (accessed March 13, 2017).
30. Akin Akingbulu, *Public Broadcasting in Africa: Nigeria* (Johannesburg: Open Society Initiative for West Africa, 2010), 111.
31. Ibid., 111.
32. Koblowe Obono and Oluchi Madu, "Programming Content of Nigerian Broadcast Media: Towards an Indigenizing Paradigm," *Estudos em Comunicação* 8 (2010): 82.
33. Obafemi Lasode, *Television Broadcasting: The Nigerian Experience (1959–1992)* (Ibadan, Nigeria: Caltop, 1993), 184.
34. Ebele N. E. Ume-Nwagbo, "'Cock Crow at Dawn': A Nigerian Experiment with Television Drama in Development-Communication," *Gazette* 37 (1986): 156.
35. This argument is also made by Joe De-Goshie using content analysis, which reveals that the program privileged urban content over rural. See Joe De-Goshie, "Mass Media and National Development: A Content Analysis of a Nigerian Developmental Television Drama Series: 'Cock Crow at Dawn'" (PhD diss., Ohio University, 1985), 177–178.
36. Ume-Nwagbo, "'Cock Crow at Dawn,'" 165.
37. Ibid., 158.
38. *Good Business* (London: Colonial Film Unit, 1947). While the progressive character in *Good Business* is named Belo, the progressive farmer in *Cock Crow at Dawn* is named Bello. The coincidence is all the more striking because the former is set in Yorubaland, while the latter is set in Hausa-speaking northern Nigeria. Of course, the name Belo/Bello is indigenous to neither area, but imported to West Africa through Islam.
39. Basil Davidson, *The Black Man's Burden: Africa and the Curse of the Nation-State* (New York: Random House, 1992), 210.
40. Ibid., 211.
41. Ibid.
42. Harry M. Cleaver, Jr., "The Contradictions of the Green Revolution," *American Economic Review* 62, no. 1–2 (1972): 179.
43. Timothy Brennan, "The Economic Image-Function of the Periphery," in *Postcolonial Studies and Beyond*," ed. Suvir Kaul, Ania Loomba, Matti Bunzl, Antoinette Burton, and Jed Esty (Durham, NC: Duke University Press, 2005).

PART II

Creative Adversities and the Truly Productive State

6 "Performing Like There's No Tomorrow"

Theater, War, and Social Vulnerability in Mozambique

Luís Madureira

On the first two days of September 2010, after circulating intractably for days, rumor—"the poor person's bomb," as Achille Mbembe calls it—suddenly detonated in the sprawling, ramshackle periphery of Mozambique's capital.[1] During the preceding two weeks, anonymous text messages had insistently called for widespread demonstrations against the steep and abrupt rise in the cost of living, inciting people to oppose government-sanctioned increases in water and electricity rates, in the price of fuel, bread, and other basic food items.[2] In the early morning of September 1, shantytowns erupted as announced. Thousands of people, for the most part youths, whom President Armando Guebuza's spokespeople would later brand "vandals and thugs,"[3] seized burning tires, boulders, pipes, variously sized tree trunks, and even torn-up bus stop equipment, to block the main roadways into the cities of Maputo and Matola.

The few cars and buses that ventured into the eerily empty streets were pelted with rocks. Some were set on fire. The demonstrators looted shops, vandalized fuel stations, and, most distressingly for the ruling party, after having unsuccessfully attempted to wreck a school carrying the president's name, they trampled on posters bearing his triumphantly beaming likeness: the ubiquitous and politically strategic remnants of the 2008 electoral campaign.[4] For two seemingly interminable days, the inhabitants of Maputo's periphery kept the capital's privileged inner core in a veritable state of siege. By the time these civil disturbances had been ruthlessly quelled, thirteen people reportedly lay dead and at least three hundred wounded, mostly from the live ammunition fired indiscriminately by police, despite public assurances by the interior minister that the police force would use only rubber bullets. In all, about two dozen shops had been ransacked, a handful of fuel stations and banking institutions vandalized, and several buses as well as other vehicles destroyed or set ablaze.

These events transpired around eight months into my eleven-month stay in Maputo, where I had been conducting research on theater. Since early February, I had pored through unpublished original and adapted play scripts; I had interviewed numerous theater practitioners (actors, current and former directors and set designers, playwrights, as well as drama students and teachers from the recently founded drama school at the national university); I had attended seminars, rehearsals, and workshops as well as multiple professional and amateur theater productions, including two theater festivals, and had seen several community and forum theater performances, a number of which had taken place precisely in the neighborhoods where the disturbances of early September occurred.[5] I was trying to understand how the sustained and diverse performance culture that has thrived in Mozambique since the early 1980s entails a novel and effective mode of exercising citizenship. I wanted to gauge the extent to which, for both spectators and theater workers, drama constituted a powerful form of political participation. Ultimately, I wished to propose that Mozambican theater opened up spaces for the negotiation and rearticulation of ethnic, class, and gender identifications both against and alongside dominant nationalist discourses. Nevertheless, what happened on those two fateful days of September compelled me fundamentally to rethink my hypotheses.

The events of September made it imperative that I reconsider the theater-citizenship connection in the context of a widening social divide. I had glimpsed its early signs on the night I arrived in Maputo, as I drowsily watched an amalgam of tumbledown shanties unfurling like some peri-urban equivalent of Georg Wilhelm Friedrich Hegel's bad infinity from behind the window of the late-model, air-conditioned US Embassy van that drove me from the airport. By early September, I had become better acquainted with the meanders of those suburban precincts. Yet they remained, not just for me but probably for most of those who dwell in the urban zone of economic privilege, citizenship, and sociability, largely a foreign country. To cite Mia Couto, Mozambique's best-known writer, "the inhabitants of the concrete nation woke up to the existence of another, greater nation" on the morning of September 1.[6] On that day, Couto continues,

> the poor ceased to be the topics of workshops. The poor leaped from seminars held in luxurious hotels into day-to-day reality. The poor can bring the country of the others to a halt. Even if in the process they become poorer. For those who have little or no "tomorrow," this waste of the future is worth it. . . . The perception that a certain Mozambique has of itself was turned upside down. The periphery became the center. Poverty found its own voice, with its poor resources, its impoverished hope.[7]

As Mozambican sociologist Carlos Serra queries in a recent interview:

> What do we know of our compatriots' lives in the suburbs? What do we know of their dreams, their sorrows, their ambitions? We talk about them and make projects that involve them without ever contacting or listening to them. . . . Some, at the height of their arrogance, say that the young people from the [urban] peripheries are irrational for protesting. Irrational? There aren't people who are more rational than others, there are only people with different rationalities.[8]

As Cristiana Pereira asserts in her investigative report on the riots originally published in the magazine *Africa 21*: "The revolt laid open the asymmetries of a country where over 90% of the population live on less than two dollars a day."[9] "People [feel as though they belong to] a cardboard landscape, while big business deals go on" at the center of the national stage, comments Mozambican writer and historian João Paulo Borges Coelho.[10] The inhabitants of this uncharted, peripheral world, as Serra notes in a study on social vulnerability, are in the main excluded from the benefits and privileges of Mozambique's dominant social order. They constitute a hybrid "counter-society" that produces new rules, new values, new identities, and new forms of social representation. While those who live inside the city's confines enjoy full citizenship rights, shantytown dwellers engage in a grueling and unremitting struggle for daily survival, forever poised "on a knife's edge," immured in a kind of "infra-citizenship."[11] In the despondent words of an old Maputo beggar, the periphery's residents have been dumped "in the trash can" of national history.[12] They flit "like ghosts" before the unseeing eyes of the privileged few, while barely subsisting in the social dead zones where "God is like a longing [*Deus é como uma saudade*]," to quote the hauntingly poetic phrase of a mental institution inmate.[13]

The riots were "the way in which the populace sought to be heard," Mozambican sculptor Pekywa summed up succinctly, while Borges Coelho likewise identifies in the text messages that sparked the protests something beyond "a tactical question," indeed "a form of [spontaneous] expression."[14] Nevertheless, Pereira, the author of the *Africa 21* report on the riots, pointedly underscores the muted reaction to the revolt by organized civil society, a silence that an unnamed "diplomatic source" qualifies as "frightening."[15] For rapper and political activist Azagaia (Edson da Luz), this lack of a formal response exemplifies a fundamental crisis of political representation: "There is no dialogue between those who govern and the governed. We have a Government that insulates itself in times of crisis, but shows up to address the populace when it needs their vote."[16]

The insurrection laid bare the grievously deficient forms of political participation as well as the flagrantly unequal access to public services afforded to shantytown inhabitants. Thus, if my aim was to develop a keener appreciation of contemporary Mozambican politics and culture as well as the intricate ways in which citizenship practices could evolve in relation to drama and performance, then the September riots surely demanded that I grasp the conditions of possibility of this putative link between theater and citizenship within the problematic social terrain unfolding just beyond the urban core where much of the theater in Maputo takes place. I therefore began seriously to question whether theater could ever compensate for or supplement the quotidian denial of full citizenship rights. For it remains to be ascertained whether among the privileges denied to the "infra-citizens" of what Couto calls Mozambique's "other, greater nation" are precisely performance and active and informed spectatorship.

In a narrow sense, the incidents of September 2010 only reaffirmed what many economists and social scientists had been asserting for some time. Despite the high-flying rhetoric issuing from the president's office about the battle against poverty, for the past five years or so, both poverty and social inequality have been steadily rising in Mozambique. Thirty-five years after the country gained independence, and notwithstanding the record economic growth it has been posting since the end of the civil war in 1993, the overwhelming majority of Mozambicans continue to live in abject poverty. In the end, whether or not citizenship can ever emerge through performance and spectatorship in the badlands sprawling beyond the edges of the "concrete city," the fact remains that during those first two days of September, the social actors from Maputo's periphery effectively reappropriated and resignified social space. As Couto suggests, and to paraphrase Georges Balandier slightly out of context, the September civil disturbances downgraded political power and its hierarchies. By disrupting, or upending, the social order, they ultimately lay bare the ruling class's vulnerability. They showed that power was not untouchable.[17] Ironically, the social drama the shantytown dwellers enacted thoroughly fulfills the role that Pius Ngandu Nkashama ascribes to theater (in Africa): "through the power of its own law, theater confers upon itself the authority to attack hierarchies, challenge established rules, and contest political power."[18] Yet, precisely by dramatizing an extreme negation of a power and privilege that appear to have endured since the times when Maputo was still known as Xilinguine ("white people's city"), they also pointed to a troubling continuity between colony and nation.

In the face of this recognizably postcolonial persistence of colonial relations and conditions well into the national phase (a continuity that is all the more vexing in a country like Mozambique, which declared itself a "people's republic" during the first decade of independence), two crucial and related questions emerge.[19] First, and perhaps most evident, is the question concerning the place and role theater and theatricality have historically played beyond the urban centers, not just in the outlying boroughs I have been discussing, but in the villages and countryside. A comprehensive treatment of this question certainly exceeds the scope of the present study. However, its significance requires that I advance at minimum some preliminary and necessarily provisional arguments. This is, in fact, one of the tasks of the present chapter. Second, if "theatricality has been a major dimension for upholding and contesting power structures and social (generic) differences," and if theater remains, throughout Africa, "the most important expression of conflicts, contradictions, as well as fundamental social complexities," then it is essential to interrogate how (and indeed whether), in the course of Mozambique's tumultuous recent history, theater has ever succeeded in catalyzing, or at least symbolizing, social change and political participation in rural and peri-urban zones.[20] In the following overview of theatrical activity in Mozambique, I attempt to broach these crucial issues, without as yet reaching any definitive conclusions. In the main, I concentrate on the last two of what Serra designates the "three phases in the genealogy of Mozambican cities"—the revolutionary (1975–1986) and neoliberal periods (1986–present).[21]

Rehearsing the Revolution

During the first part of Mozambique's Afro-Marxist republic (1975–1986), several neighborhood amateur troupes, ardently committed to the principles of the revolution, cropped up in major cities and townships. The most prolific and influential of these groups by far was Grupo Cénico das Forças Populares de Libertação Nacional (Theater Troupe of the People's Army of National Liberation). Founded in 1973, in Nachingweya, FRELIMO's military training camp, by Liberation Front combatants who are now prominent members of the country's political and financial elite, the group put on various plays criticizing both the colonial order and, in more rare instances, the abuses and excesses of postindependence society. Some of their most famous productions in the 1970s include *Monomopata*, *Resistência e Vitória Popular* (*Popular Resistance and Victory*), *A Sagrada Família* (*The Holy Family*), and *Javali-Javalismo* (*Wild Boar-Wild Boarism*), reportedly the first play to have been banned by the FRELIMO regime for presenting too frank a critique of the new society.

Grupo Cénico dissolved as many of its members left the armed forces and assumed a variety of prominent posts in government and later in the private sector. Most of their plays, only a few of which survive, fell into the category of agitprop style of drama and served to propagate the same nationalist and socialist messages that the state vigorously promoted.[22] Today, when the Mozambican state has come to share with the majority of African states in the subcontinent many of the starkly coercive and unproductive features that Tejumola Olaniyan outlines in the Introduction, these texts seem dolefully out of place. According to one of Mozambique's chief economists, Mozambique's emerging capitalist class utilizes its control over natural resources (obtained through its stranglehold on the state apparatus) in order to facilitate the largely unregulated penetration of foreign capital and thereby ensure its own unrestrained "primitive accumulation."[23] Indeed, most of the country's professed "liberators" have aggressively embraced neoliberalism and "the line separating luxury and whim . . . within the ruling classes" seems to have vanished.[24] Meanwhile, the overwhelming majority of the citizenry can hardly eke out a living, in these returning "strange times [that are] / Killing hope / Sowing Despair," as Guebuza once described the colonial era.[25]

Sagrada Família, for example, a play staged by Grupo Cénico in the late 1970s, denounces the efforts by the colonial bourgeoisie and its local "lackeys" to reverse "the achievements of the revolution" in the wake of the nationalization of private housing, schools, hospitals, and farmland.[26] As the following "stage directions" illustrate, the play is especially ruthless with the "puppet managers," whom it portrays as outworn, "black-skinned" replicas of colonial bosses: "Ambrósio has no managing experience and the attitude he assumes had been surpassed long ago by his [white] predecessor. In reality, [he] is no more than a puppet manager. And, as with all puppets, his ambition is boundless."[27] The "simple life in which . . . everyone works to support himself and on behalf of the People . . . in which nobody exploits our sweat," upheld as the main aspiration of the political leadership by one of the play's young cadres, contrasts starkly with the unproductive capitalism, brazen corruption, and conspicuous consumerism that characterize the "lifestyle" of much of the current elite.[28] The latter appear, in effect, to epitomize the "black capitalists—the so-called national bourgeoisie" intent on "exploiting other blacks" with impunity precisely because it is also black—a class that "produces nothing more than a repetition of what capitalism instilled [which] creates absolutely nothing, because [it] is isolated from the people . . . from praxis," that Samora Machel, Mozambique's first president, was warning Mozambicans against on the eve of independence.[29] The "new era," whose dawn prompts the collapse of "the old Society" and the end of "the bosses' reign," forecast in the epilogue, would ring particularly hollow to a contemporary audience from Mozambique's urban peripheries.[30] It is enough to wonder, in fact, how many of Grupo Cénico's members now belong to the ranks of the "predatory" elite.[31] To cite a Mozambican political commentator's acerbic allusion to the portentous refrain of FRELIMO's anthem (see note 19), "not only has socialism not triumphed but it lies in the graveyard once reserved for capitalism. Today, the exploiters that [FRELIMO cadres] once vowed to struggle against are the [party leaders] themselves."[32]

A similar incongruity underpins a play about the Paris Commune (*A Comuna*) that dates from the same period. Purportedly the result of a collective effort, the script evolved out of a series of workshops that joined together national university students and railroad workers. Their principal objective was "to reaffirm proletarian internationalism," and guide the "people" toward the recognition that their own struggle was structurally linked to revolutionary processes occurring in other countries.[33] The play blends scenes from France's insurrectionary past and Mozambique's revolutionary "present." The Narrator intervenes frequently to establish relevant parallels between the two historical trajectories. At pivotal moments, and in a manner that vaguely recalls Bertolt Brecht's technique in his own adaptation of the Commune episode, the Narrator draws the audience's attention to the fatal strategic errors committed by the Communards (and, relatedly, to the fact that Mozambique's liberation fighters shrewdly averted similar mistakes).[34] At the end of the play, following the brutal suppression of the Commune ("In Paris, everything went back to the way it was!"), the Narrator turns to the Audience and asks: "Comrades, will we allow the bourgeoisie and imperialism to do the same with our Revolution?" To the rousing strains of the *Internationale*, originally the anthem of the Commune, the Audience roars: "No, never again!"[35]

Needless to say, not only has the bourgeoisie returned in full force, but so also has a particularly overreaching form of financial imperialism. As Castel-Branco avers, in a critique of the state that one might call foundationalist, one of the two main readings of the African state Olaniyan identifies across the social sciences and the humanities, dependency on foreign aid and investment constitutes a "fundamental characteristic" of Mozambique's economy at the turn of the millennium.[36] In 2007, for instance, 22 percent of the country's gross national product stemmed directly from development aid, a figure that is five times greater than the average for sub-Saharan nation-states, making Mozambique the eleventh most foreign-aid dependent country in the world.[37] In effect, more than a decade ago, Mbembe was underscoring what he designated the as-yet underexamined dynamics of conditionality defining the loans granted to African countries by international financial institutions, and the consequent "crumbling of African states' independence and sovereignty and the (surreptitious) placing of these states under the tutelage of international creditors," a patronage manifested in "a range of direct interventions in domestic economic management, credit control [and] even direct control of the treasury."[38] As it happens, foreign "donors wield immense and detailed power [in Mozambique], and are at the very heart of decision-making and policy formulation, from the conception of issues and options through to writing the final policy. There is a real sovereignty question here: 'to what extent should non-Mozambicans be playing such a central role?'"[39]

Castel-Branco argues concurrently that Mozambique's political elites rule almost exclusively in accordance to the donors' prerogatives and demands, rather than those of the people. As a consequence, the selection of political options and public policy involves only these two actors (the dependent state and the donors). "There is no space to develop citizenship practices in Mozambique," the economist concludes.[40] As Mbembe indicates, this particular mode of "tutelary government" by international creditors and donors imposes "new forms of subjection . . . on the most deprived and vulnerable segments of the population."[41] In this sense, the Commune's tragic flaws turn out to have been peculiarly prophetic. Like Aristotle's hamartia, the fatal error appears to have been already inscribed in the text itself. For, as the introduction elucidates, *A Comuna* was as much the successful culmination of a collective project exemplarily joining proletarians and students as the chronicle of a failure.[42]

Due to a series of disagreements among the workers and student members of the collective concerning the supposed need to research in depth not only the historical figure of Napoleon III but concepts such as bureaucracy and dictatorship of the proletariat before the play could be produced, *A Comuna* was never staged. Although the introduction does not specify it, in the main, it appears that the students advocated a stricter adherence to historical accuracy and ideological exactitude, while the workers, if one is to go by one of their testimonials quoted in the text, believed their life experiences provided them with sufficient knowledge to put on the play: "I also had never heard of Napoleon III before I came in here, just today. But that doesn't matter. I got to know very well what oppression was, and that experience will be of help."[43] Yet, the students' "error," which the introduction's authors acknowledge in hindsight, may have in fact already resided in the very conception of the project.[44]

What precluded the representation of the Mozambican Commune was, in essence, a consequence of the "the paradox of the spectator," as Jacques Rancière defines it, the notion that viewing is the opposite of knowing. From this perspective, the spectator is thought to remain in "a state of ignorance" both about the process of production of the performance or spectacle she or he views and about the reality the latter arguably masks.[45] The students' task, then, was to transform the railroad workers from passive spectators into active participants: "Our first attitude, as [railroad workers], was to present ourselves as being completely ignorant about the Commune and, for that reason, wish to be suitably enlightened in order to begin working. Our first attitude as [university students] was to assume the role of History teachers, explaining and providing texts about the Commune."[46] In keeping with the Brechtian paradigm that appears to have informed their endeavor, the students sought to compel the railroad workers "to exchange the position of passive spectators for that of scientific investigator or experimenter."[47] Nevertheless, as the dilemma that finally thwarted the staging of the play demonstrates, the logic underpinning their pedagogics essentially remained that of "straight uniform transmission: there is something—a form of knowledge . . . on one side, and it must pass to the other side. What the pupil must learn is what the schoolmaster must teach her."[48] As with most varieties of so-called critical art, this entire schema is anchored on the presupposition that the stage, the audience, and the world exist in a more or less seamless "continuum," that the autonomy and cohesion of the play, both as text and as performance, are capable not only of eliciting "ethical effects," or a particular understanding of society in the minds of the spectators, but of inducing them to undertake concrete political action "outside the theater."[49] The experience of watching a play that imputes the state of the world must, in the last instance, lead to the decision to change it. Ultimately, however, there is no reason to assume a direct link between a stage performance and the results it produces either on the minds of the spectators inside the theater or on their actions outside it. As Rancière concludes, "There is no straight path from the viewing of a spectacle to the understanding of the state of the world, and none from intellectual awareness to political action."[50]

In *A Comuna*, the plot of the drama of emancipation that the student-worker collective set out to produce had already been etched in graven letters before the first lines of the text were even committed to paper. The emancipatory promise of the revolution that the group wished to perform had therefore already been foreclosed, subsumed in advance into a preexisting international story of liberation. By subscribing to the view that the path to social transformation was reducible to an enforceable program or line, the students ended up reproducing the logic of radical state power. They thus became, paradoxically and much like the nation-state itself, "the true inheritors of the colonial tradition of rule by decree and rule by proclamation, of subordinating the rule of law to administrative justice so as to transform society from above."[51] In effect, nearly a decade earlier, Michel Cahen had suggested that from its inception FRELIMO's notion of "people's power [*poder popular*]" had always been a "complete ideological fiction."[52]

The peasant-worker government or the revolutionary-democratic dictatorship of the proletariat and the peasantry that nominally defined the nature of the Mozambican state was, according to Cahen, belied by the fusion of the party and the state at all crucial levels, from mass organizations, to elective state structures, nationalized businesses and communal villages.[53] The ultimate expression of this commanding "democratic centralism" was the tight control exercised by FRELIMO over all autonomous social movements.[54] In this vein, the power of workers and peasants became consistently reducible to their representation by the single party.[55] Of more direct bearing on the impasse between students and workers that I have been discussing was the absence of any official sanctioning or indeed support on the part of FRELIMO for the creation of urban workers' or industrial production cooperatives. Instead, the party tended invariably to nominate administrative commissions so as to sidestep the emergence of workers' self-management teams, which it anathematized for allegedly promoting anarchy.[56] For Cahen, in the final analysis, FRELIMO's rigidly hierarchical political structure produces its isolation from the citizenry and engenders a state that is fundamentally "suspended in the air."[57] In this sense, argues Cahen, the fundamental character of the Mozambican state is no different from that of other African nations, a nature that Olaniyan defines as authoritarian, unstable, and unproductive in the Introduction: it belongs to the strain of neocolonial countries. It is neither a Marxist state nor a third-world socialist nation, but rather a "peripheral" bourgeois state.[58] By a supreme irony, then, the legacy of colonial power was reasserting itself at the very moment that the Audience thunderously interdicted its return. The watchword "never again" (*nunca mais*) is consequently turned inside out, signifying, in the last instance, a tragic recurrence of the same. If the perplexity and contradictoriness of Mozambique's recent history could be reduced to the elegant economy of an Attic tragedy, then the September riots would be the peripety, or reversal of circumstances, induced by the "fatal error" that precluded *A Comuna* from ever being staged.

Independent Theater

Mozambique's first independent amateur troupe, Associação Cultural da Casa Velha (ACCV, Old House Cultural Association), arose in Maputo seven years after independence (in 1982), nominally still during the revolutionary period. It maintained a steady rate of activity, putting on multiple plays by African, European, and American authors, notably Wole Soyinka, Molière, Brecht, Federico García Lorca, Eugene O'Neill, as well as adaptations of narrative fiction by other Luso-African writers, such as, significantly, *Quem me dera ser onda* (*I Wish I Were a Wave*), Manuel Rui's mordant, child's-eye account of the plodding but inexorable rise of a parallel economy toward the end of the first decade of Angola's "Marxist Republic." The theatrical adaptation of Rui's ironic representation of the appearance of precisely these early signs of a rampant "primitive accumulation" may have nevertheless resonated with contemporaneous Maputo audiences as well. Cahen points out, in fact, that one of the FRELIMO regime's more conspicuous trends from around 1980 onward is the predisposition of its leaders, their professed Marxism-Leninism notwithstanding, to respond to each aggravation of the economic situation with increasingly pragmatic economic liberalization measures, along with a concomitant strengthening of FRELIMO's ties with the West, especially the OECD (Organization for Economic Cooperation and Development) countries. As early as 1983, the Mozambican regime had initiated negotiations for membership to the World Bank and International Monetary Fund.[59]

There is thus unquestionably a link between the rise of a thriving and largely autonomous theatrical activity in the early 1980s with the state's initial, tentative steps toward economic liberalization. As the adaptation of Rui's novella suggests, it is most likely this very neoliberal turn (or purposeful progression toward liberalization), and the related ascendance of the petite and *moyenne* bourgeoisie, as witnessed by the growing strength of black market networks, and the attendant emergence of Mozambican financiers that several of the plays staged in the 1980s decry.[60] As Couto has put it, the revolutionary ardor with which many of the artists of his generation were imbued was rapidly ebbing.[61] From the early 1980s the rift between writers increasingly disenchanted with the dysfunction of postindependence society and the ruling party becomes "ever more visible."[62] Theater begins to surface as one of the more vocal forums for this emergent contestation of the still dominant revolutionary discourse. According to Calane da Silva, a well-known writer who was a prolific theater practitioner during that decade, many artists felt compelled to express their disapproval of many aspects of the status quo, and despite a prevailing "self-censorship," "theatre itself . . . became a galvanizing force because it was a living theatre, critical of a particular reality."[63] Even celebrated author Luís Bernardo Honwana, who served as minister of culture at the time, while dismissing offhand any allegation of state-sponsored censorship, refers likewise to the tens of plays produced during his tenure that were openly critical of several government entities and organizations.[64] From devised theater as well as the frequent adoption of Brechtian and even Boalian techniques, to innovative theatrical adaptation, theater of the absurd and the production of a kind of poor theater as a strategic means of coping with the prevalent scarcity of resources, the most inventive as well as technically sophisticated theater in Mozambique was produced in the early 1980s. Indeed, during this period, theater was perhaps one of the few forms of expression (artistic or otherwise) that managed to elude the tight control exercised by the FRELIMO government over most meaningful forms of social and political expression and organization. It was arguably one of the more substantial forms of cultural productivity, which, to borrow Olaniyan's elegant formulation, began to accompany the Mozambican state's incipient unproductivity like a refractory shadow.

The Theater of War

In light of the devastating toll that the (then) five-year-old war had taken on the country, brutally obliterating both communal and familial ties, and ruthlessly targeting the more visible symbols of FRELIMO's program of modernization along with its vision of an organic and forward-moving national collective, it is not surprising that one of ACCV's first productions had the war as its central theme. It was a translation and adaptation of *Goutte de Miel* (*Honey Drop*) by the renowned pioneer of children's theater Léon Chancerel, who in turn adapted it from an Armenian tale. This dramatic fable stages the precipitate and intricate chain of events connecting a single drop of honey that falls on the floor of a grocer's shop to "the red mantle of war" being cast over "the whole of creation," an apocalyptic denouement where "there is not enough time to bury the dead. / There are mountains of corpses / and rivers of blood."[65] In a departure from Chancerel's original, where the last two soldiers to survive the war, ignorant of the cause of the devastation around them, are about to commit "an irreparable deed" but decide instead to walk away together from the desolate field of battle, in ACCV's *Gota de Mel*, the last two survivors stab each other with their bayonets and slowly fall to the ground, "shoulder against shoulder," repeating ("as life slowly ebbs away from them"), "so we'll die without knowing why."[66]

ACCV's adaptation of Chancerel's play subtly calls into question the ruling party's official account of the civil war as a well-orchestrated destabilization campaign aimed at scuttling the FRELIMO government's efforts to dismantle the social system and property relations inherited from the colonial era, as well as foiling the fledgling nation's attempt to disengage itself from international capital. In accordance with FRELIMO's official account of the conflict, the rebel movement RENAMO's sole and defining purpose was to destroy and demoralize, to erect out of the resulting wreckage a national reconstruction regime amenable to the interests of global capital.[67] "Civil war" was, in effect, not a phrase the FRELIMO government was likely to employ to refer to the brutal struggle that had been ravaging the country since 1977. In its view, a band of bloodthirsty murderers had been sowing terror, desolation, and death throughout the country. Were this the full story, however, then it would be difficult to explain how a group that started out as a mercenary unit created by the Special Branch of the Rhodesian army—and whose political strategy apparently boiled down to looting the country's scarce natural resources, blowing up schools and bridges, and butchering, raping, and mutilating women and children—was able to extend its sphere of activity to 80 percent of the national territory by 1986.

As Cahen suggests, a plausible explanation for this apparent paradox resides in the relationship that a centralized state guided by "a paradigm of authoritarian modernization" established both with "animist" religions (whose expression it often sought to repress) as well as local and traditional forms of authority, which it invariably abrogated, while failing to produce any visible signs of social progress.[68] With the reduction of its social base, induced by its particular brand of "democratic centralism," FRELIMO effectively lacked both the legitimation and the wherewithal to mobilize the rural population on a massive scale. According to Cahen, bereft of this popular commitment, the war became, in the eyes of the majority of the people, little more than "a private fight between two rival bands."[69] It was a "little" war, in Mbembe's sense, a war "between bands and, commonly, [a war] of rapine pitting one set of predators against others"; such conflicts "involve few persons and relatively simple weaponry. But, while their tactics are quite rudimentary, they still result in human catastrophes."[70] More than likely, in fact, RENAMO probably controlled no more than 50 percent of the armed gangs roaming the countryside throughout the 1980s, most of whom had obtained their weapons either from poorly trained rural militias or army deserters, who commonly made up the former's ranks.[71] It is the peculiar form of institutional violence produced by these so-called private wars, the combination of low-tech warfare and the destruction of large swathes of the population or at least their means of survival, that *Gota de Mel* points to, in the end.

This view of the war as an inordinately vicious conflict between more or less autonomous armed bands reluctant to give up the gun also underpins Mutumbela Gogo troupe's 1992 adaptation of Aristophanes's *Lysistrata*: *Amor, vem* (*Come, My Love*). Manuela Soeiro, the group's director, has indicated that the play seeks to convey the citizenry's growing sense of frustration at the seemingly interminable delays and obstructionist tactics defining the protracted negotiations between FRELIMO and RENAMO (which were to culminate in the 1992 Rome Peace Accords).[72] In effect, the Maputo market women in *Amor, vem*, who, like their upper-class Attic counterparts, resolve to deny their consorts connubial pleasure until they stop fighting, reiterate that their objective is to "end the war," and "make [their] husbands sign a swift peace."[73] By demanding to know "exactly where the people's money is ending up," they strive, at the same time, "to prevent some men from buying luxury cars while the people go hungry," thus underlining not only the widening gap between the haves and have-nots, between the urban center and its increasingly squalid and expanding periphery during the initial stages of economic liberalization and structural adjustment, but also the link between the war and profiteering.[74] In contrast with Aristophanes's original, in *Amor, vem*, the protagonist Julieta opens the play by pointedly telling the audience that what it is going to see is "a very curious dream" about "something the women did in order to bring the war to an end."[75] In the final scene, Julieta discloses the heightened anxiety surrounding the likelihood of a peaceful resolution of the conflict in the months prior to the signing of the peace accords, as she reminds the spectators that "this has been nothing but a dream, maybe it will be made possible tomorrow. . . . But the war continues."[76] This final, ironic allusion to FRELIMO's world-renowned shibboleth, *a luta continua* (the struggle continues), provides a sense of how far the dream of social justice has plummeted since the halcyon days of the revolutionary period, while simultaneously suggesting perhaps that the struggle for a more equitable and just society is already giving way to rampant class warfare.

In September 1995, three years after Mutumbela's production of *Amor, vem*, in what was dubbed as the first "Luso-Mozambican co-production," ACCV and Portugal's Coimbra-based company Teatro da Rainha (Queen's Theater) staged *De volta da Guerra* (*Back from the War*) for the theater festival organized that same year in Maputo by Cena Lusófona (Lusophone Scene, or Stage).[77] The play was an adaptation of *The Veteran* (*Parlamento de Ruzzante che iera vegnù de campo*) by the sixteenth-century Italian playwright Angelo Beolco (known as Il Ruzzante), whom Dario Fo considers not just "the true father of the *Commedia dell'Arte*," but "the greatest playwright of Renaissance Europe."[78] One year after the first multiparty elections (which returned FRELIMO to power), and three years since the signing of the peace accords, the protagonist's colorful dismissal of the war ("And shit on the regiment, on the war and the soldiers") presumably encapsulates a national "everyday experience still indelibly marked by the recent war.[79] For Fernando Mora Ramos, one of Cena Lusófona's founding members, who coordinated *De volta da guerra*'s coproduction, the play's "healthy" confrontation with the war aims to avert the ever-lurking danger of forgetting it.[80] Notwithstanding the irreducible differences between the devastating effects of the Mozambican civil war on the peasantry and the circumstances of the Venetian republic's peasant army in the wake of its crushing defeat at the battle of Agnadello by the joint armies of the League of Cambrai in 1509 (which provides the immediate historical backdrop for *The Veteran*), the appropriateness of Beolco's sixteenth-century comic play to late twentieth-century, war-torn Mozambique was never in question for Ramos, who also selected the play for the festival.[81] Perhaps the principal affinity between the two contexts lies in the protagonist Ruzzante's trajectory, which ostensibly reproduces the history of recent wars in Africa, also defined on the whole by the disruption of time-honored kinship ties, and forced migration from ancestral lands into the harsh, precarious living conditions of the straggling peripheries of Africa's major cities.[82]

Whatever the extent and specific forms of the resemblances between late twentieth-century Mozambique and Renaissance Italy, one feature that both the adaptation and the original share in common is the link between warfare and the predation of the rural populace. In *De volta da guerra*, for instance, despite his denunciation of the war "and those who invented it," the protagonist Sitoi, just like Ruzzante in Beolco's comedy, admits that "If it weren't for all the fear I felt, the war wouldn't be so bad, as far as the yield goes. In the army we call it 'scraping by' [*desenrascar*]."[83] Although the only thing he manages to "extract" (*desenrascar*) from a fellow peasant is the heavy, tattered overcoat he brings back from the war, and even though, in the end, he is forced to sell his own weapon "to one of those who sends them to South Africa" (one of the main sponsors of the rebel forces) in order "to get enough money to eat," Sitoi's goal upon setting out for battle, as his mate (*compadre*) reminds him, was always "to line his own pockets."[84] Sitoi's situation, however derivative, resonates with that of the common conscripted infantryman during the war: ill-trained, poorly equipped, undernourished, and recurrently averse to engaging in direct firefights with the enemy. As with Ruzzante, Sitoi's combat experience is reduced to "performing his duty" by fleeing "when those in front began to run away."[85] Desertions among government troops were indeed common, with the army occasionally having to resort to summary executions in an effort to curtail their high incidence.[86] At the same time, like Mutumbela's *Amor, vem*, ACCV's "free" adaptation of Beolco's comic masterpiece also endeavors to encapsulate the brisk acceleration of economic neoliberalism and its overpowering social impact in the late 1980s: not only the massive influx of war refugees into the outskirts of the major cities, especially Maputo, but the exponential rise in the absolute poverty index (50 percent in 1989, up from 15 percent in 1980), and a major upsurge in the parallel economy.[87] In effect, Sitoi's wife, like her Paduan counterpart, has, during his absence, begun to consort with the owner of a stall in the Estrela Vermelha (Red Star) *dumba nengue*, "one of those folks in the *business* [in English in the original], a dangerous type, who will slay you for real if he happens to take a dislike to you."[88]

According to Ramos, tickets for the play consistently sold out and became available on the black market for up to three times the original price. He adduces that the audiences followed the text with "extraordinary attentiveness," while the "Elizabethan" spontaneity that their responses to the performances supposedly exemplified presumably reinforced the appositeness of a text from the European Renaissance (chosen by a European set designer) to a contemporary African context.[89] João Machado da Graça, ACCV's director at the time, conjectures that the popularity theater enjoyed in Maputo during the war years was probably a consequence of the near total isolation of the capital, occasioned by the war itself, both from the rest of the country and the world. In the absence of Hollywood film distribution chains, commercial television, and other globalized forms of mass entertainment, theater emerges almost by default as the main attraction, as it were.[90] Cahen and Christian Geffray, among others, have long maintained that one of the chief causes of the civil war was the exacerbation of the urban-rural divide by the FRELIMO regime's administrative enforcement of development, the astonishing incapacity of the political leadership to construct a nationalism that did not concurrently erase "the concrete historical heterogeneity of the social groups which they wished to unite and integrate under the sign of a single national identity."[91] Insofar as these vital dramatic exchanges between mainly urban actors and audiences, about the nature and impact of the war, continued to take place within the confines of the capital, this sustained theatrical activity unavoidably reflected the urban-rural split that was in part accountable for the outbreak of civil strife. This was a conflict whose origins and consequences this urban theater was strenuously calling into question.

This rift assumes broader (global) dimensions in light of the North-South constituent of this particular coproduction. Although Ramos describes the collaborative experience as "truly multicultural," anchored in a profound mutual respect for the specificity of each contribution, Machado da Graça grasps this "complementarity" as a means of surmounting some of the key technical shortcomings afflicting Mozambican theater. While the ACCV director identifies the actors' talent and passion as their greatest assets, without expert guidance by someone well-versed in "the culture and technique of the theater," he believes, this enthusiasm and skill will ultimately redound in "what we can see today in Maputo: a repetition of the same models," distinguishable only by "the greater or lesser skill of the performers"; a theater that works well mainly because of the "great communicability" between actors and spectators, but whose artistic quality is consistently low.[92] Machado da Graça closes his assessment of the coproduction by proposing the establishment of a drama school staffed by "teachers hailing from Portugal, Brazil, etc., who may even profit from some local values."[93] With this familiar division between European technical prowess and African vibrancy and raw talent, the ACCV director apparently seeks to reinstate precisely the hierarchical exchange that Couto had called for the festival *not* to promote: "a center that conceives [ideas] and a periphery that executes [them]."[94] In this proposed transmission of knowledge and expertise by Portuguese and Brazilian instructors to gifted but untrained African theater practitioners, whose local experience may by chance contribute something of value to the pedagogic transfer, there appears to be little or no room either for the remaking of "discoveries, in lower case and in both directions," for which Couto advocated, or for Soeiro's injunction to allow Mozambican theater to develop in its own terms.[95] One may wonder, finally, whether the members of Mutumbela and *M'beu* had precisely this very coproduction in mind when they claimed in their open letter about the state of Mozambican theater that no one from Cena Lusófona ever consulted with Mozambican artists when they conceived and designed the festival, and complained that the selection of plays was "unilateral" and entirely heedless of the criteria proposed by their Mozambican counterparts.[96]

In any case, it is this hierarchized model of cultural and epistemological exchange that has, at least until 2010, underpinned the curricular structure of the drama school founded more than a decade later as part of Eduardo Mondlane's Escola de Comunicação e Artes (School of Communication and Arts). What Machado da Graça's proposal simultaneously restores, then, is the conventional antinomy (which, in spite of all its limitations, the popular theater of the revolutionary period had endeavored to transcend) between an elite or art theater performed inside a building usually in colonial languages and a theatrical activity situated "where the majority of the people reside: in the villages in the countryside and in the poor urban areas," between, on the one hand, the intellectual, technically proficient drama that appeals either to Western audiences or to a small, literate, and urban African public, and, on the other, Kenya's Kamĩrĩĩthũ open-air theater, for example, or the community theater of 1980s Zimbabwe promoted by Ngũgĩ wa Mirii, a veteran of Kenya's Kamĩrĩĩthũ experiment.[97] Such a theater would purportedly address the problems of ordinary people "in their own terms, from their own perspectives and from within their own art forms."[98] The parallel between this particular strain of post-Marxist Mozambican theater and the enforcement of structural adjustment policies as well as the almost always conditional dispensation of foreign aid that broadly characterize the neoliberal period is difficult to ignore, especially if one recalls, with Olaniyan, the crucial work of culture in normalizing and rendering plausible the entire social process.

Immediately after the 1992 Rome Peace Accords, this rift between the country and the city, between the socially and economically privileged urban centers and their precarious, ever-expanding peripheries, or between art and popular theater, was to some extent, and for a brief period, dissipated, or at least attenuated. Mutumbela Gogo, transposing the skills and material resources of its urban art theater into remote rural "areas which the war had completely cut off from the rest of the country," produced and performed a number of plays intended to facilitate the rehabilitation and reintegration of well over a million war refugees and displaced persons.[99] Mutumbela's work in the refugee camps broached, while at the same time leaving indefinitely inchoate, a potential model for relocating theater outside the city center, in the peri-urban districts and the countryside. To be sure, in his address to the 1993 annual International Festival for Theater of Iberian Expression (FITEI, in its Portuguese, Galician, and Spanish acronym), Couto relates these performances to the broader efforts of playwrights and theater practitioners to assist Mozambicans in their slow and anguished attempt to emerge from the "trauma" of war and become once again "reconciled with themselves."[100] Couto concedes that he was surprised to discover, during Mutumbela's tour through war-ravished rural Mozambique, "how much hope can resist inside the hearts" of human beings in places which the troupe expected to find drowning in despair:[101]

> Those folks were not simply an audience . . . they transformed the performance into revelry, they created, participated, took ownership both of themselves and of the moment. And as we continued to work in other areas dilacerated by the war, we became increasingly certain of one thing: the war had not taken everything away from us. There remained our initiative, our will to create, to reinvent ourselves. This [was] our task: to convert the days of blood and horror into the stuff of hope and tenderness, to create order where chaos [had] entrenched itself, to create life and beauty where death [had] spread its mantle of sorrow and grief.[102]

Couto wrote these lines at the height what Olaniyan names the postcolonial state's crisis of fragility. From the perspective of these war refugees, in effect, the Mozambican state had been reduced to a hollowed out husk, an idea bereft of content. It was theater's task at that ephemeral moment to fuel the "active will to community" that for Mbembe is the essential political meaning of decolonization among stateless "spect-actors," as Augusto Boal might have called them, who dreamed implausibly of refashioning the state in their image.[103] As Olaniyan indicates, in their stubborn belief in the possibility of devising a script for the state that would derive not from the directives of a ruling elite but from a collaborative and collective praxis, these folk may have, in the last instance, revealed themselves consummately pragmatic. Twenty years on, this short-lived experiment in imagining or devising a more productive state, ruled by law and committed to social justice, suggests that the precarious hope, which tenaciously endured through the worst atrocities of the war, has today been effectively severed. The yearning to reinvent a shattered community now seems to lie fractured and forgotten like the debris that lingers by the roadside long after the riots have been quelled, until the time comes to gather up the shards once again and stage the next destructive reclaiming, the next violent reappropriation of a social space that remains foreclosed to "those who have little or no tomorrow."[104]

LUÍS MADUREIRA is Professor and Chair of Spanish and Portuguese, and Professor of African Cultural Studies, at the University of Wisconsin, Madison. He is author of *Cannibal Modernities: Postcoloniality and the Avant-garde in Caribbean and Brazilian Literature* and *Imaginary Geographies in Portuguese and Lusophone-African Literature: Narratives of Discovery and Empire.*

Notes

Some portions of the first two sections of this chapter have been published in "'Where God Is Like a Longing': Theatre and Social Vulnerability in Mozambique," in *Imagining Human Rights in Twenty-First-Century Theater: Global Perspectives*, ed. Florián Becker, Paola Hernández, and Brenda Werth (New York: Palgrave Macmillan, 2013), 45–66. I am grateful to the Fulbright Program for awarding me a grant to conduct research on theater in Mozambique in 2010 and to the Graduate School at the University of Wisconsin, which also provided generous support for my research both in Portugal and Mozambique through a Vilas Associate Award in 2009 and 2010.

1. Achille Mbembe, *On the Postcolony*, trans. A. M. Barrett, Murray Last, Steven Rendall, and Janet Roitman (Berkeley: University of California Press, 2001), 158.

2. For example, "Mozambicans, get ready to chill [*curtir*] on the great day of the general strike, September 1, 2010," quoted in João Dias Miguel, "A guerra do pão," *Visão*, September 9–15, 2010, 64.

3. Fernando Lima, "Até à próxima crise em Moçambique," *Visão*, September 9–15, 2010, 72.

4. Ibid.

5. These play scripts exist mostly in private collections, since only two of these texts had been deposited at the national archive. In this regard, I owe an enormous debt of gratitude to Dinis Chembene, Tela Chicane, Dadivo José Combane, Paulo Guambe, João Machado da Graça, Nelson Mabuie, Rogério Manjate, Joaquim Matavel, Gilberto Mendes, Lucrécia Paco, Manuela Soeiro, and António Sopa for their incredible generosity in availing their private collections and materials to me.

6. Mia Couto, "As outras nações de Moçambique?" *O País*, September 18, 2010, 4.

7. Ibid.

8. Quoted in Celso Ricardo, "Manifestações para além do custo do pão," *O País*, July 9, 2011, http://opais.sapo.mz/index.php/entrevistas/76-entrevistas/15079-manifestacoes-para-alem-do-custo-do-pao.html. Unless otherwise noted, all translations from Portuguese and Rhonga are my own.

9. Cristiana Pereira, "Moçambique: O despertar da fome," *Buala: Cultura Contemporânea Africana*, November 2, 2010, http://www.buala.org/pt/a-ler/mocambique-o-despertar-da-fome.

10. Ibid.

11. Carlos Serra, *Em cima duma lâmina: Um estudo sobre a precariedade social em três cidades de Moçambique* (Maputo, Mozambique: Imprensa Universitária, Universidade Eduardo Mondlane, 2003), 19.

12. Ibid., 47.

13. Ibid., 47, 56.

14. Pereira, "Moçambique."

15. Ibid.

16. Ibid.

17. Georges Balandier, *Le pouvoir sur scènes* (Paris: Librairie Arthème Fayard, 2006), 53.

18. Pius Ngandu Nkashama, "Theatricality and Social Mimodrama," in *African Drama and Performance*, ed. John Conteh-Morgan and Tejumola Olaniyan (Bloomington: Indiana University Press, 2004), 243.

19. Ironically, the social inequality against which the protesters were revolting was the very same one that the FRELIMO anthem (which was until 1992 the national anthem) promised to overturn: "United with the whole world, / Struggling against the bourgeoisie / Our Fatherland will be the graveyard / Of capitalism and exploitation." FRELIMO is the Portuguese acronym for *Frente de Libertação de Moçambique* (Mozambique Liberation Front), which had been the armed anticolonial rebel movement.

20. Joachim Fiebach, "Dimensions of Theatricality in Africa," in Conteh-Morgan and Olaniyan, *African Drama and Performance*, 25; Pius Ngandu Nkashama, *Théâtres et scènes de spectacle: Études sur les dramaturgies et les arts gestuels* (Paris: Éditions L'Harmattan, 1993), 11.

21. Serra, *Em cima duma lâmina*, 21. The first phase is the colonial (ca. 1890–1975).

22. A former playwright and theater director, currently a Ministry of Education official (Luís Savel) assured me that the FRELIMO government never imposed any kind of censorship, and that the playwrights composed their proregime messages of their own free will, without any sort of official pressure or coercion.

23. Carlos Nuno Castel-Branco, "Economia extractiva e desafios da industrialização em Moçambique," in *Economia extractiva e desafios da industrialização em Moçambique*, ed. Luís de Brito, Carlos Nuno Castel-Branco, Sérgio Chichava, and António Francisco (Maputo, Mozambique: Instituto de Estudos Sociais e Económicos, 2010), 77–78.

24. Mbembe, *On the Postcolony*, 49.

25. Armando Guebuza, "Esses Tempos Estranhos," in *Antologia temática de poesia africana 2: O Canto Armado*, ed. Mário de Andrade (Lisbon: Livraria Sá da Costa, 1979), 74.

26. Grupo Cénico das Forças Populares de Libertação de Moçambique, *A sagrada família ou a crítica da crítica do javali do camaleão e do xiconhoca* (Maputo, Mozambique: Imprensa Nacional, 1980), 4. The allusion to Marx and Engels's famous text is, of course, intended.

27. Ibid., 38.

28. Ibid., 20.

29. Carlos Serra, "Graça, Marcelino e Rebelo: A frente crítica," *Diário de um sociólogo*, October 24, 2010, http://oficinadesociologia.blogspot.pt/2010/10/graca-marcelino-e-rebelo-frente-critica.html.

30. Grupo Cénico, *Sagrada família*, 51.

31. The term "predatory state" was coined by Peter Evans to define a political and economic dispensation in which "those who control the state apparatus seem to plunder without any more regard for the welfare of the citizenry." Quoted in Joseph Hanlon and Teresa Smart, *Do Bicycles Equal Development in Mozambique?* (Oxford: James Currey, 2008), 107.

32. Lázaro Mabunda, "Nossa pátria será o túmulo do capitalismo e da exploração," *O País*, February 25, 2011, http://ambicanos.blogspot.com/2012/09/nossa-patria-sera-tumulo-do-capitalismo.html?m=1. Rumor has it that Guebuza was once an actor in the troupe.

33. Colectivo de Trabalho Trabalhadores dos Caminhos de Ferro de Moçambique e Estudantes da Universidade Eduardo Mondlane, *A Comuna* (Maputo, Mozambique: Instituto Nacional do Livro e do Disco, 1979), 8.

34. *The Days of the Commune*, 1948–1949. Bertolt Brecht, *Os Dias da Comuna*, vol. 10: *Teatro Completo em 12 volumes*, trans. Fernando Peixoto (São Paulo: Paz e Terra, 1993), 11–106.

35. Brecht, *Os Dias da Comuna*, 90. The Audience (*Plateia*) is one of the play's *dramatis personae* and appears as the Narrator's recurrent interlocutor in the play. A rousing rendition of the *Internationale* was a common, perhaps obligatory, finale to dramatic performances in the period.

36. Castel-Branco, "Economia extractiva," 64.

37. Ibid., 69.

38. Mbembe, *On the Postcolony*, 74.

39. Hanlon and Smart, *Do Bicycles Equal Development?*, 131.

40. "Em Moçambique não há cidadania," *O País*, February 22, 2011, http://opais.sapo.mz/index.php/sociedade/45-sociedade/12451-em-mocambique-nao-ha-cidadania.html.

41. Mbembe, *On the Postcolony*, 74.

42. Colectivo de Trabalho Trabalhadores dos Caminhos de Ferro de Moçambique e Estudantes da Universidade Eduardo Mondlane, *A Comuna*, 12.

43. Ibid., 12.

44. Ibid., 13.

45. Jacques Rancière, *The Emancipated Spectator*, trans. Gregory Elliott (London: Verso, 2009), 2.

46. Colectivo de Trabalho Trabalhadores dos Caminhos de Ferro de Moçambique e Estudantes da Universidade Eduardo Mondlane, *A Comuna*, 10.

47. Rancière, *Emancipated Spectator*, 4.

48. Ibid., 14.

49. Ibid., 61.

50. Jacques Rancière, *Dissensus: On Politics and Aesthetics*, ed. and trans. Steven Corcoran (New York: Continuum, 2010), 143.

51. Mahmood Mamdani, *Citizens and Subjects: Contemporary Africa and the Legacy of Late Colonialism* (Princeton, NJ: Princeton University Press, 1996), 135.

52. Michel Cahen, *Mozambique: La revolution implosée* (Paris: L'Harmattan, 1987), 141.

53. Ibid., 141.

54. Ibid., 147.

55. Ibid., 141.

56. Ibid., 147.

57. Ibid., 146.

58. Ibid., 151–152.

59. Ibid., 26–27.

60. Ibid., 30.

61. Michel Laban, *Moçambique: Encontro com escritores* (Porto, Portugal: Fundação Eng. António de Almeida, 1998), 3:1000.

62. Michel Laban, "Écrivains et pouvoir politique au Mozambique après l'indépendance," *Lusotopie* (1995): 172.

63. Laban, *Moçambique*, 2:797.

64. Ibid., 2:679.

65. ACCV, *A Gota de Mel*, typescript, private collection, 8, 9.

66. Léon Chancerel, *La goutte de miel, les mauvais garçons, le tambourin de velours* (Lyon, France: Éditions la Hutte, 1943), 11 (copy in author's possession); ACCV, *Gota de Mel*, 10.

67. RENAMO is the Portuguese acronym for *Resistência Nacional Moçambicana* (Mozambique National Resistance), currently one of Mozambique's main opposition parties.

68. Michel Cahen, *Les Bandits: Un historien au Mozambique* (Paris: Fundação Calouste Gulbenkian, 2002), 4.

69. Cahen, *Mozambique*, 73.

70. Mbembe, *On the Postcolony*, 87.

71. Cahen, *Mozambique*, 81.

72. Manuela Soeiro, interview by the author, July 23, 2010.

73. Henning Mankell, ed., *Amor, vem* (Maputo, Mozambique: OMNI, 2003), 29, 13.

74. Ibid., 29.

75. Ibid., 1.

76. Ibid., 51.

77. "De Volta da guerra," *Setepalcos: Revista do Programa Cena Lusófona* 0 (November 1995): 14.

78. Dario Fo, "Against Jesters Who Defame and Insult: Nobel Lecture," *Nobelprize.org*, December 7, 1997, http://www.nobelprize.org/nobel_prizes/literature/laureates/1997/fo-lecture.html. I have consulted Angelo Beolco, *Falatório do Ruzante de volta da guerra*, trans. António Neves Pedro, Fernando Mora Ramos, and José Carlos Faria (Lisbon: Edições Colibri, 2000).

79. *De volta da guerra*, transcript, private collection, 2; Fernando Mora Ramos, "Em torno de uma co-produção," *Setepalcos: Revista do Programa Cena Lusófona* 1 (December 1996): 24.

80. Ramos, "Em torno de uma co-produção," 24.

81. Ibid., 22.

82. Ibid., 22–23.

83. *De volta*, 12, 2.

84. Ibid., 4.

85. Ibid., 6.

86. Cahen, *Mozambique*, 71.

87. Serra, *Em cima duma lâmina*, 22.

88. An informal and often illicit stall market located on the edge of Maputo's "cement city." *Dumba nengue* literally means "every person for him or herself."; *De volta*, 8.

89. Ramos, "Em torno de uma co-produção," 22.

90. João Machado da Graça, interview by the author, June 8, 2010.

91. Christian Geffray, *A Causa das Armas. Antropologia da guerra contemporânea em Moçambique*, trans. Adelaide Odete Ferreira (Porto, Portugal: Edições Afrontamento, 1991), 15.

92. João Machado da Graça, "Complementaridade," *Setepalcos Revista do Programa Cena Lusófona* 1 (December 1996): 25.

93. Ibid., 23.

94. "Mia Couto," *Setepalcos* 0 (November 1995): 30.

95. Ibid., 30, 31, 29.

96. *M'béu*, or "seed," was Mutumbela's "sister troupe," composed for the most part of younger actors. It was conceived as a kind of training ground for future Mutumbela actors. "Um teatro nosso crescendo ao nosso ritmo e medida," *Savana*, February 5, 1999, 11.

97. Ngũgĩ wa Thiong'o, *Penpoints, Gunpoints, and Dreams: Towards a Critical Theory of the Arts and the State of Africa* (Oxford, UK: Clarendon, 1998), 52.

98. Oga S. Abah, "Creativity, Participation and Change in Theatre for Development Practice," in *The Performance Arts in Africa: A Reader*, ed. Frances Harding (New York: Routledge, 2002), 159.

99. Maria Couto, *FITEI: pátria do teatro de expressão ibérica, 1977–1997*, ed. Carlos Porto (Porto, Portugal: FITEI, Fundação Eng. António de Almeida, 1997), 234.

100. Ibid., 234.

101. Ibid.

102. Ibid.

103. Achille Mbembe, *Sortir de la grande nuit: Essai sur l'Afrique decolonisée* (Paris: Éditions La Découverte/Poche, 2013), 10.

104. Couto, "As outras nações," 4.

7 Fissures of Trespass

Women as Agents of Transgression amid National Disenchantment

Névine El Nossery

> Order and harmony exist only when each group respects the *hudud*. Any transgression necessarily leads to anarchy and misfortune, and women were thinking only of transgressing the boundaries.
>
> —Fatima Mernissi, *Dreams of Trespass: Tales of a Harem Girlhood*

WITHIN THE FORMATION of new nation-states in the Maghreb, especially after several decades of colonial ruling, social segmentation has been one of the means used by the state to establish and reinforce its own centralized power and absolute authority. The existing collectivities—ethnic, tribal, religious, linguistic, or gender-based—were considered a threat to the state, therefore alliances were regulated, if not completely condemned and disbanded. According to Mounira Charrad, "the establishment or extension of state domination entails a rearrangement of the nexus of social solidarities."[1] Considering that women in most Middle Eastern and North African cultures play a central role in supporting and sustaining social groups that often function as alternative centers of collective power in the patriarchal diktat and, by extension, their nations at large, it is easy to understand how and why the repression of women became a priority for the state. It was in the state's best interest to maintain the existing arrangements, therefore religion and religious laws were and continue to be invoked in order to regulate gender issues and to limit women's rights.

Crossing boundaries or defying the *hudud* established by the patriarchal diktat is a serious transgression for an Arab woman. In doing so, not only is she breaking the rules that are rigorously enforced by the social groups to which she supposedly belongs, but she is stepping into the public sphere, a space that has often been forbidden to her.[2] The separation between public and private spheres, based on a gendered hierarchy, represents the culmination of a long-standing state manipulation of religion. Ruling entities have a long history of tactically appropriating religious teachings and regulations in order to prevent social change and greater equality for women in the family and the society at large.

In this chapter, I introduce an overview of how Islam, from its inception, has been instrumentalized first by the *umma*, the Islamic community, and then by the new independent states in the Maghreb in order to maintain absolute control. I also demonstrate how both Algeria and Morocco can be considered paradigms of the effects of strategic political use of Islam in modern history.

A result of the long and demoralizing experience of colonization, postcolonial regimes were able to easily rely on orthodox Islam in order to establish and assert national control. To illustrate the long and complex relationship between women and the version of Islam that dominated during the formation of the new nation-states in the Maghreb, I explore how the effects of policies such as the physical and metaphorical veiling of women's potency are reflected in the contemporary literature of the region. I mainly focus on two literary works that challenge the exclusion of women from the public sphere by representing what I call fissures of trespass, voices and movements that challenge dominant discourse. In particular, I consider certain practices and strategies in francophone autobiographical narratives that function as fissures that break through the inviolable and sanctified walls of the private sphere, that seclude women and portray them as the source of *fitna*, seduction, and therefore pose a threat to the homogeneity of the nation. The two literary works on which this chapter focuses can be considered as counternarratives that question the boundaries between the public and the private and explore the nation-state's crisis of identity in an attempt to understand and ultimately dismantle the barriers, or *hudud*, that keep social groups segregated in this kind of society.

An overview of the statization of Isalm, or the misappropriation of cultural-religious traditions by the state, would explain the spread of Islam throughout North Africa in the seventh century. It served the patriarchy well and has been used by political rulers to maintain the status quo for more than fourteen centuries. Needless to say, Islam is not a monolithic religion. It is a complex set of variable practices and beliefs that differ widely from one country to another. When it comes to women's status within the Islamic structure, it is important to stress that the origins of the devaluation of women's role and place in society predates the advent of Islam. In the Mesopotamian region, for instance, laws governing the family were rather harsh with regard to women. The Hammurabi code (ca. 1752 BC) gave men the right to divorce their wives for any reason, whereas a woman who disobeyed her husband might have had her teeth ground with bricks.[3] With the rise of Islam in the seventh century, however, the misogynistic and demeaning image of women, inherited from Christianity and Judaism, would continue to persist. Although Islam had forbidden the infanticide of female children, it certainly had not granted any more power to women. On the contrary, before

Islam, women in North Africa had more sexual freedom and lived in a rather matrilineal society.[4] With the expansion of Islam and its increasingly important social and political role within the main cities of the region, women gradually lost the power and privileges that they had previously enjoyed.

One can say that religion, throughout the history of the Muslim world, has been an instrument used by the state in order to coerce, to intimidate, and to assert its control over various groups. The physical distinction of private and public spheres was another means with which to further stratify society according to class, race, and gender. It is important to note that with the advent of Islam, the architecture of the places in which the Prophet lived created a space where private and public life were barely distinguishable. Physical thresholds were hardly obstacles, and the house of the Prophet opened directly onto the mosque. For this reason, the mosque played a decisive role in the lives of women, and it defined their place in politics. In other words, the Prophet converted the mosque into a democratic space for public debates on the affairs of the state.[5] However, this proximity created discontent among radical Muslims and led to the revelation of a Koranic verse demanding a curtain be placed between the men and the Prophet's wives, when the latter were addressed.[6] After the death of the Prophet and within the caliphal state, this public democratic space became an oppressive institution, especially for women, as they were discouraged from attending mosques.[7]

This separation was the basis for women's reclusion behind the veil and would eventually cause a schism between the leading class, the *khassah*, and the people, the *'amma*. The desire to veil women represented the suppression of resistance of any kind against the autocracy in place. As a result, women became foreigners within the *umma*, and would come to symbolize alterity, due to their heterogeneous, even indomitable nature, as Fatima Mernissi states: "Islam, as a culture and a political entity, is imbued with the idea that a woman is an uncontrollable force—an unfathomable 'other.'"[8] It is important to point out that the Arabic language has a word, *al-nashiz*, exclusively reserved for the woman who rebels against her husband's will and who does not yield to her matrimonial obligations.[9]

Thus, her alterity represents not only a threat to the religion, but also to the *umma*, insofar as any variance—whether sexual, ethnic, or social—disrupts the group's stability and homogeneity and encourages pluralism. The effort to keep this quality of otherness physically and symbolically invisible resulted in further concessions by the lower class to privileged elites, who could speak in the name of the groups they intended to marginalize.

This agenda and subsequent strategy are comparable to what is introduced later in this chapter regarding the formation of new nation-states within the contemporary era, during and following the independence of Morocco and Algeria.

In these two countries, as well as in other parts of the Arabic-Islamic world, the relationship between women and the state remains exceptionally complex. On the one hand, women have been invaluable members to their communities and to institutions and groups that support the nation's political agenda. On the other hand, they make up a social category that plays specific roles and fulfills certain duties—namely, those of reproduction and transmission. Nira Yuval-Davis and Floya Anthias summarize the five roles reserved to women:

> (a) as biological reproducers of members of ethnic collectivities;
> (b) as reproducers of the boundaries of ethnical/national groups;
> (c) as participating centrally in the ideological reproduction of the collectivity and as transmitters of its culture;
> (d) as signifiers of ethnic/national differences—as a focus and symbol in ideological discourses used in the construction, reproduction and transformation of ethnic/national categories;
> (e) as participants in national, economic, political and military struggles.[10]

One can say that within the nation's formation and throughout history, both before and after colonial rule, the state established its control through the instrumentalization of religion, which consists of a regulation system that governs individual rights and responsibilities even within the family. Under these tenets women are condemned to play a subordinate role while the liberties allotted to men are affirmed and defended. In challenging these regulations, not only will women be discharged and removed from the political body and national discourse, but they will also be made strangers to their own bodies, perceived under the aegis of a reductive vision of alterity and as a source of insubordination, or *fitna*.

Regarding decolonization and independence that was attained later than most, as was the case in Algeria and Morocco, nationalist discourse often focused on women's issues in its fight against the colonizer as a means of resisting any form of Western imperialism. After the independence of Maghrebi societies, state apparatuses sought to control more effectively the whole territory in the absence of bureaucratized states in the precolonial period. The states' intervention was particularly existent on the economical level but also aimed to bring stability and to consolidate its power and hegemony at particular periods of its history. The states that were recognized as new states after attaining independence frequently weakened after colonial rule and became mostly fragmented into minority groups based on ethnic, tribal, religious, linguistic, or gender distinction.[11] New nation-states, therefore, had to reorganize in order to establish new social cohesions. This process of state intervention in the formation of social organizations would have significant consequences on gender relations. Postindependence reforms sought to reorganize the dismantled states after colonial rule, but in doing so, as Mahmood Mamdani stresses, "each reproduced a part of that legacy, thereby creating its own variety of despotism."[12]

Women had been a driving force in the fight for independence, therefore imposing severe limits on their civil liberties had become a measure taken by the state in order to maintain control. The enforcement of Islamic law, especially the Maleki version that has historically dominated in the Maghreb region, has long been a method of regulating gender relations. It has also served to prevent social progress or change of any kind and to inhibit gender equality. According to Charrad, this interpretation of Islamic law gives "male members of the kin group extensive control over key decisions affecting women's lives."[13]

In short, in religious discourse, the woman's body is perceived as an *'awra*, that is to say, a source of shame that must be covered, "defined as sacred, *h'aram*, and that must be inscribed in bodily terms."[14] In nationalist discourse, women are the guardians of traditions, cultural and spiritual authenticity, and must remain at home, so that men are able to exercise their power out in the public sphere. On this subject, Elleke Boehmer notes that the role of men in the national scenario is usually "metonymic," whereas women are vested with a "metaphoric or symbolic" role.[15]

Thus, religious, national, and patriarchal discourses have always found ways of characterizing any expression of individuality, let alone personal ambition, interests, or desires, as something that is "unhomey," selfish, or antitraditional with regard to their bodies and their homes.[16] The female body itself is demonized. For their part, women realized that any transgression of the *hudud* or other boundaries, whether physical or intellectual, actual or symbolic, would have to begin within themselves, within the bodies that they were expected, not only to not acknowledge, but, in a sense, to condemn. The psychological weight of this paradox is reflected in the work of contemporary authors such as Malika Mokeddem and Fatima Mernissi. In Mernissi's highly acclaimed novel *Dreams of Trespass*, Aunt Habiba advises the young Fatima that "if society is hard on you, fight back by pampering your skin. Skin is political [*A-jlida siyasa*]. Otherwise why would the imams order us to hide it?"[17]

Both Algeria and Morocco, in the various periods of modern history, could be considered paradigms of the effects of strategic political use of Islam. As I argued earlier, the relationship between women and the state has always been conflictual. One of the results of the long and painful experience of colonization was that the postcolonial regimes often had recourse to orthodox Islam in order to assert national sovereignty. The new authoritarian and centralized states in Algeria and Morocco were modeled after the Jacobinism of the French occupation.

In Morocco, this complex relationship knew different junctures starting with the political instrumentalization of Islam of the mid-1940s as a means of resistance against French colonization. After independence was attained in 1956 and under a rigid monarchy, political ideology was used to enforce the king's authoritarian regime. During the period known as the Years of Lead, the three decades following independence, and with the support of religious discourse, women and their sexuality were associated with the honor of men and families.[18] The Moroccan monarchy aimed to maintain synergy between tradition and modernity in order to conserve its power; therefore it supported some women's issues and rejected radical Islamists that threatened Moroccan autocracy. It is important to keep in mind that even when the feminist movement was flourishing in the 1970s and 1980s, because women represented a potentially great political force, the political parties were using women to lead their own battles. Morocco did not experience political progress or relative democratization until the mid-1990s.[19] In 2004 the adopted family law, the *Mudawana*, was reformed to some extent to give women and men equal rights, while remaining consistent with the spirit of Islam: "women are no longer regarded as inferior but are now formally equal to their husbands within the family."[20] This revision was an extremely important development for the women's movement and for the participation of new political actors; however, it largely remained consistent with the spirit of Islam in that it did not entail democratization nor did it increase collective control as the reform process remained under the power of the monarchy.[21]

If women in Algeria played a crucial role in the war for independence, which started in 1956, they were reminded immediately afterward of their main role in the private space as guardians of familial traditions and symbols of national cohesion. Moreover, and under the regime of the one-party government, the National Liberation Front (*Front de Libération Nationale*, FLN) adopted some archaic values of Islamic traditionalism as a way of promoting its nationalism, as Partha Chaterjee points out: "the story of nationalism is necessarily a story of betrayal." He explains that "nationalism confers freedom only by imposing new controls, defines a cultural identity for the nation only by excluding many from its fold, and grants the dignity of citizenship to some because others could not be allowed to speak for themselves."[22] Nationalism in Algeria as well as the marginalization of assimilationists and minorities began in the 1940s with a greater mixing between the nation and the community. With support of Marxist groups opposed to the FLN, the feminist movement, which had been imprisoned in the framework of a one-party state, finally came out of hibernation in the 1980s. The movement focused its energies on the revision of the famous family code that was approved in 1984 by an FLN National Assembly, which was based on Islamic sharia law. In this regard, Fatima Sadiqi points out that the discourse of the Islamists vis-à-vis women's roles was never very different from that of the FLN. Both designated the private sphere of the family home as the women's space and maintained that women should leave their jobs for the thousands of young unemployed men.[23] Let's remember that just after attaining independence in 1962, the *Mujaheedates* (women fighters) were deeply disillusioned when they were asked to return to their homes and to their roles as mothers and guardians of the nation's traditions and values. However, it is worth noting that when President Houari Boumédiène removed Ahmed Ben Bella after an organized military coup in 1965, Algeria experienced a period of egalitarian socialist rule in which all minority groups were integrated and welcomed into the democratic project of the country. It was under the rule of Chadli Bendjedid in 1978 that Islamists started to gain more influence in the public sphere; as Benjamin Stora states, "in the twenty years following independence, religion was used as an instrument to contain possible advances in the secular and democratic currents, and, above all, as a weapon for the legitimization of power."[24] The economic crisis of the mid-1980s resulted in high unemployment rates and food shortages throughout the region as well as an enormous drop in oil prices worldwide. At this moment, Islamists saw an opportunity to recruit unemployed young men to propagate their extremist views, especially toward women. The government initially attempted to quell popular frustration and discontent by allowing for some reforms and calling for democratic elections in 1991. These elections were ultimately canceled when it became clear that they might have resulted in victory for Islamists. Several groups, such as the Islamic Salvation Front (*Front Islamique du Salut*, FIS) and the Islamic Armed Group (*Groupe Islamique Armé*, GIA), emerged immediately after the cancelation of the elections. These groups reacted fiercely to this repression and, as a result, for more than a decade, Algeria was devastated by a barbaric civil war, not only directed toward all that the Algerian regime represented but against the civilian population as well.

Despite the fact that women were the main victims of terrorist violence, they were at all times active in their society. In January 1992, women were the first to stage massive protests in major cities across Algeria, calling for the cancelation of the electoral process and warning of the dangers of becoming an Islamic republic. In 1999, after what was called the Black Decade, President Abdelaziz Bouteflika was elected. He promised to bring peace and social justice and to promote the cause of Algerian women. In 2004 the family code was slightly revised to give women more independence, especially regarding the requirement of having a matrimonial guardian.

Throughout modern history, in both Morocco and Algeria, women's efforts to attain independence were challenged on all fronts partly because their cause was often considered to be a movement that was heavily influenced and inspired by the West. Women's demands were portrayed as being a threat to the nation's authority. Any attempt at modernization threatened the purity of the nation and its values, thus representing the eternal debate between advocates of a discourse that lauds the return to tradition, and therefore authenticity, or *asalah*, and those who support progress, modernity, and the right to be different, a concept that traditionalists and nationalists deemed *bidaa*, a novelty that will turn into a type of heresy.

The history of these two countries in the postcolonial era has proven that political liberation from colonization did not lead to women's emancipation. Through their struggle against colonization and later against conservatism, women have always shown resistance against dogmatism and imposed gender hierarchy, expressing their disillusionment with the nationalist project through multiple means, whether through political vectors or various forms of self-expression, highlighting women's role in society as agents of transgression.

La transe des insoumis (*The Trance of the Rebellious*), a novel by Mokeddem, and *Rêves de femmes: Une enfance au harem* (*Dreams of Trespass: Tales of a Harem Girlhood*) by Mernissi, brilliantly illustrate the ongoing struggle that exists for those living in postcolonial states that have yet to find a manner in which to achieve social integration. These two semi-autobiographical accounts demonstrate how the deconstruction of the foundation of monolithic thinking and practice has to start from the inside, symbolically the home, in order to go beyond its walls and access the public space and to change the status quo. In other words, and in the social and political arena, these literary accounts emblematically support the notion that women, in order to gain more agency, have to challenge the patriarchal structure from its roots. Identifying the boundaries, especially those often drawn to confine women to the private sphere, is the first step toward crossing these boundaries. Finding fissures through which the feminine subject can begin to weaken and dismantle them would bring some vicissitudes. In this vein, these two narratives, among many others, can be classified as what Barbara Harlow calls "resistance literature." Long marginalized and often influenced by a specific geopolitical situation, this literary category, nevertheless, creates an atmosphere that allows for "a vision of new relational possibilities which transcend ethnic, class, and racial divisions as well as family ties."[25]

Furthermore, these texts encourage a reimagining of national identity, not only relating to the constitution of a nation-state after attaining independence but also aspiring to a transnational concept of identity, in the context of accelerated globalization in which the dividing lines between the local and the global tend to blur. Making reference to their own situations, both Mokeddem and Mernissi demonstrate that the boundaries imposed on women remain ambivalent and fluid, even often imagined or invented. Thus, these narratives represent the qualities of the national identity crises that have manifested in countries such as Morocco and Algeria, where there is perpetual hostility toward any group that threatens the stability of the nation-state.

Renowned sociologist Mernissi has written a number of essays with a feminist slant, as well as her celebrated fictionalized memoir, *Rêves de femmes*. Throughout her work, Mernissi has emphasized that women's oppression by

Islamic states is part of a larger effort to suppress democracy. She also argues that the misinterpretation of Islam and its regulations by male leaders is intended to maintain the status quo of women's long subordination. As she stresses: "Not only have the sacred texts always been manipulated, but manipulation of them is a structural characteristic of the practice of power in Muslim societies."[26]

Mokeddem, a prominent contemporary francophone writer, was born in Algeria and was forced into exile to escape from familial and social burdens and to seek education opportunities in France. Through her literary works, Mokeddem has explored several topics related to exile, nomadism, and wandering. She has also employed storytelling techniques in order to narrate an alternate version of Algerian history from a feminine and feminist perspective. In most of her novels, the female characters are, like Mokeddem, nomads who are also defiant figures in a society that stifles their freedom and their right to think and behave differently, "always rebels who never belong to any established system."[27]

Mernissi's memoir portrays a multitude of women in their struggle to obtain some degree of independence and agency. The memoir can be considered as a collective autobiography. In other words, if the female protagonist reveals herself as a singular voice and stands up to the community, whether patriarchal or national, a slippage toward the integration of other female voices takes place, representing Fatima's story and that of others. First, the feminine subject creates a form of personal historiography, or as bell hooks terms it, a "bio-mythography," or a "writing down of our meaning of identity . . . with the materials of our lives" through which the subject fuses "myth, dream, and reality in a process of self-narration that entails self-construction and self-recreation."[28] She gives narrative authority to other women who will in turn pass it on from one woman to the next. Therefore, Mernissi's narrative can be considered as a cultural autobiography, or what I call a sociobiography, in the sense that the traditional, autobiographical "I" transcends its individuality and becomes a collective one. In a gesture of solidarity, Mernissi demonstrates that she will have recourse to other women to dismantle the walls of the harem, and by extension, the nation. Throughout the text, we witness the profusion of polyphonic and embedded narratives, transmitted by her circle of female surroundings.[29] Furthermore, Mernissi challenges the norms of the traditional autobiography in order to insist on the porosity of the boundaries that separate genres by filling the narrative with intertextual references and metadiscursive comments, and at the peri-textual level, endnotes that inform the text with historical details from a feminist perspective. It is thus enriched, offering another type of knowledge and another typically female vision that in some ways transcends the official knowledge of the nation, challenging the nation's absolute control.

A single question seems to haunt the narrator—namely, how to identify and define the boundaries, or *hudud*, that confine women to their homes and, ultimately, how to find ways to dismantle them. As Mernissi explains in the memoir, "looking for the frontier has become my life's occupation."[30] By focusing on the multiple definitions of the word *hudud* in Arabic and by consulting a wide range of books including stories and legends, she demonstrates that the use of the word remains problematic due to its ambivalent nature. One must first know what side one is on, that of the dominator or the dominated. However, if "any transgression necessarily leads to anarchy and unhappiness," states Mernissi, "but women dreamed of trespassing all the time."[31]

If for women the harem is synonymous with prison, for men it might be thought of as a way to protect women from foreigners, in this case the colonizers. These distinctions are all the more important, since the harem can differ from one place to another; the urban harem is described very differently from the rural one where "there were truly no limits to what women could do on the farm."[32] The dividing lines were often blurry, as indicated by Fatima, a city girl, who could not sleep during her first nights spent at the harem in the country, because "there were no closed gates to be seen anywhere, only wide, flat, open fields where flowers grew and animal wandered peaceably about."[33] As I mentioned before, rural women in Morocco, even illiterates, were not passive. They developed empowering strategies of oral communication, using Berber and/or Moroccan Arabic, through which they expressed their views on politics and religion. Even dreams are fissures that can make the boundaries disappear, as Aunt Habiba states: "dreams can change your life, and eventually the world. Liberation starts with images in words."[34]

Furthermore, while the harem is a place where women can be shut in, it can also be a place, ironically, where powerful groups can protect themselves. During the occupation, the French built the new city as a sort of harem, only this time because they were afraid of getting lost in the old city of the natives. Like the women, the French didn't have the right to freely go into the Medina; "the Ville Nouvelle was like their harem."[35] Consequently, Mernissi underscores the fact that even men could have an internal harem of their own. When a man met an unveiled woman in the countryside, it was he who would cover his head with the hood of his *djellaba* and, in this case, explains Yasmina the grandmother, "the harem was in the peasant's head, inscribed somewhere under his forehead."[36] In addition, the possibility of having a harem remains a question of economic status; we see proof of this in the character of Hamed, the doorman for the harem, who is married and lives in a small house with his wife and their five children.

The recourse to orality, examined in this chapter, is one of the fissures that can contribute to the dismantling of the private-public boundaries, even in a symbolic way. Storytelling is a powerful method of subversion for women. In many cases the stories that are told and circulated among women are radically different from the original versions. These stories and their many variations and interpretations consequently challenge the history of the nation and, due to their tautological nature, evolve over time, serve new purposes, and propose new perspectives.

According to these works there are spaces within the home itself that can function as metonymies that shake the boundaries that separate the subject from the nation. For Mernissi, the hammam represents not only a space of female agency but also of resistance to patriarchal authority and to Western neoimperialism. For Mokeddem, the "guest room" is not only the space that the female narrator takes over, but it is also a space that allows for a deterritorializing of sorts. The narrator in this case symbolically creates a kind of transnational identity. Her takeover of this room will render the female character "unhomey" and therefore a stranger in a familiar space.

Fissures of Orality

In both autobiographical narratives of Mernissi and Mokeddem, storytelling is a powerful tool for subversion, as the act of oral transmission represents a form of shared agency. First, it is important to recall that Arab culture favors oral tradition over written record, especially given that the Koran was delivered and circulated orally until the death of the Prophet. The first sura in the Koran starts with this command: "Proclaim! [or Read!] in the name of thy Lord and Cherisher." Furthermore, the Arabic language has very different meanings when it is recited rather than written, since in the written form, the voweling, or *tashkil*, is not necessarily available to indicate the meanings of words. As for women, even in the pre-Islamic period—the *Jahiliya*—they could participate in the high culture of their society by sharing their poetry in front of large audiences. In the Arabian Peninsula, where the primordial genre was poetry, many women (about sixty, according to sources) were considered to be well-known poets, including al-Khansa, who had surpassed her male peers in one of the most prestigious genres at the time, the elegy (*ritha*). In addition, the most ancient texts from the Maghreb were women's oral accounts, dating back to the beginning of the nineteenth century. Known as *Al-Ruba'iyah*, this classic Bedouin poetic genre originating in Fez, Morocco, was sung until the mid-twentieth century to express women's visions about religion. In the postcolonial era and especially in the rural areas, women, mostly illiterate, spoke Berber and/or Moroccan Arabic in order to convey their political and religious views. Moreover, orality came to play a significant role in Morocco's struggle for independence and "women's oral sources in this respect are primary sources. The colonizers themselves were aware of the importance of such texts as the collections of Berber poetry gathered by Arséne Roux and his collaborators during the 1930s and the 1940s show."[37] And because this oral expression could be a threat to the patriarchal status quo and established order, the regime in power would always find ways to subjugate its role and status.

According to Sadiqi, "the absence of female oral literature in Moroccan official culture is mainly due to a rigid patriarchal system regulating gender behavior whereby women are excluded from public authority. Paradoxically, the anonymous aspect of oral female literature freed women's self-expression from social constraints and gave it space."[38]

As previously mentioned, resorting to storytelling is undeniably a resistance strategy. This is demonstrated in Mernissi's narrative by the theatrical performances that take place on the harem's terrace, an exclusively female place, forbidden to men. Not only were tales and legends from *One Thousand and One Nights* performed there, but changes were also made to the original stories, and certain stories were favored over others or certain parts of the story were emphasized, in particular those that encourage revolt or change, as in the tale of the winged woman who could fly away from the court when she wanted. Thus, these performances, enhancing the oral tradition, introduced all kinds of heretical interpretations and distortions. Moreover, it is significant that during these performances, cousin Chama, assisted by a whole team of actresses, technicians, and even acrobats, staged the lives of certain women who represented models of emancipation, such as the singer Asmahan who "showed Arab women that a life filled with deliberate self-indulgence, as short and scandalous as it might be, can be better than a long and respectable one devoted to a lethargic tradition."[39] Other heroines such as Egyptian and Lebanese feminists, the pioneers for women's rights—among others Aisha Taymur, Zaynab Fawwaz, and Huda Sha'rawi—were frequently portrayed. A transnational vision of history is emphasized, not only because the lives of these feminists coming from all the Arab countries were represented but also because history books on Sudan, the kingdoms of Songhai and Ghana, were being read.[40]

In bringing a vision from the past into contact with that of the present, these performances had a certain narrative authority that challenged the single accepted version of history as well as the standardized rhetoric of the nation, insofar as transmission proved to be important and to have an impact on the public, which was primarily composed of women and children. In other words, these creative presentations resisted the dominant official vision and in so doing, shook off some of the impermeable, unwavering boundaries erected by those who claimed to speak on behalf of the nation and whose objective was to maintain the status quo. The restricted space of the terrace thus became the emblem of creativity, fulfillment, and liberation, as Fatima affirms: "Chama's theater provided wonderful opportunities for all of us to discover and show our talents, overcome our shyness and develop some self-confidence."[41]

Finally, even if these performances took place in the private sphere and only women and children had access to them, they did provide for each woman an opportunity to discover and demonstrate her talents, by having a role in the plays and by overcoming her shyness and developing her self-confidence. Consequently, the idea of having a role and participating in a collective project elevated her self-image.

In all her books, Mokeddem favors the oral tradition as a means of communication, through tales, laments, and proverbial narratives, inspired by *One Thousand and One Nights*. In *La transe des insoumis*, the grandmother reaffirms: "The immobility of those who stay-at-home is a death that has already taken hold of me by the feet. Now, I only have traveling through words."[42] The imaginary created through words constitutes one of the fissures through which the female narrator frees herself from the confines of the private sphere. It also seems to be the only way to resist the culture of immobility and to preserve a nomadic lifestyle in the face of progress that is imported, even imposed, by the colonizer and the new nation-state. According to the narrator, the nomadic culture, through words and storytelling, "when it vibrates with emotion, nourishes the spirit, enriches the memory."[43] It stands in opposition to print culture—a facet of the nation-state in the modern sense of the word—and "is paralyzed by prohibitions and erected as prison."[44] Storytelling thus underscores the taking on of a narrative voice, which can lead to a kind of awareness and brings to light its revolutionary scope, challenging all that is forbidden insofar as it is during her wakeful nights. In reaction to a story relayed to her, the narrator says, "It's the first love story I've been told. I don't know what this word love entails. But the load of mysteries and taboos it carries with it has an effect."[45]

It is worth noting that the narrator's insomnia symbolizes another fissure through which Mokeddem can free herself from familial constraints. She transgresses the bounds of her own family's natural rhythm in that she lies awake and reads books with fervor under her blanket and sleeps during the day: "To read all night and sleep in the morning, to live out of sync with the others—like an American [as her mother scolds her]—allows me to escape from the activities that devour my days and terrify me."[46] Insomnia also reinforces her displacement, given that it erases the borders between the states of wakefulness and sleep and becomes a site of resistance; a right that she appropriates for herself: "The right to insomnia is the right to have my own body, separate from the family unit that I am conquering."[47] This seems to be Mokeddem's position, favoring the "in-betweenness" that allows her to travel all over, tirelessly, thanks to the power and magic of words, in her desert lost forever.[48]

Storytelling and theatrical performances thus become ways to retell the story of the nation from a different perspective that incorporates the Other.

Places of Resistance

In the two narratives, as previously mentioned, the foundations of the nation would be dismantled from within the home, thanks to the fissures through which the narrators undertake a transgression of the patriarchal laws that weigh on them. Furthermore, the house located in the indigenous neighborhood in the two narratives is a place that represents a contrast to the French neighborhood that remains closed off like a harem, a place where, Mernissi seems to imply, the French protect themselves from the natives. For Mokeddem, on the other hand, the two quarters were separated by the path she took to go to school every day, the path that symbolized, as she explains, a "space of meeting in sum, of cohabitation whose threshold for tolerance is very low, if not insurmountable."[49]

For Mernissi, the hammam functions as a metonymy for liberation through which the women attempt to dismantle the boundaries of the harem and, by extension, the nation. In the rigid architecture, as with Islamic art, the hammam seems to be the only place that evades strict patriarchal norms. It becomes a liberating space insofar as it gives women the power to demonstrate solidarity among themselves. A symbol for reclusion and passivity in the Orientalist imagination, the hammam is transformed into a space of autonomy, even agency, as one of the characters in the narrative confirms: "as far as Aunt Habiba was concerned, women's liberation had to start with skin toning and massage."[50] The hammam, as experienced by Mernissi, was very particular in the sense that it was a beauty salon; men were prohibited, as was Western influence. By using a variety of local natural products including rose water, henna, almond oil, dates, and honey, these women rejected commercialized products and manufactured cosmetic treatments that husbands had brought over from France. Thus, the hammam, an indigenous salon par excellence, turns into a place of resistance, the only place where women became masters. In addition, the desire to control the appearance of their bodies deconstructs the image of the Oriental woman who is passively reclining in the hammam and endures with nonchalance the imposing gestures of a masseuse, and thus challenges the objectification of the Oriental body prevalent in Western discourse.

The guest room for Mokeddem is another metonymy for the deconstruction of the patriarchal space and, by extension, the nationalist discourse. An unused room, since it was reserved for guests who rarely came due to the challenges of travel at the time of colonization, is taken over by Malika, feeling the growing oppression and hostility that her family is demonstrating toward her because of her rebellious nature, while the sixteen other family members pile in on top of each other in the other three rooms. Barricaded in the guest room, Mokeddem proclaims:

> Never a servant, no. I am the Guest. I intrude on my own family as a guest. Amidst orality, I live buried in my books. Books are my only friends. I even put in three shelves for them in *the guest room*. It's my own little revolution! The sign that I am in the process of becoming a stranger among my own. Removed from their days and their nights. A life on the margins. I'm obsessed with the idea.[51]

Within this room, Malika literally and symbolically constructs another wall, doubly protecting herself from social subjugation, by piling books up around her to push away any threat coming from the outside world, like "a paper rampart to protect against bottles, soups, screams, piss."[52] However, even if books condemn her to solitude, the fact remains that they offer incommensurable possibilities for liberation and enjoyment, and the narrator emphasizes: "A euphoria comes over me at this unexpected discovery: my book, my notebook are undecipherable for my mother. Impenetrable spaces, they keep her at a distance."[53] It is worth noting that books and reading could function as another means of transgression and of putting boundaries between herself and her family, which is for her a source of menace.

With these two narratives, I have tried to illustrate some fissures that female subjects have identified and utilized as a way of renegotiating the terms of their own space. Even if these fissures are temporary, imperceptible, and at times imaginary, and thus do not create radical changes, the fact remains that they give female protagonists self-awareness and a certain control, however limited, over their own voices and bodies.

Thus, the narratives of both Mokeddem and Mernissi demonstrate the confusion and turmoil of the times as well as the consequences of living in a nation-state that discourages solidarity and manifests hostility toward any group that could potentially threaten its stability. They also show, however, that boundaries that demarcate the nation-state are no longer impermeable, especially when the nation loses its legitimacy and authority. The crisis of legitimacy is due, in part, to the complicated national identity crisis that has been facing Algeria and Morocco for many years now. On the one hand, it is a national project of a moral nature that hides its political agenda and relies on traditional religious discourse to encourage the establishment of a national sense of community. On the other hand, references to state of laws call for compliance and good citizenship in the name of democracy and progress.

In the face of the erosion of these self-sustaining governments as well as the intense development of popular opposition, the loss of credibility and power is unavoidable, thus demonstrating the need for that which these two countries are still struggling to attain—namely, the creation of a national project that would integrate minority groups into society in a manner that would allow them to continue to think and behave as individuals. For their part, and by refuting homogeneity encouraged by the state, Mernissi and Mokeddem have succeeded in symbolically demystifying national histories by insisting on the importance of the role of those who belong to minority groups who are often excluded from participation in the state discourse. The stakes are more complex when those minorities reside in more than one state or when their home territory extends beyond the boundaries of the nation and is replaced by a supranational structure.

The strategies described in these narratives offer ways to bridge cultural divisions imposed by dictum, creating a crossing of boundaries and therefore a transgression that would allow for women protagonists, as Mokeddem describes them, "without borders and without taboos."[54] Keeping women confined "inside" results in turning those women, and possibly the nation as whole, into what Gloria Anzaldua calls "boundary subjects."[55]

Another factor that further complicates the identity issue for women in Algeria and Morocco, one that distinguishes them from other Arab countries, is their unavoidable cultural hybridity, or *métissage*, due to their multilingualism (mother tongues: Berber, classical and dialectical Arabic) and multiculturalism (French, Arabic, Berber, and Jewish cultures in Morocco), and what Abdelkébir Khatibi calls "The Multifarious Maghreb."[56] This plurality renders them unique and may serve as an advantage in that by embracing both Islamic and Western cultural commodities, these women are innately shaped by a transgressive mode of thinking that may allow them to experience a new social and personal equilibrium. This level of understanding and balance, which stands in stark contrast to the polarizing national disenchantment of the times, might inspire the region to move gradually and intuitively toward modernization and progress.

NÉVINE EL NOSSERY is Associate Professor in the Departments of French and Italian, and African Cultural Studies at the University of Wisconsin, Madison. She is author of *Temoignages Fictionnels Au Feminin: Une Reecriture Des Blancs de La Guerre Civile Algerienne* and coeditor of *The Unspeakable: Representations of Trauma in Francophone Literature and Art.*

Notes

1. Mounira Charrad, "State and Gender in the Maghrib," in *Arab Women Between Defiance and Restraint*, ed. Suha Sabbagh (New York: Olive Branch, 1996), 222.

2. *Hudud*, the Arabic word حدود, is the plural of حد and means "limit or boundary." In a religious context, it refers to the laws enforced by God.

3. In her seminal book, *Women and Gender in Islam: Historical Roots of a Modern Debate* (New Haven, CT: Yale University Press, 1992), Leila Ahmed examines these significant transformations through time and space.

4. A quick example, and a very well-known one, is of Khadija, the Prophet Muhammed's wife, who, before marrying him, was a widow and enjoyed a relatively flourishing economic position, which she had attained thanks to her prosperous business. She had employed Muhammed to manage her affairs and monitor her caravans between Mecca and Syria before asking him to marry her, at the age of forty, while he was only twenty-five. Furthermore, she remained his only wife until her death at sixty-six years old. It was after the death of the Prophet in 632 and with the relative establishment of Islam in the Arab Peninsula, not only

as a religious institution but also as a political entity, that a certain animosity toward women began to emerge. The caliph Omar Ibn El Khatab, whose reign extended from 634 to 644, was very harsh toward his wives. He also chose a male imam to lead women's prayer, whereas in the time of Muhammed, a woman, Umm Waraka, was the imam designated for women by the Prophet.

5. For more details, see Fatima Mernissi, *Le Harem politique: Le Prophète et les femmes* (Paris: Albin Michel, 1987).

6. A semantic slippage from "curtain" to "veil" occurred based on this verse from the Koran: "And when you ask [his wives] for something, ask them from behind a *partition*. That is purer for your hearts and their hearts." Sura 33, verse 53, https://quran.com/33 (emphasis added). The word *hijab* in Arabic could mean "curtain," and not necessarily a scarf to be worn. However, this separation, at first reserved for the wives of the Prophet Muhammed, would later be interpreted as a veil to cover women's hair and body.

7. Mernissi, *Le Harem*, 136.

8. Ibid., 30.

9. Whereas the verb نشز literally means "an elevated place," when used as an adjective, it means "discordant" and could refer to an overbearing or scolding wife.

10. Nira Yuval-Davis and Floya Anthias, *Women-Nation-State* (Hampshire, UK: Macmillan, 1989), 7.

11. As in Clifford Geertz, *Old Societies and New States: The Quest for Modernity in Asia and Africa* (New York: Free Press, 1963).

12. Mahmood Mamdani, *Citizen and Subject: Contemporary Africa and the Legacy of Late Colonialism* (Princeton, NJ: Princeton University Press, 1991), 8.

13. Charrad, "State and Gender," 223.

14. Pierre Bourdieu, *La Domination masculine* (Paris: Seuil, 1998), 33 (my translation).

15. Elleke Boehmer, "Stories of Women and Mothers: Gender and Nationalism in the Early Fiction of Flora Nwapa," in *Motherlands: Black Women's Writing from Africa, the Caribbean and South Asia*, ed. Susheila Nasta (London: Women's Press, 1991), 5.

16. Homi Bhabha, "The World and the Home," *Social Text* 10, no. 2–3 (1992): 143.

17. Fatima Mernissi, *Dreams of Trespass: Tales of a Harem Girlhood* (New York: Perseus, 1994), 226.

18. Fatima Sadiqi, in her article "Women, Islam, and Political Agency in Morocco," points out that the rise of political Islam and the return of conservatism were due mainly to the success of the Iranian Revolution in 1979, the downfall of the Soviet Union in 1981, the emergence of the United States as a superpower, the invasion of Iraq, the Israeli occupation of Palestine, and the spread of ideas by globalization. In *Women in the Middle East and North Africa: Agents of Change*, ed. Fatima Sadiqi and Moha Ennaji (New York: Routledge, 2011), 39–42.

19. Morocco witnessed "the first ever socialist government in 1998, a new and more open king in 1999, a quota system in the 2001 elections, 35 women in the Parliament in 2002, a new family Law in 2003, and more women in the highest religious offices in 2004." Sadiqi, "Women, Islam, and Political Agency," 40.

20. Julie Pruzan-Jørgensen, "Islam, Gender, and Democracy in Morocco: The Making of the Mudawana Reform," in *Gender and Islam in Africa: Rights, Sexuality, and Law*, ed. Margot Badran (Washington, DC: Woodrow Wilson Center Press, 2011), 233.

21. Ibid., 254.

22. Partha Chatterjee, *Nationalism Thought and the Colonial World: A Derivative Discourse* (Minneapolis: University of Minnesota Press, 1993), 154.

23. Sadiqi, "Women, Islam, and Political Agency," 43.

24. Benjamin Stora, *Algeria 1830–2000: A Short History* (Ithaca, NY: Cornell University Press, 2001), 171.

25. Barbara Harlow, *Resistance Literature* (New York: Methuen, 1987), 142.

26. Fatima Mernissi, *The Veil and the Male Elite: A Feminist Interpretation of Women's Rights in Islam* (New York: Addison Wesley, 1992), 8–9.

27. Malika Mokeddem, *Les hommes qui marchent* (Paris: Ramsay, 1990), 70 (my translation).

28. Quoted in Caren Kaplan, "Resisting Autobiography: Out-Law Genres and Transnational Feminist Subjects," in *Women, Autobiography, Theory: A Reader*, ed. Sidonie Smith and Julia Watson (Madison: University of Wisconsin Press, 1998), 330–334.

29. While the narration opens in the first person with the narrator telling bits and pieces of her personal life, it also tells pieces about other women who populated her past and her childhood, and ultimately uses, through caustic writing in the last pages of the story, narration in the present about women in general.

30. Mernissi, *Dreams of Trespass*, 3.

31. Ibid., 2–3.

32. Ibid., 55.

33. Ibid., 25.

34. Ibid., 114.

35. Ibid., 23.

36. Ibid., 62.

37. Sadiqi, "Women, Islam, and Political Agency," 44.

38. Ibid., 41.

39. Mernissi, *Dreams of Trespass*, 107.

40. Sadiqi, "Women, Islam, and Political Agency," 129–130.

41. Ibid., 126.

42. Malika Mokeddem, *La transe des insoumis* (Paris: LGF, 2005), 56. All quotes from *La transe* are my translation.

43. Ibid., 27.

44. Ibid.

45. Ibid., 46. This motif comes up in several of Mokeddem's novels. In *Les hommes qui marchent* (*The Men Who Walk*), the grandmother reminds Leïla, "un conteur est un être fantasque. Il se joue de tout. Même de sa propre histoire. Il la trafique entre ses rêves et les perditions de la réalité. Il n'existe que dans cet entre-deux / Un 'entre' sans cesse déplacé" (A storyteller is fanciful. He plays with everything. Even with his own story. He traffics it between his dreams and the reality's perditions. He exists only in this in-between / An "in-between" constantly moved), 10 (my translation). In *Le Siècle des sauterelles* (Paris: Ramsay, 1992), we read, "Conter, c'est échapper à l'instant. C'est refuser de n'être jamais qu'une borne de sa course. Conter, c'est le saisir en plein temps. C'est le déplier en éventail de mots. Tu t'en éventes et le railles. Puis tu le replies, fermé dans le nœud de la narration. Tu en cueilles un autre et tu recommences à l'effeuiller" (Telling stories is to escape the moment. It is to refuse to just being one of its limits. Telling stories is to grab it at once. It is to unfold it as a fan of words. You fan yourself with it and then you rib it. Then you fold it again and close it at the node of the story. You pick up another and you start again to pluck it), 46 (my translation).

46. Mokeddem, *La transe*, 141.

47. Ibid., 157.

48. Ibid., 11.

49. Ibid., 110.

50. Mernissi, *Dreams of Trespass*, 226.
51. Mokeddem, *La transe*, 147 (emphasis added).
52. Ibid., 141.
53. Ibid., 156.
54. Yolande Helm, "Entrevue avec Malika Mokeddem," *Le Maghreb littéraire* 3, no. 5 (1999): 14.
55. Gloria Anzaldua, *Borderlands/La Frontera: The New Mestiza* (San Francisco: Spinsters/Aunt Lute, 1987), 165.
56. Abdelkébir Khatibi, *Maghreb pluriel* (Paris: Denoël, 1983) (my translation).

8 The Sudanese Nation and Its Fragments

Tayeb Salih's Literary Archaeology

Sofia Samatar

Tayeb Salih did not live to see the official division of his country: he died in 2009, two years before Sudan became the two nations of Sudan and South Sudan. Yet Salih witnessed the years of nearly constant civil war from independence in 1956 until his death, and *Bandarshah*, his final work of long fiction, represents this conflict as an unfinished quest for national identity. *Bandarshah* approaches this problem through an exploration of the relationship between community and authority, a double preoccupation expressed in its title, as Salih explained in a 1977 interview: "I have chosen the name . . . because our problem is the search for the City (*bandar*), and also the search for a form of government that suits us—authority (*shāh*)."[1] The goal of the quest is a unified social body, gathered under a single ruler; for Sudan, this quest was already hampered by grave difficulties in the 1960s and 1970s, when *Bandarshah* was conceived and written. The challenge of reaching consensus on national identity among the population of the south, most of whom practiced Christianity or traditional African religions and identified themselves as African, and the largely Muslim population of the north, who identified themselves as Arab, led directly to a second problem: the development of a constitution and system of law that would be acceptable to all Sudanese.[2] These intertwined problems, which concern community (*bandar*), on the one hand, and state and civil authority (*shāh*), on the other, are approached in Salih's text through a family drama. Through the representation of three generations, Salih reveals the manner in which the construction of an Arab-Muslim Sudanese national identity, a project launched from a subordinate position vis-à-vis colonial authority, became an oppressive authority in its turn. Excavating fragments of black African identity from his northern Sudanese setting, Salih attempts to trace a buried genealogy of Sudan, in search of an alternative and more pluralistic "narrative of community."[3]

The two volumes, originally titled *Dau al-Beit* and *Meryoud*, of Tayeb Salih's *Bandarshah* appeared in 1971 and 1976. The 1996 English translation combines these two novels into a single volume. This work was to have had at least four parts: "It may reach five parts. . . . God knows," Salih said in a 1977 interview.[4] Salih never published the rest of *Bandarshah*, nor has any information regarding a possible manuscript version come to light since his death. *Bandarshah* must be taken at face value, then, as a pair of linked novels. Like all of Salih's novels and short stories, this work is set in Wad Hamid, an imaginary village in northern Sudan. In discussing his choice of setting, Salih described his method as one of excavation, in which he explored an area that "was Pharaonic, heathen, Christian and then . . . Muslim" in order to dig deeply into its past: "I am trying to work as though digging archaeologically."[5] *Bandarshah* brims with the results of this imagined excavation. Its epigraphs include quotations from the Arab-Persian poet Abu Nuwas and from *Kalilah wa Dimnah*, an Arabic version of an Indian collection of fables, highlighting the links between the Arabic literary tradition and a larger Asian culture. The different tales centering around the text's eponymous hero reveal further cultural variety: Bandarshah is not only a powerful personality of Wad Hamid but also, in the different accounts, a Christian Nubian king, a pagan king, and an Abyssinian prince.[6] The representation of diverse cultural elements is underscored by a formal heterogeneity: *Bandarshah* is exceedingly episodic and disjunctive, employing different narrators, switching between first- and third-person point of view, and leaping back and forth in time. Yet together with a rich cultural diversity, Salih's text depicts a patriarchal and Arabized authority that excludes women and black Africans from full participation in the community. In what follows, I examine the two major symbols of this authority, the name and the whip. Taken together, these symbols illuminate the workings of the dominant *shāh*, whose victimization of the nation's unassimilable fragments relegates the *bandar* to an ever-receding horizon.

To begin with the name: the title of the text, *Bandarshah*, is the name of the grand figure of the village of Wad Hamid, a formidable and ultimately tragic man, the father of eleven sons. The name "Bandarshah" is not Arabic in origin, but Persian, a childhood nickname attached to the character: the village children called him "Bandarshah" because of his fine clothes, and also perhaps because his father was a foreigner of unknown origin. The name of Bandarshah's father is Dau al-Beit; this name serves as the title of the first volume of *Bandarshah*. The title of the second novel, *Meryoud*, is the name of Bandarshah's grandson. These titles frame the text within Bandarshah's genealogy. It is a genealogy marked by violence, prefigured by the Oedipal drama that introduces the narrative: the main character, Meheimeed, returns to his home village of Wad Hamid to find that his friend Mahjoub, once the head of the village cooperative, has been deposed by his own nephew. Mahjoub opens the novel, seated in the first sentence, "like an old tiger."[7] This tiger is toothless, rendered obsolete by a younger group known as "Bakri's boys." "From that day on," a friend of Meheimeed's informs him, "[Mahjoub] walks the face of the earth as though dead."[8]

The new generation leaves its elders "dead": at first glance, a rather banal occurrence, painful to those on the losing side of the Oedipal struggle, but natural enough. Yet at the heart of *Dau al-Beit* lays a most unnatural murder, an event so appalling that it is covered with a veil of allusive language. It is a "catastrophe that defies description, be it in a single journey or in several," the deep event below the surface event of the battle for the village cooperative.[9] This "catastrophe" is mentioned in chapter two, but its details are not revealed until chapter seven, and even then the facts are stated in the gnomic language of fable, so that it is easy to miss the actual deaths that have occurred in the village:

> They were eleven brothers, slaves to what had passed and to what would not come about in a clearly defined form. One day they rebelled and destroyed the two of them together. Houses were made desolate, tracks were obliterated, and the soldiers came and led them off to prison.[10]

This is the catastrophe that defies description: the obliteration of three generations overnight. The eleven brothers are Bandarshah's eleven sons. They are enslaved to "what had passed"—Bandarshah himself—and "what would not come about in a clearly defined form"—Bandarshah's grandson, Meryoud. The image of a future infinitely deferred recalls Antonio Gramsci's interregnum, in which "the old is dying and the new cannot be born"; the rebellion of the eleven brothers, a "morbid symptom" of apocalyptic proportions, destroys grandfather and grandson together.[11] *Dau al-Beit* is subtitled "A Tale of How a Father Becomes a Victim of His Father and His Son," but this is more than a tale of the father's victimization. It is a tale of the father's counterviolence, of the brutal and fruitless—because eventually "led off to prison"—revenge of the present.

Gramsci's interregnum describes a "crisis of authority," in which the popular masses have grown apart from the ruling ideology, so that this ideology can only be maintained through force.[12] The description resonates with *Bandarshah*, in which the interregnum takes the form of a closed circle created by Bandarshah and Meryoud. Meryoud is "a complete replica of his grandfather," we read, so that "when you stood between them, it was as though you were standing between two mirrors placed opposite each other, each reflecting the same image in an endless extension."[13] This continuity is introduced as positive, as the villagers admire Bandarshah's powerful and successful family, but it also has a sinister side, expressed in the scene immediately following the preceding quotation, when Meryoud, "the complete embodiment of [Bandarshah's] authority," bullies Meheimeed's grandfather into selling him a calf at a low price.[14] Meheimeed's grandfather easily acquiesces to the demands of Meryoud, a fifteen-year-old boy, and accepts being greeted by name rather than addressed as "Uncle" or "Grandfather." "At any rate," he reflects philosophically, "dealing with the boy is better than dealing with his grandfather."[15] This scene introduces the idea that the authority of Bandarshah/Meryoud is in fact tyranny—that is, authority in crisis. It also hints at an affinity between Bandarshah and Meheimeed's grandfather, who is "happy at that abnormal event," and whose companions express "reverence" and gaze at Meryoud as if at "an angel that has descended from above."[16] Waïl Hassan notes how the unexpected delight of the elderly men at Meryoud's insolence reveals a desire for power: "As the mirror image and extension of his grandfather—a 'reconciliation' between past and future—Meryoud is the embodiment of the elders' desire for continuity, free from the threat of their sons' Oedipal impulses."[17] Meheimeed, too, is drawn to this idea of a "reconciliation" with the past, but is overcome by an otherworldly vision that emphasizes its dangers: amid howling winds, leaping afreets and images ephemeral as "specks of dust," he observes one striking sight, and the tense of the paragraph shifts from past to present:

> Then, with a rushing and a roaring, the images are welded together, mingle and form a tangible shape, that of Bandarshah in the form of Meryoud; or Meryoud in the form of Bandarshah; and it is as though he is sitting on the throne of that hubbub, gripping the threads of chaos in both hands, amidst it and above it at one and the same time, like a resplendent and destructive ray.[18]

In this vision, the past and the future, represented by Bandarshah and Meryoud, become one, and claim an unnatural and paralyzing authority over the present. The stasis of the "destructive ray," untouched by the chaos it controls, recalls the shining, closed circle of the doubled mirror. The present is trapped in that circle. It is like Bandarshah's eleven sons, observed by Meheimeed in another waking dream: he enters a magical citadel in the desert where he sees Bandarshah, seated on a throne, ordering Meryoud to flog the eleven brothers. Here the whip figures as a symbol of oppressive authority: "The universe was silent: deaf, dumb and blind but for the whipcracks on the backs of Bandarshah's sons, within sight and earshot of their father, and performed by the grandson on behalf of the grandfather."[19]

What is the origin of this terrifying authority? Despite his foreign nickname, Bandarshah was born in Wad Hamid; yet his father, Dau al-Beit, was a stranger to the village, and there is much to suggest that he was a soldier in the Ottoman army. Wounded and suffering from memory loss, Dau al-Beit was cast up from the Nile near Wad Hamid, dressed in the uniform of a Turkish soldier, and the villagers, choosing to believe that his presence would bring them prosperity, gave him an Arabic name that means "The Light of the House."[20] Dau al-Beit's wedding to a daughter of the village is a key moment in the text, a lyrical expression of communal joy:

> Tonight every old man is young, every young man is infatuated with love, every woman truly feminine, every man an Abu Zeid al-Hilali. Tonight everything

> is alive. . . . Every limb walks with a swinging gait, every breast trembles, every buttock quivers, every eye is darkened with kohl, every cheek is smooth, every mouth is honeyed, every waist slim, every action beautiful—and all the people are Dau al-Beit.[21]

As in the earlier passage describing Meheimeed's vision, there is a shift into the present tense here, but while the earlier unity that present-tense language evoked was that of Bandarshah and Meryoud alone, the unity here is that of Dau al-Beit and "all the people." The eroticized language of the passage, employing well-known tropes of Arabic love poetry (the slim waist, the honeyed mouth), celebrates Dau al-Beit's physical union, through his bride, with the Arabic-speaking people of Wad Hamid. It is a joyful absorption of his foreign body, through which all the men in attendance become Abu Zeid al-Hilali, the hero of the famous Arabic folk epic. Yet this wedding will produce tragedy, and the tragedy is embedded, like a portent, in the wedding ceremony itself. Immediately following the statement that "all the people are Dau al-Beit," the bridegroom is represented as "standing in the center of the circle brandishing a whip of hippopotamus hide above the women dancers, while the men sprang one after another into the circle to vie with one another, and he would strike about him as he pleased."[22] The scene represents the practice of *al-buṭān*, the whipping ceremony of traditional northern Sudanese weddings, in which male guests remove their upper garments in order to be whipped by the groom.[23] A test of endurance and fearlessness expressive of a masculine ideal, *al-buṭān* requires men not to flinch under the lash. It is linked to the ethos of chivalry and physical prowess expressed most richly in the pre-Islamic poetry of Arabia, which is considered the highest moment of Arabic literature.[24]

By taking up the whip at his wedding and lashing the men of Wad Hamid, the foreigner Dau al-Beit confirms his kinship with them and becomes heir to their traditions. Yet his participation in *al-buṭān* cannot be read as merely an expression of his new communal ties. The joy of the moment is compromised by two earlier whipping scenes: Meheimeed's vision, in which Bandarshah's sons are whipped by his grandson, and the whipping contest among the boys of Wad Hamid, including the young Bandarshah.

The story of the boys' whipping contest is related in the fourth chapter of *Dau al-Beit* by Hamad Wad Haleema, a childhood friend of Meheimeed's grandfather. In this chapter, the tropes of the name and the whip are woven together, beginning with a reflection on the process of naming. "This business of names is extraordinary," Hamad says.[25] He lists a number of village nicknames, including Bandarshah's, and then moves on to the story of his own name, which was given to him by the bully Mukhtar Wad Hasab ar-Rasoul. Hamad, the narrator of the chapter, is known as "Wad Haleema," a derogatory appellation, as it names him "son of Haleema," his mother, rather than "son of Abdul Khalek," his father.

Hamad recounts how the boys of Wad Hamid used to take turns whipping one another, to see how long each of them could stand it, and how the bully Mukhtar habitually mocked Hamad, who feared the lash: "Whenever he met up with me," Hamad says, "he'd make fun of me, calling me by my mother's name because of the great contempt he had for me."[26] Finally, Hamad relates, he avenged himself by numbing his body with red pepper before the whipping contest. He was then able both to bear the lash and to whip Mukhtar senseless, as well as humiliating him by calling him by *his* mother's name: "Wad Maymouna."[27]

This anecdote introduces the name of the mother. In so doing, it highlights the fact that authority in Wad Hamid is under the male name. The perfect symmetry of Bandarshah and Meryoud, which creates a closed circle of oppression, is only possible because both characters are male. The whipping contest extends the problem of the doubled maleness of Bandarshah and Meryoud into the lives of other characters. It shows how the dangerous Bandarshah/Meryoud continuity, characterized by coerciveness, violence, and an absolute maleness in which the mother's name has no place, is not only accepted but fully inhabited by the community. Both Meheimeed's vision of the whipping in the citadel, and the whipping contest among the boys, comment on the whipping ceremony during the ecstatic moment of Dau al-Beit's wedding. The whip moves from the outside (a fantastic vision out in the desert), to the fringe of the community (boys playing games), to the heart of the village: the wedding, the greatest celebration of the continuity of Wad Hamid. Its significance also expands, from the Bandarshah family, a particular group of individuals, to the village boys, to "all the people." That double movement, from outside to inside, from the particular to the general, undoes the uniqueness of Bandarshah and his sons, the special status claimed for them in chapter two by the admiring villagers, who declare: "Bandarshah and his sons aren't like us."[28] This putative difference is challenged by the implied symmetry between Bandarshah and Meheimeed's grandfather, and also by the practice of naming grandsons for grandfathers, which is common in the village, and results in what Hassan calls a "monotonous pattern of names."[29] These hints that Bandarshah's family is not outside the culture of the village, but emblematic of it, are confirmed in the wedding scene. The ceremony of *al-buṭān* both prefigures the violent future of Dau al-Beit's family and marks that future as socially sanctioned.

There is a critique of gender norms here, focused on the privileging of aggressive masculinity and the absence of the female name. This line of thought is inseparable from a second critique, which addresses the suppression of ethnic difference. This second critique also emerges during that pivotal moment, the celebration of Dau al-Beit's wedding, through two statements: the claim that "all the people are Dau al-Beit," and that "every man [is] an Abu Zeid al-Hilali."

To claim "all the people are Dau al-Beit" is to claim that all the people are foreigners with amnesia. Dau al-Beit, after all, is a foreign invader and colonizer; he is able to integrate himself into Wad Hamid only because he has lost his identity. The reference to Abu Zeid al-Hilali emphasizes the condition of the amnesiac foreigner: Abu Zeid is the hero of the famous Arabic folk epic *Sīrat Banī Hilāl* or "the saga of the tribe of Banu Hilal," which is based on the invasion of the Maghreb by a tribe of Bedouin Arabs in the eleventh century. The Banu Hilal had migrated to Egypt from Arabia during the eighth and ninth centuries and were mobilized by the Egyptian Fatimid leaders in the eleventh century against the ruler of the Tunisian littoral.[30] Fourteenth-century historian Ibn Khaldun writes that the Banu Hilal arrived "like a cloud of locusts."[31] This historical incident provides the raw material for a cycle of tales known throughout the Arabic-speaking world, where it continues to circulate both in printed versions and in oral performance.

Abu Zeid, the hero of the epic, is black. His blackness is essential to the workings of the narrative, for the drama of *Sīrat Banī Hilāl* turns on the refusal of Abu Zeid's Arab father to accept his black son, and the eventual rise of this black Arab outcast to the leadership of the tribe. The story of Abu Zeid al-Hilali expresses, Bridget Connelly writes, "the traumas still fresh in Arab-African identity"—what Sayyid Hurreiz has called "the dilemma of the Sudanese."[32] In the many versions of the epic that proliferate across northern Africa, Abu Zeid's physical description signals his mixed heritage: he may be black with blue or green eyes, or black with "white features" or even "piebald."[33] This description is almost precisely that of Bandarshah, Dau al-Beit's mixed-blood son: "black of face like his mother, his eyes green like those of his father: a person apart, resembling neither this nor that."[34]

It is worth noting that of all the Arabic folk epics or romances featuring black heroes, *Sīrat Banī Hilāl* is the most amnesiac.[35] 'Antarah, for example, the other widely known black hero of the genre, is the son of a black slave woman, while Abu Zeid's tale avoids the admission of black ancestry by invoking a miracle. According to the story, Abu Zeid's mother, Khadra, went down to the river with ninety maidens to bathe and saw a powerful black bird scattering all the other birds away from the water. She wished for a son as powerful as that bird, and Abu Zeid was the result.[36] Khadra is the daughter of the Sharif of Mecca, and her husband, Abu Zeid's father, is a Hilali, the leader of the Banu Hilal. Abu Zeid, then, is black by accident. He is Arab on his father's side, and on his mother's side he is not only Arab but also a descendent of the Prophet Mohammed.

This story, based on an Arab movement into Africa, featuring a black hero, and insisting that this hero is not African, but Arab, does indeed express a Sudanese dilemma. This dilemma is bound up with the history of slavery in Sudan and its effects on Sudanese national identity, a fragment Salih unearths in *Bandarshah*. In chapter four of *Meryoud*, Meheimeed gathers a number of folk histories that yield conflicting versions of Bandarshah's genealogy: Bandarshah is declared to be a Christian king, then a pagan king, and then an Abyssinian prince. A fourth version, the most detailed, calls him "a man of fair complexion who had arrived in Wad Hamid—no one knows from where" and built a marble palace similar to the marvelous structure observed by Meheimeed in his vision.[37] The story continues:

> This Bandarshah's greatest pleasure was to sit on the throne of a night, after eating his fill and drinking till he was drunk, then order his slaves to be herded in, shackled in irons. He would order his executioners to flog them with thick whips made of hippopotamus hide until the blood flowed down their backs and they fainted. . . . This went on till the night they rebelled as one man and fell upon him and killed him, then they hacked him to pieces and threw them into the palace well.[38]

Bandarshah's sons are, in this episode, his slaves. This version of his story reveals a new layer in Salih's tripartite Oedipal drama. The oppressed present, formerly the space of the son, now becomes the domain of the slave, and the role of Bandarshah's grandson and proxy is played by the executioners. It is here that ethnic difference is explicitly brought into play, for "slave" is a racialized insult in Sudan.[39] Through the story of Bandarshah and his sons, the text represents the black slave as an element that must be continually flogged in order for Bandarshah to maintain his supremacy. The repeated flogging, which can only be stopped through even more extreme violence, is a continuity of the perverse: a morbid symptom. Its location in the magical space of the palace allows it to function in both the historical and the psychological domains. In terms of the oral histories collected by Meheimeed, the flogging serves as evidence, drawn from the collective memory, of the Sudanese slave trade that, during the second half of the nineteenth century, was one of the most intense on the African continent.[40] In the psychological domain, which the text invites us to consider through the similarity of this story to Meheimeed's vision, the flogging represents the suppression of black African identity.

These two domains are, of course, intertwined, and the period of their most powerful mutual reinforcement is also the time in which *Bandarshah* is set—that is, from the Turco-Egyptian period (1821–1884) through the postindependence era. The use of slaves in Sudan predates the Turco-Egyptian period, as does the association in Arabic discourse of blackness with servility.[41] However, before the nineteenth century, slave ownership was the privilege of the nobility in the Fur and Funj kingdoms that would become modern Sudan. The use of slaves did not become pervasive and general until the Turco-Egyptian period. Significantly for this reading of *Bandarshah*, one increase in slave use during this time was in the military: Mohammed Ali of Egypt used Sudanese slave soldiers in Sudan as replacements for Egyptian and Turkish troops, among whom there was a high rate of death and desertion. It is likely that we see one of these deserters in Dau al-Beit. Certainly his Turkish uniform dates his appearance to this period, when Sudanese slave labor not only buttressed the ruling military but also became the dominant source of agricultural labor in Sudan. Dau al-Beit represents not only cultural hybridization but also a specifically modern colonial legacy, one that directly engenders the tyrant Bandarshah.[42]

The link between slavery and ethnicity in this context arises from the fact that Muslim law prohibits the enslavement of freeborn Muslims: slaves must be either the children of slaves or non-Muslims captured in war. As Islam and Arabic spread in northern Sudan, slaves were obtained from further south, in Dar Fertit, the Nuba Mountains, and the Upper Blue Nile. The slave-raiding frontier was not only geographical but also ethnic and ideological: as such, it was moveable. Ahmed Sikainga describes Dar Fertit as a "state of mind": "as the slave raiders moved southward, Dar Fertit was pushed further south."[43] The ethnic and ideological factors determining who was, and who was not, enslaveable, greatly increased the importance of genealogy. The preoccupation with genealogy in *Bandarshah*, the high value placed on Muslim names "handed down from father to son," reflects the immense symbolic capital invested in Arab-Muslim heritage.[44] From the time of the eighteenth-century Funj kingdom, when contact with Egypt and the Middle East increased—partially, of course, through the slave trade—the indigenous merchant class had been claiming Arab identity "by constructing genealogies tracing their origin to an Arab ancestor."[45] The importance of Arab-Muslim identity intensified in nineteenth-century Sudan, as slave usage became more prevalent.[46]

This ethnic division was further exacerbated during the period of British rule. Although during this period the slave trade, if not the use of slaves, was suppressed, labor remained divided along ethnic lines: "British officials," writes Sikainga, "conceived of labor in ethnic terms," considering the Arabic-speaking slave owners lazy and the slaves, or ex-slaves, "suitable for hard and unskilled labor."[47] Colonial policy established educational projects that focused on northern and central Sudan, with the result that most postcolonial elites were Arabic-speaking northerners.[48] On decolonization, these elites promoted an Arab-Muslim Sudanese identity, regarding the southern Sudanese as a "lost brother" seized by the British who could now be returned to the fold.[49] This repressive interpretation of kinship surfaces in *Bandarshah* in the form of the whip Meryoud brings down on the backs of his uncles, under the watchful and approving eye of his grandfather. A future generation, in order to mirror one chosen part of its heritage, beats down a rejected part—the part that is, in fact, closer to it in time.

The promotion of Arab-Muslim identity in postcolonial Sudan focused on education and language, and implemented the *taʿrīb*, or Arabicization, of administrative and school systems.[50] The policy, which had been officially adopted on decolonization, was widely enforced in the mid-1960s and 1970s, when *Bandarshah* was conceived and written. Its purpose was to spread the Arabic language, and with it Islam and a Sudanese Arab identity, as quickly as possible through a vast territory where multiple languages are spoken.[51] The program was intended to reverse the imposition of an English-language school system during the colonial period, but it was also an attempt to absorb the "lost brother" of southern Sudan, where an armed struggle for a political voice had continued sporadically since independence. The explicit goal of *ta'rīb* was to foster an Arab-Muslim Sudanese identity. Qāṣim 'Uthmān Nūr, writing favorably of the program in 1988, notes among its benefits the "development of national feeling and strengthening of cultural ties between students" and the "attention to the Arab culture and literary heritage," and stresses that the use of Arabic in schools is important "especially in the regions of linguistic interference."[52] On the linguistic front, the program was quite successful: Arabic remains a lingua franca even in South Sudan. As a postcolonial policy of national integration, *ta'rīb* was clearly a failure: especially after 1983, bilingual or multilingual education became a rallying point for antigovernment struggle in the south, among the very "regions of linguistic interference" where national feeling was meant to develop through Arabic-language education.[53] The issue was not the imposition of the Arabic language per se—after all, English had been imposed by the British—but the link between the Arabicization of the schools and a nationalist discourse that strongly privileged Arabness and rejected Africanness. Al-Baqir al-Afif Mukhtar describes this nationalist perspective, in which the adjective "Sudanese" is inseparable from "Islamic and Arabic culture," as simultaneously "exclusionist" and "assimilationist": "Those who misfit the new definition of Sudani [Sudanese] are either to be cut off from the body politic . . . or to be changed in order to fit (i.e. to be turned [into] Northerners)."[54]

The *ta'rīb* of administrative and education services, a policy designed to make Sudan into an Arab country by rejecting the notion of an African Sudan, amounts to an officially sanctioned and indeed enforced amnesia. It echoes the miraculous conception of the hero Abu Zeid, an Arab who just happened to be black. Both types of amnesia erase not only difference, but the violence by which difference is assimilated. In *Bandarshah*, too, a violent history is forgotten: Dau al-Beit forgets that he is a colonizer, and the inhabitants of Wad Hamid, in identifying themselves as Arab, forget their own history of violent cross-cultural contact. *Bandarshah* exposes these shards of history. These shards interrupt the moment of highest joy, the wedding scene, when a marriage between two people of different ethnic backgrounds is solemnized with a whip, and they resurface in Bandarshah's palace, a site of torture. Dau al-Beit produces Bandarshah, and Bandarshah produces Meryoud, suppressing the memory of the link between them: Bandarshah's slave sons.

The text unifies patriarchy and conquest through the image of the whip, which is at one time an instrument of the torture of slaves and a symbol of an idealized masculine spirit of conquest, raised in celebration at the taking of a bride. In opposition to this gendered and ethnic violence, the text proposes the power of love as a generator of new forms of sociality. Maryam, Meheimeed's childhood sweetheart, represents human love, which is linked to the structures of civil society. Bilal, Bandarshah's black son, represents divine love, expressed through the mystical language of Sufi Islam. While each of these models has its problems, they are worth examining by way of conclusion, as shards of possibility raised in the course of *Bandarshah*'s archaeological project.

Maryam is an energetic character, unintimidated by traditional mores, who once disguised herself as a boy in order to go to school; Hassan notes that it is Maryam who speaks most passionately of the *bandar*, the city, as the site of a liberating modernity.[55] Hassan also argues that it is unfortunate for the text, in ideological terms, that by the time of Meheimeed's return to his village, Maryam is dead: her death, Hassan writes, is "the death of a dream for a better future."[56] Yet Maryam's impulse toward social change persists in the form of the politically active young women of Wad Hamid, who stage a demonstration that helps depose Meheimeed's friend Mahjoub from the leadership of the village cooperative. Indeed, one of the principal differences between the old "Mahjoub's gang" and the new "Bakri's boys" is that the latter group admits the participation of women. Salih's text does not posit the cooperative as an ideal political form: the old men of Meheimeed's generation consider the government in general worse than useless, characterized by the empty language of "up withs" and "long lives," a burden whether its platform is religious or secular.[57] Still, despite the cynicism of the older generation, there are signs of change: the opposition party in the village collects signatures to hold a general meeting of the cooperative, "something that had not happened since its formation."[58] This unprecedented move suggests a means of relating to the cooperative as a functional social form rather than a necessary evil. The general movement of Wad Hamid, including its young women, to depose Mahjoub after his twenty-five-year reign, works by taking the structure of the cooperative at its word, implementing processes, such as the collection of signatures, abandoned by Meheimeed's generation. The young people's belief in the democratic process despite its quarter century of dysfunction, as well as the success of their demonstration, prefigures the movements of the Arab Spring, and the power of "Maryam's way," which is, Meheimeed remembers, "to think that everything was possible."[59]

Bilal, a mystic inspired by divine love, is the counterpart to Maryam. Like her, he is both a representation of difference and an idealized, flawless character. His story immediately follows the tale of Bandarshah and his slaves, and carries the motif of the oppressed slaves/sons into new territory. In this version of

Bandarshah's story, Bandarshah again has eleven sons, but this time he also has a twelfth son, a black son, Bilal, his child with a black slave woman. Unacknowledged by his father and brothers, Bilal is blessed with a spiritual father, a sheikh who declares that Bilal is no one's slave; he is the slave of God.[60] Bilal embraces the life of a mystic and becomes a muezzin, like the Bilal for whom he is named, the Abyssinian freed slave whom the Prophet Mohammed made the first muezzin. "I am walking in the paths of the people of the Presence," he says, not "the people of this world."[61]

The spiritual vision of the desired *bandar* is carried by Bilal, who, with his mixed heritage and Sufi Islam, expresses "the fermentation of the Sudanese consciousness . . . born from the seed of two cultures, Islamic and African."[62] He is separate from the tyrannical continuity of Bandarshah/Meryoud, removed from the signs of authority that are so prevalent in the text: he rejects the whip, symbol of conquest, in his embrace of divine love, and his position as an unacknowledged son of a slave woman leaves him no access to the power of the male name. Absorbed in spiritual matters, Bilal offers no direct confrontation to the despotism of Bandarshah. However, if Maryam and the young women activists advance a new vision for civil society, Bilal holds out the possibility of a type of community rooted not in law, either secular or religious, but in a Sufi concept of unity that forms an important current throughout Salih's work. This current resonates with Partha Chatterjee's explication of a "narrative of community" that is "not domesticated to the requirements of the modern state, and yet persistent in its invocation of the rhetoric of love and kinship against the homogenizing sway of the normalized individual."[63] Bilal's doctrine of love takes shape in the same spiritual domain as the nationalist discourse that privileges Arab identity and demands Islamic law, but it opposes these terms with African identity and popular Sufi Islam. Bilal's role as the source of an alternative to the Bandarshah/Meryoud narrative is confirmed by his son, Taher, whom Bilal engenders in the one night he spends with his wife before dissolving the marriage in favor of spiritual contemplation. The relationship between Bilal, his wife Hawwa, and their son Taher is the only wholly positive example of kinship in the text. It constitutes a new genealogy, one characterized by acceptance and love rather than repression and violence. Where Meryoud flogs the previous generation, Taher embraces it: significantly, that embrace includes both his father and his mother, and both are mentioned by name. Taher assures Meheimeed that on the Day of Judgment he will tell God, "Your wretched servant, Taher Wad Bilal, the son of Hawwa bint al-Oreibi, stands before You empty-handed, devoid of merit, having nothing to place in the scales of Your justice but love."[64] Taher, whose identity is both "Wad Bilal" (son of Bilal) and "son of Hawwa," is also in a sense the father of *Bandarshah* the text: it is he who convinces Meheimeed to begin collecting oral histories, to "get down to work and record" the life stories of the villagers.[65] Thus *Bandarshah*, the record of Meheimeed's explorations among the buried histories of Wad Hamid, can be seen as the continuation of a new "narrative of community" positioned as an alternative to the reigning national narrative.

And yet it seems Meheimeed has not done enough. A call to action concludes the second novel, *Meryoud*. In this final scene, Meheimeed mourns the dead Maryam. He recalls her funeral and a vision in which she spoke to him from beyond the grave, exhorting him to answer the call of life. In this passage Meheimeed and his grandfather are equated with Meryoud and Bandarshah. Maryam, in fact, addresses Meheimeed as Meryoud, her nickname for him, which means "beloved." We read:

> "O Meryoud. You are nothing. . . . You have chosen your grandfather and your grandfather has chosen you because the two of you are most weighty in the scales of the people of the world. And your father is greater than both of you in the scales of justice. . . . He dreamt the dreams of the meek, and he partook of the provisions of the poor; he was tempted by glory but he restrained himself, and when life called him—when life called him—"
>
> I said yes. I said yes. I said yes. But the way back was harder because I had forgotten.[66]

This is where the text stops. Hassan writes: "Meheimeed cannot be saved until he remembers—but that event does not occur in *Meryoud*. The last word in the text, 'forgotten,' confirms the condition of amnesia from which he and his society continue to suffer."[67]

Hassan, emphasizing Salih's critique of Islamic fundamentalism, reads *Meryoud* as a condemnation of patriarchy. *Meryoud*, he writes, "counters the paradigm of patriarchal tyranny and violence with a mystical one based on love."[68] Meheimeed must remember his own complicity with patriarchy—something he fails to do, as is clear from the reference to his career as a browbeaten schoolteacher forced against his will to teach girls.[69]

The recurring trope of the whip suggests that we expand this analysis to include ethnicity as well as gender. Maryam's call asks Meheimeed to remember his father. It equates Meheimeed with the Meryoud who carried out the whipping in Meheimeed's vision. It equates Meheimeed's father with Bandarshah's eleven sons, who are described in one version of the story as eleven slaves. Meheimeed is complicit with a patriarchal system, and also with the oppression of his own "slave" father—a figure who, locked away in the inner world of the vision, may be read as Meheimeed's own African heritage, his own black self. Maryam's words, like the whipping scene in Dau al-Beit's wedding, extend the significance of Bandarshah's family drama, allowing it to comment on Meheimeed and through him on his whole community. The challenge to Meheimeed is that he refuses to become the Meryoud who is a mirror image of Bandarshah, the "man of fair complexion" who, to maintain his identity as a slave owner, must violently suppress the slaves who are his kin. Bilal, Bandarshah's unacknowledged son, is also Meheimeed's unacknowledged father. Here Salih uncovers a buried genealogy, referencing a history of oppression based in both gender and ethnicity. Slave women in Sudan were used for sexual services and valued for biological reproduction: female slaves were often hired out as prostitutes, and the children of these women, lacking legitimate fathers, were also considered slaves, thus increasing the master's holdings.[70] *Bandarshah* references these actual unacknowledged descendants through the character of Bilal, and also transforms them into metaphor. The unacknowledged and oppressed slave son becomes a figure for an African fragment in Sudanese identity, one that must be recognized and reclaimed in order to break a cycle that does violence to both the nation and the self.

The exposure of these shards of identity marks an important development in Salih's oeuvre: while ex-slaves and the children of slaves figure in both of his previous novels, *The Wedding of Zein* and *Season of Migration to the North*, *Bandarshah* is the only one of Salih's works to elaborate a sustained critique of Sudan's slave-owning history and its effect on national consciousness. *Bandarshah*—especially the second part, *Meryoud*—proposes a narrative of community that will gather the broken shards of Sudanese history and identity. Yet ultimately, the narrative of *Bandarshah* remains suspended, cut off in midair, stranded in the interregnum. It is worth noting here that while the text insists that any viable Sudanese community must, like Bilal, claim a mixed, black heritage rather than a strictly Arab one, it also imagines that community through Islam. In this sense, it stops short of advocating a community that would embrace all the shards it unearths. Moreover, the text struggles to extricate itself from the Bandarshah/Meryoud circle represented in its pages, and to imagine collectivity beyond the family. Even the women activists are evaluated in kinship terms; defending them, one of Meheimeed's friends declares: "Good luck to the girls who demonstrate: modest, polite and well-educated. Our daughters and the daughters of our sons. And if I found one of them who'd marry me . . . I'd do it tomorrow."[71]

The perception of *Bandarshah* as an incomplete text perhaps accounts for the lack of critical attention it has received in comparison with Salih's other works. It is possible, however, that the interest of the text is heightened rather than damaged by this apparent flaw. If "to make a claim on behalf of the fragment is also . . . to produce a discourse that is itself fragmentary," then the "incomplete" text may signify a particularly uncompromising engagement with a situation that does not admit of closure.[72] Be that as it may, the fractured, unfinished text of *Bandarshah* effectively represents a nation that became two nations two years after Salih's death and continues to suffer fissures along ethnic lines: a region whose future is burdened by questions of nationhood as kinship, and threatened by what Salih named the revenge of the present.

SOFIA SAMATAR is Assistant Professor of English at James Madison University. She is also author of *A Stranger in Olondria* and *The Winged Histories*.

Notes

1. Waïl Hassan, *Tayeb Salih: Ideology and the Craft of Fiction* (Syracuse, NY: Syracuse University Press, 2003), 134.
2. Ann M. Lesch, *The Sudan: Contested National Identities* (Bloomington: Indiana University Press, 1998), 3.
3. The phrase comes from Partha Chatterjee's *The Nation and Its Fragments: Colonial and Postcolonial Histories* (Princeton, NJ: Princeton University Press, 1993), 238.
4. Constance Berkley, *The Roots of Consciousness Molding the Art of Tayeb Salih: A Contemporary Sudanese Writer* (PhD diss., New York University, 1979), lxxix.
5. Ibid., xxxviii.
6. Tayeb Salih, *Bandarshah*, trans. Denys Johnson-Davies (London: Kegan Paul, 1996), 104.
7. Ibid., 3.
8. Ibid., 29.
9. Ibid., 9.
10. Ibid., 35.
11. Antonio Gramsci, *Selections from the Prison Notebooks*, ed. Quintin Hoare and Geoffrey Nowell Smith (London: Lawrence and Wishart, 1971), 276.
12. Ibid.
13. Salih, *Bandarshah*, 10.
14. Ibid., 10–11.
15. Ibid., 11.
16. Ibid.
17. Hassan, *Tayeb Salih*, 151.
18. Salih, *Bandarshah*, 12.
19. Ibid., 31.
20. Ibid., 67.
21. Ibid., 76.
22. Ibid.
23. Long associated with rural weddings, *al-buṭān* has moved into the cities of Sudan, including the capital, Khartoum, according to a 2010 Reuters report: "Young Sudanese Men Lashed in Traditional Wedding Ceremony to Show Bravery," *Reuters*, September 29, 2010, http://www.itnsource.com/shotlist/RTV/2010/09/29/RTV2470710/?v=1.
24. Salma K. Jayyusi, *Modern Arabic Poetry: An Anthology* (New York: Columbia University Press, 1987), 2.
25. Salih, *Bandarshah*, 20.
26. Ibid., 21.

27. Ibid., 22.
28. Ibid., 10.
29. Hassan, *Tayeb Salih*, 151.
30. Susan Slyomovics, *The Merchant of Art: An Egyptian Hilali Oral Epic Poet in Performance* (Berkeley: University of California Press, 1987), 1.
31. Quoted in Ibid.
32. Bridget Connelly, *Arab Folk Epic and Identity* (Berkeley: University of California Press, 1986), 220; Sayyid Hamid Hurreiz, "Afro-Arab Relations in the Sudanese Folktale," in *African Folklore*, ed. Richard M. Dorson (Bloomington: Indiana University Press, 1972), 161.
33. Connelly, *Arab Folk Epic*, 196, 301.
34. Salih, *Bandarshah*, 77.
35. There are several black heroes of the *sīrah* genre: Peter Heath writes that "the Arabic *sīra* seems to have become infatuated with the idea of the black hero." *The Thirsty Sword: Sīrat 'Antar and the Arabic Popular Epic* (Salt Lake City: University of Utah Press, 1996), 272.
36. Slyomovics, *Merchant of Art*, 49.
37. Salih, *Bandarshah*, 105.
38. Ibid., 106.
39. Heather J. Sharkey, "Arab Identity and Ideology in Sudan: The Politics of Language, Ethnicity, and Race," *African Affairs* 107 (January 2008): 28.
40. Ahmad A. Sikainga, *Slaves into Workers: Emancipation and Labor in Colonial Sudan* (Austin: University of Texas Press, 1996), xi.
41. Ibid., 5; Helmi Sharawi, "The African in Arab Culture: Dynamics of Inclusion and Exclusion," in *Imagining the Arab Other: How Arabs and Non-Arabs View Each Other*, ed. Tahar L. Djedidi (London: I. B. Tauris, 2008), 106.
42. Sikainga, *Slaves into Workers*, 5–6; 16; 19.
43. Ibid., 5.
44. Ibid., 8.
45. Ibid.
46. Ibid., 6–7.
47. Ibid., xiii, 68.
48. Ibid., 167.
49. Lesch, *Sudan*, 22.
50. Sikainga, *Slaves into Workers*, 22.
51. Sharkey, "Arab Identity," 21.
52. Qāṣim 'Uthmān Nūr, *Al-ta'rīb fī al-waṭan al-'arabī ma'a ishārah khaṣṣah li al-sūdān* (Khartoum, Sudan: Khartoum University Press, 1988), 33 (my translation).
53. Sharkey, "Arab Identity," 25.
54. Al-Baqir al-Afif Mukhtar, "The Crisis of Identity in Northern Sudan: The Dilemma of a Black People with a White Culture," in *Race and Identity in the Nile Valley: Ancient and Modern Perspectives*, ed. Carolyn Fluehr-Lobban and Kharyssa Rhodes (Trenton, NJ: Red Sea, 2004), 224.
55. Hassan, *Tayeb Salih*, 167.
56. Ibid.,168.
57. Salih, *Bandarshah*, 49, 25.
58. Ibid., 27.
59. Ibid., 117.
60. Ibid., 109.
61. Ibid., 112. "The Presence," *al-ḥaḍārah*, shares a root with *al-ḥāḍir*, "the present."

62. Muḥammad al-Mahdī Bushrā, "Taḥdīd al-jins al-fūklūrī fī ibdā' al-Ṭayyib Ṣāliḥ," in *Al-Ṭayyib Ṣāliḥ: dirāsāt naqdīyah*, ed. Haasan Abshar al-Ṭayyib (Beirut: Riyāḍ al-Rayyes, 2001), 335 (my translation).
63. Chatterjee, *Nation*, 238–239.
64. Salih, *Bandarshah*, 113.
65. Ibid., 100.
66. Ibid., 122.
67. Hassan, *Tayeb Salih*, 168.
68. Ibid., 162.
69. Salih, *Bandarshah*, 51.
70. Sikainga, *Slaves into Workers*, 23.
71. Salih, *Bandarshah*, 38.
72. Chatterjee, *Nation*, 13.

9 The African Postcolonial Predicament

A Logic of Revenge, Prison Poetry, and Becoming Human

Ken Walibora Waliaula

> The question remains for us to see in what ways postcolonial Africa continues to be complicit in a prison experiment that uses a logic of revenge, and does little to restore hope or humanity.
>
> —Mechthild Nagel, "'I Write What I Like': African Prison Intellectuals and the Struggle for Freedom"

OYEKAN OWOMOYELA'S ESSAY "Dissidence and the African Writer: Commitment or Dependency?" represents one of the most trenchant critiques of what he calls the "academic-literary elite," whose claim to humanistic and nationalistic motivations he strongly discounts and doubts.[1] Owomoyela attributes the acrimonious contestation between African writers and rulers of their independence states to the writers' desire to share power with or usurp it from bona fide politicians. Westernized African writers, Owomoyela claims, arrogate to themselves the modern equivalence of traditional bards who were part and parcel of the royal court. They therefore lament their exclusion from political power in their respective African states and take to dissidence to appeal to their European patrons and sponsors. Illustrative of the explicit expression of thirst for power, Owomoyela explains, are the remarks of Ghanaian writer Ayi Kwei Armah and Nigerian Wole Soyinka. He quotes Armah as having pronounced in a speech at the University of Wisconsin, Madison, in 1979 that the "exclusion of (writers) from power by modern-day rulers represents a breach with African ethos."[2] Armah's plaintive cry resonates with Soyinka's assertion earlier on in Stockholm in 1968: "When the writer woke from his opium dream of metaphysical abstractions he found that the politician had used his absence from earth to consolidate his position."[3] One could say these dissident African writers, in Owomoyela's view, look up to the European gaze in their quest for the political power they have missed out on. The writers' portrayal in their fictional and nonfictional works of leaders of independent Africa as inept and corrupt belies their own unbridled megalomania.[4] Indeed, the list of who's who of Africa's political prisoners includes well-known writers who were or are deemed antigovernment both for their writing and their activism. For these groups of African elites, Owomoyela has no sympathy, and he is appalled by efforts to demand their release from prison for their antigovernment stances.

The struggle between academic elite writers and rulers in postcolonial Africa is a divisive issue, with different individuals taking sides. Owomoyela, by tendentiously denouncing the literary output and activism of the academic literary elite, obviously takes sides with the rulers whose underbelly he decidedly refuses to expose. Yet the controversy is an index of the complexity of the postcolonial state in Africa. It is a controversy from which it is almost impossible to remain neutral, objective, and balanced. The controversy speaks to multiple narratives and counternarratives that are told to make sense of the political quagmire of postcolonial Africa. When Owomoyela says that writers conceive of themselves as the positive side in the struggle "between enlightenment and anomie," we are made to confront both the writers' conception of themselves and their world and how their detractors conceive of them.[5] The writers, ostensibly, see themselves as special and should therefore be a part of African governments; the governments, however, see them as antigovernment and deserving of exile, detention, or death. Both sides of the divide have strong opinions on the question of the postcolonial state in Africa, whether it is characterized by enchantment or disenchantment, and whether there is sufficient respect for democracy and human rights.

It bears clarifying that this chapter does not attempt to extrapolate at length on the intricacies of human rights theory and the intellectual skepticism around it; that is perhaps a matter for another day. However, suffice it to say, discussions on human rights are inextricably tied to the alluring "idea that every person anywhere in the world, irrespective of citizenship or territorial legislation, has some basic rights, which others should respect."[6] But a sizable number of critics have pointed at the conceptual weaknesses underpinning the theory and praxis of human rights, of which failure to justify universalizable interest is one. As Mark F. N. Franke correctly asserts, human rights tends to be geographically oriented.[7] Human rights activists, however, routinely deny or diminish the boundedness of human rights. As Amartya Sen states, drawing on Karl Marx, activists in their zeitgeist, eager to change the world without necessarily interpreting it and apprehending its multifaceted nature, routinely resent any critique of human rights.[8]

African writers who have been imprisoned for political reasons have often particularly come face to face with the reality or uncertainty of their individual and collective humanity while behind bars. Thanks to the dehumanization, deprivations, and denials of basic human rights (otherwise taken for granted), writers are compelled to ponder their sense of being human. For most of them prison becomes the locale for writing themselves into existence, regaining sanity, surviving. Unable or unwilling to use the gun, the writers resort to wielding the pen as their weapon against what they perceive as despotic regimes in postindependence Africa. In their moment of crisis as prisoners, these writers are bound to use writing as a means of reflecting on their place within the confined world of the prison walls and the world beyond the prison walls. More importantly, they would be thinking about the reason for their incarceration. Writing in prison, then, becomes a voyage of self-discovery, a quest for the sense of being human, of the right to be human. And as Ioan Davies asserts, the prison writer almost always asks the question, "What did I do wrong?" to which Owomoyela would answer, hastily, of course, for your being power hungry, for your antigovernment activities, including your writing.[9]

As Tejumola Olaniyan and Ato Quayson contend, "One dirty little secret of the African literary tradition is the flourishing of the form of writing we could call 'writer's prison diaries,' that is, poems, fictional and non-fictional prose, and dramatic works by writers about their experience in the jail of the postcolonial state as political prisoners."[10] In the twentieth century, Africa witnessed a tremendous increase in its incarcerated intellectuals and activists, creating an endless list of works typifying African prison writing, what Olaniyan and Quayson term as the "dirty little secret" emerging in "adversarial contexts." Nelson Mandela remains perhaps the most famous of African prisoners of conscience, thanks to his twenty-seven-year jail term by the apartheid government of South Africa. In general the colonial encounter in Africa had produced its long list of political prisoners from the rank and file of indigenous peoples who sought to break free from the colonial yoke. The treatment of the colonized during this turbulent period underscores the excesses and abuses of empire as it clung to its illegitimate overseas sphere of influence. Thousands were incarcerated, persecuted, maimed, raped, or castrated across Africa in some of the most appalling and atrocious instances of human rights violations in modern times.

Indeed, although the level of bloodshed and human rights violations in colonial Africa differed from country to country and from region to region, it was generally a tale of wanton and egregious violation of the human rights of indigenous populations. Incidentally, quite a number of the founding fathers of postindependent African states met the full force of the colonial tyranny, becoming prisoners themselves. Ghana's Kwame Nkrumah and Kenya's Jomo Kenyatta, who soon became first presidents of their respective independent nations, were themselves imprisoned, hence victims of the colonial attempt to silence opposition. Could it be said that, in a sense, Nkrumah and Kenyatta were convicted criminals who later became leaders of their nations? Was not the British colonial presence in Africa criminal in and of itself?

The devastating colonial encounter and its attendant violation of human rights completely sullied the pretentious and spurious civilizing mission in Africa that the empire had arrogated on itself. As Robin D. G. Kelley, following Aimé Césaire's polemical *Discourse on Colonialism*, would argue, the rape, torture, violence, and immorality imperial Europe unleashed on the colonized was the most telling evidence of how "colonialism 'decivilize[d]' the colonizer."[11] Even those Africans not included in the hundreds of thousands who were literally incarcerated were virtually under the figurative colonial prison. The state of unfreedom in colonial Africa was similar to the prison life in apartheid South Africa, of which Winnie Mandela would speak of as the "prison inside and the prison outside."[12] In other words, it mattered little that one was in literal prison, being outside prison was equally incarcerating, stifling, and suffocating. Not surprisingly, indigenous Africans, in the prison inside and the prison outside, began to use their inventiveness and ingenuity to come up with means to survive the hellish ambience that surrounded them.

Moreover, the victims' penchant for narrating incarceration as a survival mechanism, as a therapeutic exercise, as well the tendency to mask meaning to the oppressor in the oral narratives of colonial Africa, anticipated the written narratives of incarceration that would come in the postcolonial period. It is a paradox of our times that the unfreedom that existed in colonial Africa persisted in the so-called postcolonial Africa. In contemplating this paradox and the love-hate relationship between the modern African state and prison, one comes closer to understanding the depth and width of what Kelley would call Africa's "postcolonial predicament."[13] The conditions that necessitated the narration and thematization of literal and figurative prison in colonial times seem to have continued almost unabated in postcolonial Africa. It is the state's determination to thwart the human spirit, to curtail freedom in colonial and postcolonial Africa that impelled victims to tell stories to capture their experiences, to survive. Additionally, fear of further reprisal and victimization motivates prison narrators to turn to fascinating inventiveness and circumlocution in colonial and postcolonial Africa.

The list of texts that constitute the corpus of narratives of incarceration in postindependence Africa is legion as are the circumstances that produced them. For instance, in Ethiopia the popular revolution that brought down Emperor Haile Selassie was followed by disenchantment and then grievous human rights violations by the military junta under Mengistu Haile Mariam, who hijacked the revolution. Former political prisoners have written chilling accounts of this dark chapter in Ethiopian history, detailing the abuses and excesses visited by the state on the populace in the prison inside and the prison outside. The Ethiopian corpus of firsthand political prisoner accounts includes Taffara Deguefe's *A Tripping Stone: An Ethiopian Prison Diary* (2003), Dawit Shifaw's *The Diary of Terror:*

Ethiopia 1974–1991 (2006), and Nega Mezlekia's controversial memoir, *Notes from the Hyena's Belly* (2002), while Ethiopia/Eritrea has Abeba Tesfagiorgis's prison account, *A Painful Season and a Stubborn Hope* (1992).

In Kamuzu Banda's Malawi, jailed poet Jack Mapanje wrote *And Crocodiles Are Hungry at Night* (2011) and the *The Chattering Wagtails of Mikuyu Prison* (1993), while his contemporary and senior civil servant Sam Mpasu wrote *Political Prisoner 3/75 of Dr. H. Kamuzu Banda of Malawi*. In Yakubu Gowon's Nigeria, detained Wole Soyinka came out with his prison memoir, *The Man Died: Prison Notes* (1972), and a prison poetry collection, *A Shuttle in the Crypt* (1987), while in Sani Abacha's Nigeria, Kunle Ajibade wrote *Jailed for Life* (1981). In Zanzibar, Shafi Adam Shafi fictionalized his incarceration after the 1967 revolution in the semi-autonomous islands in his Swahili novel *Haini* (2000), while in Idi Amin's Uganda, P. M. O. Onen narrated his confinement in *Diary of an Obedient Servant During Misrule* (2000).

In apartheid South Africa, examples of political prisoner writings include Breyten Breytenbach's *True Confessions of an Albino Terrorist* (1984), Dennis Brutus's *Letters to Martha and Other Poems from a South African Prison* (1968), Molefe Pheto's *And Night Fell: Memoirs of a Political Prisoner in South Africa* (1983), Frances Baard's *My Spirit Is Not Banned* (1986), and Tim Jenkin's *Inside Out: Escape from Pretoria Prison* (2003).

However, the production of prison narratives is not the preserve of sub-Saharan Africa. One of the better-known prison writings is Nawal el Saadawi's personal prison memoir, *Memoirs from the Women's Prison* (1983), recounting her detention without trial in Anwar Sadat's Egypt as well as her fictionalized account of a real woman's life in *Woman at Point Zero* (1975). In Morocco, poet Abdellatif Laâbi wrote his French prison memoir, *Le Chemin des ordalies* (1982), which has been translated in English as *Rue du Retour*, to capture his prison experience for crimes of opinion or thought.

The relationship between state tyranny and the emergence of prison writing in Kenya presents a fascinating scenario that perhaps qualifies as a touchstone for the rest of Africa. Indeed, Kenya is a supreme example of how independence did not translate into complete emancipation, of how there was transition from hope to despair due to tyranny and curtailment of freedom. The reign of Kenya's founding father, Jomo Kenyatta (1963–1978), and his successor, Daniel arap Moi (1978–2002), witnessed a proliferation of prison writing. A former political prisoner and detainee himself, Kenyatta took a cue from the colonial potentate to detain and imprison, and even assassinate, critics and dissidents. The assassinations of Pio Gama Pinto, Tom Mboya, and J. M. Kariuki are attributed to his state terror machine. Both Abdilatif Abdalla and Ngũgĩ wa Thiong'o were survivors of the brutalities of Kenyatta's regime, telling their stories in *Sauti ya Dhiki* (*Voice of Agony*, 1973) and *Detained* (1980), respectively.

Moi, Kenyatta's vice president, succeeded his former boss, ruling Kenya for twenty-four years with an iron fist until his retirement in 2001. Initially a moderate political leader, Moi seemed to have been jolted into dictatorship by an abortive military coup mounted against his regime in August 1982. He espoused what he fondly called the "Nyayo philosophy" (the Swahili word *nyayo* means "footsteps"). On ascension to power Moi vowed to walk in his predecessor's footsteps, which he claimed meant clinging tenaciously to the principles of "love, peace, and unity" in order to foster truly prosperous Kenyan nationhood.[14] But that love, peace, and unity epitomized by the Kenyatta era is a theme found only in the official authorized Kenyan national narrative.

The alternative narrative has it that Kenyatta set the pace and precedent for silencing opposition through detention, imprisonment, and assassination. Kenyatta is, therefore, painted in this version of the Kenyan story as one whose example it was dangerous for anyone to follow. According to this alternative national narrative, Moi became more and more inclined to emulate his predecessor's worst qualities, following Kenyatta's footsteps in turning Kenya into a virtual police state. Moi's regime saw a monumental increase in political detentions, censorship of media and books, and ruthless crackdown on opposition activism in every area of the country. The assassination of foreign affairs minister Robert John Ouko in 1990 was the apex of political intolerance in the Moi regime. Leftist intellectual Alamin Mazrui and journalist Wahome Mutahi are examples of survivors of the state terror and tell their experiences in *Chembe cha Moyo* (*Arrowhead in My Heart*, 1988) and *Three Days on the Cross* (1991), respectively.[15] As an analysis of Mazrui's prison poetry demonstrates, Kenya under Moi was an instance of Africa's postcolonial predicament, Kelley's characterization of the continent that echoes Basil Davidson's idea of the "black man's burden."

Davidson's book *The Black Man's Burden: Africa and the Curse of the Nation-State*, widely regarded as his magnum opus, is audacious and unequivocal in pinpointing nation-statism as what ails Africa, the main reason for the continent being in "deep trouble."[16] Nation-statism is the curse and burden breaking the back of postcolonial Africa, in Davidson's view. Davidson argues that the lights have gone out in Africa because of the pernicious imposition of nation-statism, an alien concept or ideology, at the expense of effective indigenous African systems of governance that thrived in the precolonial moment. Nation-statism, Davidson argues, came with the invention of untenable and incompatible national and group identities that hardly cohere. At the same time, imposition of nation-statism was characterized by rejection and denigration of the values and vitality of African precolonial governance ethos. In this regard, pioneer Western-educated African elites such as Obafemi Awolowo and Nnamdi Azikiwe stand accused of being complicit in aiding the introduction of the destructive and incongruous Eurocentric notions of governance that have led to "general and continental failure in Africa."[17] In his magisterial text, Davidson enacts a juxtaposition of African nationalism and Eastern European nationalism to justify his central argument that nationalism is necessarily unsuited for African realities. Nevertheless, he argues that it would be foolhardy to entertain despair regarding the present crisis in Africa and therefore suggests a rather hazy "escape route" that looks to African solutions to African problems, indeed a sort of mass-character democracy that overlooks the place of human rights.[18] It is to the meditation on the impact of an African state's recourse to what Mechthild Nagel terms the "logic of revenge" and denial of an individual poet's human rights that we now turn.[19]

Mazrui's collection of prison poems invites us to meditate on a poetics and a politics of pain and relief for the political prisoners. If the poems in *Chembe cha Moyo* capture the anguished perception of tragedy and trauma that detention signified for Mazrui, they also underline the love-hate relationship between the poet and his Kenyan state. *Chembe cha Moyo* as a text is centrally situated within the context of incarceration and political struggle for change. It essentially grapples with issues of personal and collective dignity and freedom in the wake of human rights abuses, despotism, and decay in the postcolonial or neocolonial moment. Mazrui wrote *Chembe cha Moyo* while locked up as a political detainee during the Moi era in the 1980s.

By the time of his detention, Mazrui had already burst onto the Kenyan literary scene in a powerful way. His literary oeuvre had begun with *Kilio cha Haki* (*Crying for Justice*, 1982), a predetention play that placed him among the leading East African playwrights, principally because of its superior aesthetics and anticapitalist stance. The publication of *Kilio cha Haki* would become both a blessing and a curse; imprinting indelibly Mazrui's name in the canon of Swahili literature and incurring the ire of the paranoid Moi regime. One could say Mazrui's detention seemed to have been essentially linked to the regime's displeasure with the publication and popularity of *Kilio cha Haki*.

Mazrui's poetry of incarceration, *Chembe cha Moyo*, has not elicited as much critical attention as his preincarceration play. Critical responses to *Chembe cha Moyo* are few. It is germane to bring to the fore not only Mazrui's thematic preoccupations but also the ethos underlying his prison poetry. In this regard, it is appropriate to ask questions such as: What is the connection between the text of Mazrui's poems and the detention context within which they were written? How and to what extent does he thematize truth? What is the place or role of the pronoun "I" in Mazrui's poetic world? Does the "I" enter the stage in multiple guises as expressions of the poet's various ways of self-narration? How is the "I" related to the "we" of the collective identity? This study also addresses the questions of trauma as they are related to the text and context of the carceral imagination and experience.

Mazrui was dragged from the classroom at Kenyatta University in March 1983 during the first round of detentions in the Moi era under the Preservation of Public Security Act, chapter 57, of the Laws of Kenya. He joined the long list of officials of the newly proscribed university faculty union who were detained, such as Dr. Willy Mutunga, Kamoji Wachira, Professor Edward Oyugi, Maina Kinyatti, and Mukaru Ng'ang'a.[20]

One of the most salient aspects of *Chembe cha Moyo* is the apparent silence on the back cover and in the introduction on detention as the place of writing. The back cover vaguely dwells on generalities, merely stating that "*Chembe cha Moyo* ni mkusanyiko wa mashairi yenye mdundo wa kisasa kututongolea hisia za ndani zinazotokana na mazingira mapya katika mataifa ya Ulimwengu wa Tatu [*Chembe cha Moyo* is an anthology of poems with a modern resonance revealing inner feelings that emerge from a new environment in the Third World nations]."[21] The back cover does not say whose "inner feelings" are at stake, and it presumes that those feelings are typical of all individuals in the third world! Neither does it account for the presumed newness of the environment in the third world.

The loudness of the silence regarding the where of *Chembe cha Moyo*'s writing is accentuated by the militant tone of the poems in the collection. Yet it is difficult to surmise the why of the writing of *Chembe cha Moyo* without also unearthing the where. It is, I think, in unraveling the connection between where and why that we can come close to fully understanding the interplay between context and text in Mazrui's poetry. Mazrui has disclosed that he had indeed discussed unequivocally the question of why and where in his original introduction of the anthology.[22] Nonetheless, fearing that such candid revelation would short-circuit the book's distribution and sales, the editorial team at the Nairobi office of Heinemann publishers decided to elide it altogether. The introduction that remained in the published version is, therefore, a mutilated vestige of the original manuscript, dwelling as it does on the safe stylistics and aesthetics of Swahili poetry in general and making no mention about why and where Mazrui wrote his collection of poems.

However, whereas the peritext succumbs to the culture of silence that the Moi regime perpetuated and perfected, it is still not impossible to speculate about the motivation for Mazrui's poems. For one thing, the bulk of the poems are preoccupied with incarceration with some of them being quite explicit in this regard. The first poem, "Niguse" (Touch Me), is a case in point.

Nitokapo Kizuizini
Nitamwomba yeyote mwendani
        aniguse
                taratibu
                pole pole
                        lakini
                        kwa yakini

Niguse tena
Unijuze tena
Unifunze tena
          maisha yalivyo
          maisha yaonjavyo
                    ladha yake ilivyo

Nipo hapa nimekukabili
Niguse tena tafadhali
Niguse!
Niguse!

[When I come out of Detention
I will beseech any of my beloved ones
     to touch me
          softly
          slowly
                    but
surely

Touch me once again
Let me know once again
Instruct me anew
about how life is
     about how life tastes
          the taste of life
Here I am facing you
Please touch me once again
Touch me!
Touch me!][23]

From the very first line of the first poem, Mazrui foregrounds the reality of incarceration, alluding to the moment "Nitokapo Kizuizini [When I come out of Detention]." The plea "Niguse" in the title and repeated throughout the poem underscores the deprivation of human contact, human rights in general and in particular, and the denial of human touch that the speaker in the poem has experienced in detention. The plea is indicative of the speaker's desperate yearning for human touch and contact, literally and figuratively, and envisions the momentous and joyous moment of release that would make such contact both possible and probable. The reference to "Kizuizini" (Detention) is overt, not tacit, amplified as it were, with the initial uppercase K. And yet this allusion to the condition of detention in particular and incarceration in general is not isolated but indeed suffuses *Chembe cha Moyo* far too much to assume that it is accidental.

Because the silence on the facticity of detention in the introduction and back cover deprives us of potentially useful hints as to the motivation for writing, we are left to speculate from what we can glean from the poems themselves. Thankfully, the poems do not disappoint in this regard, as "Niguse" illustrates. Other poems that explicitly mention or thematize incarceration include "Kifungoni" (Incarceration), "Kizuizini" (Detention), "Nayeyusha Pingu" (I Am Melting Handcuffs), and "Hakuna Yeyote" (Alone).[24] Mazrui wrote a play, *Shadows of the Moon*, and *Chembe cha Moyo* under the depressing conditions of detention and against the wish of prison authorities. Prison authorities generally tend to be antibooks and antiwriters. As Nagel cogently notes, religious books such as the Bible seem to be the only "innocuous" texts one is allowed access to while behind bars.[25] Prison, like boarding houses across most of sub-Saharan Africa, is home to dog-eared copies of the Bible, presumably reminding inmates of their sinfulness and/or their proximity to sin as well as their need to make peace with their Maker. One could argue that for the political prisoner the presence of the Bible in the cell is an implicit message that by sinning against the state he or she has sinned against God and should therefore make amends.

That is not to suggest that prisoners find the religious text antithetical to their ideals. As Ethiopian political prisoner Deguefe's prison diary, *A Tripping Stone*, illustrates, the prisoner's quest for solace in religious texts and tenets is sometimes integral to maintaining sanity or coping with the trauma of incarceration. In his diary Deguefe repeatedly recounts how a pattern of prayer and sermons sustained him and other believing detainees in the early 1970s after the fall of Ethiopian emperor Selassie.[26] In his diary *Detained*, Ngũgĩ, too, records how spiritually inclined fellow detainees turned to religious activities as a means of coping with the trauma of incarceration.[27]

If the presence of the Bible was meant to woo Mazrui toward a spirit of repentance and contrition, to lead him toward submission to secular authorities, it perhaps achieved little or nothing in this regard. And yet the Bible made possible Mazrui's search for solace in ways that the prison authorities least expected or desired. Mazrui was least interested in simply reading and imbibing the wisdom of the Bible given to him by prison authorities; instead, he used the margins to scribble his poems and play. Also, he resorted to stealing pens from prison warders and once from a pilot to be able to write. On the whole, the write-and-hide game he had to play indicates that writing under prison conditions needed more than a simple will to write.

Writing, then, appears to have been a compulsion, something that needed to be done in spite of or because of the antiwriting detention surroundings. In answering the question concerning the where of the writing, one should also take into account the locale. Why write from such an unlikely place? As the title of this chapter suggests, seeking solace in writing was evidently an important motivation for Mazrui's prison writing. The therapeutic properties of writing seem to play a crucial role in the writer's motivation, particularly in the genre of poetry, which lends itself toward free release of pent-up feelings and emotions. But this self-expression also enables and enhances self-narration, albeit in the somewhat incoherent and circuitous poetic form. This brings us to the grammatical "I" of Mazrui's *Chembe cha Moyo.*

There are multiple "I" pronouns in Mazrui's prison poetry that reflect and refract the poet's self and reality as a real historical person detained for political reasons. Or perhaps to put it more accurately, these "I" pronouns project the poet's wide spectrum of invented selves. They range from optimistic to nihilistic, from militant to resigned, from devout to almost irreligious, from confident to doubting, from cultural nationalist to Pan-Africanist, and so on. In "Niguse" the "I" refers to an incarcerated yet optimistic self. There is optimism, if cautious, because the yearned for desire for authentic human interaction is now more than just a remote possibility due to the apparent prospect of freedom. In this opening poem, Mazrui presents a self that needs to learn to be human again as the second stanza suggests:

> Touch me once again
> Let me know once again
> Instruct me anew
>   about how life is
>   about how life tastes
>   the taste of life[28]

This is an "I" whose selfhood hangs onto a receding sense of being but that takes refuge in the knowledge of the real possibility of becoming human again, of belonging yet again in the human fold, of enjoying one's unalienable human rights once more. Through the desperate tone of the narrating and narrated "I," Mazrui compellingly reveals how life in detention and outside detention are worlds apart. The experience in detention has almost erased the speaker's memory of what it means to be free outside the prison walls. His experience is similar to that of Moroccan political prisoner Laâbi, whose prison memoir, *Le Chemin des ordalies,* demonstrates the extent to which the "spatial configuration of the prison yard itself affects the narrator [Laâbi] to his very core. It affects his physical relationship to the world around him. . . . Again the moment of release is both a time to rejoice, and a time of trepidation; it is a move from the known to the unknown."[29] For the incarcerated inured to being treated as nonhuman, release signifies a new learning experience in the business of normal human existence. Indeed, incarceration had taught Mazrui to forget what it meant to be truly a free human agent. Clearly, by using the "I" in transition from nonbeing to human being, the poem reveals profoundly the magnitude of dehumanization that detention may work on individuals.

The same sense of cautious optimism is expressed in the poem "Nitangojea" (I Will Wait) in which the narrating "I" projects itself as exercising patience and looking forward to reunion with a beloved one.[30] Yet expressing or representing oneself in terms of the possibility of release and relief in the foreseeable future despite the present moment of crisis accords with the search for refuge in poetry that underwrites the ebb and flow of *Chembe cha Moyo.*

But the optimistic "I" is sometimes replaced by a doubting, even nihilistic "I" in the range of poems in the anthology. In "Mtabiri" (Seer) one encounters an "I" presenting itself as a prophet of doom bereft of any iota of hope for a better future.[31] The speaker in the poem predicts assertively:

sauti tishi zimenijia
kusudi kunitabiria
hatari zilotukalia
    na kutukamia

[fearful voices have come to me
warning me of what is yet to come
about the danger we are bound to face
    dangers that are about to engulf us][32]

The narrator then lists a host of oddities that, according to his predictions, are set to occur (e.g., a female goat bearing through the mouth a grotesque offspring that is neither completely goat nor sheep, a human mother giving birth to a deformed child with a wound in place of the eyes, and the human population being pounded by the "mvua ya mauti" [rain of death], etc.). The speaker concludes by suggesting that the upheaval in the system of things shakes even angelic hordes:

Ndimi mtabiri
Mwona Mbali
Nami naogopa

[I am the prophet
The far-sighted one
And I am fearful][33]

It is possible to perceive this tremor or transformation of the social equilibrium as an emblem of social revolution, the kind envisioned by political activists who are not contented with folding their arms and watching their societies crumble under tyranny and misrule. The leftist ideology that underpins Mazrui's entire literary output in general seems to lend credence to this supposition. However, the grotesque and unattractive images of the changes that ensue undercut the possibility of the prediction of an expedient revolution whose outcome is positive change. The speaking self in the poem is overwhelmed with fear, ending the poem with little or no hope of a bright future as the lines "Naogopa [I am fearful]" clearly indicate.

If in "Mtabiri" the poet predicts impending doom and gloom in the not so distant future, he is no more sanguine in his estimation of the present in "Mashindano" (Contest). The poem opens with the persona describing a tireless porter toiling to fend for himself and countless dependents:

Nimuonapo hamali mwenye tumbi ya midomo
yote yataka kulishwa
Huona mja asukumaye jabali liso kikomo
juu ya mlima usokwisha
Kwa kujikaza hulisogeza kidogo
Shubiri baada ya shubiri ilonyumbuka
Na chini ya kivuli cha huu mzigo
Humwona amejikita kwa tambo liloumbuka

Mishipa huvimba na kuiva rangi
Damu ikakimbilia usoni kwa wingi
sasa akishindwa
sasa akishinda
akishindilia vidole katika ardhi yenye mashaza
kimya kimetanda
roho inampaa
moyo ukimdunda
Katika muda huu wa hatari
muda wa kifo na nusuri
Ole wangu wee! . . .
jabali hili litamshinda huyu mpweke
limvuruge chini ya nguvu zake
likititimka kurudia kwenye kiza cha mauti?
Kimya . . . mashindano yaendelea
ya wawili katika ndoto

[Whenever I see a porter with many mouths
All needing to be fed
I behold a person heaving a limitless boulder
Towards a limitless mountain

He exerts himself to move it a little bit
Inch by inch he moves it
And in the shadow of this burden
I behold him standing erect with a disfigured figure

Veins swell and his color darkens
Blood rushes to the face
Now he wins
Now he loses

He digs his finger into the shell covered soil
There is quiet everywhere
He is distraught
His heart pounds
At this perilous moment
The moment of life and death.

Oh! Woe unto me! . . .
Will this boulder conquer this loner
Will it crush him under with its might
As it tumbles back to the darkness of death?

Silence . . . the contest continues
between the two in the dream.][34]

It is the risk, danger, and futility of the porter's onerous task of moving a huge boulder uphill that the persona foregrounds. And yet the porter is undeterred in doing the impossible and perhaps profitless job of heaving the boulder uphill; he is impelled by the plight of the countless mouths that depend on him for food. The narrator poses the disturbing question: Will the boulder crush the porter to death? If the question appearing at the end of the poem remains unanswered, it also diminishes the need for the question of wages that may accrue from the task. In other words, the possibility of death supersedes the issue of whether the porter gets paid. Clearly, in "Mashindano" the poet reenacts the Greek narrative of Sisyphus who continually rolls a boulder uphill only for the boulder to come tumbling down.[35] Although the speaker in the poem alludes to a third person struggling to heave the rock up an endless hill, one is bound to discern that the person in question is indeed the narrating self from the line "Ole wangu wee! [Oh! Woe unto me!]" in the final stanza. Also, although the rock is not directly said to be rolling back in "Mashindano," the sense of futility that pervades the poem suggests such possibility.

It is tempting to read this poem as being primarily concerned with the economic imperative, to interpret it as a classic case of a hardworking porter trying to make ends meet in a thankless economic system that has perfected depriving and denying workers. Given Mazrui's leftist orientation, such interpretation may seem plausible. While not altogether discounting such an interpretation, I think being attentive to the context of the poem points toward Mazrui himself as the porter and hence is suggestive that the task of heaving the stone uphill symbolizes activism against the Moi regime. Incarceration allows for self-scrutiny for the revolutionary, enabling the detainee to take stock of his or her individual role in particular and the general direction of the struggle. Mazrui seems to acknowledge the enormity of the task at hand. In this poem Mazrui creates a self that is a "loner" or lone ranger thrust into loneliness and solitude through the isolation concomitant with detention. He may strive to push the boulder of Moi's tyranny up the mountain, but the danger of it rolling back and crushing him looms large. The exclamation "Ole wangu [Woe unto me]" is therefore applicable to Mazrui the political detainee pondering the "perilous moment" of detention and being uncertain of his release, much less the success of the revolutionary struggle for which detention has made him an ineffectual lone ranger. Or is he that ineffectual? One could say that Mazrui heaves the boulder of the Moi tyranny fundamentally and solely through writing while incarcerated. At the perilous moment of detention, he continues writing without knowing whether or when these works of literature created in captivity would see the light of day. He has no clue at that moment whether prison authorities will find his resistance literature and confiscate or destroy it, crushing him and his precious prison oeuvre.

However, in trying to present various versions of the "I" that tend to reflect and refract his selfhood, Mazrui does not always foreground the ideological at the expense of the essentially human. The sense of being or becoming human that his various "I" pronouns in *Chembe cha Moyo* aspire to or despair aspiring to is not obscured by a quest for ideological abstractions. This is so despite or because of the poet's manifestly Marxist stance. Granted, Mazrui's uncle, Ali Mazrui, has aptly characterized his nephew as a Kenyatta University instructor "who was detained without charge by the Moi regime for being a left-wing Kenyan academic."[36] But in the poem "Mimi ni Mimi" (I Am Me), there is ostensibly a vehement disavowal of ideologues and the ideologies and ideals with which they identify themselves or are characteristically identified.[37] The narrating "I" refuses to be branded in accord with any ideological orientation:

Waniita mkomunisti
Waniita mkapitalisti
Na mimi ni binadamu tu,
Kwani hilo halitoshi?

[They call me a communist
They call me a capitalist

And yet I am just human
Isn't that enough?][38]

The narrating "I" in this poem conceives of a selfhood that is not mediated through opposing ideological branding or paroxysms. Ideologies or ideological branding, whether accurate or inaccurate, glosses over the quintessential human attributes embodied in the self. Furthermore, emphasis on ideological differences tends to overlook our common humanity, or that we are fellow passengers on the train of life. To the poet humans everywhere face challenges so similar as to make fiery arguments over ideology or ideological identification and differentiation count for little or nothing. But by tending to reject ideology and invoking his sense of humanity, the speaker in the poem may be said to be seeking solace in a fundamental truth that humans have flagrantly trampled on throughout history. The detaining authorities do not fully appreciate or acknowledge the humanity of the detainees as they do their own, otherwise they would not subject them to extreme dehumanizing conditions as they often do. Nagel's allusion to the overriding "logic of revenge" in the postcolonial African prison industrial complex in this chapter's epigraph underscores this negation of humanity. When and if my humanity is denied or negated as now, the self in Mazrui's poem seems to be saying, it behooves me to console myself with both the declaration and the knowledge that I am still human. The poem is, therefore, the poet's attempt to stake a claim on subjectivity as opposed to being regarded as a mere object. Only that staking a claim on humanity appears to come at the expense of repudiating something held dear.

The apparent disavowal of ideological identification or taxonomy in the poem, including that of the leftist variety that undergirds Mazrui's activism, should only be accepted with a caveat. The poet creates an image of a self that renounces ideology; rather it is a self that values the fundamental sense of just being human. Yet there is a level of inherent contradiction or irony in this self's disavowal of ideology, since the disavowal itself is based on ideology, the ideology of devaluing ideology. At the same time, by deigning to claim he is not to be branded a communist and any number of ideological tags, the self seems to point to the rehabilitative propensity of detention, its capacity to reform a detainee hitherto corrupted by hated and dangerous ideology. The Kenyan state would not have been more pleased than to hear a detained leftist intellectual recanting any and all ideology, including his leftist stance. It is supposedly a true measure of the success of the prison system. Nonetheless, I think the disavowing self and voice in the poem is only a ploy the poet employs to hoodwink the authorities that he has reformed. As Barbara Harlow states in *Barred: Women, Writing, and Political Detention*, "penal institutions aim to function as part of the state's coercive apparatus of physical detention and ideological containment."[39] And the tenor and thrust of Mazrui's poem tends to delude the state into celebrating its victory over the poet. But is the state really triumphant in this regard, earning for itself this ostensibly double success of effecting on Mazrui both "physical detention and ideological containment"?

Implicated in this humanist impulse in Mazrui's poetry is an acute awareness of personal tragedy and trauma. It is true that some of the poems are concerned about the global village, about humanity, and about disenchantment with the postcolonial situation in Africa and other all-encompassing issues that affect larger collectivities or entities. But *Chembe cha Moyo* is more than a chronicle of the faceless "inner feelings" of the third world as the writer of the back cover purports; it is also, if not more, about what the back cover and the introduction do not say—namely, meditation on the personal trauma and tragedy of incarceration. The poems in the anthology amply demonstrate how incarceration, isolation, torture, and trauma are inextricably bound up together. Therefore, poems like "Niguse," which thematize incarceration, do not only locate detention as the site for writing but also bring to the fore the extent of the site's traumatizing potential. Apart from "Niguse" there are a number of poems in the anthology that underwrite this sense of trauma in Mazrui's poetic narration of self and confinement. For example, in "Kifungoni," the speaker relates both the desolation of his sense of self and the dissipation or disappearance of hope for recovery:

Kwa kuangalia juu mbinguni
Na kulia sana kwa matumaini
Samawati imeingia
Mwangu machoni.

Kwa kuota mahindi mashambani
Na kulia sana mahuzuni
Manjano imeingia
Mwangu machoni.

Waache majemadari waende vitani
Wapenzi waende bustanini
Na walimu mwao darasani
Ama mimi, tasbihi nipeni
Na kiti cha kale, cha zamani
Niwe vivi nilivyo duniani:
Bawabu mlangoni
Katika kingo ya maumivu ya ndani
Maadamu vitabu, sheria na zote dini
Zitanihakikisha mauti
Nikiwa na njaa au kifungoni

[Because of looking up in the heavens
and weeping so much with optimism
The color blue has entered
into my eyes.

Because of the sprouting of corn in the fields
and weeping so much with sorrow
The color yellow has entered
into my eyes.

Let the commanders go to war
Lovers to the park
And teachers to their classrooms
As for me give me prayer beads
And an ancient chair, an old one
So that I can remain the way I am in the world:
A Sentry at the door
On the banks of inner pain
So long as books, the law and every religion
Will ensure my death
In my famished or incarcerated state.][40]

The speaker's "kulia sana kwa matumaini [weeping so much with optimism]" in the opening stanza is not a mark of optimism, but a postoptimism reevaluation of his state as an incarcerated individual. At any rate, that weeping has borne no tangible benefits. To the contrary, his eyes have turned blue, for nothing, one could say, because the much hoped for divine intervention has not materialized, much less changed his material reality. It is instructive that the initial "weeping with optimism" soon turns into "kulia sana mahuzuni [weeping so much with sorrow]." The trauma is intensified by the knowledge that while one languishes in detention, other people such as army generals, lovers, and teachers go about their duties as if there is nothing amiss.

But for the speaking "state guest," incarceration is never business as usual because of the attendant traumatizing deprivation of basic human rights and agency that it causes. The recourse to "tashbihi" (prayer beads) is not driven by optimism or deep religious devotion but a resignation to one's despondent destiny. The speaker in saying "Maadamu vitabu, sheria na zote dini / Zitanihakikisha mauti [So long as books, the law and every religion / Will ensure my death]" is fundamentally voicing a death wish. When the speaker alludes to "inner pain," he seems to imply the deep psychological trauma that gnaws at him in his incarcerated state. This inner pain is certainly related to what the back cover writer terms "hisia za ndani" (inner feelings) except that the inner pain here points to

Mazrui's imaginative projection of the trauma of detention rather than the hazy and faceless third world to which the back cover points.

The poet's "weeping with optimism" and "inner pain" are, then, to be regarded as both individual and collective, touching on his own lived experience as an incarcerated artist and the lived experience of Africa's postcolonial subjects. As someone incarcerated and objectified, he yearns for subjectivity and utilizes prison poetry as the means to achieve this end. "Weeping with optimism" is oxymoronic, but suggestive of the underlying hope amid the hopelessness of "weeping with sorrow" in postcolonial Africa. There is weeping because there is cause for weeping; African leaders have bungled independence and turned against their own people. It is not weeping for one's own sake, however. The lamentation is tinged with hope for a better future. In other words, postcolonial Africa is at once in a state of optimism and pessimism, simultaneously eliciting Afro-optimism and Afropessimism. Therefore, in trying to humanize himself, Mazrui uses his prison poetry to point to the dialectical duality of Africa's postcolonial predicament. If prison writing such as Mazrui's is a part of the "dirty little secret" of African literature, it is because the conditions of its emergence are a testament to the complexity of the postcolonial predicament. But for the individual incarcerated poet, composing such prison poetry is an escape route from despair and deprivation to the sense of becoming human again.

KEN WALIBORA WALIAULA is author of *Siku Njema* and *Narrating Prison Experience*. He currently works for the National Media Group, East Africa's leading media group.

Notes

1. Oyekan Owomoyela, "Dissidence and the African Writer: Commitment or Dependency?" *African Studies Review* 24, no. 1 (1981): 83–98.
2. Ibid., 83.
3. Ibid., 87.
4. Ibid.
5. Ibid., 85.
6. Amartya Sen, "Elements of a Theory of Human Rights," *Philosophy and Public Affairs* 32, no. 4 (2004): 315.
7. Mark F. N. Franke, "A Critique of the Universalisability of Critical Human Rights Theory: The Displacement of Immanuel Kant," *Human Rights Review* 14 (2013): 368–385.
8. Sen, "Elements of a Theory of Human Rights," 317.
9. Ioan Davies, *Writers in Prison* (Oxford: Basil Blackwell, 1990), 54.
10. Tejumola Olaniyan and Ato Quayson, *African Literature: An Anthology of Criticism and Theory* (Hoboken, NJ: Wiley-Blackwell, 2007), 139.

11. Robin D. G. Kelley, "A Poetics of Anticolonialism," introduction to *Discourse on Colonialism* by Aimé Césaire, trans. Joan Pinkham (New York: Monthly Review, 2000), 8.

12. Winnie Madikizela Mandela, *Part of My Soul Went with Him*, ed. Mary Benson (New York: Norton, 1984), 105.

13. Kelley, "A Poetics of Anticolonialsm," 28.

14. Njuguna Mutahi and Mugo Theuri, *We Lived to Tell* (Nairobi, Kenya: Friedrich Ebert Stiftung, 2003), 13.

15. Alamin Mazrui, *Chembe cha Moyo* (Nairobi, Kenya: East African Education Publishers, 1988); and Wahome Mutahi, *Three Days on the Cross* (Nairobi, Kenya: East African Education Publishers, 1991).

16. Basil Davidson, *The Black Man's Burden: Africa and the Curse of the Nation-State* (New York: Random House, 1992), 9.

17. Ibid.

18. Pieter Boele van Hensbroek, "Review: Cursing the Nation-State," *Transition*, no. 61 (1993): 114–122.

19. Mechthild Nagel, "'I Write What I Like': African Prison Intellectuals and the Struggle for Freedom," *Journal of Pan African Studies* 2, no. 3 (2008): 73.

20. Mutahi and Theuri, *We Lived to Tell.*

21. Mazrui, *Chembe.* All translations from Swahili are mine.

22. Alamin Mazrui, email communication with the author, March 6, 2007.

23. Mazrui, "Niguse," in *Chembe*, 1.

24. Mazrui, *Chembe*, 14, 27, 33, 40.

25. Nagel, "'I Write What I Like,'" 78.

26. Taffara Deguefe, *A Tripping Stone: Ethiopian Prison Diary* (Addis Ababa, Ethiopia: Addis Ababa University Press, 2003).

27. See Ngũgĩ wa Thiong'o, *Detained: A Writer's Prison Diary* (Nairobi, Kenya: East African Education Publishers, 1981), 6. See also Kunle Ajidabe, *Jailed for Life: A Reporter's Prison Notes* (Ibadan, Nigeria: Heinemann, 2003), 107–109. In his prison memoir, Ajibade points to the sustaining power of religious activity and narrates how "We [Nigerian political prisoners] found solace in Christianity and Islam as we waited for [President Sani] Abacha to decide our fate" (107).

28. Mazrui, "Niguse," 14.

29. Alexander Elison, "Opening the Circle: Storyteller and Audience in the Moroccan Prison Literature," *Middle East Literature* 12, no. 3 (2009): 294.

30. Mazrui, "Nitangojea," in *Chembe*, 8.

31. Mazrui, "Mtabiri," in *Chembe*, 52.

32. Ibid.

33. Ibid., 53.

34. Mazrui, "Mashindano," in *Chembe*, 31.

35. Ibid., 31.

36. Ali Mazrui, "Pan-Africanism and the Intellectual Rise, Decline and Revival," in *African Intellectuals: Rethinking Politics, Language, Gender and Development*, ed. Thandika Mkandawire (Dakar, Senegal: CODESRIA, 2005), 60.

37. Mazrui, "Mimi ni Mimi," in *Chembe*, 12.

38. Ibid.

39. Barbara Harlow, *Barred: Women Writing, and Political Detention* (Hanover: Wesleyan University Press, 1992), 24.

40. Mazrui, "Kifungoni," in *Chembe*, 13.

10 "Jesus Christ, Executive Producer"

Pentecostal Parapolitics in Nollywood Films

Akin Adesokan

THE MUCH-BEMOANED inability of the political postcolonial state to serve as the generator of social hope has had a remarkable impact on the growth of Pentecostal churches, which proliferate so fast and within such a logic of informalization as to make a reliable estimate of their number practically impossible. In many Nigerian cities, especially in the southern parts of the country, there is hardly a major street, not to say a neighborhood of a few thousand inhabitants, where one will not encounter at least a score of these churches. Sociologically, the explosion of Nollywood films is very much linked to the logic of informalization at work in the growth of these churches. In this chapter I stress the socio-aesthetic process of generating performative idioms from the conception of religious observation, charismatic self-presentation generating and feeding off yearning for material prosperity. A mode generically evocative of instrumental performances such as advertising on the streets and inside public transports is transposed into Nollywood aesthetics where spectacular self-presentation reinforces the mutuality of a moral-religious injunction and its embodiment in the personality of an admired actor, either as a performer of "turns" or as a glamorous figure. From looking at specific scenes in a Pentecostal-themed Nollywood film (*Scores to Settle*) and a film in which such acting is decisive (*Ogun Abele Tije?* [*Why Civil War?*]), I develop an argument about the relationships between actual and metaphorical deployment of Christ as a parapolitical authority in strategic alliance with kinship structures and agents of a failing bureaucratic state.

What does Dr. Sign Fireman of Perfect Christianity Mission have in common with Arthur, the narrator of Ben Okri's short story "Stars of the New Curfew"?[1] They are both unreal; the atmosphere in which Fireman luxuriates is so otherworldly, so uncanny, as to morph seamlessly into the fictional hallucinogenic world of Okri's characters. Fireman introduces his church as the place "where the supernatural is natural, and Jesus is Lord."[2] They are also both salesmen; one hawked POWER-DRUG to hapless passengers inside public transport in Lagos in the 1970s, while the other sold prosperity to hopeless Lagosians in the 1990s. This second feature, the status of both men as salesmen, is the more consequential for what I discuss in this chapter. That Okri's world is fictional is taken for granted, and to focus here on the surreality of characters like Fireman and thousands of others in that genre is ultimately a banal undertaking akin to debating which, between fiction and reality, is truer. In fact, I think that the world of Fireman is also taken for granted by its denizens, hence the non-ironic naming of Jesus Christ as the executive producer of a Nollywood film, for which I am obviously grateful, being saved the trouble of inventing a title for this chapter.[3]

My interest lies in the socio-aesthetic process through which the idioms of performance that are characteristic of salesmanship have been so formalized as to become permanent features in a variety of spheres—social, economic, religious, and political. First, I use the cinematic practice we call Nollywood as the mode in which this process is currently most active, and examine its aesthetic manifestation in the genre of films that promote the chiliastic worldviews of Pentecostalism. Since my larger interests are in the process by which the dramatic idioms characteristic of salesmanship are deployed in the service of parapolitical authority to substitute or supplement the failing bureaucratic state, I focus on Pentecostalism, but in relation to other types of self-conscious and instrumental performances such as advertising, political speech making, and preaching. What is significant in the deployment of these performative modes in Nollywood films is the sense of a sociality where acting, as spectacular self-presentation, is crucial. Thus, I also discuss films that do not advance a religious agenda but draw their power from the presence of actors who possess the skills of a salesman.

As a cinematic tradition, Nollywood is both absorptive and generative of these idioms, and if we pay very close attention to how this process unfolds in the different spheres, I think we will see more clearly the structural, and perhaps also causal, links between the crises of the political, postcolonial state in Nigeria and the variety of forms that constitute a cultural response to it. Thus, the commonplace separation of spheres in sociological terms is less useful for my purposes than the conceptual understanding of this cinematic practice as an ongoing aggregation of incommensurable spheres.

Secondly, I propose that parapolitics—that is, the self-contained mode of sociopolitical organization and rationality that is parallel to official politics—has existed in different forms in West Africa prior to its current manifestation as a result of neoliberal economic logic. It exists parallel to the operations of the political state, and is even permitted by them, as political scientist Paul Nugent's recent exhaustive study on African state makes clear.[4] Although the forms of social contract (coercive, productive, and permissive) that Nugent identifies between national and local elites are strictly about governance and the exercise (or lack) of sovereign control, I think that the vertical relationships he describes between the two tiers of governance inform politics so deeply as to impact on the horizontal one between, say, political and religious actors—that is, between the president of a country and the leader of a Pentecostal church. This fact has the potential of broadening the range of the permissive as a form of contract to the degree that, taken with the aggregation of spheres that I have suggested as a conceptual fact in Nollywood, it can incorporate the mode we think of as parapolitics.[5] These forms have become intensified in the poststructural adjustment era because the logic of structural adjustment as an instrument of neoliberal economic practice is to put limits on the direct impact of the state on economic activities. Concepts current in anthropology and economic history such as clientelism, informalization, parallel economy, and so on, were developed from analyses of forms of parapolitics—although they were not perceived or spoken about as such. It has been difficult to think of them in this manner because, as Nugent again claims, in both the structural and the historical explanations for the character of the contemporary African state "there is relatively little that seeks systematically to account for the reproduction of state institutions or modes of operation over time."[6]

Third, I also propose that parapolitics exists side by side with another process, that even within the Pentecostal movement, which makes parapolitical practice possible, there is also what some scholars have termed the "theocratic class."[7] This is the emergence and consolidation of a formation through which religious leaders use their position as spiritual counselors to political figures to advance the ideologies of their movements. This is a more complex development, drawing on a variety of sociopolitical practices that are quite diffuse, and each of which has been theorized in different ways. Its reemergence in the wake of a new generation of African leaders (think of the rumored visits of the presidents of Ghana and Zambia to Pastor Temitope Joshua's Synagogue of All Nations in a Lagos suburb) has to be conceptualized in a slightly different way from the prevalent critical analysis of nonstatist political organization through the prism of informalization or clientelism. Clarifying the precise operation of these two processes requires that I shift focus to Pentecostalism, especially its use of the cinematic media to advance its goals.

In their essay "Pentecostalism, Islam and Culture: New Religious Movements in West Africa," Brian Larkin and Birgit Meyer characterize the religious formation known as Pentecostalism as combining "the prospect of prosperity with deliverance from evil forces such as witchcraft, ancestral spirits and other demons" and thus these churches "have had tremendous appeal for people, and in particular young men and women, who desperately seek to make progress in life."[8] Sociological analyses of the Pentecostal movement in its various forms are certainly a vibrant branch of academic scholarship. What distinguishes the phenomenon addressed by current scholars such as Larkin and Meyer is its inflection with technological and cultural imaginaries, the fact that new processes of global formation play a major role in the emergence and direction of what we refer to as Pentecostal movements. These movements are effective as new modes of socialization, of identity, to the extent that, as I learned from conversation with a member of one such church, they conceivably replace the traditional kind of sovereignty once identified with the nation-state.[9] Pentecostal leaders have also been effective in using mass media in the propagation of their ideas, and the remarkably accessible format of video appears ready-made for the dissemination of popularizable ideas.

Pentecostal movements are not the only social formations that use charismatic self-presentation for dramatic purposes in Nollywood, nor are the methods they adopt exclusive to Christianity. There are denominations of Islam that rely on mass media, especially television and radio, to proselytize, using the rhetoric of melodrama to make political critique along moral lines. But the usage by Pentecostal churches is the most spectacular and best developed. This is not surprising. Pentecostal churches number among the fastest-growing socioreligious communities in Nigeria and beyond, and they proliferate within a logic of informalization very much linked to the processes that resulted in the development of Nollywood itself. As scholars Moradewun Adejunmobi, Obododimma Oha, and Onookome Okome have argued, Christian film production is an important aspect of spiritual instruction and proselytizing among Nigerian Pentecostal churches.[10] The most famous of these groups involved in film production is Mike Bamiloye's Mount Zion Faith Ministries International, which had a serial, *Agbara Nla* (*The Mighty Power*), running concurrently with Alhaji Yekeen Ajileye's *Koto Orun* (*The Fatal Abyss*) on primetime television in Lagos and its environs in the mid-1990s. Bamiloye is also the proprietor of Institute of Drama at a place named Habitation of Faith (on Ile-Ife Road in Ibadan), where students could study for certificates in Christian drama arts, with concentrations in such areas as church growth and church planting. This information is usually presented in advertorials or promotional introductions in films produced by the company.[11] There is also Liberty Films, owned and operated by Prophetess Helen Ukpabio, who recently achieved international notoriety for her claims of exorcising demons from so-called witch-children in the southeastern state of Akwa Ibom. Also noteworthy is the work of scholar Foluke Ogunleye (d. 2016), who began as a producer-director of evangelical films but has latterly focused on writing about Nollywood as an African-centered cultural practice.[12]

Primarily designed for evangelical purposes, Pentecostal films draw on different rhetorical tactics to expand the scope of religious conversion and instruction, and most directly, to dramatize the conflict between evil and godliness. From the perspective of Bamiloye's Mount Zion Faith Ministries and similar organizations, the films are spoken of as Christian dramas, and special courses are organized to train writers in that particular genre. They—the films—extend to the screen what routinely takes place inside churches, which themselves exist as forms of theater, it being understood that a church without a television slot is not fulfilling its pastoral injunction to the optimum. Instructively, with the advent of private broadcasting in the early 1990s, televised evangelization began to occupy the same time slot as television serials, which, considering the effects of commercialization and privatization, were already transforming into video dramas.

In their mise-en-scène, Pentecostal films combine faith healing with charismatic self-presentation by pastors on prime-time television and yearning for material prosperity, which performers and audiences alike believe to be both attainable and destined. The standard dramatic conflict is staged as an exorcism session, with prayers, cajoleries, and imprecations, ending with the ubiquitous "To God Be the Glory" in the credits. In fact, in her rich and informative essay "Technorality, Literature, and Vernacular Literacy in Twenty-First-Century Africa," Adejunmobi makes the important claim that "rhema—the word of God endowed with transformational power"—is deployed in Pentecostal films through "technologically mediated performances" (or technorality) as part of "alternative practices of orality" to neutralize the power embedded in traditional orature.[13] She goes into great detail in drawing a historical connection between literacy, writing, and the proliferation of Christian churches in Western Nigeria, claiming that Nigerian and Yoruba charismatic churches "take the literacy of members and potential converts for granted," and argues convincingly that a similar process is at work in the deployment of technological media—film, video, television—by today's Pentecostal churches.[14] The difference is that the usage of audiovisual media to proselytize depends less on literacy, or rather on a different kind of literacy, one that privileges the critical communicational interface of the oral and the visual. For example, discussing one Pentecostal film, *Àpótí Èrí* (*Treasure Chest of Testimony*), she writes of the eponymous protagonist's (Àpótí Èrí) "mother holding the Bible while praying and teaching her children Bible stories, including one about the Ark of the Covenant," but notes that the character is not shown simply reading or writing.[15] What matters in this context is not so much the literacy signified by the Bible as *rhema*, the uttered word of God endowed with transformational power.

Besides this issue of the communicability of biblical and religious ideas through dramatized speech, Pentecostal filmmakers also find Nollywood to be useful for their objectives because the form's low-intensity mode of production fits with the informal, improvisational character of a religious formation given to endless proliferation. The story of the emergence of Nollywood as an economic necessity spurred largely by the strictures of adjustment programs in the late 1980s is by now well known. This economic context and the ideological orientation of the films' dominant producers in contrast to the intellectual tradition shaping filmmaking in the decades prior (in Nigeria and in West Africa) have encouraged an analytical tendency to downplay the aesthetic aspects of the films. It is as if the professionals (as directors, actors, or producers) are too preoccupied with the need to turn a profit, and quickly too, to be bothered by the finer, technical details of a film's role as a mode of signification. Thus, we have a myriad of metaphors—"aesthetics of hunger," "imperfect cinema," "the art of man-must-wack" (the last phrase once used by the present writer)—to describe the formal orientation of the films. These terms are not inaccurate, but the economic does not exhaust the material context of Nollywood's immediate origins. Indeed, the primarily commercial needs of the cinematic practice can only be fulfilled within specific technological, formal, and infrastructural conventions.

As works of art, Nollywood films have a number of features that are so commonly found in film after film as to be characteristic of the form itself. These include narrative, proliferation, exhortation, and spectacle, although the emphasis on these features in a given film may be uneven depending on the contingencies of its production. Of these features, exhortation is the most relevant to the argument I am making here. By exhortation, I mean the conception of the dramatic conflict as a force field of moral injunctions. The explicit narrative, the spectacular development of the plot and the proliferative deployment of specific tropes, styles, "turns," and so on, are calculated to advance larger arguments about morally consequential conduct. The use of exhortation in the films usually requires the presence of an actor (either as a glamorous figure, a performer of accustomed mannerisms and idiolects, or as a physically compelling personality) to be effective. This is because the plausibility of a moral injunction depends equally on its philosophical ring and on the personality of the agent through whom it is dramatized. The spectrum of the persona ranges from a star—a leading man or woman—(i.e., Ramsey Nouah or Genevieve Nnaji) to a "talker" (i.e., Osuofia, Eleso, or Binta Ayo Mogaji) to the midget or giant (i.e., Akin and Pawpaw). My focus on the actor here is deliberate because it draws attention to the instrumental nature of Nollywood for the larger politics of films—Pentecostal or otherwise—that mobilize the performative skills of the salesperson. It means that not only Christian but also Islamic varieties of moral exhortation are admissible, and that similar skills can be put to service in films with purely secular objectives.

In order to clarify the point I am making here, I draw on sequences from two films, *Ogun Abele Tije? I* and *II* (*Why Civil War?* Parts I and II), released in the wake of intraethnic violence in Southwestern Nigeria in the late 1990s, and *Scores to Settle* (1998).[16] *Ogun Abele Tije?* is an attempt to critically discuss the spate of fighting (a communal war, to all intents and purposes) between residents of Ile-Ife and Modakeke in Osun state. The relevant sequence focuses on a visit by the president, a native son, who had previously chided his people—one of the warring sides—for letting him down. The current visit is designed to paper over that testy encounter, but before his arrival, a leader of the community (referred to as *Mogaji* or neighborhood/clan head) works the crowd, prepping it for the president's arrival. The actual visit is very brief, cannily indicative of the depth of rapport between state functionaries and the general populace, and is notable for consisting of an appropriately monologic stump speech. The text of that address, in Yoruba, is worth quoting here:

> Mo ki yin leekansii, eyin eniyan mi. E woo, e je ki nyo'go loju, oju loro wa. E pele, e ku ojo meta. Se e binu ojoonii? E ma binu si mi. Bo se ye kin se loju alejo ni mo se'hun. E ma pe mo kan yin labuku. Se Yoruba bo, won ni, Bi a ba ta ara ile eni lopo, a o le rira lowon-on. Amo, emi o ta yin lopo. Mo se ojuse mi bo se ye ki nse ni. Se Yoruba naa lo bo, won ni, Eeyan meji kii padanu iro. To difa fun ode meji to re igbo ode. Ti okan ni, O yo, ti ekeji ni, Mo ki i. [Ekini] ni ki lo ki? [Ekeji] ni ki lo yo? Hen-hen. E wa a je ki nsododo oro fun yin o. Ile ni mo wa yi o. Eyin ni temi, emi si ni tiyin. Oririn mi si niyii. Ododo ibe nipe, kii se eyin nikan ni mo nse ijoba le lori o. Bi mo tin se fun Hausa, beeni mo nse fun Ibo. Gbogbo eya ti nbe lorile-ede yii pata ni mo nse ijoba le lori. E waa gbo mi: Kii je ti baba ati omo ko ma laala. Eyiun naa tun ye yin? Ti e ba ti wa nfe nnkan lodo mi, ilekun mi ko ti, sisi lo wa nile. E maa beere, n'o si maa se e fun yin. E waa seun. Gege bii ileri mi, awon nnkan ti n'o maa se fun yin, gbogbo ohun ti Olorun ba fun mi nikapa ni. E wa a maa fi adura ranmi lowo. Emi naa o si maa ranti yin, ni gbogbo igba, n'o si maa fi adura ran yin lowo. Se e wa a ri baba Mogaji yii, ti e ba fee beere nnkan lowo mi, e maa ri won. Ti e ba ti nran won si mi, n'o si maa ri won, n'o si maa se e fun yin.
>
> [Greetings again, my people. Wait a minute, let me remove my eye-glasses (removes glasses) because understanding is a matter of direct contact. Yes, it's been a few days. Hope you're not upset over my conduct the other day? Don't be angry. That was the best way to conduct myself in front of outsiders. I did not damn you on purpose. After all, it is the Yoruba who say, "If one sells one's family on the cheap, one cannot buy it back at a high price." But I did not sell you out cheaply; I was only doing my duties. It is the Yoruba who, again, say, "Two people do not lose on account of a lie." Such it was with two hunters who go hunting. The first says, "It's come out!" and the other says, "I grab it!" The first asks, "What did you grab?" and the second retorts, "What came out?" Heh-hen, you understand. Let me tell you the plain truth: Here I am at home. I am yours, and you are mine. This is my origin. The truth of the matter is that you are not the only group upon whom I preside. I am the president for the Hausa, the Igbo, and the rest of the ethnic groups in the whole country. There's another saying, "A farmland may belong to father and son, but there must be boundaries nonetheless." You understand that as well? If you need anything from me, remember that my door is always open. You only need to ask, and I shall do as you request. Thank you. According to my promise, my duties to you have to fall within my capabilities. You will help me with prayers. I will in turn keep you in mind, at all times, and remember you in my prayers. Now, look at this man, your Mogaji. Whenever you need anything from me, just send him to me. Once I see him, I will send him back to you with your requests (my translation).]

In this minute-long speech, the president deploys two proverbs and one parable, all primed to elicit approving noises from the crowd. This actor's rhetorical gifts are of great significance here. He is famous with audiences of Yoruba films for his gift of the gab, his easy and assured way with proverbs and idioms. In this role, with his bulky frame and ethnic facial marks, he is deliberately cast to look like President Olusegun Obasanjo (1999–2007). The speech is full of internal contradictions (having promised to provide all his community wants, he soon declares that he will only act within his capability), non sequiturs, and plain rhetorical word games. The point is that the proverbs, idioms, and parables need not be suitable for the occasion; it is sufficient that they come from him and are sufficiently weighty to confirm his gifts and suitability for the role. This point has to be placed in context: the actor working the crowd just before the president's arrival is a trained Muslim cleric, and his rhetoric and demeanor are those of a persuader. In fact, part of his costume is the rosary of a Muslim cleric, worn round his neck. It is also important to add that *Ogun Abele Tije?* was directed by Alhaji Yekeen Ajileye (d. 2006), himself a Muslim cleric with a slew of titles in film and television. His popular but controversial television serial *Koto Orun* aired on television in the early 1990s and was sponsored by yet another Muslim cleric, Alhaji Abdul-Jabar, one of the many *marabouts* patronized by Nigeria's former military ruler, General Ibrahim Babangida (1985–1993).

There are two issues here that are pertinent to this chapter's argument. First, the presence of the two actors gives us an idea of a narrative sequence in which physical appearance, demeanor, and rhetorical skills are all indispensable to its successful execution. In this case, the skills needed are those of the salesman, the political speechmaker, and the preacher. The president's speech is funny, but he does not deliver it the way a comic actor might. By contrast, the Mogaji is all rhetorical aplomb: he meanders through the seated crowd, speaks to no one in particular, but in such a manner that everyone gets the point of his persuasion. He successfully works the crowd. Second, in the very figure of Alhaji Ajileye, the film's director, we have an Islamic equivalent of a member of the theocratic class. It is true that this film is different from *Koto Orun*, through which one can draw a connection between the serial's ideological argument—that sorcerers are responsible for the world's ill—and Babangida's patronage of Abdul-Jabar, the serial's sponsor. The relevant point, however, is that both works originate from the same ideological premise and that this premise is constituted in the conjunction of the rhetoric of moral suasion and actual clientelist relationship between the man of God or Allah and the man of power.

With the other film, *Scores to Settle*, the ideological premise of Pentecostal parapolitics comes into full relief. This film tells the story of a woman, Mabel, who as a child had been bewitched but who, becoming a born-again Christian as an adult, thus finds herself an unaware pawn in the game between the forces of evil (the marine spirits) and good (Christ). The decision of the leader of the marine spirits to get back at her through Charles, her only surviving son, points to the titular settling of scores. Indeed, Mabel's life has been a series of misfortunes—the death of her husband, the death of her first son, perennial homelessness, and sundry miseries. All of this is her punishment for breaking ranks with the marine spirits. In an important sequence toward the end of the film, we see a fine example of the classic scene of Pentecostal exorcism. The leader of the marine spirits has caused one of her members to transform herself into a beautiful maiden who goes about town luring men into bed and "harvesting" their genitals. Finally, she becomes Charles's girlfriend and is now living with him. A pastor and an aide arrive on a social visit to see Charles and to inquire why he has not been attending church lately. After the usual pleasantries, the pastor asks about Charles's mother. Embarrassed and struggling with complicated emotions, Charles tells the pastor: "My mother is a witch. She's been trying to kill me since. I had to send her back to the village." This statement is of extreme importance in terms of the wider context in which Pentecostal parapolitics has come to be a representational option in Nollywood. Charles's first declarative sentence echoes *Aje Ni Iya Mi* (*My Mother Is a Witch*), perhaps the most famous of the titles that the merchant Kenneth Nnebue produced for Yoruba theater-practitioners-cum-filmmakers before the making of *Living in Bondage*, in 1992.[17]

From this point to the end of the sequence, everything follows a simple causal, indeed predetermined, track. We see a direct link between the visit, the nature of the inquiries, the request for permission to pray for Charles, and the nature and force of the prayer. As Adejunmobi observes with respect to *Àpótí Èrí*, the crucial force is *rhema*, the manifestation of the power of the word of God for which the Bible becomes an accompanying fetish but not necessarily a book from which to read.[18] As the Bible-wielding pastor prays, noises filter in from an upstairs room, attracting Charles's attention, and forcing him to momentarily scurry away to check on his girlfriend. What he sees horrifies him, and he scrambles downstairs again, to ask for the pastor's help. All three men bound for the bedroom and the pastor resumes his prayers, further amassing the forces of good. The most potent tool in this encounter between good and evil is the prayer, and it is not a benediction but a jeremiad, a stream of ferocious imprecations aimed at the evil of a genital-harvesting sea monster in the form of a beautiful woman, whose true identity as a cobra is made concrete on the strength of prayer. In fact, the pastor's statement drives the point home as he warns Charles to step away from the writhing snake-woman: "this is a clear case of demonic manifestation."

Variations of this scene are present in dozens of Nollywood films such as *Omasiri* (2003) and *Violated* (1996), where spells previously cast on characters are shattered through prayers. My point is that religion matters at all in the first example (*Ogun Abeje Tije?*) to the extent that Islamic identity functions in the demeanor and rhetoric of the first actor, and to the extent that some of Ajileye's work could be understood in the spiral of patronages between him and Abdul-Jabar and between Abdul-Jabar and Babangida. At the time *Scores to Settle* was produced, the actor playing Charles (Richard Mofe-Damijo) was a member of the famous Pentecostal church Household of God, whose founder-pastor, Kris Okotie, is the author a book titled *The Last Outcast*.[19]

These kinds of dramatizations, especially the second film, may seem so distinct and transcendental as to be incompatible with the kind suitable for salesmanship, and which, as I claim with reference to Fireman, puts the preacher and the peddler in the same box. However, if we think of Pentecostal persuasion in instrumental terms, as a rhetorical attempt to work the imagination of the audience—internal or external—through spellbinding/breaking performances and conjurations (or the psychological means of projection, identification, and transference), we see that the immediate objectives are the same. Personally, I have witnessed occasions on the public transport in Lagos (*molue* [minibus] and ferry) where the drug peddler and the preacher competed to be the first to take the floor.[20] They appeal to the same band of commuters who could use a bit of tonic for body and soul, and enjoy a good performance in the bargain. (Incidentally, Arthur, the character in Okri's story, claims that he was initially regarded as a failed salesman because he entertained commuters more than he sold drugs.) Once one steps out of the molue, the jingles coming from drug hawkers on stationary vans selling antidotes to venereal diseases and sterility and from the public address system now ubiquitously used by bus loaders simply seeps through the Muslim call to prayer and especially into Christian church services to create a sensory overload, synesthesia, in the middle of the day.

The case of Fireman makes the comparison even more compelling. He is an example of the contemporary Lagos Pentecostal preacher, and since this type is ubiquitous, special skills are required to elevate oneself about the common run. By being made the subject of a documentary feature by BBC Channel 4 television, *Nigeria's Millionaire Preachers*, Fireman achieves this status, one for which his identity (turning out in suits and vehicles of the same color—for the documentary the color is gold) easily paves the way.[21]

At the beginning of the feature, we see the preacher in his church, calling forth people with infirmities and commanding the devil to come out of them. A small boy (ostensibly a middle-aged man whose growth is stunted by evil spirits) walks gingerly across the church floor, demonstrating the changes he has gone through. A young lady rises, contorts, writhes, and flops onto the floor, screaming and kicking. Fireman, microphone in hand, yanks off his designer jacket and yells back at the woman, who is now the very figure of the devil that has possessed her, damning her to hell and worse. There are no Bible-wielding gestures, not to mention quotations from the scriptures. After these shows of miracles, parishioners stream forth to praise the work of God by throwing cash into huge bags to the accompaniment of church songs. The service is over, and the narrator of the documentary (Seyi Rhodes) comments that those supposedly cured of their ailments can be seen leaving the church exactly as they had arrived, the only difference is that they are leaving without their money. In itself, the exorcism sequence of the documentary is basis enough for arguing that Fireman is a salesman fronting as a man of God. His acting skills are compelling and are deployed to signify him as a deliverer, in a show of Jeremiah-like damning of the forces of evil, very much reminiscent of the exorcism scene in *Scores to Settle*. There is also the bald fact of church members exchanging cash for the wonderful work of deliverance, gestures that are so integrated into the service they could well be daily tithing.

Yet there is more to come. The feature moves to a second part in which the viewer is led into Fireman's office. At the front desk is a female receptionist who, according to the narrator-presenter, was the same young lady who had been possessed by the devil. She is asked about that particular incident, but she denies any knowledge of it. To all appearances, she is now one of Fireman's employees. Past the front desk, we see the preacher addressing a roomful of people on the duties of a preacher. The addressees have books or notebooks opened before them, not unlike line salesmen taking coaching lessons from the chief personnel manager in a commercial business establishment. Here is the flamboyant preacher reproducing his own kind. This understanding of the practical purposes of the Pentecostal movement is at the root of the deployment of the mode in Nollywood, and it explains why the actor is indispensable to its realization, especially when the dramatic purpose manifests itself in the larger context of a commercial undertaking. There are two different ways that this instrumental use of the Pentecostal religious movement advances political objectives in the general direction of substitution or supplement to the orthodox authority of the postcolonial state.

First, there is the conception of the dramatic form as the basis of practical politics, but in the shadow of the routine legal structures of governmentality. It is in this sense that I use the term "parapolitics"—that is, as a self-contained mode of sociopolitical organization and rationality that is parallel to official politics. The films in this category are concerned with good and evil, which are respectively to be rewarded and punished, and Pentecostalism and traditional practices remain the spaces where hopes of such redress are conceivable. The bureaucratic state is hardly present in daily life, except as a specter of political manipulation or control: social amenities are notable for their perennial absence; the police would frame victim and culprit alike; and the courts would take bribes and deliver justice to whomever can pay. This is the commonplace view of these institutions, although there are also films committed to a constructive depiction of them.[22]

Just as scenes of exorcism are a routine aesthetic procedure in Pentecostal-themed Nollywood films, different modes of parapolitical deliberation occur as a tried-and-tested feature in certain categories of films. We see this in the use of the family gathering—the visit of the pastor and a friend to Charles's house at the end of *Scores to Settle* is an abridged example of this mode, which is well developed in the work of Tunde Kelani and a few other directors. There is also the format of the court as a means of arbitration, which points to a constructive depiction of the institutions of modernity and represents a secular attitude to the recuperations of the ideals of the modern state. Indeed, the recourse to the court or the police shows a fidelity to the modern state as such, and in the calculations of the filmmakers, it is adjudged a more enlightened worldview than the knee-jerk resort to sorcery or religious imprecation. Finally, there is the view of the church as a self-contained site in which the values of orthodox political society are shown to be inadequate for, and indeed constitutes an impediment to, spiritual grace. There is a case of self-fulfilling prophecy here (no pun intended) because, as I said earlier, one objective of the structural adjustment regime is to demarcate the power of the state as an economic actor, to limit its power as such. The consequence of this process for formations like Pentecostalism has been to fully supplant the state in precisely these areas. But this is a partial picture.

To paint a more complex picture, we need to think of the emergence, even within this Pentecostal movement, of the rise of the theocratic class—that is, the consolidation of a class of religious leaders whose role is to leverage their position as spiritual counselors to political figures to advance the ideologies of their movements. Following Jeff Haynes's formulation, Ebenezer Obadare has made a compelling argument about the rise of the "Pentecostal presidency" in Nigeria, especially in the wake of the second presidential rule of Obasanjo, who presented himself in the late 1990s as a "Born Again" president.[23] The nature of the relationship between political figures like Obasanjo and others without his prestige and Pentecostal pastors is a complex example of parapolitics. In this case, the interest is in the orthodox political state but in terms of controlling it, or at least controlling those who control it. This relationship, between Pentecostalism and state power, is quite entrenched in public consciousness. While Obasanjo's opportunistic deployment of the sentiment as abstract humanism in his book *This Animal Called Man*—published just before he was nominated as the presidential candidate of the People's Democratic Party in 1998—might not have caught popular imagination, his subsequent patronage of religious leaders both conventional and Pentecostal did blaze a trail.[24] As Obadare has explained in detail, Obasanjo emerged from years of imprisonment during the Sani Abacha regime to proclaim his "spiritual rebirth" and subsequently held Thanksgiving church services.[25] A society securely in the grip of superstition and religious fatalism would readily accept the narrative of divine intervention in the series of events surrounding Obasanjo's second coming as president of Nigeria: a man sentenced to life imprisonment, whose former deputy, General Shehu Yar'Adua, was medically murdered in jail, and who was overwhelmingly supported by the nation's power brokers to run successfully as presidential candidate.

That Obasanjo's dalliance with Pentecostal religious leaders became fashionable with political officeholders was in evidence when, in 2011, soon after his election, photographs of President Goodluck Jonathan kneeling in prayer before Pastor Enoch Adeboye, General Overseer of the Redeemed Christian Church of God, were widely circulated in all the media. The relationship between Abdul-Jabar and Babangida, which I discussed earlier, is of this kind, in addition to the fact that Abdul-Jabar's importance lay in his charismatic qualities (performed for the camera).[26] The example of African presidents visiting Pastor Joshua's Synagogue is well known, but I doubt that it can rise, or has risen, to the level of putting the pastor in the class of the theocratic elite. This mode of operating the levers of power is quite complex, and Nollywood films have not systematized it as they have the parapolitical mode, outside of standard depiction of such powers behind the throne as charlatans.

Indeed, Nollywood films have not been able to systematize the theocratic elite mode of political patronage in part because, in representational terms, such systematization would expose the unreliability of the narrative of Pentecostalism as primarily unworldly. After all, a movement that presents its interests in spirituality is hard put to justify this kind of involvement in temporal governmentality.[27] Ultimately, though, the question is not so much whether the Pentecostal movement can justify such an involvement as that Nollywood, in aesthetic and ethical terms, has not found a way of broaching narratives of this kind. Of course, such representations of the attitudes of religious personages to power and their temporal obsessions are well known in Nigerian cinema and theater. Right from Wole Soyinka's iconic figure of Brother Jero in the plays *The Trials of Brother Jero* and *Jero's Metamorphosis*, the figure of the religious leader as a charlatan has been part of the cultural repertoire.[28] The figure once attained something of a type, especially among the traveling theater professionals. The themes of lust for power, money, and other material possessions were a staple of comic and melodramatic scenarios in stage plays, radio broadcasts, and photoplays.[29] The same figure has appeared in Nollywood films, such as *Iru Oka* (*The Viper's Tail*, 2002) and Kelani's *Agogo Eewo* (*The Sacred Gong*, 2002), although the emphasis in these films is on the practice of seeking divine intervention through the instrumentality of a cassock-wearing pastor, not on the figure as such. What appears to have changed is this: the depth of the involvement of Pentecostal Christianity in everyday life in Nigeria is so total that the resources available to the cinematic practice, tried and tested for the melodramatic Jero type and routinized for commercial realism, do not seem capable as yet of rising to the representational challenge.

To focus on this issue as a technical problem is to address a central philosophical problem in Nollywood—the fitful understanding of political critique. Generally, political critique in Nollywood films operates either as customary injunction, using moral language to address sociopolitical issues but ignoring an analysis of systems, or as politically sophisticated critique that unfolds through culturally specific forms of allegory. The majority of Nollywood films proffer the first kind, while the work of Kelani and Tade Ogidan, and recently Jeta Amata exemplify the second. It is clear, however, that a cinematic representation of the theocratic elite subgenre of Pentecostalism cannot productively deploy either of these forms of political critique. For this reason, the new directions in Nollywood indicated in the work of younger producer-directors like Emem Isong, Kunle Afolayan, Kenneth Gyang, Seke Somolu, and Sandra Obiago are both welcome and intriguing. These are young directors more invested in the technological and social possibilities of contemporary realities, and whose historical references are profoundly complex if not inchoate. Some of Afolayan's most recent films (*The Figurine* [2010], *Phone Swap* [2012]) are remarkably indifferent to the kind of ideological investment underwriting Pentecostal films, and to the status of the state, whether failed or thriving.

Another noteworthy development that further underlines the ideological limitations of Nollywood as a field of representation is the emergence of Pentecostal pastors who engage in political preaching and progressive politics to the point of becoming involved in mainstream party politics. An excellent example of this trend is Pastor Tunde Bakare of Latter Rain Assembly, who rose to become a leader of the Save Nigeria Group, an activist coalition that came into existence in the context of the intrigues surrounding the fatal illness of President Umaru Yar'Adua in mid-2010. From keeping up his fiery sermons and appearances at political events, the pastor moved quickly to party politics, becoming the vice presidential candidate to General Muhammadu Buhari of Congress of People for Change, one of Nigeria's major political parties in the general elections of April 2011. The challenge that this latter development presents is both to representation and critique.

While it is the case that three spheres of representation—political, religious, and artistic—exist as concentric circles, it seems that the artistic sphere is the one without sufficient awareness or consciousness of this challenge. The nomination of Professor Yemi Osinbajo, a constitutional lawyer and pastor of the Redeemed Christian Church of God, as the vice presidential candidate of the All Progressives' Congress, and the party's electoral victory in the 2015 general elections are further evidence of the troubling, if successful, alliance of official politics and Pentecostalism. In a country where Pentecostalism exerts the kind of influence discussed so far, the act of identifying a pastor as a viable option for electoral gains is politics in a strict sense, and it sidesteps the question of whether Pentecostal parapolitics can become a process of government. To argue that Osinbajo is both a successful lawyer-politician and a respected pastor would be to ignore the fact that the candidate's status as a lawyer is less of a factor in a society where the theocratic elite already have much political weight. What such an alliance means for the state where this has happened is a question that Nollywood can begin to address only when it develops enough reflexivity to imagine such reality as the basis for artistic exploration.

AKIN ADESOKAN is Associate Professor of Comparative Literature and of Cinema and Media Studies at the Media School, at Indiana University, Bloomington. His books include *Roots in the Sky*, a novel, and *Postcolonial Artists and Global Aesthetics*.

Notes

In the course of researching this chapter, I received invaluable support from Gbemisola Adeoti, Sola Olorunyomi, Bond Emeruwa, and Joe Dundun, and I wish to express my sincere gratitude to them. I also wish to acknowledge the feedback from Tejumola Olaniyan as well as the anonymous reviewers of this chapter.

1. See Ben Okri, "Stars of the New Curfew," in *Stars of the New Curfew* (New York: Penguin, 1989), 81–144.
2. *Nigeria's Millionaire Preachers*, dir. Matt Hann (Silver Media for Channel 4, 2001).
3. *Majemu Ikoko* (*Secret Covenant*), dir. Debbie Animashaun (His Glory Drama Ministries, Nigeria, PAL, 1998).
4. Paul Nugent, "States and Social Contracts in Africa," *New Left Review* 63 (May–June 2010): 35–68.
5. Ibid., 56.
6. Ibid., 42.
7. Ebenezer Obadare, "Pentecostal Presidency? The Lagos–Ibadan 'Theocratic Class' and the Muslim 'Other,'" *Review of African Political Economy* 110 (2006): 665–678.
8. Brian Larkin and Birgit Meyer, "Pentecostalism, Islam and Culture: New Religious Movements in West Africa," in *Themes in West Africa's History*, ed. Emmanuel Kwaku Akyeampong (Oxford, UK: James Currey, 2006), 290.
9. See Akin Adesokan, *Postcolonial Artists and Global Aesthetics* (Bloomington: Indiana University Press, 2011), 12.
10. See Moradewun Adejunmobi, "Technorality, Literature, and Vernacular Literacy in Twenty-First-Century Africa," *Comparative Literature* 60, no. 2 (2008): 164–185; Obododimma Oha, "Nation, Nationalism, and the Rhetoric of Praying for Nigeria in Distress," *Interventions: International Journal of Postcolonial Studies* 7, no. 1 (2005): 21–42; and Onookome Okome, "'The Message Is Reaching a Lot of People': Proselytizing and Video Films of Helen Ukpabio," *Postcolonial Text* 3, no. 2 (2007), http://postcolonial.org/index.php/pct/article/view/750/419.
11. These advertorials are presented as trailers to films coming out of the stable of Mount Zion Faith Ministries, in much the same way that non-Pentecostal films advertise the products

and services of their sponsors or executive producers. For a classic comparison, see the promos of the herbal medicine manufacturer Yem-Kem, in Alhaji Kareem Adepoju's film, *Ekun Oko Oke* (*The Indomitable*, 2002).

12. For an overview of her work in the two spheres, see Foluke Ogunleye, ed., *African Video Film Today* (Manzini, Swaziland: Academic, 2003).

13. Adejunmobi, "Technorality," 177, 176.

14. Ibid., 173.

15. *Àpótí Èrí*, dir. Mike Bamiloye (Mount Zion Faith Ministries International, Nigeria, PAL, 2002); Adejunmobi, "Technorality," 175.

16. *Ogun Abele Tije?*, dir. Alhaji Yekeen Ajileye (Oyedele Production, Nigeria, PAL, 1999); *Scores to Settle*, dir. Chico Ejiro (Ossy Afason Production, Nigeria, PAL, 1998).

17. This complex relationship between Pentecostalism and supernatural belief in sorcery points to a pattern of values in which the so-called African religious worldviews, which smack of the occult, collude with Pentecostalism, both shown to be closely related and having more in common with each other than we currently think. This connection remains to be carefully theorized.

18. Adejunmobi, "Technorality," 177.

19. Kris Okotie, *The Last Outcast* (Lagos, Nigeria: Marskeel, 2001).

20. See Akin Adesokan, "A Lagosian Original: Preliminary Notes on the Speech of the Street," in *Art, Parody and Politics: Dele Jegede's Creative Activism, Nigeria and the Transnational Space*," ed. Aderonke Adesola Adesanya and Toyin Falola (Trenton, NJ: Africa World Press, 2013), 155–167.

21. *Nigeria's Millionaire Preachers.*

22. Films such as *Idaamu Agbodegba* (*The Informer's Dilemma*, 2003) and *Morolayo Ajifa* (*Morolayo the Freeloader*, 2004) belong to what may be categorized as police–public relations genre of films.

23. Obadare, "Pentecostal Presidency?," 666. See also Jeff Haynes, *Religion and Politics in Africa* (London: Zed, 1996).

24. Olusegun Obasanjo, *This Animal Called Man* (Abeokuta, Ogun: AFL, 1998).

25. Obadare, "Pentecostal Presidency?," 665.

26. The "message from our sponsors" segments during the broadcast of *Koto Orun* featured clips of the cleric in preaching mode. Instructively, during the mass protest following the annulment of the presidential elections of June 12, 1993, Abdul-Jabar's house and central mosque in Ketu, a Lagos suburb, was attacked by demonstrators apparently because of his association with Babangida, who had annulled the results.

27. Obadare argues that the pressure group Christian Association of Nigeria (CAN) used to be less engaged in politics until the imagined "creeping 'Islamization' of the country" forced it to change tactics and become proactive ("Pentecostal Presidency?," 668).

28. See Wole Soyinka, "The Trials of Brother Jero" and "Jero's Metamorphosis," in *Collected Plays 2* (New York: Oxford University Press, 1974), 143–171; 173–213.

29. In this connection, see Karin Barber's observations in "Radical Conservatism in Yoruba Popular Plays," *Bayreuth African Studies Series* 7 (1986): 5–12.

11 Hi-fi Sociality, Lo-fi Sound

Affect and Precarity in an Independent South African Recording Studio

Louise Meintjes

For its working-class clientele, Shirimani Studios is perfectly situated above the taxi rank on a crumbling edge of inner-city Johannesburg. Close to transport, but above its din on the eighth floor of an office block, the studio is adequately equipped (more or less) for run-of-the-mill digital production. Joe Shirimani has put few resources into the look of the studio, or its upkeep in this dark and grungy building, save for a coat of strawberry-pink paint and a security gate at the entrance. But the enterprise is there, with Shirimani's silver discs hanging on the wall from his glory days as a Shangaan disco artist. Two young African house engineers cater to Shirimani's clientele.

Low budget and independent, Shirimani Studios is symptomatic of the rationalized music industry in South Africa of the new millennium. Yet it is also a sign of new forms of postapartheid empowerment for African entrepreneurs, studio personnel, and musicians. For musicians who are trying to make do and also still make art, studios like this offer an opportunity even while they limit artists' range of sound production and professional possibilities. I look closely at a Shirimani recording session in order to consider how musicians manage these lived tensions in the course of their creative practices. I focus on the alternative networks they cultivate to enable their studio work and then on their in-studio social play and technological choices. Improvisations among the participants point to their underlying sense of precarity and to their resolve to combat it. What are the affective dimensions entailed in working toward a future at the turn of the millennium in South Africa? That is, how do traditional Zulu musicians take hold of the promises proffered by a new democracy while struggling under the burden of an increasingly rationalized state shaped by the racialized history of colonialism and apartheid?

Migrant Zulu men who sing and dance in the *ngoma* and *maskanda* styles struggle and play from positions of political and economic precarity in relation to the contemporary state. Siyazi Zulu and his musical compatriots—the musicians in the studio session I analyze—are poorly, partially, or temporarily employed, if they have work at all. In Johannesburg, they live in decrepit conditions, in men's hostels, informal settlements, shared rooms in inner-city apartments, or in backyard rentals in the townships. They speak of themselves as politically marginalized, unrepresented by an African National Congress that has failed to create jobs and to deliver anticipated resources in their home area in rural KwaZulu-Natal (an area that had fully supported the Zulu nationalist Inkatha Freedom Party during the liberation struggle).

Such musicians are also undervalued in the music industry. They are catalog artists playing in styles considered by musicians and industry alike as traditional, rather than pop icons who are feted and branded. That is, they are professionals who have enjoyed some success in the past and have a regional market of consumers who mostly live in poverty. Some were once under contract to a record company, though no one in this Shirimani session is currently. Once riding the wave of South Africa's dominating presence on the world music circuit in the mid-1980s to mid-1990s, and now struggling to sustain local musical careers or to find alternative employment, they are like the many wage laborers who have become expendable to the state.[1] They hover beneath the radar of the national culture industry, hustling for performing and recording opportunities. Trying to live as responsible breadwinners for their rural households while sustaining their city life and mobility, these musicians hope for a professional break and work toward it.[2]

This predicament is not unique to South African musicians. Global cultural production has rationalized. The vertical and horizontal integration of its multinational industries has increasingly excluded most world music and Afropop musicians from international circulation networks.[3] The sense of failed promise may be heightened for South Africans. At the time when the lifting of apartheid's racist restrictions opened new opportunities for Africans, the restructuring of the global and domestic music industries further curtailed access for many musicians. Not only this, but the industry's streamlining followed South Africa's dramatic flourish on the international stage that Paul Simon's *Graceland* album (1986) had catalyzed. For Zulu musicians like Siyazi and his compatriots, the decline was perhaps especially felt, for Zulu-identified musical styles and Zulu musicians (Ladysmith Black Mambazo, Mahlathini and the Mahotella Queens, Johnny Clegg and Savuka) had dominated the South African roster overseas.

Sidelined by the new state and the changed multinational industry at the turn of the millennium, Siyazi and his compatriots live, earn, and create music in a provisional space. I want to understand the production choices such artists make as they settle for poorer quality recorded sound than necessary in this provisional political space. In part, this is a political issue: How do musicians utilize a low-budget studio (a limited resource) to counteract the lived effects of the limitations of the state? In part, this is an aesthetic issue: Why settle for representing your musical ideas with poorer quality sound than necessary when alternative choices available to you could result in higher fidelity? Why make production choices that compromise the clarity of sound that makes close listening rewarding? Why not spend the resources you have on fewer hours in a more expensive studio and thereby work with more experienced studio technicians? These choices also have implications for expanding their markets: better fidelity—coming as close as the musicians could to major industry production standards—would enhance the chance that professional opportunities would ensue beyond the reach of their own relationships. Better fidelity would facilitate their (re)entrance into the major industry networks, the "official highly regulated forms of media trade" linked to the "official world economy."[4] That is, a product of higher sound fidelity would offer a better chance of counteracting the state's limited delivery to these migrant musician-citizens than would a recording of poor sound quality. Whether through borrowing, negotiating, or otherwise scraping together the money, these artists expend scarce resources to record in a studio. Yet for comparable cost, they make decisions about technology and studio practice that involve goals other than getting the best sound they could.

Changes in the studio landscape of the city enabled by advances in recording and sound processing technology influenced the musicians' choices. With developments in digital sound technology and gear designed and marketed for home use, small studios proliferated in the early 1990s. While the premier recording studios associated with the parastatal South African Broadcasting Corporation and the major or multinational recording companies offered state-of-the-art professional studio space, some of the small, independent production sites proved that they could also produce hits. The explosion of home and small recording studios is a global phenomenon, the rise of which predates South Africa's political transition, but Zulu migrant musicians largely view them as part of the postapartheid musical landscape, offering new freedoms from white rule. While the big companies carried the baggage of apartheid's labor relations and of white capital, many of the new independents were black-owned and staffed with black expertise.[5] They offered black African musical professionalism at an affordable rate. To access a recording booth, small-scale musicians no longer needed to work through company gatekeepers—A&R men (artist and repertoire staff), in-house producers, or established independent producers. Indeed, they could work their own social networks to access the necessary resources to record. They could extract favors, call on obligatory relations, offer cuts, make deals, request loans, and expedite processes on the basis of promises to their friends and affiliates who themselves were working the margins and building alternative networks.

After three recordings produced and released in 1988, 1991, and 1994 through Gallo (Africa), South Africa's major domestic recording conglomerate (and subsequent to his renowned producer's tragic death), Siyazi turned to self-production.[6] For his next seven recordings he hoped to use the major companies to distribute his CDs, and on the first three occasions secured contracts with them (EMI in 1997 and 1998, Gallo [Africa] in 1999). For most projects he picked coproducers. For the Shirimani recording he chose Philemon Hamole, drummer from the Makgona Tsohle Band that backed Mahlathini and the Mahotella Queens as they toured the world. Siyazi also picked his musicians, Zulu *maskandi* (singer-songwriters) who could add instrumentation to support his lead ngoma vocals and the backing vocals mostly sung by members of his male song and dance troupe. To realize these recording projects, having lost access to the major companies (like many traditional musicians had), he secured backing capital, albeit precarious, for each recording from small-scale black entrepreneurs with whom he was acquainted. Enoch Nondala, once a salesman in the apartheid music industry and now an independent producer-promoter, backed the Shirimani project. Stanley Dladla, an Inkatha Freedom Party politician-cum-businessman who lived in a neighboring chiefdom and who had entered the entertainment industry, backed another.[7] Siyazi was set to do his own projects his own way.

I argue that affectively cultivating a sense of self-reliance in a precarious context is a tenet of good Zulu manhood in rural and migrant working-class communities. In its contemporary register, this requires of artists such as Siyazi that without work (in the form of employment) they nevertheless continue the practice of working (as a gesture of effort). They pursue cosmopolitan relationships in acts of laboring. Their engagement is premised on the hope of experiencing the enchantments African cosmopolitanism offers: visibility and audibility beyond the homestead, dignity despite contending with living conditions of decrepitude, equitable encounter and exchange beyond the community, recognized social citizenship, and the standing of responsible men at home.[8] Effectively, they respond as self-reliant, respectable Zulu men to an unresponsive state, to the failed promises of a new democracy. I show in what follows that recording studio practice enables these men to perform and produce respectable manhood, at once engaging the professional world and cultivating the sociality of Zulu men for the pleasure such relationships offer as well as for their support.

In their precarious predicament in relation to the state, these musicians are like many other South Africans; in their tenuous relation to the culture industry, they are like many underserved artists in the Global South. But their predicament is differently inflected: the brutal peculiarities of apartheid and the striking late-apartheid presence of South African music internationally heighten the stakes of participation as Zulu men in the world via the mediated arts. Such dynamics, along with the digital advances in sound recording that facilitate self-help, prompt these traditional Zulu musicians to turn to Shirimani Studios.

Hi-fi Sociality

"Sing, men," instructs Nothi Ntuli, maskandi guitarist and session musician, spurring the Shirimani recording session on, on the first day of a three-day recording session, July 24, 2002. Fellow musicians laugh, for Nothi is picking up a phrase in the lyrics and addressing it to his friends. Sing, men.

"Soyishela kanjani intombi ephuza ugavini? [Who would woo a girl who drinks liquor?]" sing the backing vocalists, Pat and Mkhize, to the rhythm tracks emanating from the speakers in the control room.[9]

Lahl'Umlenze is comping on his concertina. He inserts a trickling treble run here and there. Nothi complements his concertina groove, adding cyclical guitar riffs. Pat and Siphiwe are learning the backing vocals. Composer, producer, and lead singer Siyazi is singing along. Coproducer Philemon listens, joining them in their circle of moving bodies in Shirimani's tiny control room. (No one wants to use the recording booth.) They are enjoying themselves. The sound engineers are working at the console programming a rhythm track. Guided by the feel of the singing, they are layering bass drum, snare, tom, and high hat lines to create the basic groove. I am recording them recording.

"Uyaphuza ayabhema uyayadakwa [She drinks, she smokes, she gets drunk]," the musicians sing in close harmony.

"Soyishela kanjani intombi ephuze ugavini emakhaya? [Who would woo a girl who drinks liquor at home?]"

Nothi complains. It's an old-fashioned lyric Siyazi has written, citing the girls alone. Add in the men, he prompts.

Siyazi experiments, hooking the word *amadoda* (men) onto the end of the phrase.

"*Madoda*!" states Pat approvingly. He likes the way Siyazi is singing it, with a high tone in this tonal language. "*Madóda*!" others copy, chuckling. They are enjoying the reference not just to "men"—with a straight tone—but to a large group of men standing together, adult men in solidarity, citizens. Themselves, now.

"So you like 'amadoda' [(sung with a high tone) in the lyrics]?" Nothi is seeking Pat's agreement.

Collectively they try "amadoda" as the end to the chorus line, shifting the lyrics from a call to all citizens to stop the actions of girls, to one to curtail irresponsible men as well.

While figuring out the finesse of these lyrics, Nothi also coaches Pat and Siphiwe to sing in a more fashionable style, not "kicking the voice hard" like Siyazi does. He proposes they sing with less stridency, bringing out the "sweetness" of Pat's upper line and the blend of the two, and ensuring that their phrase end, "amadoda," won't "clash" with Siyazi's overlapping lead. A different timbre will differentiate the two in a busy arrangement.

"We can always cut 'madoda' off [edit it out] if it isn't feeling right," Nothi advises them, momentarily taking charge of the recording process as they work on their arrangement.

"Uyaphuza ayabhema uyayadakwa [She drinks, she smokes, she gets drunk]," they sing over and over, all of them together while the concertina and guitar riff on.

"Soshela kanjani intombi ephuze ugavini emakhaya? [Who would woo a girl who drinks liquor at home?]"

"Don't sing like you're from the township!" shouts out Lahla over the dense sound of playing together. He demonstrates his preferred glissandi (ornamental pitch glides between two notes of a melody) by swooping his index finger up and down as his voice slides up to key pitches and off others, in traditional Zulu vocal style. Soon Pat and Siphiwe have shifted their singing to match his, in their sweet timbre.

"Now we are on the right track!" Lahla affirms, getting in position to dance. But it is time for a concertina run so he swings the instrument into place and squeezes his way back into the song.

As the playing winds down and Pat and Siphiwe drop out of the groove having grasped their parts, Philemon picks up their melody and tweaks the lyrics to sing a sexual joke.

Umzansi Zulu Dancers' recording sessions are long, boisterous ones. Without a company producer whom they would have had in an apartheid studio or would have were they recording in a premium studio, all the musicians arrange and rearrange their songs.[10] They improvise their parts, co-conceive of the backing tracks, and dance to their creations in the control room of the studio. Without a white engineer, isiZulu becomes the lingua franca. In the midst of the camaraderie of *madoda*, men, *madóda*, men of the world, these musicians finesse their songs. Distilling the difference between singing a high tone on a single syllable and maintaining the pitch level through a fast-moving utterance (a distinction that will be hard to hear on the recording), or tweaking the meaning of the lyrics with a phrase extension, or inflecting the timbre of the backing voices for sweetness and contrast, or working on the glissandi, these musicians attentively craft the detail of their recording. They collectively negotiate a sound drawing on their repertoire of urban and homely Zulu gestures and new and old styles. In the process of settling on a sound, they voice changing generational ideas and reference values of contemporary manhood. These debates are embedded in the resulting sound while positions on them are staked out among the speakers. For example, Siyazi is criticized as outdated in how he genders his lyrics. With discourse about rights now circulating in the national arena, and the earnings of young mobile women supplementing the domestic shortfall within the homestead, the musicians modify his lyrics that single out girls' immoral behavior.[11] At the same time, the backing vocalists are castigated for the fashionable township sound in which they sing those lyrics, a sound that forgets the rural homestead.

There are two kinds of work being done here: the work of recording a song and the work of cultivating sociality (that is Zulu, contemporary, male, and migrant) in the studio. These two processes become one and the same, with seamless shifts in register, when *madoda* in the song becomes self-referential, or the lyrics are tweaked into a male sexual joke after the song ends. Likewise, criticism of a township-sounding vocal becomes an assertion of a self that incorporates rural, migrant affect along with the urban and wider world consisting of the township, the city, and the studio. Such moments create a sense of home in the song: home as city, homestead, and street, home as having mobility through these spaces. Simultaneously, these moments play a role in shaping personhood in the studio through ways of relating to the music and to one another. The cultivation of this Zulu, contemporary, male, and migrant sociality not only happens in the studio; it also becomes of the studio. The musicians make their way of being together into a local studio practice.

At other times during the session, artists privilege the work of cultivating sociality over the professional task at hand, at the expense of recording efficiency. When Jabu the bass player arrives, he doesn't have a plectrum. They send him out into the city below to purchase one. Maskanda needs the clipped and percussive sound of the attack a plectrum produces when it strikes a string, not the longer (and hence gentler—weaker in these musicians' terms) onset of a note that a fleshy finger produces as it pulls the string. With Jabu's plectrum in place, the musicians start to coach him in the bass lines they want. He is a stranger to most in the group, and he doesn't know their songs. They play with his trials, sing with him, and vocalize his lines. It takes forever, but they persist. They want the bass amp miked. For maskanda it must be amped and miked, they say.[12] They send him into the recording booth. Set your sound on your amp, they say, otherwise the engineers will take control of it. There is extraneous noise on the bass. They need the engineers to isolate and remove the glitch. They wait. The young engineers call Shirimani to help them solve the problem. The engineers can't figure it out. Well, we'll do it DI (direct inject, plugging straight into the console rather than using an amp), the musicians eventually agree, because it is only a guide bass line.[13]

So much attentive crafting for a line that will be replaced for the master recording! Later in the week, bassist Robert Bhengu will lay down the final version. Yet the musicians attend precisely to Jabu's melodic lines, glissandi, and rhythmic patterns, even though he is a stand-in for Bhengu. They spend studio time shaping the sound of his bass, and they articulate strong preferences about the right recording process to render the ngoma/maskanda sound till a glitch prompts them to compromise.

In the way these deliberations unfold, the musicians perform their professional experience with recording to one another. (They make it evident to their peers that Jabu's ineptitude as a session musician in this style irritates them.)[14] *Amadóda*. But collectively conceiving of Jabu's bass lines in this way takes up hours of studio time. In other recording processes this would probably have happened in a rehearsal room. For laying down a temporary bass guideline, other musicians might not have spent studio time refining the sound, or worrying about the technique of recording them (DI or through the amp). They could have directed the time and money on finessing sounds that would become fixtures in the final project. Laying the guideline in this arduous collaborative way provides the musicians with an opportunity to compose, arrange, and rehearse. It is a creative process through which they perform competence to one another as fellow musicians, as ngoma and maskanda artists with studio experience, and as friends. The process puts them in charge of the control room space and the pacing of the session.

Against the backdrop of the programmed percussion, Jabu and Lahla are playing along while Nothi records his guitar part. Siyazi, Pat, and Siphiwe dance together. Lahla dances with his concertina.

Siphiwe tries to imitate Siyazi's footwork and dance turn. There is danced joviality.

"Hey, *madoda*," Nothi calls out over his guitar riff. "Hey, you young men," he calls again, "You're disturbing me. I can't manage to avoid you. You're too close to me."

"I noticed you thought about stopping," Philemon says to Siyazi, who with an eye on the recording process underway had hesitated at one moment in the cramped dancing space.

"Okay, sorry, we'll leave it," says Siyazi, folding his arms and stepping back. "It's the armbands that are waking up!" he jokes using a Zulu-specific reference that deflects responsibility onto the spirits for spurring him on, and, by implication, onto the music for evoking the irrepressible feeling in his body to dance. Traditionally, a belt fastens an herbalist's pouch onto a man's forearm, giving him extra power and surges in spiritual energy.

"You can dance next time," proposes Nothi with a gesture of easy dismissal.

"But then you people must also stop playing such nice music!" Siyazi quips back.

The problem was that Nothi was drawn to following the dancers when he should have been playing straight, laying down a rhythm track, Siyazi reflected later. The dancing in that cramped space that day hindered the recording process, potentially compromising their end product. Yet such dancing, improvisational and competitive in style, is a form of ordinary male sociality.

There are other ways, too, that the musicians bring forms of appropriate sociality into the studio, which compromise the performance being recorded. When Siyazi, a teetotaler (who has promised session fees to the musicians), criticizes the musicians for wasting time on liquor and by his disapproval constrains their time for consumption, they make a plan.

"We'll go back to Jeppe [hostel (a migrant men's residence nearby)]," to have a quick drink, prompts Nothi.

"Now there's the problem starting!" quips Siyazi.

Pat intervenes with indirection and polite address: "*Malume akazame* [Uncle, Nothi must try (by his own means)]." He addresses Siyazi as *malume*, mother's brother, instantiating Zulu ways of relating in the studio. Pat's mother is of the Zulu clan. He implies that Siyazi, as host, should provide them with beer as would be expected of him were they at home. Pat makes the studio into the homestead, with the lead and owner of the project, Siyazi, as *umnumzane*, head of household.[15]

"Get someone else to go and get it. It's not far to Jeppe," instructs Siyazi, compromising.

When the drink arrives in a plastic shopping bag, Siyazi makes the gesture of a host: "Those who want to drink," he says, "there's the plastic bag." It is a gesture of goodwill though he himself believes that alcohol quickly dulls the attention needed to produce a tight-knit project.

Musicians also at times privilege the pleasure of relating through music over the demands of the task at hand, another choice that compromises the potential for the best sound quality on the final product. Nothi is bobbing and rocking in his seat as he plucks runs on his guitar. The engineer stops him to correct a setting on the console. When Nothi chides the young engineer for interrupting, he is reprimanding him for breaking his groove. He is skeptical that the engineer has a good reason for doing so. Later, the engineer holds up his hand because the programmed drum is erroneously off beat and he wants to fix it. No one really attends to his sign, though it is a standard in the industry. No one really stops playing because they are into their groove. When Lahla flatters the engineer for a moment of good listening that enabled quick identification and rectification of a mistake, Lahla is being attentive to studio efficiency. But he is also after the sociality that a less disrupted groove can produce.

In recent ethnographies that focus on the expressive practices and related entrepreneurial endeavors of African men living precariously elsewhere on the continent, the reliance on intense sociality to produce useful alternative networks is a shared theme, as is, in some cases, the easy dissipation of alliances.[16] Marginalized men are necessarily often hustlers, making do in order to make good. The mercurial, the ephemeral, the ironic, and the possible are conditions that coproduce the struggle to accumulate that which facilitates the life process of making good, and they are qualities that are also drawn on in attempts to override that struggle. Maneuvering from within the global shadows, whether with sweat and through danger, or playfully and creatively, they are engaged with the world beyond the state, but on an uneven cosmopolitan terrain.[17] They are expendable bodies in the global and national order of things, perhaps, but they are not disconnected. Steven Feld's tracing of trans-Atlantic connections and postcolonial entanglements through Ghanaian artists' storytelling and Danny Hoffman's accounts of the intricate Sierra Leonean and Liberian mercenary and military networks dramatize the ephemerality of futures and of relationships, unless one works on them.

In Shirimani Studios, voiced or performed assertions in favor of pleasurable grooving are forms of relating that are facilitated by new forms of empowerment in the postapartheid democracy, in particular by the changed demographics in the studio. The sound engineer is young and African: it is easier to openly disregard his instructions and to reprimand him than it would have been in an apartheid studio where the engineer was middle class, usually white, usually expert, and usually older than the youth at Shirimani's console. In contrast to apartheid-era studio sessions, in these studio sessions difficult professional relationships across language, race, and class lines are erased (although participants sometimes point to ethnic difference to account for differing knowledge bases). But in their place are contentions on the basis of age and practices of respect. In addition, in apartheid studios, musicians like Siyazi and his compatriots did not learn how to ask for the sounds they imagine. Now, they are ill-equipped to coax a desired sound out of an engineer.[18]

The house engineer at Shirimani Studios learned his trade as a fan of kwaito, South Africa's youth music of the 1990s, a form of electronic dance music. With friends as mentors, he taught himself how to use sound-processing computer programs in order to create kwaito.[19] He knows the basics of the digital recording process—how to cut, paste, sync tracks, boost the bass, set the volumes, add some reverb, compress the vocals, and equalize a little. When he discusses components of the recording process during the session, he gestures to the computer's screen that has become a focus of visual attention in the studio. He works visually, relying heavily on the computer graphics to identify the detailed makeup of the sounds. He has yet to develop an engineer's hearing acuity and the technological skills to translate the musicians' poetic lexicon into the language of acoustic and electronic science, though his dream is to apprentice with the renowned producer Quincy Jones. The musicians notice, correctly, that he has a lot to learn at the console, even while they acknowledge their own lack of technological expertise.

During the sessions, naming play is elaborate and often clever within a context in which there are practices of respect on the basis of men's seniority and with regard to kinship, and in which individuals are subject to multiple terms of endearment and forms of address. Flattery and insults circulate in friendly masculine sparring. Forms of address are strategically employed—or misemployed—to social effect, whether to cultivate camaraderie, to specify its hierarchical terms, or to get preferred sounds recorded. Musicians joke using age-inappropriate or standing-inappropriate forms of address for Zulu men, as they do sometimes using denigrating forms of endearment. "*We Mjita* [Yo, dude]," Nothi risks addressing Siyazi, who is older than he is. "The black person's ox can really play guitar!" teases Siyazi later, with double-edged flattery of Nothi, at once granting him the power of an ox and denigrating his friend with a racial slur from the apartheid era. "Take the song out/run with the song, *mkhulu* [grandpa]," encourages Lahla addressing his junior, Nothi. "*Yeyi wenzizwa* [hey, you young men], you are disturbing me with your dancing!" complains Nothi addressing his seniors and age-mates.

"Let's go, *mdala* [old man]," says Nothi to the engineer, pressing to move on to the next song.

"That young guy [the engineer] is old?" Lahla responds quizzically. "He's a small one, that one!" he corrects Nothi, unduly diminishing the engineer's age.

"He's an old one, this guy," Nothi insists, nodding his head in the direction of the console. "Can't you see he's an *ikhehla* [grandfather, one who wears a head ring]?"

"Let's go," instructs the engineer, having readied the console to begin recording the next song. Perhaps he is oblivious to his clients' banter. Perhaps he is appropriately enduring this hazing from the senior men.

An excluding jab that marks difference can work as an inclusionary move with the help of a successful comeback. "You're going to be a good teacher for Zulus," remarks Nothi to Philemon, as he helps Pat and Siphiwe to learn Siyazi's Zulu lyrics. "The problem is you haven't got a scar on your head."

"A scar for a snake? A scar for what?" Philemon dismisses the emasculating criticism by which Nothi marks Philemon's ethnic difference from the rest of the group. Were Philemon Zulu rather than Sotho, Nothi implies, he would have toughened up through the boyhood punishment that makes strong men. Whether hit by a stone propelled from a slingshot, or scarred by older boys roughing up younger ones when herding cows, or in boyhood stick fighting, a scar becomes a valued marker of past courage. Here, Nothi undercut's Philemon's status in the studio as a respected worldly musician and the coproducer by means of exposing his lesser cultural competence. He doesn't have a scar. The momentary equalizing move cultivates intense camaraderie in the control room among the fully adult men.

Sing, men. Hear the recording process of *madoda*. Hear the pleasure of men relating. Hear their trickstering, the clever bantering, the competitive Zulu poetics. The jostling and joking, the reversals and hyperboles, the expressive displays in a men's space. The singing of a sexual joke about women that holds the melody and tweaks the lyrics of a backing chorus just learned. Vocables that stand in for the energy of a dance step in a space too cramped to dance it out. The armbands, *amabhande*, are juicing me up! Hear the infusion of the studio's professional relationships with Zulu cultural practices. The density of this studio camaraderie is, one might say, a form of hi-fi sociality, on which a premium is placed by these ngoma men.[20] Hear their poetic play against the backdrop of struggle.

The recording process and sound outcome are also demonstrations of another kind of relationship that the musicians recognize and work on—namely, that between *madóda* and *madoda*, between the world at large in which they participate as cosmopolitan men and the world at home in which they participate as respectable men. This is always a provisional relationship. "Something might be happening, or it might not be happening," Siyazi says. Potential is always present. Respectability at home is enhanced by the signs of work to make it happen.

In fact, the Shirimani Studio project never came to fruition. Resting as it was on precarious affiliations, it produced affective results, not material certainty. Nondala never produced the promised backing money, so the studio retained the master recording. With his reputation in jeopardy with his friends, Siyazi eventually borrowed money to pay his musicians. The Scorpions, South Africa's anticorruption unit (disbanded under President Jacob Zuma), raided Nondala's township household and left him bare. Shirimani was later arrested and charged with buying stolen studio gear.[21] In this case, Siyazi's alternative infrastructure disintegrated, at least for now. Siyazi would gather a group of his musical friends again in another poor studio four years later.

Lo-fi Sound

The low-budget independent studio is a postapartheid infrastructure that seems to make room for the expression of particular registers of Zulu masculinity, and for men to experiment with and improvise around gendered values. At the same time, Zulu masculine ways of being—and styles of comportment—seem equally to facilitate changes in studio practice, wresting new control into their independent hands by articulating the terms of relating within this intensely social and cosmopolitan site in ways that are Zulu, male, and musical.

Good sociality is, of course, necessary studio practice, in whatever the culturally specific gendered and genre specific terms might be. To record is a social event that involves the careful management of relationships to good aesthetic effect. The social challenges vary in form from location to location, studio to studio, and musical style to musical style, as evidenced in case studies in Johannesburg,

Austin, Istanbul, and Canada's northern plains.[22] All recording sessions involve creative experimentation and some degree of recomposition and musical arranging. Yet, arising from South African historical circumstances, some of the choices these musicians make in how to use their studio time are counter to efficient use of their limited resources. But the question is not only one of efficiency. It also concerns technology and aesthetics: the desire for production autonomy and, once in the studio, performances of authority compromise the possibilities for high-fidelity sound. Indeed, the pleasures of camaraderie and that camaraderie's constant negotiation often results in low sound production values, lessening the chances of a crossover listenership and so limiting the range of options that a recording might open up for them.

When musicians eagerly and liberally use preprogrammed sounds and fill up the sound spectrum, and inexperienced young engineers lack the skills to finesse the sonorities and to nuance the mix of a preferred dense and busy sound, the sonic result is muddy, making distinctive musical lines and expressive effects unclear. With the technical capacity and aural acuity of a well-trained engineer, clichéd preprogrammed sounds could be remade into nuanced acoustic ideas. As these artists become disembedded from state and global institutions, and increasingly participate in informal and alternative infrastructures, they in relation with others connected into an informal infrastructure create "an aesthetic, a set of formal qualities that generate a particular sensorial experience of media marked by poor transmission, interference, and noise" by the sound of the recording process' improficiency.[23]

Poor production quality is a constraint with which postcolonial listeners and musicians contend the world over, and which they in turn treat as a resource. I am reminded of Nigerian *jùjú* musicians who fed their instruments through cheap amplifiers and public address systems and punctured their loudspeaker membranes, exploiting the distortion to effect a buzzy African aesthetic.[24] In Indonesia, R. Anderson Sutton was confounded by the use of poor-quality amplification when listeners could hear the music well without any amplification at all.[25] From his perspective initially, Indonesians unnecessarily suffered through loud, distorted playback of recordings or performances with stylistic details muffled and lost. He went on to articulate the circumstances in which such "bad sound" carried social valence for Indonesians. For example, the loud volume of amplification identified a social or ritual event, thereby drawing a crowd, while the noise worked as a means of averting malevolent spirits. When Siyazi and his musical compatriots exploit the electronic resources and the working relationships at hand to effect a dense aesthetic, they are producers repurposing sound technology to render aesthetics in local terms (as in the Nigerian case), and they are consumers making do with poor sound technology and investing it with social value (as in the Indonesian case). They bring a sound ideal into the studio drawn from their experience as performers and from years of listening to Zulu performances at weddings, parties, festivals, ngoma dances, and staged maskanda events. The approach to sound at such events is multilayered and densely textured. Percussiveness excites the overall effect. At issue in Shirimani Studios is the degree to which personnel, recording equipment, conditions, and competing desires allow for an artful mix when producing this aesthetic in the studio. At times, the difference between being able to hear the interplay of voices in performance and a muddy mixdown that obscures those voices dismays the musicians, as does the discrepancy between the desired sound quality of individual voices and the limitations in communicating those specificities and in rendering them electronically. Where it has seemed possible to him, Siyazi has worked his contacts to effect some remixing on review of a master recording. At other times, the musicians listen through the marks of poor transmission to hear and celebrate their sound.

Yet such musicians face enormous difficulties in mobilizing the networks that would launch them into the official, regulated media trade. As the alternative infrastructure produced by Nigerian videocassette piracy attests, media dissemination enables connections to the world—all be they connections that are easily disassembled. But at the same time, the quality of that disseminating media emphasizes the marginality of those it represents.[26] In this way, the musicians' aesthetic choices risk detaining them in circumstances that as citizens they seek to overcome.

Culture, Agency, and the State

In their reach for an exacting and enduring space, what makes musicians settle for something provisional? Why does an exacting and enduring space always seem so far out of reach? The artists' compromise in their sound's production value enables them to gain some creative control over their own representation. Their willingness to compromise in order to enhance their creative control is a consequence of the history of apartheid in the music industry and of apartheid's studio practices in which migrant musicians had little say. But their compromise is also a means by which they hold onto their agency as they find themselves pushed further into the precarious zone of postapartheid's neoliberal economy. The championing of men's social space and working relationships in the studio, and the use of the recording process to cultivate the camaraderie of respectable men, affectively counters some of the obstacles these men face to sustaining responsible manhood in the broader context of diminished wage labor brought on by the neoliberal restructurings of the postcolonial state.

Under the radar of the national culture industry, with the difficulties of gaining access to formal media infrastructure and then sustaining a presence within it, Siyazi and his compatriots' intense studio sociality bears significance in the present and for the future. Hi-fi sociality is rendered in sound as the sound of low production quality. That the musicians have to make do with "hi-fi sociality" as affectively dense consolation for lo-fi sound is, in effect, a consequence of the inadequacies of the state. It is a position to which musicians who are living under postcolonial, postapartheid constraints are consigned.[27] As an ethical stance, hi-fi sociality is a way of holding open the question of better times to come. With the musicians' male, migrant, Zulu, cosmopolitan sociality restructuring studio practices, they gain some control over the process of their own representation. By calling on alternative networks and working at solidifying them, they also gain some control over the wider production process. When those networks fail, there remains the work achieved for the future through the sustenance and animation of their own music-making relationships.

Umzansi Zulu Dancers' studio practice is an expression of hardworking, principled masculinity: self-reliance even in precarious times, albeit that a provisional political space enables only a provisional sound. If this recording right now doesn't render results (connections, opportunities, money, fame), then perhaps it will later. "And if not—well, never mind," Siyazi quipped. The studio in this case is a site for doing the work of men—namely, producing connections to the world including to one another, so that "something may be happening," whether at home, on stage, within a record company, or maybe one day overseas. Coupled with the cultivation of alternative professional networks, the gendered studio play of Shirimani's musicians is sometimes productive, even while compromised by the infrastructural limitations to which their improvisations bear a contingent relation. Possibility is kept alive in the struggling South African state. "Sing, *madoda*," instructs Nothi.

LOUISE MEINTJES is Associate Professor of Music and Cultural Anthropology at Duke University. Her monographs are *Sound of Africa! Making Music Zulu in a South African Studio* and *Dust of the Zulu: Ngoma Aesthetics After Apartheid.*

Notes

This chapter was previously published in an expanded form as "The Digital Homestead: Having a Voice and the Sound of Marginalization," in *Dust of the Zulu,* Louise Meintjes. Copyright 2017, Duke University Press. All rights reserved. Republished by permission of the copyright holder, www.dukeupress.edu

1. See Timothy Taylor, *Global Pop: Global Music, Global Markets* (New York: Routledge, 1997); and Louise Meintjes, *Sound of Africa! Making Music Zulu in a South African Studio* (Durham, NC: Duke University Press, 2003). The release of the first two LPs of Siyazi Zulu's

group, Umzansi Zulu Dancers, coincided with the group's tours in France (1988, 1989). See *Bayekeleni*, Gallo Record Company, 1988, LP; and *Emzini*, Gallo Music Productions, 1991, LP. Anne-Maria Makhulu's detailing of mobile and precarious South African biographies in chapter 15 demonstrates the effects of diminishing wage labor.

2. While family structures are diverse, numerous households, especially of older patriarchs, are polygamous in the community where I work in Msinga, KwaZulu-Natal. Polygamous households tend to be large.

3. See Jocelyne Guilbault, "On Redefining the 'Local' Through World Music," *World of Music* 35, no. 2 (1993): 33–47; Reebee Garofalo, "Whose World, What Beat: The Transnational Music Industry, Identity and Cultural Imperialism," *World of Music*, 16–32; and Steven Feld, "A Sweet Lullaby for World Music," *Public Culture* 12, no. 1 (2000): 145–172.

4. Brian Larkin, *Signal and Noise: Media, Infrastructure, and Urban Culture in Nigeria* (Durham, NC: Duke University Press, 2008), 218.

5. I detail how apartheid's race and class relations impinged on the politics of studio relationships, and so on the shaping of South African sounds, in *Sound of Africa!*

6. See Umzansi, *Bayekelen*; Umzansi, *Emzini*; and Umzansi, *Khuzani*, Gallo Music Productions, 1994, LP.

7. Dladla was later charged with embezzlement of state and municipal funds. Nathi Olifant and Agiza Hlongwane, "Contractors Took Millions, Failed to Deliver," *Sunday Tribune*, August 26, 2012, http://www.iol.co.za/news/politics/contractors-took-millions-failed-to-deliver-1369753.

8. See Tejumola Olaniyan, Introduction.

9. Literally: "How will you woo a girl who drinks liquor?" Siyazi Zulu transcribed, we translated, and I edited Zulu dialogues that I recorded in the studio.

10. A topflight studio would not require that clients work with a producer. However, these musicians would be unable to afford such a studio without company backing, which would probably come with the insistence they use a company producer.

11. For more on this topic, see Mark Hunter, *Love in the Time of AIDS: Inequality, Gender, and Rights in South Africa* (Bloomington: Indiana University Press, 2010).

12. *Omaskandi* (maskanda musicians) strongly prefer miking the amp. One session I documented folded on a disagreement over this issue, and musicians, producer, and the sound engineer went home disgruntled (Meintjes, *Sound of Africa!*, 144). In another, a guitarist surreptitiously refined his amp settings while the engineer worked to control the sound from the console (Ibid., 106).

13. A guideline (usually a vocal) is a basic but key melodic part that is recorded first, along with a skeletal rhythm track. Musicians then synchronize and elaborate their parts in relation to it. In the end, the guideline is replaced.

14. I use a pseudonym.

15. Hunter's ethnography, *Love in a Time of AIDS*, of intimate relations in an informal Zulu settlement, shows why and in what forms pressures are brought to bear on the dignity of household heads in the time of diminished wage labor (and AIDS). Hylton White's ethnography of rural domestic reproduction highlights related challenges for men ("Outside the Dwelling of Culture: Estrangement and Difference in Postcolonial Zululand," *Anthropological Quarterly* 83, no. 3 [2010]: 497–518). Benedict Carton's history of stick fighting performances reminds us of the long socialization into competitive forms of Zulu male virtue ("Zulu Masculinities, Warrior Culture and Stick Fighting: Reassessing Male Violence and Virtue in South Africa," *Journal of Southern African Studies* 38, no. 1 [2012]: 31–53). Robert Morrell frames masculinity in relation to a history of violence and racism through colonialism and apartheid to which men necessarily responded (*Changing Men in South Africa* [London: Zed, 2001]).

16. See Bob White, *Rumba Rules: The Politics of Dance Music in Mobutu's Zaire* (Durham, NC: Duke University Press, 2008); Brad Weiss, *Street Dreams and Hip Hop Barbershops: Global Fantasy in Urban Tanzania* (Bloomington: Indiana University Press, 2009); Alex Perullo, "Imitation and Innovation in the Music, Dress, and Camps of Tanzanian Youth," in *Hip Hop Africa: New African Music in a Globalizing World*, ed. Eric Charry (Bloomington: Indiana University Press, 2012), 189–209; Danny Hoffman, *The War Machines: Young Men and Violence in Sierra Leone and Liberia* (Durham, NC: Duke University Press, 2011); and Jesse Weaver Shipley, *Living the Hiplife: Celebrity and Entrepreneurship in Ghanaian Popular Music* (Durham, NC: Duke University Press, 2013).

17. James Ferguson, *Global Shadows: Africa in the Neoliberal World Order* (Durham, NC: Duke University Press, 2006); Hoffman, *War Machines*; Steven Feld, *Jazz Cosmopolitanism in Accra* (Durham, NC: Duke University Press, 2012).

18. Thomas Porcello makes clear how sophisticated a sound engineer's professional linguistic expertise is, combining talk about the science of acoustics, histories of listening, knowledge of technologies, and elaborate improvised poetic reference. "Music Mediated as Live in Austin; Sound, Technology, and Recording Practice," in *Wired for Sound: Engineering and Technologies in Sonic Cultures*, ed. P. D. Greene and T. Porcello (Middletown, CT: Wesleyan University Press, 2005), 103–117.

19. Pakie Mohale, interview by the author, Johannesburg, July 29, 2002.

20. R. Murray Schafer proposed a continuum from hi-fi to lo-fi soundscapes. Clarity and communicative reliability characterized hi-fi soundscapes, epitomized by the natural world. Industrialization, for him, increasingly compromised high fidelity. I apply his idea to a high-tech social space. See *The Soundscape: Our Sonic Environment and the Tuning of the World* (1977; repr., Rochester, VT: Destiny Books, 1993).

21. Jonathan Mangena and Mandla Motau, "Joe Shirimani Arrested for Stolen Goods," *Daily Sun*, October 22, 2003, 3.

22. See Meintjes, *Sound of Africa!*; Porcello, "Music Mediated as Live in Austin"; Eliot Bates, "Mixing for Parlak and Bowing for a Büyük Ses: The Aesthetics of Arranged Traditional Music in Turkey," *Ethnomusicology* 54, no. 1 (2010): 81–105; and Christopher A. Scales, *Recording Culture: Powwow Music and the Aboriginal Recording Industry on the Northern Plains* (Durham, NC: Duke University Press, 2012).

23. Larkin, *Signal and Noise*, 218–219.

24. Christopher Waterman, *Jùjú: A Social History and Ethnography of an African Popular Music* (Chicago: University of Chicago Press, 1990).

25. R. Anderson Sutton, "Interpreting Electronic Sound Technology in the Contemporary Javanese Soundscape," *Ethnomusicology* 40, no. 2 (1996): 249–268.

26. Larkin, *Signal and Noise*, 218–219.

27. Olaniyan contributed this point.

PART III

The State in the City: Urban Negotiations of the Necessary

12 Talibé Trafficking

The Transformation of Koranic Teaching in Senegal

Lark Porter

In 2000, the United States enacted the Trafficking Victims Protection Act (TVPA) and the UN adopted the Protocol to Prevent, Suppress, and Punish Trafficking in Persons, Especially Women and Children (Palermo Protocol). These measures are among the first of their kind to call on the international community to "[criminalize] all acts of trafficking—including forced labor, slavery, and slavery-like practices."[1] Together, the TVPA and the Palermo Protocol declare that "all forms [of trafficking] should be criminalized, victims of all forms [deserve] protection, and prevention of all forms [must be undertaken] to attack the problem at its core."[2] As of May 2010, 137 countries have adopted the Palermo Protocol, including Senegal.[3]

For the past twenty years, national, regional, and global governments have taken an increasing interest in the sociocultural situation surrounding young male Koranic students—known as *talibés*—living in West Africa.[4] Since the 1980s, the Senegalese talibés have been the focus of local and regional human rights advocacy programs because their Koranic teachers—known as *marabouts*—force them into exploitive begging, rather than only asking them to beg for their meals.[5] Because almsgiving is one of the five pillars of Islam, and strict adherence to this practice is an expectation, marabouts have historically been able to avoid the obligation of feeding their talibés by requiring them to beg on the street for their meals. However, as evidence of the more heinous ills associated with exploitation and trafficking surfaced, the Senegalese government has adopted and attempted to enforce more stringent laws designed to protect the safety of the nation's children.[6]

Yet Koranic schooling remains popular to this day. A centuries-long tradition motivates parents to temporarily transfer guardianship of their sons, ranging in age from five to twenty-five, to a marabout. The aim of this tradition is twofold. First, Senegalese child-rearing customs dictate that boys be educated in a physically, mentally, and emotionally disciplined atmosphere.[7] Second, the boys would have the opportunity to study the Koran and the Islamic faith, thereby becoming "virtuous adult[s]."[8] The extreme poverty of many Senegalese parents is conveniently offset by being able to educate their children by sending them away to Koranic schools. But in the past several decades, this custom has led to nefarious practices by many marabouts. Despite compelling physical evidence that points to this fact, and due to the customary noninterference in Islamic religious education practices, many Senegalese are extremely hesitant to support movements to modify the practices that comprise Koranic teaching.

Some unscrupulous marabouts have transformed their schools into domestic and international human trafficking rings by viewing their talibés as a large force of free labor. They victimize the boys and force the talibés to beg all day while not receiving any religious training, following which they must surrender the money to the marabouts. This practice perpetuates while the talibés do not receive adequate food, shelter, or education for their own benefit. Many of these boys are placed in constant risk of becoming subject to drugs, violence, and even sexual exploitation.

To make matters worse, Senegal's geographic location facilitates the quick, illegal transportation of these boys to Europe and other parts of Africa.[9] The country's orientation in the midst of several politically unstable countries that are vulnerable to Islamic jihadists also poses a national security threat. Historically, Senegal has been a fairly stable country. However, events during the summer of 2012 illustrate that terrorism has encroached on the country.[10] Terrorist cells are located along the northern and eastern borders, and on July 5, 2012, Senegalese security forces arrested ten terrorist militants, several of whom are known to be students in Senegalese Arabic schools.[11] Because the Senegalese government does not regulate Koranic schools, corrupt marabouts and their trafficked talibés might easily fall prey to Arab extremists in the future.[12]

In an article on postcolonial African fiction, Ayo Kehinde states, "African literature engages in imaginative presentations of the woes and vicissitudes of the lives of the pauperized masses. . . . They imaginatively chronicle numerous abuses to which the African masses have been subjected. . . . In fact, postcolonial African writers have a sensitive perception of a world of desolation, alienation, hopelessness, insecurity and the like."[13] Senegalese authors are no exception to this observation. I employ the definitions of human trafficking set forth by government documents in order to examine the transformation of Koranic teaching in Senegal as it is reflected in postcolonial Senegalese fiction. Two novels, Cheikh Hamidou Kane's *L'Aventure ambiguë* (*Ambiguous Adventure*) and Aminata Sow Fall's *La grève des Bàttu* (*The Beggars' Strike*), will serve as the historical and literary basis of the analysis. *L'Aventure ambiguë*'s position as one of Senegal's foundational literary oeuvres "places [the] talibés at the center of debates about modernity in Senegal," and *La grève des Bàttu* deconstructs society's application of begging as well as giving and receiving alms.[14] Since African writers' works are inspired by current events (which we will also examine), the novels allow us to gauge just how much the relationships and begging that comprise Koranic teaching have been subverted in today's world. Similarly, brief corresponding analyses of the Senegalese government's response to crimes against children will elucidate the state's disregard for the protection of its most vulnerable population.

Child Trafficking

As defined by the US Department of State and the UN, the terms "trafficking" and "exploitation" can be, but are not necessarily, interchangeable. First, "trafficking" has a double meaning: most specifically, it refers to the capture and subsequent movement/gathering of individuals as carried out by perpetrators. The UN Office on Drugs and Crime (UNODC) website defines this aspect of trafficking as "the recruitment, transportation, transfer, harboring, or receipt of persons" via "threat or use of force, coercion, abduction, fraud, deception, abuse of power or of a position of vulnerability and giving of payments or benefits."[15]

The TVPA elaborates on this definition in the following statement:

> A person may be a trafficking victim *regardless* of whether they once consented, participated in a crime as a direct result of being trafficked, were transported into the exploitive situation, or were simply born into a state of servitude. *At the heart of this phenomenon are the myriad of forms of enslavement*—not the activities involved in international transportation.[16]

Second, traffickers exploit the victims for various purposes such as "sexual [favors], forced labor, slavery or forced servitude, and the removal of organs."[17] "Exploitation" embodies that which the victims are forced to do. Third, the TVPA further stipulates that "a victim need not be physically transported from one location to another in order for the crime to fall within [the] definitions [of trafficking]."[18] Hence the two terms can rotate on their own axes, yet they can also simultaneously converge under the umbrella term of "trafficking." Consequently, this second, universal use of "trafficking" groups the actions of the perpetrators and the modes of exploitation into an all-encompassing and synonymous denotation. When used in this comprehensive sense, when a victim is exploited, he or she is trafficked, and when that same victim is trafficked, he or she is exploited. Usually when one thinks of the term "trafficking," one assumes that it is limited to the movement of persons from one locale to another. As the prior definitions explain, this is not the case. In order to more fully understand the scope of human trafficking and its associated horrors, one must forsake this stereotypical and inaccurate conclusion and view the vice through a broader lens. Unless otherwise noted, I use the terms "trafficking" and "exploitation" interchangeably throughout, as defined and prescribed by the US Department of State and the UN.

The US Department of State's *Trafficking in Person's Report* (*TIP*) *2010*, *TIP 2011*, the US Department of Labor, and UNICEF records show the extent to which Senegal is implicated in the global trafficking market. These organizations all report that Senegal is a "destination country for children trafficked from surrounding [West African] countries" such as Guinea-Bissau, Guinea-Conakry, Mali, and The Gambia.[19] Senegal's country profile in *TIP 2010* describes the country's trafficking market:

> Senegal is a source, transit, and destination country for children and women subjected to trafficking in persons, specifically forced labor, forced begging, and commercial sexual exploitation. . . . Trafficking within the country is more prevalent than transnational trafficking. . . . Transnationally, boys are also trafficked . . . for forced begging by unscrupulous marabouts.[20]

As this quote indicates, Senegal's trafficking woes partially center around the talibés and the exploitive begging that their marabouts mask under the disguise of integral aspects of Koranic education, that is the time-honored practice of learning humility through begging.

On May 10, 2005, following the signing and ratification of several international laws and conventions, including—but not limited to—the Palermo Protocol, International Labor Organization (ILO) Forced Labor Convention 29, and ILO Abolition of Forced Labor Convention 105, the Senegalese government drafted and signed Law No. 2005-06, which outlaws forced begging. Convicted individuals face two to five years of imprisonment and a fine of five hundred thousand to two million CFA francs (US$986 to US$3,942). The law also states that if the offense is committed against a minor, the court will not stay its ruling.[21] At its inception, child rights advocates, international governments, and concerned Senegalese applauded the law, and it generated new hope that exploited talibés would finally receive protection.

The euphoria was short-lived, however. From September to October 2010, one of the greatest disappointments in the fight against child begging occurred. In an unprecedented ruling, nine marabouts were sentenced to prison after they were found guilty of coerced begging. Despite the court's decision, President Abdoulaye Wade (2000–2012) caved to both the internal pressures within his cabinet and the backlash created by enraged religious leaders. He overturned the verdict because he "disagreed" with the 2005 ban and he felt that the victimized children "were seeking alms"—a practice "recommended by religion"—rather than begging. The convicted marabouts were immediately released, and Wade's intervention "effectively ended further arrests and prosecutions."[22] Wade's actions dealt a heavy blow to a society already disenchanted with the government and its abnegation of legal responsibilities toward its most defenseless citizens. They also conveyed a powerful message: the state considered children's rights of tertiary importance, following those of powerful religious institutions and adult males. To this day, the Senegalese government fails to enforce this law.

Senegalese postcolonial literature frequently reflects the issues of greatest import to the people. By studying the trajectory of Senegalese literature and journalism, one easily recognizes the frustration and disillusionment that many Senegalese feel toward the state concerning the plight of the talibés and the practice of begging. On the one hand, it denounces the corruption of Koranic education, as well as the state's failure to uphold its own laws. On the other hand, it urges the state to assume its responsibility toward the talibés. The literature serves as both a condemnation and a clarion call to action.

Child-rearing, Self-mastery, Perfection, and Allah

Historically, Senegal's application of Sufi Islam places great emphasis on the spiritual education of its disciples, and the marabout-talibé relationship has always been highly revered. A popular Sufi maxim states, "He who does not have a [marabout] will have Satan for a guide." Therefore, the marabout and his talibé "walk [together] on the [path] proscribed by Islam." In addition to his responsibility of teaching the Koran to his talibés, the marabout is also expected to discipline them in such a way as to mold them into God's slaves, a concept that embodies meekness, obedience, and faithfulness. The marabout teaches discipline by exposing the talibés to the ravages of hunger, cold, lack of hygiene, beatings, lack of sleep and medical attention, discomfort, hard physical labor, begging, and separation from family.[23] Donna L. Perry explains that, culturally, the "Wolof people . . . see such stresses and tensions as constructive, rather than destructive, of character."[24] When internalized, harsh discipline trains the talibés to overcome physical and mental weaknesses and to more fully serve God. The degree to which the talibés exercise complete submissiveness toward their marabouts and Allah directly correlates to their ability to withstand the difficulties of life.[25]

We can see the manifestation of these beliefs in Kane's 1961 semi-autobiographical work, *L'Aventure ambiguë*. It takes place during the colonial period and follows the life of Samba Diallo, a prince of the Diallobé ethnic group. The novel's continued appeal rests in the fact that Kane allows the reader to experience the psychological and spiritual conflict of a young man who is torn between his Islamic faith and the secularized world offered by assimilation into French culture. The first quarter of the book details his life as a talibé at a Koranic school named Foyer Ardent, wherein Kane details the hardships and abuse Samba endures at the hands of le Maître, his marabout.

The novel opens with a startling scene centralized around the violence with which le Maître treats Samba, then just a young boy, when he makes a mistake while reciting the Koran:

> He had seized Samba Diallo by the fleshy part of his thigh and . . . had given him a long hard pinch. The child had gasped with pain. . . . Threatened by sobs which were strangling him in the chest and throat, he had had the strength to master his suffering; in a weak voice, broken and stammering, but correctly, he had repeated the verse from the holy Book which he had spoken badly in the first place. . . . Samba Diallo's whole body was trembling, [trying] to restrain the whimpering that pain was wresting from him. . . . The child succeeded in mastering his suffering, completely. He repeated the sentence without stumbling, calmly, steadily, *as if his body were not throbbing with pain.*[26]

Throughout this scene Samba is in constant pain. Yet if we focus too much on his agony, we may miss the significance of his state of being at the end of the experience: he succeeds in mastering his body. Le Maître's violent actions toward Samba force the boy to battle through a cat-and-mouse interplay between physical weakness and its antithesis, strength of mind. Will he give in to external forces that cause temporary pain or will he continue forward, focusing on God and His word? It is important to recognize that this example of accentuated self-mastery presents itself at the very beginning of the novel. Hence the struggle for and the implications associated with the concept of self-mastery are of paramount importance to the rest of the story.

As the scene indicates, self-mastery engenders perfection. But what sort of perfection is he searching for? The narrator reveals the answer during the novel's begging scene, and the words that the talibés chant unveil one of the reasons some marabouts support child begging. The boys call out, "Who will feed the poor disciples today? Our fathers are alive, and we beg like orphans. In the name of God, give to those who beg for His Glory."[27] The phrase "beg *for* His Glory" proves significant on two levels. Initially, it seems fairly straightforward, yet when read more attentively, one realizes that the wording can be interpreted in ways that either hide or reveal the whole basis of Koranic education. A cursory reading may cause individuals to assume that the phrase means "we are begging *in the name of* His Glory" and technically, that is correct. Yet a deeper and more transcendental implication rests just under the surface. Hungry individuals beg because they need, desire, and fervently hope to receive food. When we substitute the verb "to beg" with "to receive," the significance of the phrase changes dramatically: "In the name of God, give to those who hope to *receive* His Glory." What is God's glory? It is perfection. When one receives the glory of God, he or she is perfect like He is. When interpreted in this manner, *L'Aventure ambiguë* elucidates the claim that begging is symbolic to the disciple's quest for self-mastery; with Allah's help, self-mastery gives way to the highest spiritual form of perfection.

This brings us to the second noteworthy aspect of the text. The liturgy of all religions indicates that supreme perfection belongs to God. It is His and His alone to give. According to the Islamic faith, the Word—or the Koran—is perfect.

A perfect God uttered a perfect Word, and disciples must recite it perfectly. Hence the reason young Samba exerts such effort to master his physical emotion while being punished. The text states that the Word "demanded" suffering.[28] Perhaps this is why, despite his love for Samba, le Maître does not hesitate to subject him to the suffering and humiliation associated with begging, neither does he think twice about physically abusing the boy. The text also indicates that to Samba, his suffering was akin to physical death. All the hours Samba spent begging turned on that same axis: first, being of noble blood, he had to "kill" and "bury" his social status and pride, don the rags of humility, and then beg for his most basic necessity. Secondly, Samba's mournful chantings uttered while begging all referred to death and dying. But is not the death of one's imperfect self the very essence of the road to mastery and perfection? Kane explains, "We must remember that in Muslim Sufism, the highest level of the mystical quest is to die within oneself in order to meet the Friend and to fuse with Him."[29] Despite his young age, Samba understands that the Word is perfect and that perfection demands suffering. The most telling manifestation of his determination resides in the fact that, despite all the suffering caused by physical humiliation, Samba never begs for the suffering to stop.

By the end of his Koranic education, Samba had mastered his ability to memorize the Koran. When he returned home to his family, he was honored and deeply touched to be able to perfectly recite the Koran—the Word "that he loved"—to his parents.[30] On the one hand, this implies that he mastered his mind and his mouth. On the other hand, it indicates that the Word triumphed over and dwelled in his heart. The difficult and sometimes harrowing experiences that Samba had to endure due to violence and coerced begging eventually enabled him to perfect his discipleship and to have a portion of God's perfection dwelling within him.

Ambiguous Adventures

As the previous section illustrates, Kane's narrative contains several manifestations of events and behavior that fall loosely within the definitions of trafficking: Samba is in a position of vulnerability; he is forced to beg and he suffers various forms of corporal punishment. Yet overall, Samba's experience in the Koranic school system is a positive one. With the help of his marabout, he stands as the representation of a talibé who successfully internalizes and exercises the discipline that Koranic teaching seeks to instill. This literary representation approximates society's real-life cultural-religious ideals and expectations, and it stands as a literary testimonial to its history and the rewarding influence the Koranic school system had on the lives of Senegalese boys. When guided by a marabout who has not been corrupted, it can still positively shape their lives. However, other works have been produced since *L'Aventure ambiguë*'s publication that reflect real-life evolutions in marabout-talibé ties and the implementation of disciplinary tactics. Just as Samba questions his faith and experiences uncertainty as he grows up, the role of begging in the name of religion has become more vague, exploitative, and debated.

Specifically, Sow Fall's 1979 novel, *La grève des Bàttu*, denounces a modern subversion of the *zakat* (alms), one of the most basic and sacred Koranic teachings. A detailed analysis of the doctrine is beyond the scope of this chapter; however, the following verses highlight the administration of the zakat and the blessings that Muslims believe they will receive as they practice it. First, "believers, men and women, are protectors of one another . . . they observe regular prayers, practice regular charity, and obey Allah and His Apostle. On them will Allah pour His mercy"; second, "if ye publish your alms-giving, it is well, but if ye hide it and give it to the poor, it will be better for you, and will atone for some of your ill deeds"; and lastly, "establish worship and pay the poor-due [the zakat], and lend unto Allah a goodly loan. Whatsoever good ye send before you for your souls, ye will find it with Allah, better and greater in recompense."[31] The Koran also commands the poor and other recipients of alms to pray for those who extend charity. It states, "of their goods, take alms, that so thou mightest purify and sanctify them; and pray on their behalf. Verily thy prayers are a source of security for them."[32] Together, these teachings illustrate the preeminent emphasis placed on loving and caring for one's neighbor and paying particular attention to the poor and needy. In return for adherents' charitable offerings, Allah promises forgiveness of wrongdoings and great rewards both on Earth and in heaven. Almsgiving is one of the most important commandments, but so is the injunction to pray for those who give and asking Allah to bestow blessings on them. In short, both parties are their brother's keeper and they rely on each other to receive temporal and spiritual blessings.

When one understands the sacredness that Muslims attach to almsgiving, it is easier to recognize the audacity of the main character of *La grève des Bàttu*, Mour Ndiaye, director of the Department of Public Health and Hygiene, as he seeks to rid the capital city of the beggars that encumber the streets. Ndiaye's character is an allegorical representation of mainstream society as he laments the overabundance of disabled, talibés, marabouts, lepers, and poor—people whom he disdainfully calls "human waste"—because they "assault" and "attack" passersby for money.[33] After their displacement to a neighboring village, the beggars gather in a compound and manage to find financial means to survive. One of the beggars, Nguirane, exclaims in anger:

> They need to give charity because they need our prayers; wishes for a long life, prosperity, the opportunity to pilgrimage to Mecca, they like hearing [the

> wishes] each morning to chase away their nightmares from the night before and to maintain hope for a better tomorrow. You think those people give out of kindness? No, but out of instinct for preservation. . . . It's not for us that they give, but for them! They need us so they can live in peace![34]

Both Ndiaye's attitude toward the beggars and Nguirane's outburst indicate a divergence from Islam's teachings concerning the purposes of giving and receiving alms. Muslim scholars have written that the Islamic faith emphasizes the "cultivation" of goodwill among all human beings, including providing "maximum assistance to fellow beings for ensuring their welfare and happiness in all respects, and it regards the economic welfare of the people as a thing of vital import" specifically the "destitute and the needy."[35] Thus Ndiaye, who despises his fellowman, and the individuals that Nguirane describes who disregard the true purpose of giving alms, are all disregarding the true nature of one of the most important teachings of Islam.

Yet, paradoxically, beggars can be just as hypocritical. Their prayers and well-wishes are forced and half-hearted. The lackadaisical and bitter attitude that they display during their displacement borders on a sense of entitlement, and they claim that their discontent stems from others' refusal to let them beg according to Koranic custom. Similarly, during the centuries that spanned the precolonial era until at least the late colonial period, Senegalese marabouts cited Koranic teachings concerning almsgiving as the primary reason they forced the talibés to beg for sustenance.[36] Here we must note the subtle irony that colors Sow Fall's text and the foundation of talibé begging: neither the Koran nor the Hadith condone flagrant begging. There is a significant difference between self-reliance occasionally subsidized by others and the outright refusal to support oneself through one's own efforts. Islam strongly discourages the latter.[37] Because misunderstandings exist on both sides of the issue, the novel illustrates that "exploiters of Islam are to be found in all segments of society."[38]

When one reads the previously quoted scene from *La grève des Bàttu* with the understanding of the Koran's intended application for giving and receiving alms, one recognizes Sow Fall's bold accusation that modern Senegalese are not respecting the true ideals of charity. During an interview conducted in 2012, Sow Fall stated:

> Begging is a crutch for this society . . . it is a need that we *created*. It is not an inherent need. We've twisted certain teachings in the Koran . . . [and in denying individuals] access to the most basic of necessities, instead of creating a system where we can be charitable by not relegating someone to destitution . . . we have trained ourselves to think that we must keep people in poverty so we can follow the teachings of our religion. . . . Do we need to be charitable? By all means, yes! But we forget that we can do it in another way.[39]

In uttering this statement, and in conjunction with the observations found in her novel, Sow Fall parallels the griots of old who acted as counselor to kings and ethnic leaders. She criticizes the Senegalese state by underscoring the fact that absolutely no overarching national, social framework—let alone a comprehensive government program—exists to relieve the suffering of the poor.[40] Its failure to socially and juridically address a practice that prevents personal and social progress intentionally keeps people in poverty. In the same vein, Mbye B. Cham writes that "in exploring the divergence between the principle and practice of zakat in Senegal, Sow Fall strongly indicts society's obsessive materialism which fosters a psychology of dependence easily exploited by charlatans masquerading as venerable marabouts."[41] Additionally, when asked to respond to the Senegalese government's lack of initiative regarding the talibés, Daha Chérif Bâ elaborates on Sow Fall's and Cham's commentaries when he underscores the following:

> This issue will take a very long time to resolve, if it is resolved at all. Do you really think that our politicians want to resolve it? No, of course they do not. Why? Because they have a personal interest in its existence! [*La grève des Bàttu*] was correct in showing that they need to give alms to ensure their success, to keep their office, to keep their riches. Who do they have to give alms to? The beggars. Which demographic makes up most of the beggars? The talibés. No, the talibé as we know him today will always exist.[42]

When compared to Kane's archetypal representation of the traditional marabout-talibé relationship, these three observations indicate a major shift in contemporary motivations behind talibé begging. Albeit a cursory commentary, Sow Fall's decision to include the critique in her novel reveals her sensitivity to the infiltration of questionable practices among the marabouts. Similarly, her 2012 interview indicates that the marabouts are not the only individuals taking advantage of the talibés. As she and Bâ illustrate, the Senegalese state itself exploits them for personal gain by not enforcing national and international laws.

Talibé Trafficking in Current Events

After the "[fall of] world peanut prices, desertification and mass migration to Senegal's urban centers during the 1970s," some men began claiming that they were trained marabouts and were qualified to teach talibés the Koran when they actually were not.[43] World Vision Africa, part of a global Christian relief organization, says that "during the decades since, poverty has continued to push rural parents, who cannot support their children, into sending their boys to marabouts [or to so-called marabouts] . . . in the city" for an undetermined amount of time.[44] It is estimated that between fifty and one hundred thousand talibés are forced to beg on the streets of Senegal's cities, and in Dakar alone, UNICEF has identified approximately seventy-six hundred talibés.[45]

Because many of the talibés spend approximately ten unsupervised hours per day out in the streets begging for money, they are also highly vulnerable to sexual abuse and exploitation.[46] In 2008, workers at a child aid center in Dakar received verbal accounts from the talibés of instances where they had been raped by either older talibés or the marabout himself. However, when one worker pressed charges on behalf of the victims, "all the . . . marabouts, and even the local population, became angry with her. She [said] no one wanted to believe that a man could sleep with a boy. She [said] no one wanted to listen to what she was saying."[47] Her colleague elaborated on the issue and stated that the modern-day corruption among "marabouts and in the daaras is 'a permissive situation,' where everything can be done, and everyone can do whatever they want. He said it leads to pedophilia, violence against minors."[48] Additionally, the talibé are vulnerable to drugs and serious illness.[49] When they are not roaming the streets, they spend their time in their daara, which is usually humid, cramped, and airless, and lacks bathroom facilities and running water.[50]

Reports have also indicated that marabouts tend to resort to beating the boys if they fail to collect the daily arbitrary quota of money that the marabout requires. For example, in 1996, *New York Times* reporter Howard French explained that "beatings are common for those whose earnings are judged too sparse."[51] Furthermore, stories of cruelty and neglect toward talibés in Senegal have become increasingly publicized. In 2011, Amanda Fortier, a reporter for *Voice of America News*, wrote, "a recent case in the local media told of two 8-year-old talibés who were so badly beaten and burned by their marabouts that they were hospitalized for three weeks."[52]

The Senegalese written and television media often enter the dialogue revolving around the talibés, and one of the latest events receiving major national and international coverage occurred during the days and weeks following the evening of March 3 and 4, 2013, when nine children, eight of which were talibés, were killed in a fire; one child escaped with serious burns.[53] Fifty talibés, forty of which were crammed into the tight, one-room daara, sleeping, and several families were crowded into the multistory structure. Firefighters were "unable to arrive in time because [they had] difficulty accessing the building."[54] Unable to find their way out of the inferno, the eight talibés were burned alive, and they were so badly mutilated that it took approximately one month to identify their bodies. On April 2, 2013, they were buried together in the same grave in a cemetery in a neighborhood to the north of Dakar.[55] The victims were all under ten years of age.[56]

The day following the fire, March 4, 2013, President Macky Sall and several members of his cabinet visited the site. Later that day, Sall announced that the government would "close daaras that were not up to standards," that the government would begin enforcing "the repatriations of foreign talibés," and that it was time "to end the exploitation of children."[57] He continued by saying, "we are not against charity, but we are against child begging. Very severe measures will be taken [against anyone] who continues, in the name of so-called 'Islam,' to organize [this type of lifestyle], which, as we experienced today, can lead to the deaths of many children [who live] in completely inhumane conditions."[58] The Senegalese government has since repatriated most of the talibés affected by the fire back to their families in Guinea-Bissau.[59] However, the victims' marabout has not been identified or found, and therefore no one has been brought to justice for their deaths.

Conclusion

These statistics, details, and stories are quite sobering. Yet it must be understood that in bringing this information to the fore, the purpose of this chapter is not to suggest that all marabouts are corrupt or have cruel intentions toward their talibés. One cannot fail, however, to recognize a diametric shift from the overarching respectability that used to permeate the whole of the Koranic teaching system as represented in Kane's novel. Today, many marabouts consider their talibés to be nothing more than expendable objects that act as a source of income and/or sexual pleasure and that can be abandoned in moments of extreme danger and left to die. Preventative measures have been put into place by national, regional, and international governing bodies that are designed to protect, strengthen, and help ensure a better life for every individual of the global community. Yet, because the Senegalese government does not enforce its laws regarding child begging, immoral marabouts know they will not be held accountable for the crimes they commit. This political stalemate essentially accords marabouts the freedom to do as they please while the talibés continue to suffer the worst forms of human trafficking. Such behavior on the part of members of the government's highest echelons is an indicator of "the failure of the society to guarantee [the] rights [of children] as proscribed by International Conventions," which Senegal adopted more than a decade ago.[60] By using the written word as a tool to engage the public in a dialogue that focuses on the talibés, authors and journalists seek to give a voice to the victims and spur the state to act.

LARK PORTER is a PhD candidate in French and Francophone African Literature at the University of Wisconsin, Madison.

Notes

1. US Department of State (USDOS), Office of the Under Secretary for Global Affairs, *Trafficking in Persons Report 2010* (Washington, DC: US Department of State, 2010), 5. Report hereafter referred to as *TIP 2010*.

2. Luis CdeBaca, "Trafficking Victims Protection Act: Progress and Promise," Department of Justice's National Trafficking Conference, Washington, DC, May 3, 2010, https://geneva.usmission.gov/2010/05/06/trafficking-victims-protection-act/.

3. Ibid.; USDOS, *TIP 2010*, 363.

4. The Wolof word *taalibe* is taken from the Arabic root word for student, *talib*. The French derivative is *talibé*. Because francophone African literature refers to Koranic teachers and students by using the French adaptations of Wolof words, I use the French orthography of *talibé* throughout.

5. See Donna L. Perry, "Muslim Child Disciples, Global Civil Society, and Children's Rights in Senegal: The Discourse of Strategic Structuralism," *Anthropological Quarterly* 77, no. 1 (2004): 66. *Marabout* is the French word used to refer to a number of professions in Senegalese culture. When one speaks of marabout, he or she can be referencing either a talisman confectioner, a secretary to a chief, a Koranic teacher, or, if referring to ancient times, a specific type of warrior. For more information, see Mamadou Ndiaye, *L'Enseignement arabo-islamique au Sénégal* (Istanbul: Centre de Recherches sur l'Histoire, l'Art, et la Culture Islamiques, 1985). When I use the term "marabout" in this chapter, I refer only to the Koranic teacher. Finally, begging for meals has long been entrenched in the traditions of Koranic teaching. This concept will be discussed later in the chapter.

6. See USDOS, *TIP 2010*, 363, for a complete list of all laws and treaties signed, adopted, or ratified by Senegal.

7. For a detailed analysis on this point, see Perry, "Muslim Child Disciples."

8. Ibid., 59.

9. On pages 120, 163, and 186, *TIP 2010* states the following: "Men, often former talibés . . . are the principal traffickers. In most cases they operate in the open, protected by their stature in the Muslim community; Senegalese children [boys and girls] are [frequently] sent to Italy."

10. For more details, see Bakari Gueye, "Senegal Faces al-Qaeda Threat," *Magharebia*, June 26, 2012, http://magharebia.com/cocoon/awi/xhtml1/en_GB/features/awi/features/2012/06/26/feature-02 (accessed March 21, 2017).

11. See Jemal Oumar, "Senegal: Terror Suspects Arrested Along Mauritania Border," *Magharebia*, July 17, 2012, http://www.eurasiareview.com/17072012-senegal-terror-suspects-arrested-along-mauritania-border/.

12. Studies conducted by Senegalese and US soldiers highlight the concern that military forces have for the instability of the *daaras* (Koranic schools) and the talibés. For a brief overview, see Alhousseyni Ly, "West Africa: A New Recruiting Front for al-Qaeda?" (master's thesis, Air Command and Staff College, 2009).

13. Ayo Kehinde, "The Image of Africa in Postcolonial African Fiction: The Example of Meja Mwangi's *Going Down River Road*," *Journal of Cultural Studies* 6, no. 1 (2004): 96–97.

14. Perry, "Muslim Child Disciples," 67.

15. UN Office on Drugs and Crime (UNODC), "What Is Human Trafficking?" (New York: United Nations, 2012), http://www.unodc.org/unodc/en/human-trafficking/what-is-human-trafficking.html.

16. USDOS, *TIP 2010*, 8 (emphasis added).

17. UNODC, *Human Trafficking: An Overview* (New York: United Nations, 2008), 11, http://www.ungift.org/docs/ungift/pdf/knowledge/ebook.pdf.

18. USDOS, *TIP 2010*, 8.

19. US Department of Labor (USDOL), "Bureau of International Labor Affairs: Senegal," https://www.dol.gov/ilab/reports/child-labor/findings/tda2010/senegal.pdf (accessed March 22, 2017); see also UNICEF, "Enfants mendiants dans la région de Dakar," Understanding

Children's Work Project Working Paper Series (New York: UNICEF, 2007), 7, http://www.ucw-project.org/attachment/child_labour_enfants_mendiants_Dakar20110628_154329.pdf.

20. USDOS, *TIP 2010*, 287–288.

21. See République du Sénégal Primature, "LOI no. 2005-06 du 10 mai 2005 relatif à la lutte contre la traite des personnes et pratiques assimilées et à la protection des victimes," *Journal Officiel de la République Sénégalaise* (Dakar, Senegal: Primature, 2005), http://www.jo.gouv.sn/spip.php?article3640.

22. "Senegal: Protect Children from Forced Begging," *Human Rights Watch*, March 31, 2012, http://www.refworld.org/docid/4f7abde12.html. See also "Le président Wade cherche à réorganiser la pratique de l'aumône, selon le PM," *Agence de Presse Sénégalaise*, October 8, 2010, http://www.aps.sn/articles.php?id_article=72899 (accessed March 21, 2017); and "Wade demande la levée de l'interdiction de la mendicité," *Xibar.net*, October 9, 2010, http://www.xibar.net/Wade-demande-la-levee-de-l-interdiction-de-la-mendicite_a27820.html.

23. See Perry, "Muslim Child Disciples," 59, 63; and Murray Last, "Children and the Experience of Violence: Contrasting Cultures of Punishment in Northern Nigeria," *Africa* 70, no. 3 (2000): 359–393. While Last's article deals primarily with Nigeria, many parallels exist between the sufferings experienced by the talibé in Nigeria and those in Senegal.

24. Perry, "Muslim Child Disciples," 74.

25. For more details concerning these concepts, see Perry, "Muslim Child Disciples."

26. Cheikh Hamidou Kane, *Ambiguous Adventure*, trans. Katherine Woods (New York: Walker, 1963), 3–5 (emphasis added).

27. Ibid., 13.

28. Ibid., 4.

29. Cheikh Hamidou Kane, "The Clash of Culture and Faith in Colonial Africa: An Ambiguous Adventure," *Lingua Romana* 10, no. 1 (2011): 31.

30. Kane, *Ambiguous Adventure*, 4, 71–73.

31. *The Holy Qur'an*, trans. M. H. Shakir (New York: Tahrike Tarsile Qur'an, 1983), Online Book Initiative, 9:71–72, 2:271, 73:20, http://quod.lib.umich.edu/k/koran/.

32. Ibid., 13:19.

33. Aminata Sow Fall, *La grève des Bàttu* (Dakar, Senegal: Nouvelles Editions Africaines du Sénégal, 1979), 5. All translations from the novel are my own.

34. Ibid., 32, 53.

35. Muhammad Fazl-ur-Rahman Ansari, *Qur'anic Foundations and Structure of Muslim Society* (New Challi, Pakistan: Center for Islamic Studies, 1977), 233.

36. See Ibid., 255: "Food being the most primary and most basic physical need of a human being, feeding the indigent has been classed as one of the outstanding virtues; hence it is duty."

37. For more details on this subject, see entries on begging in the Hadith, particularly Book 5, which deals with the zakat. See also Ansari, *Qur'anic Foundations*, 82: "[one] should not beg from all sundry, namely he should not adopt beggary as a profession. Professional beggary, which is a debasing form of acquiring easy money, is therefore completely ruled out of the Holy Koran. Indeed, it has no place in Muslim society."

38. Mbye B Cham, "Islam in Senegalese Literature and Film," in *Faces of Islam in African Literature*, ed. Kenneth W. Harrow (Portsmouth, NH: Heinemann, 1991), 171.

39. Aminata Sow Fall, interview by the author, December 19, 2012 (emphasis added; my translation).

40. A simple internet search on social aid programs in Senegal that address poverty and begging—specifically child begging—reveals that, by and large, the Senegalese state has invested minimally in changing the status quo. A single shelter, le Centre Ginddi, receives funding from the government.

41. Cham, "Islam," 170.

42. Daha Chérif Bâ, interview by the author, March 18, 2013 (my translation). Bâ is a history professor at Université Cheikh Anta Diop (Dakar), and he specializes in the sociocultural histories of marginalized populations in Senegal, including child beggars and the talibés.

43. In *Islamic Society and State Power in Senegal* (Cambridge: Cambridge University Press, 1995), Leonardo A. Villalón explains that "a marabout is simply one if people say he is, and if some are willing to declare themselves his students or disciples" (129).

44. "Senegal," *World Vision Africa*, http://wvafrica.org/index.php?option=com_content&view=article&id=147&Itemid=164 (accessed March 31, 2012).

45. Elizabeth Dickinson, "Dakar Journal: Spare Change Is Big Business in a Culture of Generosity," *New York Times*, August 21, 2006, http://www.nytimes.com/2006/08/21/world/africa/21senegal.html; see also Adam Nossiter, "Senegal Court Forbids Forcing Children to Beg," *New York Times*, September 12, 2010, http://www.nytimes.com/2010/09/13/world/africa/13dakar.html; and UNICEF, "Enfants mendiants," 7. The UNICEF report is very careful to differentiate between talibés and other children who live and/or beg on the street. Also, the figure quoted in this chapter does not include talibés found in other areas of Senegal.

46. "Retrait et réinsertion des enfants de la rue: Le Parrer dévoile son plan d'action," *Sendeveloppementlocal.com*, October 15, 2007, http://www.sendeveloppementlocal.com/RETRAIT-ET-REINSERTION-DES-ENFANTS-DE-LA-RUE-Le-Parrer-devoile-son-plan-d-action_a2346.html. Senegal's entry on World Vision Africa's website states the following: "Up to 80% of the street children have been sexually abused, making them vulnerable to AIDS," http://wvafrica.org/index.php?option=com_content&view=article&id=147&Itemid=164 (accessed March 31, 2012). For the more detailed account of sexual exploitation used in the text, see "Senegal Aid Workers Express Concern About Abuse of Child Beggars," *Voice of America News*, October 27, 2009, http://www.voanews.com/a/a-13-2008-03-10-voa24-66636642/556934.html.

47. "Senegal Aid Workers." It is also interesting to note that some male authors living in Nigeria who have written autobiographies and (semi)fictional accounts of childhood in Africa "conveyed . . . something . . . violence or the threat of violence as it is (or was) experienced by children. In these recollections Muslim teachers are depicted as notoriously hard on their pupils, albeit in the name of religion. . . . But what children experienced was sometimes less than religious: abuse, physical and sexual, is very occasionally hinted at. . . . Not surprisingly, few autobiographers admit to being sexually abused as children or to seriously shaming experiences, let alone bullying others; the few instances of abuse . . . were all recounted . . . privately and hesitantly, yet at the same time were not thought to be particularly unusual." Last, "Children and the Experience of Violence," 362–363.

48. "Senegal Aid Workers."

49. For more details, see USDOL, "Bureau of International Labor Affairs: Senegal," and UNICEF, "Enfants mendiants," 4, 27.

50. See "Senegal," *World Vision Africa*.

51. Howard W. French, "Dakar Journal: Children of Islam, Piously Seduced into Begging," *New York Times*, January 16, 1996, http://www.nytimes.com/1996/01/16/world/dakar-journal-children-of-islam-piously-seduced-into-begging.html.

52. Amanda Fortier, "Senegal Child Help Hotline Offers Safety for Victims of Abuse," *Voice of America News*, June 29, 2011, http://www.voanews.com/english/news/africa/Senegal-Child-Help-Hotline-Offers-Safety-for-Victims-of-Abuse-124809954.html.

53. All the major Senegalese media outlets, including the *Agence de Presse Sénégalaise*, *Le Soleil*, *L'Obs*, *Senenews*, *Seneweb*, and *RTS*, covered the story following the fire, and op-eds continued to appear in the papers for several weeks after the incident. To avoid redundancy, I do not list all the articles that addressed the event. A simple internet search in French or

English will provide interested readers with several pages of pertinent results. The fire and deaths of the talibés were covered by many of the major international news networks including the BBC, *Guardian*, *New York Times*, and Associated Press.

54. "Vidéo: Le marabout aurait pris la fuite au moment de l'incendie, selon des témoins," *Rewmi.com*, March 4, 2013, http://www.rewmi.com/Video-Le-marabout-aurait-pris-la-fuite-au-moment-de-l-incendie-selon-des-temoins_a75126.html; Jean-Gervais Ndjimbi-Ndong, "9 morts et un brulé grave dans une incendie à la Médina," *Sud Quotidien*, March 3, 2013, http://www.sudonline.sn/9-morts-et-un-brule-grave-dans-un-incendie-a-la-medina_a_12719.html. This observation indirectly criticizes the state's lack of zoning and building laws. Shanty-like structures often encumber the narrow, winding streets of Dakar and its surrounding neighborhoods. Unless otherwise noted, all translations of media sources are my own.

55. "Incendie de la Médina—les 9 talibés enfin inhumés à Yoff," *Seneweb.com*, April 2, 2013, http://www.senenews.com/2013/04/02/incendie-de-la-medina-les-9-talibes-enfin-inhumes-a-yoff_56735.html.

56. "L'Incendie de la Médina fait le menu des quotidiens,"*Enquête Plus: Revue de presse Sénégal*, March 5, 2013, http://www.enqueteplus.com/content/revue-de-presse-au-senegal-lincendie-de-la-m%C3%A9dina-fait-le-menu-des-quotidiens.

57. Ibid.; "Des enfants meurent sous les flammes dans une école coranique," *Radinrue.com*, March 5, 2013, http://www.radinrue.com/article8007.html (accessed March 21, 2017).

58. "Des enfants meurent."

59. Elisabeth El-Khodary, interview by the author, May 29, 2013. In 2013, El-Khodary was an economic officer at the US Embassy in Dakar, and she wrote *TIP* reports and cables for Senegal and other countries in the West African region.

60. "Mendicité—Cheikh Hamidou Kane, sur le phénomène des enfants de la rue: 'C'est un signe de l'échec de la société sénégalaise,'" *Plate-form des acteurs non étatiques*, October 18, 2011, http://www.plateforme-ane.sn/MENDICITE-Cheikh-Hamidou-Kane-sur.html (my translation).

13 Tradition of Resistance in Nigeria's Print Media

An Example from TheNEWS

Kunle Ajibade

The press has been magnificent, heroic and, one of these days, when there is more pleasure, we are going to erect a statue. I am going to see personally to this, that a statue for heroism of the press is erected at a prominent place in this country. We must never ever forget.

—Wole Soyinka, *The Guardian*, October 17, 1998

You can see that there is no easy walk to freedom anywhere, and many of us will have to pass through the valley of the shadow again and again before we reach the mountain tops of our desires.

—Nelson Mandela, *Chambers Book of Speeches*

On February 22, 2012, the world lost two of its most courageous and gifted journalists in a bomb explosion in Homs: Marie Colvin, an award-winning American war correspondent, who wrote for *The Sunday Times* of London, and Rémi Ochlik, a French freelance photo-journalist. They had sneaked into Homs, the Syrian city under army siege, to tell the story of the dying and the dead, the story of the deprived and the vulnerable. Why would President Bashar al-Assad bomb defenseless journalists? Why would he turn the center they were using to file their stories into a pile of rubble? He was obviously afraid of the fire in their words, the power in their simple lines and the sting and eloquence of their images. President al-Assad could not stand to be ridiculed and exposed for he desperately wanted to cling to power even if it meant killing his own people. That is the way of tyrants. But the way of conscientious reporters is different. For them the nobility and grace of journalism lie precisely in making life difficult for every dictator, or any antagonist of humankind. To Colvin, just one story could lead to a change of public opinion; it could shed light on hidden undertows. Enormously courageous, Colvin believed in serving humanity through journalism and was willing to pay the ultimate price for that cause. She infused her reportage with empathy, superior intelligence, and moral indignation.[1] Colvin paid with her life to get the truth out, the truth that she found in what she described as "a sandstorm of propaganda when armies, tribes or terrorists clash."[2] She succeeded, like Martha Gellhorn before her, in fixing her inspiring and astonishing character in our minds. Because she bore witness in places torn by chaos and death, I dedicate this chapter to her courage. In a profoundly moving speech in London in November 2010, honoring fallen journalists, Colvin, who had lost her left eye in a hand grenade explosion while covering war in Sri Lanka in 2001, explained why reporting in dangerous places is necessary: "The public have a right to know what our government, and our armed forces, are doing in our name. Our mission is to speak truth to power."[3]

Speaking truth eloquently and forcefully can be very dangerous, particularly when you are doing so to some mad dogs in power: journalism under murderous dictators is a very hard, perilous calling. I should know because for three-and-a-half years I suffered the indignity of their madness in Makurdi prison, Nigeria. I was jailed for life in 1995 by a special military tribunal set up by General Sani Abacha, then the maximum ruler of the country. The tribunal was ordered to sentence all military officers and civilians who were found to have conspired to overthrow his regime. Based on a document sourced from a special investigation panel, which preceded the tribunal, our magazine, *TheNEWS*, published a cover story titled "Not Guilty: Army Panel Clears Coup Suspects," which proved the innocence of the forty-one people arrested. Abacha had made up his mind to crush any opposition that would prevent him from transforming into a civilian president—he wanted to extend his stay in power by at least eight more years. The arrest and trial of people for this phantom coup was meant to instill fear in his perceived potential enemies. Freedom and madness wrestled. It was a very dangerous time to practice as critical journalists. But that was what we had to do to help prevent our country from being reduced to a primitive arena of absolute terror. Abacha's killer squad, known officially as the Presidential Strike Force, coordinated by Major Hamza al-Mustapha, his chief security officer, had the license to kill anyone. We were, therefore, taking a big risk. The military investigators wanted me to disclose the source of our story. I refused. If I had cooperated, the officers who had given us the information would have been killed. I was then summarily sentenced to life imprisonment. Following an international outcry that followed our case, Abacha reluctantly reduced my prison term to fifteen years. If he had not died suddenly, and mercifully, on June 8, 1998, he would have preferred that I served out my prison term.

I was not the only journalist jailed for life: Chris Anyanwu, Ben Charles-Oni, and George Mbah, who worked for different media houses, were also jailed. And it was not only journalism that was under attack. It was very difficult for many business organizations to survive. Civil rights organizations were repressed. Dr. Beko Ransome-Kuti, the younger brother of the notable musician Fela Kuti, who was campaigning for our release, was subsequently arrested and jailed for life. As a mark of humiliation, they locked up the two of us in a single cell for a long while. I had been in jail less than two months when the writer and minority rights activist Ken Saro-Wiwa and his Ogoni brothers were hanged. M. K. O Abiola, publisher of the *National Concord* newspaper and other titles, who won the June 12, 1993, presidential election, was sent to prison where he later died. His wife, Kudirat, who was campaigning for his release, was gunned down on the streets of Lagos.[4] Retired generals Olusegun Obasanjo and Shehu Musa Yar'Adua, the former head of state and his deputy, who were then asking Abacha to democratize the polity, were dragged before the tribunal. While Obasanjo was given life imprisonment, Yar'Adua was condemned to death. He died in his dingy cell in Abakaliki prison on December 8, 1996.

A year before, Wole Soyinka, our much-respected winner of the Nobel Laureate in Literature, and a relentless critic of Abacha and his regime, had been hounded out of the country like a terrorist. He was declared wanted dead or alive. Ogaga Ifowodo and Akin Adesokan, two of Nigeria's award-winning writers, were arrested at the border on their way back to Nigeria after attending a conference in Europe, partly because the security agents found on them photographs they took with Soyinka. Niyi Osundare, the multiple award-winning poet and respected columnist for *Newswatch*, was interrogated by agents of the State Security Services for dedicating his poem on the state of that anomie to me. Injustices flourished. So the list of the victims of that tyranny is long. Of all the media houses in Nigeria, ours suffered the most: our editor-in-chief, Bayo Onanuga and his deputy, Dapo Olorunyomi, had to flee to the United States. Ladi, Olorunyomi's wife, was detained in place of her husband. Babafemi Ojudu, our managing editor, almost died in detention. Our general manager, Idowu Obasa, simply went underground. At one point, eleven members of our staff were in detention. Our Kaduna correspondent, Bagauda Kaltho, who was arrested in 1996, was never able to return to the office, or to the warm embrace of his wife and two children. He was killed in detention. Carting away our magazines from the vendors meant a big financial loss, which was easy to account for. But it has been very difficult for my colleagues and me to measure the pain inflicted on us by the death, in that tragic circumstance, of that brilliant journalist.

Yet that was not the first time we would be in trouble with generals in power. One morning in May 1993, the soldiers of General Ibrahim Babangida, who was the predecessor of Abacha, carted away about one hundred thousand copies of *TheNEWS* from the printing press. The edition was critical of Babangida's tactics of domination through bribery, patronage, deceit, and elimination of his political enemies. Using Niccolò Machiavelli's *The Prince* as a theoretical anchor, we analyzed the psyche of a ruler who wrote the rules of the game to suit a perennial reinvention of himself. Babangida raged furiously against that story. He shut down our office. We, who had made our office cozy, were forced to go underground to practice what is now popularly called guerrilla journalism. We were not going to allow the regime of Babangida to crush us. But it was set to be a fight between David and Goliath, for 1993 was a year of draconian decrees against critical publishing and defiant civil society. It was as if the self-styled president wanted a plain field on which to ride roughshod over Nigerians, who were simply fed up with his rule. Since our office was closed toward the end of the month, the first major problem was how our undercapitalized company would pay the salaries of its workers.[5] The second major problem was how to get the entire staff to remain very alert and continue to be part of the struggle. The following Monday, we called a meeting at the office of Sani Kabir, one of our directors, to solve the second problem. We assured our staff that we were going to carry on because the closure and occupation of our office was illegal. It was a threat to our livelihood: we had no other way of earning a living.

The response to that mobilization was spontaneous. We found that our staff shared our courage and doggedness. Although we reassured the staff that we were going to go on, none of us knew the form the journey would take. We next opened a bank account under a name different from one known to the government. We quickly transferred all our money into the account and informed our distributors and sales officers to ensure that payment for our products was made into it. We did not want Babangida to freeze our account as he did *Newswatch*'s in 1987 for six months because that weekly magazine, whose editor-in-chief, Dele Giwa, had been parcel-bombed in 1986, published the Cookey Political Bureau report before the government could tinker with it. We got some agents to pay in advance for the magazine. That was how we were able to pay salaries at the end of the month. That gave everyone a boost. Even those who might have had some doubts simply said, if we get paid and we enjoy what we are doing, why don't we just continue doing it? The risk was great, but our staff discounted it. Their disgust over the action of the junta, which ignored a Lagos High Court order to leave our office, was palpable. The staff became a source of inspiration to the rest of us.

In the meantime, the transition-to-democracy program for which Babangida had spent close to forty billion naira had crumbled. The sharks within the military were about to devour themselves. Many of the politicians in the Social Democratic Party (SDP) and the National Republican Convention were jostling to surrender to Babangida. We reported the political events of those giddy days as if we were producing in the comfort of our offices. We were the first to publish the comprehensive results of the June 12 presidential election, which showed that M. K. O. Abiola of the SDP was the winner. We followed that up with an insider's story of the big conspiracy to abort that election and the democratic rights of

Nigerians. We had reported then that General Joshua Dogonyaro and Brigadier-Generals David Mark, Anthony Ukpo, John Shagaya, and Halilu Akilu were the major officers goading Babangida to cancel the presidential election. We had reported the hijack of Nigeria Airways airbus by the Movement for the Advancement of Democracy led by Jerry Yusuf, whose main reason for the hijack was that Abiola was prevented from becoming president. The most popular of our editions from the underground was the special interview with General Muhammadu Buhari, in which he offered a scathing criticism of the incumbent dictator. He said, among other things, that Babangida was going to be tried for drug pushing before he overthrew him. When vendors started selling that edition secretly all over Nigeria, security men went after them.

We kept at it for a few weeks before Babangida brought out a backdated decree with which he proscribed *TheNEWS*. We ignored it. Indeed, on the cover of one of the editions we published at that time, we actually announced that the reader was reading a proscribed publication. That was not meant for the reader, who already knew. We were merely spitting in the face of the tyrant. That defiance was meant to counter the regime's defiance of the law. But then, Babangida's soldiers started beating up our vendors; they started arresting distributors for selling an illegal publication; they started seizing thousands of copies of *TheNEWS* from distribution vans. The five founding editors, Onanuga, Olorunyomi, Babafemi Ojudu, Seye Kehinde, and I were declared wanted on the network news of state-controlled radio and television stations. Our correspondent in Abuja, the new capital of Nigeria, Yinka Tella, was detained. At this point, we felt that it was not fair that people should suffer so much on account of *TheNEWS*. We decided in July 1993 to publish *TEMPO*. Because we wanted the market to know that it was just a change of name, not editorial policy, the first edition of *TEMPO* was exactly the same as *TheNEWS* in terms of form and content: A4-size, glossy cover, and so on. Our printers had just completed the tedious production process when some fully armed soldiers came to cart away every copy. It was a huge punch in the gut. We did not cry, but there was bitterness in our hearts toward the bandits who were some of the people running the affairs of our country. We resolved to fight to the very end. Many of us were in our early thirties then. It was one of those moments when we were not sure we would win, but we were just sufficiently motivated by some noble ideals that we thought would make our country outlast hopelessness.

We had one of our strategy meetings that night, but we really could not arrive at anything except a foggy idea of publishing books or bulletins or pamphlets of facts periodically. There was so much outrage. We had been courageous for six weeks. Our attempts at decoy had been defeated. But by the following morning, the idea of *TEMPO* in tabloid form came up. We thought it would have the advantage of being produced with speed. We were not going to allow the edition that had been seized to die, so we reproduced it in tabloid form. It was so successful that there were no returns. When they locked up our computers, they thought that they had paralyzed us. They underestimated the goodwill of so many Nigerians, who encouraged us by buying the magazine. Those who were working for the government fed us official information. It was a very empowering factor because the same people gave us information whenever the state security was set to unleash its terror on us. We used Gbenga Fagbami's business center as a production point. Nobody would expect that we, who were being hunted, would go to Bamgbose in Lagos Island (close to the former State House at Dodan Barracks) and do our job right under their noses. It was a very strategic place.

We identified those staff that needed to be involved in the aspect of production. We split the production into two major units: typesetting and printing. We limited access to the computers to very trusted typesetters. We asked the rest to go on leave. What that meant was that those who were chosen, like Jacob Inegbedion, had to work extra hours. Once you entered the place, you did not leave until production was finished. Staff who had nothing to do with computer production had no access to the location. Only those senior persons who needed to be involved at the point of editing were allowed into the bunker. Remember, the internet, mobile phones, and social media were not available at that time. The use of analog phones was restricted and unreliable. We divided into cells. There was another location where editorial people met, given to us by a relation of one of our shareholders. There was really no need for the entire editorial staff to meet together any longer. If you were a desk head, only your reporters had access to you. You only met other desk heads to put the stories together. We ensured that we had no situation where more than four or five persons were together at a particular place at the same time. We had a link person who was doing the dispatch.

As for the printing, we simply turned our sales staff into a production crew. No reporters knew the place except the founding editors. This was the aspect that the junta mythologized. All those times it was said that we were printing at the American Embassy or in Cotonou, Benin Republic, it was L. K. Jakande, former president of the International Press Institute and first executive governor of Lagos State, who was printing for us. He was touched by our audacity. But he was not doing it within his own premises at John West House on Acme Road, Agidingbi. He had a secret location where he had another press. The security forces could not locate the place. When it was no longer safe to stay at Jakande's place, we moved over to Jim Nwobodo's Satellite Press.

Having divided into cells, the founding editors met several times in Gbile Oshadipe's house in a suburb of Lagos before we shifted our base to Bamgbose. It was not possible for us to have visitors. We discouraged them and simply dropped out of circulation. Obasa turned half of his flat into an administrative office. He also turned part of his mother's house into a store. I asked him why he chose to do that. He said that it was imperative that we continued to operate. Since we had agreed to divide into cells, it was important to use the most unlikely places. For Obasa, the last place that anybody would expect him to keep the administrative, sales, and account staff that were under his supervision as general manager was at his mother's house. He reckoned that nobody would question it. "Why would an old woman be the storekeeper of *TEMPO*? You know, it was very unlikely to expect my old mum to understand what we were doing, not to talk of being an active part of it."[6] Obasa also observed that we were not caught because of the goodwill of his neighbors, who must have noticed our clandestine movements but chose not to turn us in.

Tensions in the country were so high that any spark could have set off a big explosion of protest. Babangida, a short man with a super-size ego, had annulled the presidential election on June 23, 1993. He had actually tried to stop it through Francis Arthur Nzeribe's Association for Better Nigeria, which asked Justice Bassey Ikpeme of the Abuja High Court on June 10, 1993, to stop the National Electoral Commission (NEC) from conducting the election scheduled for June 12 and to disqualify the presidential aspirant, Abiola. The court gave the ruling, but the NEC disobeyed it. It was when that failed that the government issued the annulment statement. Nduka Irabor, press secretary to the Chief of General Staff, Admiral Augustus Aikhomu, distributed the unsigned press release that voided the election to journalists in Abuja that morning. The annulment was first announced in the foreign media before it was aired on Radio Kaduna and the network service of the Federal Radio Corporation of Nigeria (FRCN). The release explained that the election was annulled "to protect our legal system and the judiciary from being ridiculed and politicized both nationally and internationally."[7] It was a great insult to all those who knew that Babangida had engineered the judicial anarchy that followed the elections. He had never wanted peaceful elections. One pointer to that was the ultimatum to get out of the country within forty-eight hours, which he gave Michael O'Brien, director of the United States Information Service, for saying on June 11, 1993, that "any postponement of the election would cause grave concern to the US Government."[8] Babangida closed down, on July 22, six media houses that were lending support to the deannulment of the June 12 election: *National Concord*, *The Punch*, *Daily Sketch*, *Observer*, *Ogun Radio*, and *Abuja Newsday*.

The country, particularly the South West, erupted in anger. Many people took to the streets in protest. The soldiers mowed down many of them. The more people the soldiers killed, the more defiant the protesters became. Many Nigerians were now afraid that there would be another civil war. For that reason, a lot of them traveled to their home states in panic. Many died on the way. Using the Nigerian Television Authority (NTA) and the FRCN as effective propaganda tools, Uche Chukwumerije, secretary of information, drummed up war beats in a way that reminded Nigerians that he had been a propagandist in the Republic of Biafra during the Nigerian civil war from 1967 to 1970. In that climate of uncertainties, *TEMPO* was a dependable source of information. The regime, which was now under pressure, started another round of manhunts for our journalists.

It got to the point that vendors were scared to collect *TEMPO*. We had to mobilize our staff, friends, and family to sell the magazine on the streets for three weeks. The state security was confused. Femi Falana, a famous lawyer and human rights activist, collected and sold copies through his office. Adeolu Ademoyo, a teacher at the University of Ife, Ile-Ife, always collected copies for sale. Other concerned professionals also rose to the challenge of selling the magazine. Eventually, the vendors themselves found the courage to resume sales. They collected the paper at agreed-on drop points in the night.

Babangida was smart enough to know the limits of his own chicanery. He "abdicated the throne" on August 27, 1993, because of a security report that he was about to be abducted and assassinated by some officers he had thought were his allies. When Babangida addressed the joint session of the Senate and the House of Representatives on August 17, 1993, which was his birthday, he had thought that the politicians would pass a vote of confidence in him and then ask him to carry on. But that did not work out. He said, among other things, "Following lengthy deliberations with my service chiefs, I offered as my own personal sacrifice to voluntarily *step aside* as the President and Commander-in-chief of the Armed Forces of the Federal Republic of Nigeria."[9] It was the limit of hubris that he considered it a personal sacrifice to relinquish power after eight years in government. Before he "stepped aside," he retired all other service chiefs except Abacha, who was made secretary of defense, in the Chief Ernest Shonekan–led Interim National Government (ING), which he inaugurated on August 26, 1993. Justice Dolapo Akinsanya of the Lagos High Court declared ING illegal on November 11.

Our company's frosty relationship with Babangida started during our days at the Concord Press of Nigeria Limited. In 1992, he shut down the entire premises because of a story published in the April 13 edition of *African Concord*. The story "Has IBB Given Up?" was anchored by Olorunyomi. It was a trenchant criticism of the economic and political mismanagement of the regime. It was one of the paradoxes of that time that the peg of the story was the rare interview the gap-toothed military president granted the *Sunday Times*, a paper in which the federal government had a controlling share. In that interview, thanks to the paper's liberal outlook when Dr. Yemi Ogunbiyi was the managing director, the general admitted that his regime was incapable of fixing the economy. It was a very unpopular thing to say to the people who were expecting a positive change in an economy that had impoverished them; an economy that depended on the prescriptions that were harsher than the ones packaged in the International Monetary Fund's structural adjustment program. The cover story, which contained a caustic essay by Adebayo Williams entitled "The Game Is Up," and a critical interview by one of the old frontline nationalists, Mokwugo Okoye, annoyed Babangida considerably. He banned the magazine. All the appeals of Abiola, the publisher of the magazine and Babangida's friend, fell on deaf ears. The president was too angry to see him, and Abiola began to count his losses as a government contractor. After a frustrating wait, the government started talking to Abiola through Colonel Halilu Akilu, director of the Directorate of Military Intelligence. The condition for lifting the siege was unambiguous: go and bring a letter of apology for what *African Concord* has done. Onanuga, the editor, refused. Instead, he resigned. I also resigned. So did Olorunyomi, Ojudu, and Kehinde.

On November 17, 1993, Abacha took power in a military coup and said that he would deal decisively with anyone who attempted "to test our will."[10] This was the period when some prodemocracy activists and many politicians, including Abiola, fell for the deceit of Abacha, believing that he would only rule for six months to stabilize the country before Abiola would take over. Except for members of the National Democratic Coalition, not many people knew that it was a lie until Brigadier-General Mark, in an interview with *Newswatch* in 1994, told the nation that Abacha's real plan was to stay in power for at least five years.[11] Mark, who had lost out in the power struggle that put Abacha in power, further said that the intention to remain in power for five years was a betrayal of the hopes and aspirations of Nigerians. Abacha was furious. Top editors of *Newswatch*—Ray Ekpu, Dan Agbese, and Yakubu Mohammed—were rounded up and detained. Mark, too, was declared wanted. Abacha's reign would be characterized by such deceit and incredible capacity for infinite meanness and greed, but Abiola had entered the trap before he realized it. Afterward, he tried to fight back, declaring himself president on the eve of the first anniversary of the annulled June 12 presidential election. He said that from that day, he had begun to run a government of national unity as a president and commander-in-chief and called on Abacha and members of his ruling council to resign. He also called on the people of Nigeria "to emulate the actions of their brothers and sisters in South Africa and stand up as one person to throw away the yoke of minority rule forever."[12] He naïvely forgot that the struggle in South Africa had had a long gestation period. By the time Abiola made that speech, called the Epetedo Declaration, the political ground beneath his feet had already shifted: many of the politicians around him had ditched him. For instance, his vice president-elect, Baba Gana Kingibe, had joined the government of Abacha. Demonstrating that his government was in control, Abacha arrested Abiola.[13] He was to remain in detention until he died four years later, one month after Abacha himself passed on.

Because of our critical coverage of his rule, Abacha marked our company as one of his arch opponents, but unexpectedly flattered us by hiring hacks to produce fake copies of *TheNEWS* and *TEMPO* along with *TELL*, the other critical magazine, with stories singing his praises. Our readers were not fooled. By vigorously probing his regime, we were merely fulfilling part of the promise that we had made at our first outing. We had resolved to dedicate ourselves to the principles of nationalism, democracy, liberty, and equality of the various ethnic groups of the Nigerian federation. In doing this, we had promised to adhere strictly to the ethics of the profession and to give our compatriots products that would be aesthetically satisfying.

If *TheNEWS* had responded to the military regimes in a combative manner, the putative democracy that they fostered clearly met the magazine in a critical mood. General Obasanjo, who was jailed with me, became the civilian president on May 29, 1999. When we saw massive corruption in that democracy, we reported it. When we saw autocrats who were parading themselves as democrats, we punctured the balloons of their hypocrisies. When crooks and hooligans contested and won elections, and became governors, lawmakers in the Senate, House of Representatives, and our Houses of Assembly, we exposed them. We were the first to report that James Ibori, who was then trying to become the governor of Delta State, was a fraud. But he bought his way through the constitutional processes and won the governorship election. In what could be regarded as a vindication of our story, he was jailed by a UK court for money laundering in 2012. The prosecution counsel described him as a crook in government.[14] We reported many cases of big-time international fraudsters who were giving our country a bad name around the world. When the government of Obasanjo secretly began to bribe members of the Senate and the House of Representatives to elongate his stay in power, *TheNEWS* and our evening paper, *PMNEWS*, exposed the illegal move. On account of that, the federal government stopped all its agencies from placing their advertisements in *TheNEWS*. Nuhu Ribadu, the famous boss of the Economic and Financial Crimes Commission (EFCC), whose work we had strongly supported, pleaded with his colleagues in government to no avail.

They didn't want to offend President Obasanjo, who was apparently determined to kill *TheNEWS*. Following a story of contract scandal involving his wife, Stella, in the 8th All Africa Games hosted in Abuja in 2003, the magazine was sued.[15] We engaged Gani Fawehinmi, the intrepid Lagos-based lawyer, who frontloaded his bulky statement of defense with Stella Obasanjo's past dirty deals. The press was awash with high expectations of a cause célèbre. But then, Stella suddenly died in a Spanish hospital of complications from tummy tuck surgery. The president of the Organizing Committee for the All-Africa Games, Dr. Amos Adamu, also sued *TheNEWS* for 2.3 million naira. He had become lord and master of the Nigerian Sports administration: one of the untouchables in the corridors of power. He rose to become an executive member of FIFA. But on October 17, 2010, an undercover reporter from *The Sunday Times* of London recorded him on video asking for a bribe of five hundred thousand pounds to be paid into his company account in exchange for his vote to influence the 2018 FIFA World Cup bid. He brought shame on Nigeria.[16] This bribe-for-vote scandal had more than justified the story of *TheNEWS*. It was with vengeance that Bode George, the deputy national chairman, South West, of Obasanjo's party, People's Democratic Party (PDP), instituted a libel case against *TheNEWS* when we ran a story of how he and other members of the board of Nigerian Ports Authority (NPA) looted the kitty of the board: "N85 Billion Scam at the Ports: Bode George's Board Indicted." At every sitting of the case before Justice Olubunmi Oyewole of Ikeja High Court, George, a Lagos chief, would come with many of his party members in uniform traditional attire with drummers and other entertainers in tow. The day Onanuga, the editor-in-chief, was cross-examined, hired thugs swooped on him in the court premises. They slapped him, poured water on him, and rained abuses on him. Justice Oyewole had to warn all parties in the case to desist from taking the law into their own hands. On judgment day, October 26, 2009, for reasons best known to himself, George was still cocksure he was going to win. For him and his party members, it was a carnival.

Knowing how corrupt the Nigerian judiciary had become, we were not sure which way the pendulum would swing. However, one by one, Justice Oyewole dismissed George's claims. He then sentenced him and other board members to Kirikiri Maximum Security Prison. Because of George's assumptions and claims that as chairman of the board, he was really not the one who stole, Justice Oyewole, in his judgment said, among other things,

> Persons acknowledged out of millions of Nigerians by the President of the Federal Republic of Nigeria to be of proven integrity and of cognitive experience in relation to the activities of the NPA cannot claim ignorance or simply play Pontius Pilate when obviously irregular contracts placed before them were approved without question. It amounts to willful blindness and must have its consequences. By section 10 (3) (b) and (5) (c) of the NPA Act, the board of NPA is given powers to control the managing director and the executive directors. The board was also given express powers in the said Act to obtain advice from non-members and co-opt such special members for specific purposes. Such a board cannot claim inadequacy. After all, as the ancient wisdom says, you cannot bear the title of eagle and be unable to prey on chickens. The culpability of the defendants in this regard is direct and not vicarious.[17]

George's fall from grace is similar to that of Tafa Balogun, the inspector-general of police (IG) under President Obasanjo. *TheNEWS* of July 28, 2003, had carried an exposé on Balogun's diversion of 1.5 billion naira in police funds among other crimes. We called it "The Greedy Police Boss." As soon as the story was published, the IG invited other media houses for an interview in which *TheNEWS* was roundly condemned. When the EFCC had the courage to look into the case, however, Balogun was found guilty and dismissed from service: the first time ever that an IG would be publicly disgraced. In the same manner, the first Speaker of the House of Representatives, Salisu Ibrahim Buhari, had to step down, weeping like a baby, in the wake of *TheNEWS* investigative story. In July 1999, his scandalous claims that he read Business Administration at the University of Toronto, Canada, that he was thirty-six years old, and that he had done the one-year compulsory national service after his diploma in accountancy at the Ahmadu Bello University, Zaria, became known. The University of Toronto told *TheNEWS* that the new Speaker never attended the university. From other records, we also found out that he had lied on oath about his age. When the story, "The Face of a Liar: House Speaker Buhari Deceives His Nation," hit the newsstand, Buhari asked his men to buy up all the copies in Abuja. The following week, he engaged one of the best lawyers in Nigeria, Rotimi Williams, to sue *TheNEWS*. We did not relent; we did a follow-up titled "Buharigate: An Inside Story." Our lawyer, Falana, told the country that we would meet Williams in court. In the end, Buhari pleaded guilty in his trial and, on August 3, 1999, was sentenced by an Abuja magistrate court to twelve months' imprisonment or a fine of one hundred thousand naira each on the two counts of false declaration of age and forgery. He, expectedly, chose to pay the fine. Obasanjo would soon pardon the young man. But *TheNEWS* had done its job.

The robust tradition of resistance, with combative stories and pungent criticisms in Nigeria's print media, dates back to the colonial days. Beginning with *Iwe Irohin*, founded by Reverend Henry Townsend in 1859, notable papers of the period included *Lagos Daily News*, established in 1925 by Herbert Macaulay, who suffered detention many times, *Nigerian Daily Times*, *The Daily Service*, *The Lagos Weekly Record*, *Lagos Times*, *Lagos Observer*, Nnamdi Azikiwe's chain of newspapers (*West African Pilot*, *Eastern Nigerian Guardian*, *Southern Nigerian Defender*, *Daily Comet*, *Nigerian Monitor*), and Awolowo's newspapers (*Nigerian Tribune*, founded in 1949, *Midwest Echo*, *Middle Belt Herald*, *The Northern Star*, and *The Eastern Observer*). The brains behind these newspapers were some of the best in Nigeria at that time. They were graduates of Lincoln University; University College, London; Liverpool University; University of Edinburgh; and the like, and they were trained medical doctors, engineers, lawyers, teachers, wealthy businessmen, and so on. It was logical, therefore, that they would consider colonial imposition as a yoke to be combated. Before Azikiwe and Awolowo became successful politicians, they were enterprising journalists.

Awolowo was a reporter in Lagos when Azikiwe came back to Nigeria from Ghana where he had been editor-in-chief and managing director of *African Morning Post*. On his return to colonial Nigeria, Azikiwe, whose fame had preceded him, gave a series of anticolonial lectures that Awolowo covered for Nigerian *Daily Times*. Before he became a lawyer, he freelanced for *Daily Service*, which Samuel Ladoke Akintola (who would later become his deputy when he was premier in the Western Region) edited. It was for *Daily Service* that Awolowo wrote many pungent anticolonial articles using various pen names such as "Afric" and "A. O." He paid attention to details. The bulk of the articles he wrote for *West Africa* later became *Path to Nigerian Freedom*, a book that contains some of his well-argued ideas on federalism.[18] By the time Awolowo came back to Nigeria from the UK after his law degree, he simply threw himself into legal practice to make enough money, which he used for partisan politics and journalism. In the first edition of *Nigerian Tribune*, published November 16, 1949, Awolowo wrote that "the paper would have a frank tongue and a pungent pen. A tongue and a pen that would be careless of what the opponents might say or how they might feel, and would have enough courage to call hypocrisy, humbug and tyranny by their names. Such a tongue, such a pen will mortify the proud and provoke despotism to repent its ways."[19] The paper sold thousands of copies that first day. Awolowo wrote many of the editorials in the early days of the paper. In editorial after editorial, and sometimes in the choice of its stories, *Nigerian Tribune* kept faith with the yearnings and aspirations of its readers and the larger interest of Nigeria.

Azikiwe, together with his colleagues, truly played the journalistic game to the hilt. In its mission statement, *West African Pilot* said it would be independent in all things and neutral in nothing that affected the destiny of Africa. It also said that genuine cooperation between government and citizens was necessary toward the successful realization of the objectives of the state: "If government, as an agent of the state adopted certain measures which, in the opinion of the paper, would enhance the happiness of the community, *West African Pilot* would not hesitate to say so and laud the government. If on the other hand, government enunciated or applied certain measures which would militate against the best interest of the community, the paper, as a sentinel of popular liberty and guardian of civilization, would say so loud and clear."[20] The paper said it believed in social justice and that it looked forward to a better Nigeria and a more glorious future for West Africa. It is interesting to note that Azikiwe took the mission statements of the *Nigerian Times*, *Nigerian Spectator*, and *Nigerian Advocate* to the editorial meeting that crafted the mission statement of *West African Pilot*. Azikiwe fell in love with the statements because they canvassed for the need to mold strong, healthy, and vigorous public opinions as one of the duties of every intelligent and educated member of Nigeria. He was also interested in them because one of the editorials argued that what the country needed was a government that would protect the people from harsh and oppressive measures; a government that would promote the development of the social, industrial, and economic resources of the country for the benefit of its inhabitants; a government that would govern by wise and humane laws; a government that would administer justice impartially; and a government that would care for the intellectual and moral welfare of the people.[21] It is remarkable that we now have politician-publishers who believe that one sure way of consolidating their political influence and laundering their dirty images is to have their own newspapers and radio and television stations. The Awolowo and Azikiwe model remains very attractive.

In spite of all the challenges and problems they constantly face, such as prohibitive costs of production materials and unethical practices of some publishers, editors, and reporters, Nigeria's print media, particularly the privately funded ones, have been faithful, by and large, to the analytical, combative tradition of their predecessors. In the course of doing this, journalists have been harassed, detained, jailed, and assassinated—especially under the dictatorships of Generals Babangida and Abacha. That was why Soyinka, in my prefatory quote, spoke glowingly about the heroism of journalists. Today, the digital revolution sweeping newsrooms is truly popularizing the form and distribution of news; but, sadly, it is also bringing about job losses and dwindling fortunes. This is worrisome. But the good news is that with the advances in technology, dictators would find it difficult, if not impossible, to delay the publication of a story or kill it outright by shutting down the premises of media houses or carting away printed products. With the Freedom of Information Act (FOIA), signed into law on May 28, 2011, by President Goodluck Jonathan, journalists are now institutionally empowered to access more information in their open-closed society. But access to information will not prevent sloppy reporting and editing and mediocre packaging. It will not automatically confer on reporters the sharp nose for news. That will depend on individual talents and gifts and intensive training. The FOIA in a very corrupt country like Nigeria can, in fact, become a tool of blackmail. That is why I told Elliot Ross, who did a piece on the FOIA in the September 2011 edition of *Columbia Journalism Review*, that for this law to work effectively, we would need a complete overhaul of our country, which has painfully become a paradise for crooks.[22] It can be very painful reporting Nigeria's cycle of stupidities. As you send one set of charlatans and robbers in power packing, a new set takes over. In the end, the country gasps for breath.

Shortly after Jonathan's government was voted out of power in 2015, the new president, Muhammadu Buhari, who as a military dictator jailed in 1985 two of the *Guardian*'s journalists—Tunde Thompson and Nduka Irabor—because they published a story of a diplomatic posting before he announced it, appealed for the cooperation of journalists in the course of his inaugural speech. He said he needed journalists to bring about the change for which his party, All Progressives Congress, was elected.[23] The media did not have to wait long to support his war against corruption. As soon as he settled in, revelations of mindless and incredible looting of the country's treasury began to make headlines. Recently, a Lagos High Court ruled that Dr. Ngozi Okonjo-Iweala, minister of finance and coordinating minister of the economy, should explain why thirty trillion naira disappeared from the government's kitty under her watch.[24] Professor Charles Soludo, a former governor of the Central Bank, had earlier raised alarm over the missing money. When he did so, the print media feasted on it. As the nation waited for Okonjo-Iweala's day in court, the director of finance of the Presidential Campaign Committee for the reelection of Jonathan in 2015, Nenadi Usman, was already being tried for over 3.1 billion naira she got from the Central Bank in the buildup to the election. Bank details showed that the money was shared among the PDP chiefs.[25] The president himself, in collaboration with National Security Adviser Sambo Dasuki, diverted 2.1 billion US dollars approved as extrabudgetary spending for the purchase of weapons to fight Boko Haram terrorists. Investigations of the EFCC indicated that Jonathan disbursed the money to those who were campaigning for his reelection. Beneficiaries of the largesse included Tony Anenih, Olisa Metuh, Abba Dabo, Femi Fani-Kayode, Olu Falae, Tanko Yakassai, Rashidi Ladoja, Peter Odili, Jim Nwobodo, and Nduka Obaigbena, publisher of *ThisDay* newspaper, and Raymond Dokpesi, owner of *Africa Independent Television*. Meanwhile the soldiers fighting the Boko Haram insurgents were being routed by superior firepower. When Nigerian soldiers protested that they were being sent to the battlefront without adequate weapons, they were tried and condemned to death. *TheNEWS* and other critical print media rose solidly, along with Falana, their lawyer, in their defense. If Buhari had not become the president, they would have been killed. What of the missing 4.8 billion naira from the accounts of the Nigerian Air Force?[26]

What of the mindboggling details of Diezani Alison-Madueke's fuel subsidy scams in the Nigerian National Petroleum Corporation (NNPC)? What of the pension fund of millions of Nigerians that was stolen at the Pension Transitional Arrangement Directorate under Nelly Mayshak?[27] On February 3, 2017, EFCC recovered 9.8 million US dollars from the Kaduna house of a former chief executive of the NNPC, Dr. Andrew Yakubu.[28] It's a long list of executive robberies. Nigerians had not witnessed before the large-scale stealing that characterized Jonathan's years in government. Agreed, the print media did not report in detail the entire panoply of the fleece, but *TheNEWS*, *Daily Trust*, *NEXT*, *The Punch*, *The Nation*, and a few other investigative online platforms like *Sahara Reporters* and *Premium Times* did not turn a blind eye. We were critical of many of the people now on trial. At a time when the most lucrative business in town was the federal government, that meant a loss of substantial revenue. We had done critical stories in the past on the now embattled president of the Senate, Dr. Bukola Saraki, and some of the shady businessmen and politicians implicated in the Panama Papers exposé.[29]

Driven by desire for social justice, *TheNEWS* will continue to tear off the painted masks of evil in our private lives and brigandage in our public offices.

KUNLE AJIBADE, Executive Editor of *TheNEWS* and *PMNEWS*, is author of *What a Country!* and *Jailed for Life: A Reporter's Prison Notes*, which won the Victor Nwankwo Book of the Year Award in 2003.

Notes

Some portions of this chapter, reconsidered and reworked, appeared in Kunle Ajibade, *Jailed for Life: A Reporter's Prison Notes* (Ibadan: Heinemann, 2003). I also delivered part of it in an address at the PEN's Writers in Prison Committee conference, Barcelona, Spain, in 2004.

1. Marie Colvin, *On the Frontline: The Collected Journalism of Marie Colvin* (London, Harper Collins, 2012).
2. "Marie Colvin in her own words—our mission is to report the horrors of war," *The Telegraph*, February 22, 2012, http://www.telegraph.co.uk/news/worldnews/middleeast/syria/9098053/Syria-Marie-Colvin-in-her-own-words-our-mission-is-to-report-the-horrors-of-war.html.
3. Ibid.
4. On Monday, January 30, 2012, a Lagos High Court sentenced Hamza al-Mustapha to death by hanging for the murder of Kudirat Abiola on June 3, 1996.
5. To safeguard the independence and integrity of our editorial content, we had raised funds for *TheNEWS* from the following: Gani Fawehinmi, Sani Kabir, Tayo Adesanya, Beko Ransome-Kuti, Femi Falana, Bola Ahmed Tinubu, Layi Babatunde, Yemisi Shyllon, Chris Mammah, Eyimofe Atake, Adegboyega Ojora, and Wale Babalakin. None of them holds the majority share.
6. Idowu Obasa, interview by the author, October 22, 1999.
7. Kunle Ajibade, *Jailed for Life: A Reporter's Prison Notes* (Ibadan, Heinemann, 2003), 8.
8. Karl Maier, "Nigerian Voters Look for a Leader: Lagos Demands Withdrawal of US Embassy Spokesman After Washington Insists Elections, the First for 10 Years, Should Go Ahead," *The Guardian*, June 12, 1993, http://www.independent.co.uk/news/world/nigerian-voters-look-for-a-leader-lagos-demands-withdrawal-of-us-embassy-spokesman-after-washington-insists-elections-the-first-for-10-years-should-go-ahead-karl-maier-reports-1491077.html.
9. General Ibrahim Babangida's speech at the joint session of the Senate and House of Representatives was broadcast live by the NTA.
10. See the full text of Abacha's speech here: Nehi Igbinijesu, "Discover Nigeria: The Coup; Speeches of General Abacha," *Connectingnigeria.com*, November 15, 2012, http://connectnigeria.com/articles/2012/11/discover-nigeria-the-coup-speeches-of-general-abacha/.
11. Interview with Brigadier-General David Mark, *Newswatch*, April 14, 1994.
12. "Full Text of Inaugural Address of 'President' MKO Abiola on June 11, 1994," *Vanguard*, June 12, 2015, http://www.vanguardngr.com/2015/06/full-text-of-inaugural-address-of-president-mko-abiola-on-june-11-1994/.
13. He also arrested some leaders of the National Union of Petroleum and Natural Gas Workers, whose strike from June 14, 1994, had paralyzed economic activities in Nigeria. When

the Petroleum and Natural Gas Senior Staff Association joined the strike on July 12, their leaders were also detained.

14. Mark Tran, "Former Nigeria's State Governor James Ibori Receives 13-year Sentence," *The Guardian* (London), April 17, 2012.

15. "8th All Africa Games: The Many Scandals of COJA," *TheNEWS*, October 27, 2003, 18–22.

16. "Fifa Undercover: Amos Adamu," *The Sunday Times* (London), October 18, 2010, https://www.thetimes.co.uk/article/fifa-undercover-amos-adamu-wp8mm39330l; "The Scandals of Amos Adamu," *TheNEWS*, November 1, 2010, 18–24.

17. "We Are Vindicated Again," *TheNEWS*, November 9, 2009, which quoted extensively from Justice Olubunmi Oyewole's judgment.

18. Obafemi Awolowo, *Path to Nigerian Freedom* (London: Faber and Faber, 1947).

19. Obafemi Awolowo, "Fraternity of the Pen," in *Awo: The Autobiography of Chief Obafemi Awolowo* (Cambridge: Cambridge University Press, 1960), 82–93.

20. Nnamdi Azikiwe, "Founding of the Zik Group of Newspapers," in *My Odyssey: An Autobiography* (Ibadan, Nigeria: Spectrum Books, 1994), 295–296.

21. Ibid.

22. Elliot Ross, "Nigeria's New FOIA: Reporters Enjoy New Freedoms in a Long-Repressive Society," *Columbia Journalism Review*, September 23, 2011, http://archives.cjr.org/behind_the_news/nigerias_new_foia.php.

23. "Read President Buhari's Inaugural Speech," *Vanguard*, May 29, 2015, http://www.vanguardngr.com/2015/05/read-president-buhari-inaugural-speech/.

24. "You Must Account for 'Missing N30tn,' Court Tells FG, Okonjo-Iweala," *ThisDay*, May 23, 2016, http://www.thisdaylive.com/index.php/2016/05/23/you-must-account-for-missing-n30tn-court-tells-fg-okonjo-iweala/.

25. "Court Papers Show How Ex-NSA Dasuki Allegedly Shared N13.6bn Arms Money to Cronies, Politicians," *Premium Times*, December 14, 2015, http://www.premiumtimesng.com/news/headlines/195173-court-papers-show-how-ex-nsa-dasuki-allegedly-shared-n13-6bn-arms-money-to-cronies-politicians.html.

26. "Alleged N4.8bn Fraud: Ex-Chief of Air Staff, Umar, Docked, Granted Bail," *Vanguard*, May 11, 2016, http://www.vanguardngr.com/2016/05/alleged-n4-8bn-fraud-ex-chief-air-staff-umar-docked-granted-bail/.

27. Ben Ezeamalu, "Judge Orders Final Forfeiture of N34 billion liked to Diezani Alison-Madueke, *Premium Times*, February 16, 2017, http://www.premiumtimesng.com/news/top-news/223706-breaking-judge-orders-final-forfeiture-n34-billion-linked-diezani-alison-madueke.html; Eniola Akinkuotu and Ifeanyi Onuba, "Pension: EFCC Arrests Suspended DG, Others for N2.5bn Fraud," *The Punch*, April 20, 2016, http://punchng.com/pension-efcc-arrests-suspended-dg-others-for-n2-5bn-fraud/.

28. Soni Daniel, "Update: How EFCC Recovered $9.8m from Yakubu, Ex-NNPC GMD," *Vanguard*, February 10, 2017, http://www.vanguardngr.com/2017/02/efcc-recovered-9-8million-yakubu-ex-nnpc-gmd/.

29. "How Saraki, Others Looted Societe Generale Bank of Nigera; Over N1b Looted," *Sahara Reporters*, July 6, 2008, http://saharareporters.com/2008/07/06/how-saraki-others-looted-societe-generale-bank-nigeria-%E2%80%A2-over-n1b-looted; "Panama Papers: Bukola Saraki in Fresh Trouble Over Hidden Assets," *TheNews*, April 5, 2016, http://thenewsnigeria.com.ng/2016/04/panama-papers-bukola-saraki-in-fresh-trouble-over-hidden-assets/.

14 Improvisational Characteristics of an Urban Fragment

Oxford Street, Accra

Ato Quayson

> I want to insist that theories of urban modernity belong to all cities and their citizens. And instead of seeing only some cities as the originators of urbanism, in a world of ordinary cities ways of being urban and ways of making new kinds of urban futures are diverse and are the product of the inventiveness of people in cities everywhere.
>
> —Jennifer Robinson, *Ordinary Cities: Between Modernity and Development*

THE STANDARD VIEW of African cities is that they are in crisis. This is not a recent view and has some truth in it. What has been described in the standard idiom of rural-urban drift conceals another, and perhaps more pernicious, kind of drift: the increasing number of urban dwellers moving desperately from task to task in an increasingly informalized economy, something that was compounded for most African countries by the bitter structural adjustment programs handed down by the International Monetary Fund (IMF) and other international agencies in the 1980s. The immediate effect of those programs was the shrinking of the state sector, which, despite all appearances to the contrary, is still the largest employer and engine of growth in most African economies. The 2011 *African Development Report* notes how at Independence most African countries pursued import-substitution policies, some of which entailed creating large, publicly funded agricultural produce-buying agencies, with subsidies on farm implements and fertilizers, and attractive pricing policies.[1] By the 1980s the crash in agricultural commodity prices meant that these agencies and parastatals could barely sustain themselves; many of them were disbanded under pressure from the IMF, with their effect being the forcing of rural people off barely sustainable lands and into the bosom of major urban conurbations. All the inefficiencies of the state sector are immediately translated into spatial effects: more people on the streets competing for progressively scantier and more decrepit public services while also having to face up to the chicanery of their political leaders. The sorrows for the African dweller have been the subject of endless policy papers, governmental documents, and some of the scholarly literature. It is now standard fare of major contemporary discussion forums such as *Next City* and *Informal City Dialogues*, both of which have attracted major sponsorship from the Rockefeller Foundation and other like-minded charitable organizations. And despite the qualifiers that these forums insert to correct the overall bleakness of their prognoses, the emphasis is still mainly on individual enterprise in the face of scarce resources—thus, the forums' special interest in the lives of slum dwellers, for example.[2]

My own work joins the work of urban scholars such as AbdouMaliq Simone, Garth Myers, Jennifer Robinson, Achille Mbembe, and others who have applied a more wide-angled lens to the issue of improvisation in the context of urban survival and place making, with the central difference that I have a steadier interest in theoretical questions of space and spatiality and thus insist on returning to space at every turn. The turn to space in my mind involves two interrelated vectors: the first is understanding the relationality of neighborhoods—that is to say, the degree to which a particular neighborhood acquires a specific character of social aggregation not autonomously but in relation to the evolution of other neighborhoods or districts—and the second involves the microdynamics of spatial practices, what I discuss in terms of the improvisatory spatial logics to be seen on Oxford Street. For my book *Oxford Street, Accra: City Life and the Itineraries of Transnationalism*, I took this most famous commercial street as a key to open up different dimensions of Accra's urban evolution. Turned one way, it takes us to the history of demographic aggregations from the early settlement of the Accra coastland around 1655 to its specific spatial formation as a colonial port by the early twentieth century; in another direction, to the sedimented histories of stranger groups such as the returnee Afro-Brazilians (the Tabon) from Bahia in the mid-nineteenth century, the Danish Africans of Osu Township from the 1720s, and the many northern migrants that had made their way into Accra from as early as the Anglo-Ashanti War of 1874, and subsequently in different waves as settlers in the famous *zongos* (stranger quarters) in different parts of the evolving city. The urban key also gives us access to the processes of hybridity and transnationalism, such as the international circuits of salsa and body-building culture of which Accra's youth are eager participants, and also to the expressive social imaginaries of transition, encapsulated most significantly in the many *tro tro* (shared buses) slogans and inscriptions to be seen on vehicles and all across the urbanscape. Thus, my interest is in the spatial formations that instigate different forms and levels of social interaction to give Accra its peculiar cosmopolitan character. This is not to sidestep the obvious stories of urban malaise that are much in evidence in descriptions of the African city, but to point to the historical confluences that make of the malaise only one way of understanding it.

Ethno-history and the Political Economy of Spatial Formations

Space is a social relation. Elaborated variously by Edward Soja, Doreen Massey, Henri Lefebvre, and various others, this may be taken as the mantra of contemporary urban studies. With respect to the history of Oxford Street, and beyond that of Accra, the primary challenge has been how to translate this mantra into a form that is commensurate to the particularity of Accra's evolution in which space has historically taken various inflections and thus differently affected the social relationships that make up the city. At heart, and in contrast to the emphasis found in much urban policy documents, histories of Accra have largely been ethno-political histories.[3] These are marked by two essential features: first concerns the changing relations of the Ga with the long European merchant and colonial presence, and second relates to the long-standing and variegated relationships that have obtained between the Ga and the inland Akan tribes. If such ethno-political histories provide a lively picture of state formation in the face of often contradictory political and social forces, they also ignore the specifically spatial dynamic of such forces, the ways in which such forces came to sediment social aggregations in space and subsequently to alter the social relations among different segments of society.

One engine of such sedimentations may be found in the *longue durée* of political economy that not only redefined interactions between hinterland and coastal peoples but also completely altered their relative standing in relation to the transnational world. Thus, the shift in the political economy of the seventeenth and eighteenth centuries was one from the accumulation of capital primarily from the profits drawn from caravan-based trade and exchange networks to one that was defined by political-military projects and the extraction of tribute and other levies from conquered populations. As Ray Kea points out in his account of the two phases, "networks of capital accumulation were embedded in and subordinated to networks of power," but complicated by the arrival of the Europeans on the coast in the second phase.[4] The coincidence of the phase of state formation through political-military projects with the trans-Atlantic slave trade also meant the rise of different political and social agents (such as the trading *makelaar* and *caboceer*, which fused, chiefly, merchant and military functions together in direct relation to the new opportunities provided in the foreign trade, for example), and also new and powerful brokers of European and African relations (such as the Danish Euro-Africans of Osu, for example). The Atlantic slave trade also brought with it the first of the urban morphological forms for Accra and other settlements on the coast in terms of the impact of the European trade forts in organizing the specifically spatial dynamics of economic and social relations. In this respect it is pertinent to note that the Ga do not actually enter the historical record until the wars between them and the Akwamus starting from the 1640s, which led to their final defeat in 1680. This roughly four-decade period also happened to coincide with the building of Ussher Fort (1642) by the Dutch, the James Fort (1649) by the English, and Christiansborg Fort, now Castle (1659) by the Danes. The Ga kingdom had originally been headquartered at Ayawaso, about eleven miles north from the coast. Ayawaso was not only the site of the Ga court but also the location of a famous and lively market. This market was so powerful that it had a specific official who set market taxes and determined the volume of goods that flowed into the market from all directions. From the late 1640s the Ga began to impose prohibitive tariffs on goods brought from the Akan traders to the Ayawaso market and also to prevent them from gaining direct access to European merchants on the coast. This eventually exacerbated the disagreements with the militarily sophisticated Akwamus. The Akwamus defeated the Ga, beheaded their king, and decimated their kingdom, leading to the flight of the entire ruling class and their priests to the coast to shelter under the shadows of the new European forts. This was, technically speaking, the birth of Accra despite the fact that oral traditions trace the genesis of the Ga to their appearance from today's Yorubaland in the thirteenth century. The relocation of the Ga polity to the coast following their defeat also immediately had an impact on the social structure of *akutso* (quarter; *akutsei*, plural) formation and exposed them to ineluctable forces of hybridity. Thus, the Alata *akutso* was composed of slaves brought from the Allada coast in the formidable kingdom of Dahomey, on the border between today's Benin and western Nigeria. The slaves settled around the English fort and formed their own *akutso*, which gained the name of Alata, a corruption of Allada. To this day Ghanaians refer to Nigerians either as Alata people or Anago people, irrespective of where they come from in that vast country. The Nâgos (Anago) were themselves well known as the most culturally distinctive ethnic group in Bahia, and as historians such as Pierre Verger, João José Reis, and J. Lorand Matory have noted, were drawn from today's Yorubaland via the slave market of Dahomey.[5]

The spatial implications of Ga ethno-political history are not, however, exhausted from the examination of the *longue durée* of Gold Coast political economy since the seventeenth century. For ethno-political history also allows us to see the terms of boundary making among the Ga. This has turned heavily since the end of the nineteenth century on the status assigned to northern migrants in the city. As a general rule, northern migrants have always been located on the geographical margins of the evolving township. The term *zongo*, used by both sojourners and hosts to name northerners' places of settlement, facilitates this marginalization. Yet perhaps more important is the fact that in the intense debates about "making the town," to echo the title of John Parker's fine study of

2000, northern migrants have consistently been seen as outsiders to Accra's spatial formation.[6] This was also aided by the colonial policy of indirect rule, which completely abjured any form of hybridity in favor of clear-cut ethnic enclaves with autonomously constituted customs and forms. With the evolution of Accra and the pressures enjoined on the colonial authorities for cheap forms of labor from the late nineteenth century, however, the formerly marginalized geographic constituencies were progressively absorbed into the structure of the city itself but in such a way as to produce a rhythmic spatial relation between wealth and penury, and between different social ecologies. Thus, not only are all the residential districts where northerners are concentrated today poor slums, but perhaps even more significantly, there is a peculiar spatial relation of near proximity and even contiguity between such slums and the more salubrious residential and commercial areas of town. Thus, for the Central Business District (CBD) we have Tudu; for Kanda we have Nima; for Korle Bu we have Lartebiokorshie Zongo; and for Legon, Madina, in a regular relationship of middle-class to slum neighborhoods in close rhythmic affiliation to each other. While the relationship of these places appears to have unfolded on an ad hoc basis and was driven by a variety of often quite different planning impulses, the overall effect is to have generated a peculiar aggregation of volatile social distinctions in a specifically spatial relation.

How do we move from such macrolevel analyses of the African city (not by any means exhausted by the examples provided here) to the subtler and more ephemeral improvisations of everyday street life, and how are the two to be related? To this subject we must turn next.

Performative Streetscapes

The name "Oxford Street" is partly an improvisation and a chimerical projection of popular desire, for it is not the real name of the street that will be of concern to us here. It does not appear on any official maps of Accra. The source of the moniker is somewhat unclear but seems to have been popularized after the return to the country of exiled Ghanaians from various parts of the world, but especially from London following the end of military rule and the restoration of multiparty democracy in 1992. The interest of returning political exiles turns out to have been symptomatic of the larger interests of global capital as well, since this strip of the much longer Cantonments Road had all the situational advantages that made it a highly sought-after commercial corridor. Visitors to Accra will recognize Oxford Street, or simply the Street, as the roughly mile-and-a-half of Cantonments Road that stretches between Mark Cofie in the south to Danquah Circle in the north. Cantonments Road itself extends from the Osu RE (Regimental Engineers, so named after a British army unit that camped in the area during World War II) area and, merging with Second Circular Road, joins Airport Road to form a crucial south–north axis connecting Osu RE, Labone, and Cantonments, all of which are among the most prized neighborhoods in the city that since the colonial period have been the favored residential districts of the ruling elites and their satellites. A few miles to the east and west of Cantonments Road are other prestigious neighborhoods such as Ringway Estates, Ridge, Kanda, and Nyaniba Estates, all of which provide a steady stream of well-heeled shoppers to the Street. Significant also in the evolution and maintenance of its lively commercial character is its relative proximity to government buildings such as the State House, the Kwame Nkrumah Conference Centre, the Accra Sports Stadium, and the Ministries. Completed in 1924, the area popularly known as the Ministries contains the headquarters of all government departments. Combined with the upwardly mobile neighborhoods, the Street is thus fed all day and night by government and residential tributaries from every direction. This is what lends it the sense of a twenty-four-hour hub of commercial and leisure activity, irrespective of the fact that it is not in the most densely populated commercial part of town. This distinction is still reserved for Makola Market and the CBD, some two miles southwest of Oxford Street. The farther south one goes along Cantonments Road and its connecting streets, the closer one gets to the sea and, more importantly, to Christiansborg Castle, the seat of government since 1877.

On entering the Street from the north end (that is, from Danquah Circle), one is struck by how crowded it looks, with both vehicles and people, many large commercial buildings, and a proliferation of large-size billboards advertising everything from cell phone company products (MTN: "Everywhere You Go"; TIGO: "Express Yourself") to the United Emirates Airlines; from Nescafé to sanitary pads; and from the Nigerian magazine *Ovation* to DStv with the face of Jennifer Lopez staring coyly from a billboard, among many others. To enter the Street is also to be confronted by a range of features that are recognizable from high streets elsewhere in the world and yet with a decided mix of local characteristics. Your regular banks sit cheek by jowl against vendors of football paraphernalia, which increases exponentially during the years in which Ghana participates in international soccer tournaments such as the World Cup or the African Cup of Nations. Papa Ye has to contend with the vendor promising exactly the same chicken-and-fried-rice-with-Coke combo right across from the local fast-food giant, with the added enticement of a ghetto blaster with full-on Bob Marley music to accompany your food, while Woodin (retailer of beautiful print cloths) contends with ready-made variants of dresses and shirts made from the same print cloths but available for much less from street vendors. Electronic goods stores abound, as do jewelry shops, and offices of all the major cell phone companies operating in the country such as Airtel, MTN, Glo, and TIGO. Koala, a grocery store to rival Trader Joe's or Sainsbury's, is also on the Street, while the huge edifice to US fast-food retailing that is KFC opened in September 2011 to add a further transnational dimension to the food offerings. Several large Chinese and other high-end restaurants, internet cafés, hotels, B&Bs, forex bureaus, and a large Italian-themed ice cream parlor with luscious offerings make of this commercial stretch a visitor's dream and for the local dispossessed a mouth-watering nightmare.[7] On adjoining streets and byways off Oxford Street and within a roughly five-hundred-meter radius are various embassies and high commissions, the Goethe Cultural Institute and Ryan's, reputed to be the best Irish pub outside of Dublin, along with several other such watering holes and dance venues. Since at least the summer of 2006, a megasize television screen has been permanently mounted in front of the Osu Food Court streaming live TV advertisements and reality shows such as *Big Brother Africa* on a twenty-four-hour continuous loop.

Any temptation to see Oxford Street as an almost postmodern transnational commercial boulevard is quickly tempered by virtue of the many signs of cultural phenomena that reach back several generations and that may be seen in varying forms here as well as in different parts of the city and indeed in other urban areas in the country at large: the young man selling fresh coconuts whose skill for discerning the tenderness or hardness of the inside of the fruit before deftly splitting off the crown with his cutlass seems purely esoteric; the woman that sells ripe plantains roasted over a slow coal fire under a tree on the lively curbside corner (for good strategic reasons trees and curbside corners feature prominently in the life cycle of roasted plantain); the female hawkers nonchalantly walking along with their wares balanced on their heads but without the prop of hands and selling things as varied as ice cold water or oranges or roasted peanuts or even charcoal, smoked fish, onions, chilies, and cassava and plantain for the evening's *fufu*. One or two of these women may even have a young child strapped to her back. These variant features bring the mix of businesses and vendors on the street much closer to commercial districts in other parts of the city such as Makola, Kaneshie Market, Dansoman High Street, or Spintex Road, all of which are veritable beehives of commercial activity with their own distinctive characteristics.

Apart from its name and the many businesses to be found along the street, however, the most visible yet easy-to-be-missed dimension of the peculiar character of Oxford Street is actually to be experienced underneath one's feet—that is, on the sidewalk itself. In the December 18, 1926, entry to his *Moscow Diary*, Walter Benjamin wrote, "It has been observed that pedestrians [in Moscow] walk in 'zigzags.' This is simply on account of the overcrowding of the narrow sidewalks; nowhere else except here and there in Naples do you find sidewalks this narrow. This gives Moscow a provincial air, or rather the character of an improvised metropolis that has fallen into place overnight."[8] Even though Oxford Street cannot be said to have materialized overnight from the sky, it is true that here, too, one is forced to walk in zigzags. This is not merely due to the narrowness of the sidewalk. For the Oxford Street sidewalk is marked first and foremost by its almost determined evanescence as a sidewalk (i.e., it looks like anything but a sidewalk) and the fact that the distinction between it and the tarmac roadway itself is practically obliterated. One reason why the sidewalk does not look or feel like one is that as Oxford Street evolved into the high-energy commercial street that it has become today, the sidewalk progressively became not the broad strip specifically designed for pedestrians to traverse but merely a stripped-down extension of the interior of the many commercial enterprises along the street. Thus, the sidewalk in front of various businesses on Oxford Street is taken over by them, either for customer parking extending from demarcated parking areas, in front of Frankie's or Ecobank, for example, or simply for the sprawl onto the sidewalk of manufactured goods, such as in the case of the many electronic, hardware, and bicycle stores along both sides of the street. The colonization of the sidewalk by commerce from shops and stores is augmented by the presence of vendors of various kinds, both itinerant and stationary. The items that vendors peddle vary: secondhand clothes, bags, and shoes (popularly known as *obroni wa wu*, or "the white man is dead"); fruits of all vintage, but with fresh mango, papaya, and pineapple to be peeled, sliced, or diced on the spot; Coca-Cola, Sprite, and Fanta in blue ice buckets; red snapper caught fresh from the sea and at the seashore sold by women but along Oxford Street mongered by young men with connections to fishing communities. Pushcarts with various goods abound while vendors of newly manufactured products covering everything from dog chains and flashlights to soccer balls, shoe polish, toothpicks, vibrators, and pornographic DVDs peddle their wares with verve and gusto.

Cars and pedestrians mix freely on the roadway itself. Even though the sidewalk is demarcated from the tarred roadway by the notorious and practically ubiquitous open sewage gutter, the sidewalk and the road remain at an uneven height (i.e., the sidewalk is not consistently raised some four or five inches above the roadway but is at par with it for much of the length of the street). To walk along Oxford Street is also to be constantly invited to pause and look at things, not in the manner by which shop windows in commercial boulevards elsewhere pose various enticements for the pedestrian to stop, take a quick cosmetic look at their reflection in the glass, and perhaps enter the store (the shop window displays performing the function of whetting your desire and inducing a crossing of the boundary between outside and inside), but by the constant barrage of vendors of all manner of goods vying to make a sale. The invitations to treat, to use a well-known phrase in commercial law, are only an irritation if one is in a hurry to actually get to a fixed destination. If not, the invitations to treat proffered by the vendors on Oxford Street may open up into varied kinds of culturally saturated modes of haggling and bargaining, with jokes, teasing, and overall good humor thrown in for good measure. There is a distinctly carnivalesque quality to this aspect of the street. This also means that the character of walking on Oxford Street and the human interactions one has on it are very different from that of commercial streets elsewhere, such as in, say, London or Singapore or Johannesburg, to cite but three distinct examples.

Since, as we have seen, much of the length of the sidewalks on both sides of the street have been taken over by the businesses and vendors already mentioned, and cars have no monopoly over the roadway, the experience of walking along Oxford Street involves a lot of zigzagging, moving off and onto the sidewalk or roadway with the negotiation of one's perambulations amid various kinds of vehicles, vendors, goods, and pedestrians as convenience and inclination dictate. The walk on Oxford Street, as in many parts of Accra, is thus an object of improvisation.

I have also spent many fine hours watching how people walk on the Street: the swagger, the flexing with cell phones, the bemusement or otherwise irritated hurrying-to-get-somewhere-yet-being-constantly-interrupted quality of walking. With the proliferation of MP3 players and iPhones and their attendant earbuds there is also a dimension of distractedness that is introduced into people's gait. Oddly enough, listening to something else while walking on the Street is not that common; it demands attention in a way that does not allow zoning out of its ambient sounds. Oxford Street proffers a form of sensorial totality that is only unpleasant if you go against the flow of its multimodal offerings.

If there is a performative dimension to the street; it is not to be mistaken for the performativity of occasional theatrical and political events, such as the annual December carnival held on Oxford Street, or the spontaneous outpourings of jubilation whenever Ghana makes strides in the international soccer tournaments it has had the unalloyed ecstasy to participate in. Rather, the character of walking on the street that we have described exposes itself to the possibility of spontaneous events that themselves follow set performative scripts.

The messy interaction of pedestrians with other pedestrians, and with pushcarts, with itinerant hawkers on the sidewalks, and with vehicles on the roadway means that misunderstandings regularly break out as to the proper courtesies of street use. These are not reducible to the mere road-rage variety of misunderstandings. Insults may be quickly traded between pedestrian and pedestrian, pedestrian and hawker, pedestrian and motorist, or between one motorist and another. However, the traded insults turn out to be an important aspect of the spectatoriality endemic to Accra's street life, such that ultimately the fact of seeing and being seen means that everything in the heated altercation turns on the mastery of unstated yet critical cultural codes of rhetoric and delivery. Reference to various parts of the human anatomy and its effusions proliferate in such exchanges, but the hyperinflation of the body is not the real point of the scatological insults. What is important is to produce a memorable twist on a known theme or themes both to show superiority over your opponent and to raise a laugh from casual observers who have quickly gathered to enjoy a spot of spontaneous theater. Mastery may involve the clever deployment of local language proverbs, but not exclusively. My favorite of the many I have witnessed: A taxi driver is speeding toward a zebra crossing and has to apply his brakes suddenly to let a bunch of pedestrians cross. They turn round and rain all manner of insults on him as they do so, to which he lustily retorts in Twi: "*Hwe nyen ho tan tan bi, a se ngyamoa atɔ gya mu!* [Look at all you nasty people, like a bunch of cats that have fallen into a fire!]" At which general laughter and more insults are hurled at the fast-receding exhaust fumes. And yet the effectiveness of the driver's insult and its memorableness derives not so much from the mention of cats as to the domestic setting signaled by the reference to fire, something that would immediately invoke a traditional charcoal fire kitchen very well known to most denizens of Accra. Cats in a traditional kitchen evoke all kinds of chaotic scenarios, including the potential for a loud din and total confusion in the tipping over of pots, pans, and perhaps even the meal being cooked on said fire. The entire insult, then, combines implicit references to dishevelment, to chaos, and to improper and unpredictable behavior within a domestic setting, which then acts as a correlative of the confusion of the pedestrians who, in the driver's opinion, do not even know how to negotiate the city's streets—this despite the fact that it is he who is patently in the wrong for rushing to whizz past the zebra crossing before the pedestrians could successfully navigate it. The implication from the driver's insult, then, is that, despite all appearances to the contrary, the zebra crossing does not in and of itself encompass the full protocols of how to cross a busy Accra street. A similar thing can be said for motor vehicles negotiating dense traffic. Here the rules, for example, for cutting in front of another driver are highly complicated, but generally the object of tacit agreement by most drivers. The first principle when you are doing something you shouldn't do is to absolutely not make eye contact, and the second is to demonstrate determined intent—that is to say, to move your vehicle as if not afraid of hitting the other vehicle or being hit by it. Waving a quick thank-you after the maneuver must be rigorously observed, otherwise insults or road rage may quickly ensue. Taxi and tro tro drivers are experts at this, and one is quickly enjoined to learn from them if one wants to survive the hectic density of Accra's traffic.

If the anecdote of the taxi driver's insult gives the impression that those behind the wheels of motor vehicles are somehow at an advantage when it comes to such confrontations, this is quickly dispelled by other stories in which it is the pedestrian that has the last word. In one such instance, a lumbering and clearly very tired market woman makes her way slowly down from the back of a wooden tro tro. The tro tro driver honks his horn impatiently and begins to rain insults on her. Her response, in a hoarse yet pinpoint Ga: "*Okyɛ sɔme, Adwoa Atta!* [Your father's vagina, Adwoa Atta!]" (Adwoa Atta being the name for a twin girl born on Monday), to which the dumbstruck driver mumbled some incoherencies and promptly took off. Loud laughter and wagging fingers followed him in his embarrassed exit from the scene, gearbox cranking and a splutter of protest emanating from the lorry's startled engine. "Your mother's vagina!" with the upraised right thumb pointing toward the object of your derision and deliberately wiggled up and down against your clenched fingers is one of the most common insults to be heard in Accra. The insult may be translated into something like "Your mother's vagina birthed you for nothing, you useless person." It is not uncommon to hear even a mother hurling this insult loudly at her own children, in which case the implication is that she has wasted her time giving birth to them. The twist in the woman's insult at the tro tro driver turns first on suggesting that his father was not a proper man (he had a vagina instead of a penis) and second that he should be embarrassed to have emerged as only half-woman (the reference to being one of twins bearing that implication). The gender twists to the insult were not lost on the listeners because it also carried the suggestion that the driver was really an anomaly, being birthed by a man who was really a woman and he himself appearing as nothing but half of a real woman. This is then taken to account for his monstrously rude behavior toward her, a proper, full-bodied, and uncompromising market woman.

Spatial Practice and Street Life

In the definition of "spatial practice" that Henri Lefebvre puts forward in *The Production of Space*, he indicates that not only is the concept empirically observable but that it also coincides with space as structured and regimented. For Lefebvre, the reproduction of social relations is central to spatial practice. As he notes, "The spatial practice of a society secretes that society's space; it *propounds* and *presupposes* it in a dialectical interaction; it produces it slowly and surely as it *masters* and *appropriates* it" through the network of roads, motorways and the politics of air transport.[9] The various verbs he uses here attribute to spatial practice a form of active agency. He adds that the form of space approximates to the moment of communication, and thus to the realm of the perceived. A number of implications may be derived from Lefebvre's comments: first is that space as a social concept acts on space as it is experienced in the form of social relations. This aligns Lefebvre's concept of space to that of other Marxists such as Doreen Massey and David Harvey, but with the distinction that Lefebvre goes on to set up a triangular dialectical relationship between spatial practice, representational space, and represented space such that each concept is automatically entailed in the others in complex and often elusive ways.[10] An added implication from his definition of spatial practice is that individual spaces are the localized instantiations of a larger spatial logic inherent to a given society. This might be extended to mean that the concept of space in a given society is inherently hegemonic—that it procures acquiescence in social arrangements that are not always necessarily in the interests of those that ordinarily traverse space but rather of those that want to naturalize a particular hierarchy of social relationships. There is clearly something Hegelian in the link Lefebvre suggests between a social and perhaps hegemonic spatial logic and space as the instantiation of that logic. But Lefebvre does not fill out what he means by the hegemony of spatial practice, leaving us to take it in different directions. Furthermore, we also find that the social idea of space does not remain static but that while propounding and appropriating its local instantiations it also gets progressively transformed first by the communicative character of the local instantiations themselves, and second by the alterations in the overall technology of human interactions enabled by changes in the network of roads, motorways, and other means for the traversal of geographic space. We have to add to Lefebvre technologies of interaction like social media that have also come to influence how people view themselves and their relations to others. As Jenna Burrell has shown, the inherent interpretative flexibility of the internet has allowed it to materialize a space for self-making that involves both licit and illicit uses as well as an investment of the symbolic register of enchantment commonly associated with Christianity in Ghana.[11]

However, it is what Lefebvre says about spatial practice as an approximation of the moment of communication that strikes a special note with respect to the performative and highly eventful character of Oxford Street. What might be the moment of communication that reveals the contours of space? Such a moment may be taken in the form of an expressive fragment, which we might then take as encapsulating a larger totality in miniature. But the choice of expressive fragment has to be undertaken carefully. For our purposes, the expressive fragment that is Oxford Street is constituted by a number of features. This includes the proliferation of languages (Ga, Twi, Pidgin, English, etc.) and discourses (those of billboard advertising, tro tro inscriptions, etc.). However, its expressivity is only partially captured in the languages and the discourses to be found on it; ultimately, it is the interpersonal interactions that materialize different dimensions of economy, culture, and society and out of which we can derive a sense of spatial practice. The focus of the two anecdotes just described is on the intensification of language as a marker of the social relations and the links between sociality and the larger structural and cultural dimensions of which they are a part.

Thus if we return to the taxi driver anecdote, we find that the interaction between him and the pedestrians was also simultaneously an attribution of social consensus on the human interaction. This observation is also applicable to the quarrel between the woman and the tro tro driver. The idea of social consensus does not imply any direct notion of agreement but rather the recognizability of the interaction as being part of the normative social domain—that is to say, of the terms by which something might be recognized as specifically pertinent to the sociocultural norms of social interaction. The normative social domain in the taxi driver anecdote is generated specifically from the tacit understanding of the rules that govern the negotiation of zebra crossings and their distortion in the domain of usage, either by pedestrians or drivers. The taxi driver challenges the hegemony of the spatial practice signaled specifically by the zebra crossing in his rude attempt to prevent the pedestrians from crossing safely and in the insult he delivers. He is effectively suggesting that the rules of a zebra crossing (the langue, to take a leaf from structuralism) are not limited to the formal protocols of road usage (the parole), which of course are governed by the force of law and can trigger certain sanctions if contravened. Rather, we are encouraged to conclude from the metaphorical implications of the insult he delivers that spatial practice in this instance also intersects with specifically cultural rules that include the terms of urban performativity, the main characteristic of which is the fact of seeing and being seen by a potential audience on the street. In other words, in this instance the langue of the formal rules of zebra crossings is intersected by another kind of langue, but this time of urban performativity. Thus we see two distinct yet also intersecting forms of spatial practice in the taxi driver anecdote: first is the universal rule-bound nature of how to negotiate a zebra crossing, and second are the rules of how to participate in a colorful and culturally saturated altercation on the streets of Accra. Both dimensions of spatial practice regularly interact with each other on the streets but with the second regularly distorting the protocols of the first at eventful conjunctures. Such conjunctures imply the breakdown of one modality of spatial practice and the immediate invocation of an entirely different modality in its place. Thus, the fraught interaction in the taxi driver anecdote takes place within the performative theater demarcated by the rules governing road use but against which the codes of cultural exchange attempt an alteration of the terms of such rules. With the lady and the tro tro driver, however, a completely different spatial practice comes into play. At issue here are not the protocols of road use but rather those of the chivalrous relations between male and female, here obscured in its extant urban articulation as the relation between a tro tro driver and his female passenger. His rudeness may partly have been due to his assumption of a form of authority by virtue of controlling the wheels of an instrument of evident power: a passenger lorry ferrying people between destinations. What the woman does, then, is to completely invert all available hierarchies that might pertain in the relationship between driver and passenger and male and female. The ultimate point of her insult is that he is ignorant of how to treat a woman on the streets of Accra. And if he thought that the mere fact of being a man gave him some sort of authority over her, she whisks that away from him, too, by letting him know that his father was not a proper man and that he himself cannot even aspire to be a full woman. We do not intend here to glorify haphazard and improper road use or praise the culture of impunity and rudeness that may often be seen on display on the streets, but rather, through the analysis of the apparently banal form of urban altercation, we have come to understand how spatial practices—as concepts and ideologies that shape social iterations of space and yet are challenged at every turn—come to govern interactions on the streets of Accra. While what we have just described may be said to fulfill spatial practice in the Lefebvrian sense, we can at the same time assert that his notion does not quite exhaust the communicative complexity of the human interactions to be perceived in Accra.

Conclusion

The question of method becomes most pronounced when attempting to apply a new entity of interpretation to an object such as a city that is not only composed of highly variegated social, political, economic, and cultural forms but also is always changing. Thus, the challenge is always to find a means of discerning between ephemera and elements that spell more profound consequences for grasping the shape of the city in both its present and future. And yet the dichotomy between ephemera and substantive elements is also false, for in fact it is the ephemera of stories, gossip, urban legends, and plain misapprehensions that provide the transactional glue that puts all the elements of the city together. Perhaps the even greater challenge is to find a means of extracting the social relation from such ephemera and to couple the social relation to a spatial logic, whether this spatial logic is to be discerned in the large-scale dimensions of political economy or on the more modest scale of everyday life. The account we come to provide ultimately requires an interleaving of different levels of significance, sometimes placing elements to the background of the main interest but always remembering that to be background is not to be inert but always to provide a form of conceptual animation that sometimes breaks into the foreground and alters the terms by which that foreground is perceived. Thus it is that interpreting an African city becomes a form of improvisation analogous to what its denizens practice on a daily basis. If my work on Accra speaks to anything, it speaks to this spirit of improvisation.

ATO QUAYSON is University Professor, Professor of English, and Director of the Centre for Diaspora and Transnational Studies at the University of Toronto. His most recent publications are *Oxford Street, Accra* and *The Cambridge Companion to the Postcolonial Novel* (editor).

Notes

1. African Development Bank, *African Development Report 2011: Private Sector Development as an Engine of Africa's Economic Development* (Tunis, Tunisia: African Development Bank, 2011), http://www.afdb.org/en/knowledge/publications/african-development-report/african-development-report-2011/.

2. For a special focus on Accra, see Sharon Benzoni, "Accra, Ghana," *The Rockefeller Foundation's Informal City Dialogues*, http://nextcity.org/informalcity/city/accra. *Next City* and *Informal City Dialogues* also touch on Bangkok, Chennai, Lima, Manila, and Nairobi, each of which provide ample material on slums in the third world.

3. See Frank E. K. Amoah, *Accra: A Study of the Development of a West African City* (Legon, Ghana: Institute of African Studies, 1964); Irene (Odotei) Quaye, "The Ga and Their Neighbours, 1600–1742" (PhD diss., University of Ghana, 1972); and Samuel S. Quarcoopome, "The Impact of Urbanization on the Socio-Political History of the Ga Mashie People of Accra: 1877–1957" (PhD diss., University of Ghana, 1993).

4. Ray Kea, *Settlements, Trade, and Politics in the Seventeenth-Century Gold Coast* (Baltimore: Johns Hopkins University Press, 1986), 11. For a more thorough treatment of the same proposition, see especially chapters 5–7 and Kwame Yeboa Daaku, *Trade and Politics on the Gold Coast, 1600–1720: A Study of the African Reaction to European Trade* (Oxford: Oxford University Press, 1970). See also Antony Hopkins, *An Economic History of West Africa* (London: Longman, 1973); and Edward Reynolds, *Trade and Economic Change on the Gold Coast, 1807–1874* (London: Longman, 1974).

5. See Pierre Verger, *Trade Relations Between the Bight of Benin and Bahia, from the 17th to the 19th Century*, trans. Evelyn Crawford (Ibadan, Nigeria: Ibadan University Press, 1976); João José Reis, *Slave Rebellion in Brazil: The Muslim Uprising of 1835 in Bahia*, trans. Arthur Brakel (Baltimore: Johns Hopkins University Press, 1993); and J. Lorand Matory, *Black Atlantic Religion: Tradition, Transnationalism and Matriarchy in the Afro-Brazilian Candomblé* (Princeton, NJ: Princeton University Press, 2005).

6. John Parker, *Making the Town: Ga State and Society in Early Colonial Accra* (Portsmouth, NH: Heinemann, 2000).

7. Even though Accra has not known a large or even substantial Chinese population, this has not prevented the establishment of quite popular Chinese restaurants, some of which date from the late 1960s and early 1970s. Chinese restaurants in the area include Chikin' Likin', Tsing Tao, Noble Chinese Restaurant, Peking Restaurant, and Dynasty, perhaps the most well known of them all.

8. Walter Benjamin, *Moscow Diary*, ed. Gary Smith, trans. Richard Sieburth (Cambridge, MA: Harvard University Press, 2002), 31.

9. Henri Lefebvre, *The Production of Space*, trans. Donald Nicholson-Smith (Cambridge, MA: Blackwell, 1991), 38 (emphasis added).

10. Doreen Massey, *Space, Place and Gender* (Minneapolis: University of Minnesota Press, 1994); David Harvey, *The Condition of Postmodernity: An Enquiry into the Origins of Cultural Change* (Malden, MA: Wiley-Blackwell, 1989).

11. Jenna Burrell, *Invisible Users: Youth in the Internet Cafés of Urban Ghana* (Cambridge, MA: MIT Press, 2012).

15 Gaining Ground

Squatters and the Right to the City

Anne-Maria Makhulu

Introduction

> In sum, as the social movements of the urban poor create unprecedented claims on and to the city, they expand citizenship to new social bases. In so doing, they create new sources of citizenship rights and corresponding forms of self-rule.
>
> —James Holston and Arjun Appadurai, *Cities and Citizenship*

Holston and Appadurai writing of the long-standing relationship between city and nation, a relationship that at times counted as one and the same—as in the case of the ancient Greek and later Italian city-states—and at others as two quite radically distinct political projects, note that for the late twentieth century cities regained a central significance to the question of citizenship and its entitlements. They note, too, those moments in which urban social movements functioning quite autonomously of the state created not only a set of new claims to citizenship, but in so doing constituted "corresponding forms of self-rule."[1]

I am particularly struck by this last observation and for our purposes it serves well the argument laid out here in this chapter, which is concerned with the apartheid city and the ways in which black migrants laid claim to both urban space and in turn made rights claims on the state that prefigure the kinds of urban social movements that Holston and Appadurai are writing about in the late 1990s. It is as if apartheid racial policies and the racial geographies that such policies engendered, repressive as these were, encouraged practices of illegal land occupation that would anticipate much more recent movements committed to reclaiming "the right to the city," following Henri Lefebvre.[2]

Lefebvre's mostly ambiguous and open-ended articulation of a theory of the city and of claims-in-the-making within it is continuous with what it was that blacks sought to achieve, under apartheid, by inhabiting spaces within metropolitan South Africa synonymous with white rule and political sovereignty. Indeed, the reference to "metropolitan" South Africa draws on a distinction between the city and remote rural areas to which blacks were forcibly removed after 1948. As if to imply that what lay beyond white South Africa and beyond its cities somehow also lay beyond the very borders of the republic itself such that the city stood in for the nation and the entitlements that come with rights in citizenship, which blacks were in any case denied.

Insisting on the political potential of even the most repressively produced spaces, Lefebvre argues that the "violence of power is answered by the violence of subversion" making "permanent transgression inevitable."[3] The state is always likely to provoke a response, a response that has a spatial dimension. James Holston has similarly observed that in the Brazilian context where citizenship serves to distribute inequality, the conditions of "differentiated citizenship" are also "the conditions of its subversion."[4] In South Africa in the mid- to late twentieth century, the illegal migration of hundreds of thousands of people to urban areas likewise operated to renegotiate the violence of the state, producing the sorts of spaces of alterity that were the undoing of the system of migrant wage labor. Specifically, resistance to pass laws (influx controls) and a whole political economy dependent on black labor power would bring the apartheid state to its knees. As such, those who settled illegally on the edges of many of the country's cities in so doing negotiated that tenuous relationship between "threat and promise" to produce new social worlds immediately beyond any official surveillance apparatus.

This chapter, in keeping with the notion that the city and political membership in whatever form are co-constitutive, begins to explore how living in a given city in the period 1948–1994 established a unique form of access if not to national citizenship then to its promise for otherwise disenfranchised South Africans.[5] I go on to account for some of the struggles and achievements of African people who defied legislation dictating where and how they should live and work. Mostly seeking refuge in urban squatter settlements, black South Africans came to the nation's urban areas not only looking for jobs but also hoping to reconcile the ways in which African women were forcibly sequestered in remote rural outposts while their menfolk worked on temporary contract in those urban centers given over to mining and manufacturing production. The problem of the twentieth century in South Africa was not only the problem of the color line but also the problem of the black family.

A Living Politics

In the 1970s and 1980s, despite increasingly aggressive efforts to limit black urbanization, black South Africans moved in growing numbers, very often without appropriate documentation or permits, into urban areas. They did so primarily in the search for work even while restricted by pass laws that dictated where and how African people could live and love. Consigned to the countryside or to a life of permanent movement back and forth between the country and the city, for blacks such enforced mobility defined a legal regime that equated the city with the white body politic and the countryside with a series of black dummy states or Bantustans lacking genuine sovereignty. That the international community never recognized the Bantustans, also known as ethnic homelands, as sovereign takes little away from the fact that apartheid's architects hoped to use the power of geographical distance to deny blacks rights of belonging within the borders of the republic of South Africa thereby making "citizenship more exclusive."[6]

The last few years have witnessed a number of urban uprisings including the protests in Cairo's Tahrir Square, the encampments in Barcelona, and more recently the protests in Istanbul's Taksim Square, while in South Africa almost daily service delivery and anti-eviction protests persist in communities that emerged, in the main, from those subversive strategies of informal settlement I mentioned a little earlier. Notably, all such social movements have made rights claims in the city in conjunction with claims to the "right to the city"—whether because people are demanding access to municipal services, as in the South African case, or because the city comes to constitute a ground for working out the remedies to grave inequality, political repression, or financial disadvantage.[7]

Of course, human actors continually shape their environments and themselves; cities, however, represent most explicitly the physical expression of our attempts to remake and refashion our lives.[8] Recognizing this character of city life and its interplay with human beings in struggle goes some way to explaining the practices of informal settlement (including land invasion and home building) that defined the peripheries of Cape Town from the 1970s on affording not only access to work opportunities and new forms of life, but a politics as well.

Migrations

> In a country where so many homes have been demolished and people moved to strange new places, home temporarily becomes the shared experience of homelessness, the fellow-feeling of loss and the desperate need to regain something.
>
> —Njabulo S. Ndebele, *The Cry of Winnie Mandela*

The efforts of Africans invested in homes and livelihoods in the urban areas just before and immediately after the advent of apartheid in 1948 are extraordinary. Despite increasing restrictions on migration, many blacks persisted in leaving the rural areas hoping to find work in Johannesburg, Cape Town, Durban, and other metropolitan centers. Settling in the squatter areas on the city outskirts, people found ways to raise families beyond the immediate scrutiny of the state.

Arriving in Cape Town separately beginning in the mid-1970s, the Nombembes took over a decade to settle more or less permanently. They lived initially in

Unibell moving to Crossroads squatter camp in 1979 after Unibell's destruction.[9] Evelyn Nombembe recalls that very tumultuous period:

> When the bulldozers began destroying our shacks in December 1978 I was in the Eastern Cape visiting family. I heard the news over the radio and decided to remain in the rural areas for the entire year, only returning to Cape Town in 1979 when I relocated to Crossroads. We had been living in Unibell—my husband and I and our two children. My husband had previously gone to and fro between the city and Lady Frere in the Eastern Cape, but when he finally secured a permanent job with Cape Town City Council building roads we wanted to be together.[10]

After Evelyn married at age nineteen (in 1972), she had initially remained in the reserves while her husband traveled back to visit her those first four years of their marriage, as most migrant workers did, annually during the December holiday period. Eventually, Evelyn would travel to Cape Town, moving into the company-owned "single-sex" hostel where her husband was living:

> At that time, I stayed in the hostels, but we really only saw one another on the weekends. During the week my husband would go to work along with all the other men and the women who were staying there were locked in. We would spend the whole day hiding under the beds. We rarely saw the light of day. Even on the weekends the police were likely to show up, but we would risk going out of the house together. I was pregnant and hiding under the bed all day and I would become incredibly hot and uncomfortable. Eventually after six months my husband took me to my relatives in Unibell and he would come and visit me there when he could. Later we built our own shack. I was lucky, other women were arrested who were also hiding and didn't have passes.[11]

Such stories were commonplace. In a 1978 article in the *Cape Argus* newspaper, journalist John Battersby captured the paradox of African domesticity in the city: the impossibilities posed by pass laws that discriminated against African women and forced many to seek refuge in Crossroads and other settlements. Mrs. Luke, an area activist whom Battersby interviewed, described her long struggle to remain in the city of Cape Town, first living illicitly in one of the male hostels in Nyanga East, during a period of ten years: "The buildings were always being raided and I spent many nights in hiding—often having to get up at 3 am and 4 am to evade the officials. In the end I could take it no longer and decided to move to Crossroads."[12]

Most of the women with whom Evelyn was acquainted, both in the hostels and then later in the squatter areas, had little or no access to passbooks, which was not uncommon at the time given the "breadwinner's clause," which discriminated against women's search for work, granting them half-year contracts before forcing them to return to the Bantustans.[13] Many, of course, chose to remain in the city once their passes expired, and Evelyn recalled the raids that were one consequence. These occurred with some frequency, very often late into the night in the hostel complex where she lived, located in a small town past Milnerton on the way to Malmesbury "very close to the farmlands."[14]

Just before her first son, Zamikhaya, was born (in September 1976), her husband was able to secure the family a separate plot and build a shack. In the interim she stayed with cousins, relatives on her mother's side, while her husband continued to live in the hostels. Throughout her pregnancy, the two saw very little of one another and she necessarily integrated into the extended family unit—her cousin, her cousin's husband, and their two children.

Unibell was a makeshift, if organized camp, lacking the most basic amenities. Far from ideal conditions for raising family, the daily difficulties cannot be overstated. Bathing children, readying for work, or cooking meals with limited access to water and given overflowing pit latrines, squatters were compelled to organize among themselves and to engage in self-management and self-governance—those forms of self-rule with which this chapter opened. The alternatives were few if any: in the Transkei, the Eastern Cape region from which most black Capetonians ushered, there was "no work, no land, and nothing to live on."[15]

Despite the practical difficulties the Nombembes would go on to have two additional daughters and a son (Nomaxesibe, Zanele, and Nkosibile) between 1978 and 1984. This fact deserves consideration particularly in view of the labor, affective and otherwise, required to raise small children in the squatter areas—without running water, electricity, and access to toilets or other basic services including refuse removal. Complicated by conditions of hypermobility, the absence of infrastructure (including formal housing) as well as overcrowding and extensive demands on limited resources made family life a kind of "work" even as kinship requires caring, love, and companionship. Having built a shack in Unibell, the Nombembes decamped to Crossroads, once again, joining Evelyn's cousin and her family and then finally striking out separately to rebuild in Crossroads Section 4:

> There were people who were living in Old Crossroads who had moved from Unibell, but they were dispersed throughout the settlement and my old neighbors were no longer living right next door. I was living in Section 4. I wasn't too far from Memani [a Crossroads headman], near the primary school, Sizamile, which was eventually burned down in 1986.[16]

Evelyn went on to explain their negotiations with the local headmen to secure a plot and building rights—a kind of informal ground rent. Again, we ought to note the variety of forms of self-rule in play. Headmen performed civic duties providing an informal police force, organizing ground clearing and plot allocations, negotiating with state officials, and brokering development contracts. But they also, very often, raised monies that went directly to building lavish rural homesteads. The headmen functioned as state proxies; their clientelism promising to deliver housing and services even while increasing the legal, financial, and other constraints imposed on squatters as the headmen bought and sold plots, brokered for the removal of opponents, and facilitated state interference in the camps—in the most extreme instance laying the foundation for a war of counterinsurgency in 1986 and 1987.[17]

Many former residents of Crossroads attested to having been compelled to sign rent cards, which were issued illegally by an office located in the heart of Crossroads run by members of the camp's executive committee. Most paid a fixed sum of seven rand a month despite a fair degree of variation in rates. Notably, the average African household income after 1975 was approximately seventy-two rand per month, well below any poverty data estimates for the period.[18] Further, even as Crossroads rents represented a mere one-tenth of average monthly income, these were relatively inflated rates compared with those being charged for formal housing in adjacent townships where homes came equipped with toilets, taps, bricks, and mortar. In Langa, a nearby township, apparently a four-room brick home rented for 10.17 rand a month, while in Nyanga the rents were even lower (9.70 rand) despite the fact that these included indoor bathrooms and taps—a far cry from the "wood and iron structures erected by or on behalf of the occupants" of the squatter camps.[19]

As Crossroads was elevated first to the status of an emergency camp (guaranteeing at least temporary protection from the bulldozers) and later was declared its own municipality, to some degree residents were assured of relatively secure tenure. And then in 1979, through a formal process of enumeration, longer-term residents were granted temporary documents while many newcomers were dispatched to the Bantustans to reduce the camp's overcrowding.[20] Evelyn would eventually earn a temporary six-month permit. While her cousin, now eligible for permanent residency, moved to a brick home in New Crossroads, Evelyn and her family were left to relocate to another household in Nyanga Extension, *Emavundleni* (the place of the Mavundla clan), and a satellite of Crossroads. The family would move once again, this time to Section 2, first staying with relatives of her husband's and then building their own shack in 1983:

> By that time people were building their shacks next to Lansdowne Road [the main arterial leading into Wynberg]. But those homes were continually destroyed and so people decided they must find sites within the settlement away from public view and the reach of police.[21]

Living on the city limits and on the limits of law was and remains tremendously risky. Yet through transfers of local knowledge and through modes of self-governance, squatters managed to live lives if not fully hidden from view, at least partially insulated from an aggressively surveillant state. Protected from local crime by a volunteer home guard that patrolled the camp at night, Crossroads was carefully demarcated into four (and later five) semi-autonomous sections broadly overseen by a governing committee. Local headmen (*izibonda*) sat on the executive committee, echoing quasi-traditional forms of political leadership that likely had their origins in the homelands and rural areas. At the same time, these differed fairly significantly from customary institutions of the chiefship. And while doubtless inspired by the stuff of colonial rule, the headmen's relationship to so-called traditional political forms is less than clear.[22]

From very early on, Crossroads housed Sizamile and Noxolo Primary Schools (crude schoolhouses) built to accommodate the camp's sizable population of young children. Initially, without the convenience of even a communal spigot, squatters purchased water from a small neighboring colored community, adjoining Crossroads and located along Klipfontein Road. New arrivals brought their dismantled shacks from other settlements, rebuilding them in the sections to which they had been assigned by the local executive committee or in a number of expanding satellites to the west of Crossroads along Mahobe Drive.

Without any system for disposing of sewage, shack dwellers dug pit latrines eventually forcing the municipality into installing a series of bucket toilets requiring regular night soil removal. Women, on the major thoroughfares around the camp and adjacent township of Nyanga and New Crossroads, prepared sheep's heads, offal, and other cheap cuts of meat on open braziers built out of old oil drums—an accommodation to men living in the hostels who, on their return home from work, would need a substantial evening meal. There was every imaginable enterprise and institution in Crossroads: an undertaker, a diviner (*igqirha*), an herbalist (*ixhwele*), a handful of *spaza* shops (home-based corner stores), several churches, and even a bricklayer.

Historical Antecedents

During the period marking the end of the colonial republics and through the period that introduced constitutionally ordained white supremacist rule in 1948, those who were drawn into the industrial process circulated between town and country establishing what Zolani Ngwane has identified as a "culture of mobility" driven by internal and external "structural fluidities" that rarely permitted the full establishment of households in a given place.[23] These might be realized in the imagination, but in practice households had to constantly negotiate changes in patterns of wage and work that disrupted the lives of migrants and their families. This was as true of rural households and homesteads as it was of townships and informal settlements though the concern here is with the latter. Squatter experience has long been defined by regular movement, displacement, and repeated home building productive of something entirely novel that emerged in the narrow space between culture and the state. The places people settled, following arduous treks to the city in search of employment, as well as choices of location and domicile marred by legal restrictions established a very particular set of conditions under which Africans made claims to either temporary or permanent residency in urban areas.

Where did African migrants seek shelter or a haven from state interference, from its pernicious efforts to force men to work in urban centers while isolating womenfolk in the countryside? How was it that African families, and here I acknowledge domestic arrangements as complex and varied as the array of restrictions that constrained them, in South Africa's cities manage to be together when they did?[24] One way to examine these questions might be to consider the actual physical arrangement of people in space; to reflect on the critical engagements with and from state dictates that encouraged the rise and expansion of illicit settlements on the urban margins—these most often arising to accommodate men and women drawn into the orbit of industrial work.

Accordingly, squatters negotiated the pull-push of a racist state that both beckoned rural Africans to the city and then denied them rights of urban residence making squatter-proletarians both necessary and expendable. In so doing, the city margins provided a set of alternatives even as the new social formations reinscribed older colonial patterns of racial, ethnic, and class exclusions that persist even today.[25] The space of the informal settlements must, in this sense, be conceived as something materially produced; neither inert nor a priori, space "operate[s] . . . on processes from which it cannot separate itself because it is a product of them."[26] Space is always socially produced and an expression of a given political order.

Confounded by the contradictions of apartheid political economy—by the demand for and refusal to accommodate black labor in cities—squatters arriving in Cape Town relied on the sociality of the informal settlements. Recall how long and hard Evelyn Nombembe struggled to bring her family together in one place while at the same time lamenting that not all her neighbors and friends were able to regroup in Crossroads—"homegirls and homeboys" ushering from the same region in the Transkei and affording a continuity of experience across hundreds of miles. While always under threat of destruction, squatter areas afforded opportunities for work, neighborliness, and social support. They offered a qualified freedom—that is, at the very least in the sense of a relative freedom from removal, relocation, and even to some degree other forms of state coercion, detention, and physical harm.

This is a very particularly South African story, of course. The industrial revolution triggered by the discovery of gold and diamonds caught rural Africans in the warp and weft of factories, mines, and commercial agriculture in ways quite different from the rural-urban economies of other African countries in which, similarly, yet differently, people moved to cities in hopes of finding jobs and making good. Eventually populating the city limits, black South Africans would first overwhelm and then undo apartheid itself as pass laws collapsed (in 1986) and the struggle for liberation gained strength and momentum.

Two lines of inquiry might follow from my observations about the double nature of squatting—as both a radically transgressive practice and at the same time a project entailing great risk. The first line of inquiry pertains to the apartheid past, the second, which I pursue but briefly in the conclusion, pertains to our present. Consigned at once to "both 'moving around' and 'standing still,'" hundreds of thousands of people were enticed by the promise of employment in urban areas and at the same time propelled by diminishing access to land in rural South Africa.[27] Since the beginning of the century, land had already been systematically appropriated from peasant farmers and consolidated in the hands of a relatively small white land-owning class under the provisions of the 1913 Natives Land Act.

Elsewhere, in a much more sustained consideration of the challenges of city life on Cape Town's periphery, I have argued that squatting consisted in an ontology of homelessness, counterbalanced by a struggle for "presence"—a condition of "flight and inhabitation" that has historically subjected black people to a necessary and continual negotiation of place and belonging.[28] What followed from attempts to assert such claims to presence was, not a little ironically, a form of homelessness whose foundations were double. On the one hand, squatters labored in the absence of adequate shelter and, on the other hand, because of much larger processes of displacement, they urgently made great efforts to stay put giving root to a politics *in* and *of* place.

The apartheid regime worked fastidiously to control inflows and outflows of blacks within cities, beginning in the early 1950s, and in the following decade sought to consolidate the old labor reserve policy, which had relegated blacks to specific areas within the South African countryside. What now emerged was a new homeland policy—a kind of cultural defense on the part of the state—that took the form of the Bantu Authorities Act of 1951 and latterly the Bantu Self-Government Act of 1959. The act "abolished the already limited representation for blacks in parliament, and replaced it with 'local government' comprising 'tribal' chiefs and 'traditional councils.'"[29] The new legislation most critically facilitated the removal and relocation of three-and-a-half million people, some to the recently established Bantustans (this during approximately three decades), and in the process expanded the powers of self-governance and quasi-sovereignty in the homelands as part of a much larger project of separate development.

There are many ways to read such efforts to secure a white republic against the so-called *swart gevaar* or "black peril." Certainly, the apartheid state's obsession with categorization on grounds of race, gender, sexuality, and ethnicity was given extreme expression in the identification of homelands as cultural cradles of Zulu, Xhosa, Tswana, and other ethnicities. Further, the homelands were designated as labor reserves in which women were now relegated to caring for the young, the elderly, and those sick and dying from work in the mines and industry, and that in so doing women went unremunerated—a logic that assumed the superexploitation of women as the basis of industrial profit. The dual and uneven economy of metropole and periphery, so an older 1970s neo-Marxism would have it, was the basis of South African racial Fordism. Whatever the rationale, the homelands congealed a political, cultural, and economic project forcing ordinary people to find creative ways of negotiating the crosshairs of state dictates and waning profitability.

Quotidian Struggles

Squatters were metropolitan "militants" after a fashion; their motivations toward urbanization stemming from something quite apart from any explicit strategy of organizational resistance.[30] To be sure, as the decades of the 1970s and 1980s witnessed the exponential growth of squatter areas across the republic—dashing the vision of a predominantly white metropolitan South Africa—squatters were forced into direct confrontation with the state. They fought riot vehicles, live ammunition, and rubber bullets, as well as tear gas, with stones and songs of protest, smarts, and ingenuity.

And so a process of slow creep on the city limits drew on an expanding repertoire of struggle. Shack dwellers were not merely shack dwellers, of course. They belonged to banned political organizations (the African National Congress, Pan-Africanist Congress, and Black Consciousness Movement, to name only three), trade unions, churches, and local civic associations, from which they borrowed a political grammar of action (as did those organizations from their members). Despite the continual battle to win stays of eviction and temporary passes—demands to the right to the city that facilitated the expansion of peri-urban settlements—squatters appeared somehow less noble in their actions than those engaged in formal rent boycotts and labor disputes or given other direct encounters with the state, including police and military. Was it perhaps that shack dwellers were, by and large, preoccupied with the politics of the everyday as evidenced by their long hours spent in the most basic, if challenging, activities: hauling water for ablutions, cooking food over an open fire, building makeshift corrugated iron and cardboard homes and temporary schoolhouses, disposing of waste, tending to small vegetable patches, and the like?

Despite this sense of a bread-and-butter politics or politics of need—what Hannah Arendt refers to with some frustration as "historical necessity"—the very layout and architecture of many camps lent themselves to the spatial organization of political activities along lines of street and block committees, the establishment of free zones and spaces given over to reprieve from conflict for young Comrades (activists affiliated with certain of the liberation organizations) in what many referred to as "mini exile."[31] Routine activities, these nevertheless underwrote the foundational deformation, dismantling, and reassemblage of the apartheid city and eventually the dissolution of pass laws in 1986. Squatters combined their most mundane, everyday struggles for housing and home with their roles as activists and members of formal political organizations.

Conclusion: Does History Repeat Itself?

When the Nombembes settled in Crossroads in 1979, they were only minimally conscious of the strategic significance of their choice of a place to build a home. The squatter area was one of many such shantytowns that dotted the periphery of the Cape Peninsula, some dating back to much earlier than the mid-1970s, others mushrooming in the face of an urban population explosion that left the old model of carefully managed migrant barracks and formal townships inadequate to the growing numbers of Africans, mostly Xhosa speakers, searching for both work and shelter. By the mid-1980s, Crossroads was home to fully one hundred thousand people by most accounts, the overcrowding drawing the attention of both the local and national state.[32]

Today, Cape Town's largest township, Khayelitsha, comprising formal and informal housing, as well as upgraded sites lacking "top structures" (brick-and-mortar homes), accommodates an estimated four hundred and ten thousand people and continues to expand. Khayelitsha was originally a tent town, established in 1983 with the aid of the security apparatus, and intended as a spillover zone for Crossroads' residents without passes. Those who agreed to leave Crossroads were guaranteed temporary residence permits. Soon after influx control legislation was struck from the statute books and as the South African situation deteriorated in the face of growing civil unrest as well as a looming financial crisis, squatter areas became increasingly unpoliceable. They had to an extent surpassed their original purpose: no longer strictly home to illegal migrants, they now accommodated second- and third-generation Xhosas, long settled in the city, many of whom had quite tenuous ties to the countryside even as most continued to move back and forth visiting family homesteads, extended kin, and burying their dead there.[33]

To see Cape Town's informal settlements, post-1994, as purely the consequence of the country's recent history ignores the ways in which postapartheid market reforms have played a significant hand in deepening preexisting disparities between white and black and rich and poor and, as a consequence, determining the places where each chooses or is forced to reside.[34] Today, despite the political rhetoric of decent housing, townships continue to be upgraded on the city limits where bulk infrastructure is substandard or entirely lacking even as relocating historically disadvantaged communities to middle-class suburbs or the City Bowl would address many of the limitations of in situ upgrading. The poor quality of the housing stock is another indication of the difficulties of implementation, as are the unimaginative ways in which street grids and plans are laid out echoing the matchbox houses and poor design of apartheid-era townships. The parallels with the past are clear, and there is little question that the current configuration of the city derives from a much longer history of racial discrimination.[35] At the same time, speculation in property markets, restrictive land use policies, the focus on ecotourism, and, as a corollary, the neglect of human settlements (in contrast to animal habitats)—in sum, a host of practices that generally prioritize private interests—critically inform enduring patterns of segregation and inequality.[36]

For Nigel Gibson, following Frantz Fanon, the persistence of racial and class divisions stands for a form of "social treason" in which squatters are left to remind their fellow South Africans of how spatial politics play a critical role in the control exerted on poor communities of color both by the state and by capital.[37] For Gibson, the black poor suffer so immediately South Africa's persistent Manichaean social, economic, and political divisions as to stand in for Fanon's "wretched of the earth." That squatters are engaged in a politics of transformation seems for many somehow implausible, yet for shack dwellers the political value of land occupation and anti-eviction efforts is patently clear. Again, continuity with a whole historic repertoire of activism and practices of daily life blur the lines between organizational politics and the politics of making homes.

Importantly, the 1955 Freedom Charter, an anticolonial manifesto, had already articulated struggle as a struggle for resources as well as political freedoms under an all-inclusive African nationalism. The resources of the land as well as the resources beneath the land were to be shared by all peoples. A powerfully "emotive force" within the liberation movements, land has remained the signal obstacle to real reform in South Africa.[38] And while housing provision might be seen as alleviating the most precarious conditions on the edge of life, housing, by itself, eludes the realities of destitution.[39]

Land hunger and the need for agrarian land reform as the basis of both rural and urban transformation are undeniable. Still, discussion of the nationalization of land was quickly abandoned during the interim constitutional negotiation period as the new leadership embraced urban reconstruction as the key strategic initiative in the new South Africa, in part motivated by a desire to build world or world-class cities consistent with a neoliberal agenda. Consider South Africa's hosting of the World Cup in 2010. The construction of expensive state-of-the-art stadia in both big cities and provincial towns was peculiarly at odds with the enduring demand for township upgrading and housing provision. And so "former socialists acceded to neoliberalism, arguing either that 'there is no alternative' or invoking the imperatives for developing the forces of production."[40]

It would seem that the striving for a place in the city and recognition within it must continue. Squatters, likewise, will continue to enact a principled stance in relation to the problem of land, the problem of housing, and the problem of material freedom. To use an old battle cry of the struggle—*A Luta Continua*! The struggle continues! This is not simply a bid for access to the urban environment, but to a full life within it (however defined), even as the possible outcomes of urban struggles can never be fully known. Centrally, urban struggles everywhere (Occupy, the Spanish encampments, Taksim and Tahrir Squares) ask us to consider the relationship between human life and the city and how remaking the one must, inevitably, involve the remaking of the other. "The right to the city is far more than the individual liberty to access urban resources: it is a right to change ourselves by changing the city."[41]

ANNE-MARIA MAKHULU is Associate Professor of Cultural Anthropology and African and African American Studies at Duke University. Her publications include *Hard Work, Hard Times: Global Volatility and African Subjectivities* (co-editor) and *Making Freedom: Apartheid, Squatter Politics, and the Struggle for Home.*

Notes

1. James Holston and Arjun Appadurai, "Cities and Citizenship," in *Cities and Citizenship*, ed. James Holston (Durham, NC: Duke University Press, 1999), 12.
2. See Henri Lefebvre, *Le Droit à la Ville* (Paris: Anthropos, 1968), and *Writings on Cities*, trans. and ed. Eleonore Kofman and Elizabeth Lebas (Cambridge, MA: Blackwell, 1996).
3. Henri Lefebvre, *The Production of Space*, trans. Donald Nicholson-Smith (Cambridge, MA: Blackwell, 1991), 23.
4. James Holston, *Insurgent Citizenship: Disjunctions of Democracy and Modernity in Brazil* (Princeton, NJ: Princeton University Press, 2008), 9. See also David Harvey, *Rebel Cities: From the Right to the City to the Urban Revolution* (New York: Verso, 2012).
5. For more on urban spaces and national citizenship, see Renu Desai and Romola Sanyal, eds., *Urbanizing Citizenship: Contested Spaces in Indian Cities* (London: Sage, 2012); and Michael Herzfeld, *Cultural Intimacy: Social Poetics in the Nation-State* (New York: Routledge, 1997). For more on the promise of national citizenship, see Asef Bayat, *Street Politics: Poor People's Movements in Iran* (New York: Columbia University Press, 1997); and Faruk Tabak and Michaeline A. Crichlow, eds., *Informalization: Process and Structure* (Baltimore: Johns Hopkins University Press, 2000).
6. Holston and Appadurai, "Cities and Citizenship," 5.

7. On the "right to the city," see Lefebvre, *Le Droit à la Ville*, and Lefebvre, *Writings on Cities*; Holston, *Insurgent Citizenship*; and Daniel M. Goldstein, *The Spectacular City: Violence and Performance in Urban Bolivia* (Durham, NC: Duke University Press, 2004). See also Ashwin Desai and Richard Pithouse, "'But We Were Thousands': Dispossession, Resistance, Repossession and Repression in Mandela Park," *Centre for Civil Society Research Report* 9 (2003): 1–30; and Ashwin Desai and Richard Pithouse, "'What Stank in the Past Is the Present's Perfume': Dispossession, Resistance, and Repression in Mandela Park," *South Atlantic Quarterly* 103, no. 4 (2004): 841–875; Anthony Egan and Alex Wafer, "The Soweto Electricity Crisis Committee," *Globalisation, Marginalisation and New Social Movements in Post-Apartheid South Africa*, Centre for Civil Society and the School of Development Studies (Durban, South Africa: University of KwaZulu-Natal, 2004), 1–26; and Franco Barchiesi, "Classes, Multitudes and the Politics of Community Movements in Post-Apartheid South Africa," *Centre for Civil Society Research Report* 20 (2004): 1–41.

8. See Robert Park, *Robert E. Park On Social Control and Collective Behavior: Selected Papers (The Heritage of Sociology)*, ed. Ralph H. Turner (Chicago: University of Chicago Press, 1967). Also see Harvey, *Rebel Cities*, and Lefebvre, *Le Droit à la Ville*.

9. The name "Unibell" derives from its proximity to the University of the Western Cape (UWC) campus, which locals referred to at the time as the "University of Bellville." Bellville is a nearby colored suburb and UWC was previously regarded as a so-called bush school. See "Unibell Has Gone But Squatters Have Not," *Cape Times*, January 21, 1978, Press Clippings, Black Sash Collection, African Studies Library, University of Cape Town Library (hereafter cited as Black Sash Collection).

10. Evelyn Nombembe, interview by the author, February 15, 1999, Lower Crossroads, Cape Town. Also see letter addressed to the Minister of Public Works from Messrs. Mallinick, Ress, Richman & Co., Attorneys, June 30, 1977, Colin Appleton Private Papers, regarding Unibell squatter camp.

11. Nombembe, interview. Nombembe and several other women respondents reported hiding under the mattresses anticipating pass raids by the police.

12. John Battersby, "Crossroads Squatters: We Will Not Move," *Cape Argus*, August 17, 1978, Black Sash Collection. Also see Anne-Maria Makhulu, *Making Freedom: Apartheid, Squatter Politics, and the Struggle for Home* (Durham, NC: Duke University Press, 2015).

13. Passbooks were required of all urban Africans over the age of sixteen without which they were at risk of arrest and deportation to the Bantustans.

14. Nombembe, interview.

15. Bob Molloy, "Crossroads Wife Tells of Broken Families," *Cape Times*, October 28, 1978, Black Sash Collection.

16. Nombembe, interview.

17. Johnson Ngxobongwana, headman in Crossroads, would lead a counterinsurgency campaign against activists and young Comrades (members of the banned organizations and radicalized youth, generally). He was also section headman in Section 4.

18. South African Institute of Race Relations, *A Survey of Race Relations in South Africa* (Johannesburg: South African Institute of Race Relations, 1976), 276.

19. See letter to A. Dalling, an attorney, at Messrs. Fuller, Moore & Son from Messrs. Mallinick, Ress, Richman & Co, Attorneys, November 24, 1976, Colin Appleton Private Papers.

20. For a far more detailed account, see Makhulu, *Making Freedom*.

21. Nombembe, interview.

22. See Philip L. Bonner, "The Politics of Black Squatter Movements on the Rand, 1944–1952," *Radical History Review* 46, no. 7 (1990): 89–115; and Isak A. Niehaus, "The ANC's

Dilemma: Three Witch-Hunts in the South African Lowveld," *African Studies Review* 41, no. 3 (1998): 93–118. For an account of the *induna* (the Zulu term for leader or headman) system in Alexandra Township, see Justine Lucas, "Civic Organisation in Alexandra in the Early 1990s: An Ethnographic Approach," in *From Comrades to Citizens: The South African Civics Movement and the Transition to Democracy*, ed. Glenn Adler and Jonny Steinberg (New York: St. Martin's, 2000), 145–174. Also see Mahmood Mamdani, *Citizen and Subject: Contemporary Africa and the Legacy of Late Colonialism* (Princeton, NJ: Princeton University Press, 1996).

23. Zolani Ngwane, "'Christmas Time' and the Struggles for the Household in the Countryside: Rethinking the Cultural Geography of Migrant Labour in South Africa," *Journal of Southern African Studies* 29, no. 3 (2003): 683.

24. Donald Donham's work on same-sex relationships in Soweto is one example of the extraordinary variation in domestic arrangements, likewise his recent book about the mines and life in the mining compounds. See "Freeing South Africa: The 'Modernization' of Male-Male Sexuality in Soweto," *Cultural Anthropology* 13, no. 1 (1998): 3–21; and *Violence in a Time of Liberation: Murder and Ethnicity at a South African Gold Mine, 1994* (Durham, NC: Duke University Press, 1994).

25. See, for example, Steven Robins, "Bodies Out of Place: Crossroads and Landscapes of Exclusion," in *Blank ____: Architecture, Apartheid and After*, ed. Hilton Judin and Ivan Vladislavíc (Rotterdam: NAi, 1998).

26. Lefebvre, *The Production of Space*, 66.

27. Quoted in Ruth Wilson Gilmore, *Golden Gulag: Prisons, Surplus, Crisis, and Opposition in Globalizing California* (Berkeley: University of California Press, 2007), 12.

28. See Makhulu, *Making Freedom*; and Fred Moten, "Black Op," *PMLA* 123, no. 5 (2008): 1745. Also see Saidiya Hartman, *Scenes of Subjection: Terror, Slavery, and Self-Making in Nineteenth-Century America* (London: Oxford University Press, 1997).

29. Quoted in Jean Comaroff, *Body of Power, Spirit of Resistance: The Culture and History of a South African People* (Chicago: University of Chicago Press, 1985), 38.

30. See Manuel Castells, *The City and the Grassroots: A Cross-Cultural Theory of Urban Social Movements* (Berkeley: University of California Press, 1983).

31. On "historical necessity," see Hannah Arendt, *On Revolution* (New York: Penguin Classics, 2006).

32. See Surplus People Project, *Khayelitsha: New Home, Old Story, a Dossier of Forced Removals of Cape Town's African Population* (Cape Town: Surplus People Project, 1984). Also see Josette Cole, *Crossroads: The Politics of Reform and Repression, 1976–1986* (Johannesburg: Ravan Press, 1987).

33. See, for example, Hylton White, "Outside the Dwelling of Culture: Estrangement and Difference in Postcolonial Zululand," *Anthropological Quarterly* 83, no. 3 (2010): 497–518.

34. See Patrick Bond and Meshack Khosa, eds., *An RDP Policy Audit* (Pretoria: HSRC, 1999). Also see Patrick Bond and Angela Tait, "The Failure of Housing Policy in Post-Apartheid South Africa," *Urban Forum* 8, no. 1 (1997): 19–41.

35. See, for example, Vivian Bickford-Smith, *Ethnic Pride and Racial Prejudice in Victorian Cape Town: Group Identity and Social Practice, 1875–1902* (Cambridge: Cambridge University Press, 1995).

36. David A. McDonald, *World City Syndrome: Neoliberalism and Inequality in Cape Town* (New York: Routledge, 2008).

37. Nigel Gibson, "What Happened to the 'Promised Land'? A Fanonian Perspective on Post-Apartheid South Africa," *Antipode* 44, no. 1 (2012): 51; Frantz Fanon, *The Wretched of the Earth*, trans. Constance Farrington (New York: Grove, 1963), 145.

38. Gillian Hart, *Disabling Globalization: Places of Power in Post-Apartheid South Africa* (Berkeley: University of California Press, 2002), 227.

39. See Judith Butler, *Precarious Life: The Power of Mourning and Violence* (New York: Verso, 2004).

40. Hart, *Disabling Globalization*, 23.

41. David Harvey, "The Right to the City," *New Left Review* 53 (2008): 23.

16 African Urban Garrison Architecture

Property, Armed Robbery, Para-capitalism

Tejumola Olaniyan

What I call "garrison architecture" is that colorful feature of urban African landscape of residential homes enclosed by high walls spiked at the top with barbed wires or broken bottles, huge gates, and built-in iron bars on windows and room doors. Figures 16.1 and 16.2 show two examples, from Lagos and Accra, respectively.

In some instances, the barbed wires are electrified. These security measures do not in any way substitute for the usual twenty-four-hour manned entrance gate by those who can afford it. In many African cities today, a new residential house, from mid- to upscale, is not complete until the enclosing walls, barbed wires, and iron bars are firmly in place. Such protective shells have, in fact, become the number-one selling point for houses. Here is an upscale example. An online advertisement for a house selling for three hundred and seventy-five thousand British pounds in a suburb of Nairobi enticingly states in the second sentence, "This property offers a quiet enclosed compound" and goes on to repeat that it is situated in a "secure walled compound in the centre of the plot." In case you still miss the point, the next paragraph goes on to reiterate that you access the house "through a double steel gate to a high walled secure compound." Plus, "a stone guard house is situated just inside the gate," and "the gates are fitted with electric lighting."[1] In many instances, it is not just houses that are walled, but, additionally, entire neighborhoods are gated, and also manned, and with specific hours you can go in or out. It is no exaggeration to say that garrison architecture in urban Africa has become a normative, like an entrenched sociocultural trait. And, without question, one of the most effective agents of its normalization in general African consciousness today is that phenomenally popular film tradition and cultural form known as Nollywood. It broadcasts in a most alluring form an implied quintessential African upscale living that is incomplete without a well-appointed big house walled up in a seemingly most impenetrable way. Poor audiences in squalid and unsafe shacks and neighborhoods salivate in futuristic great expectation.

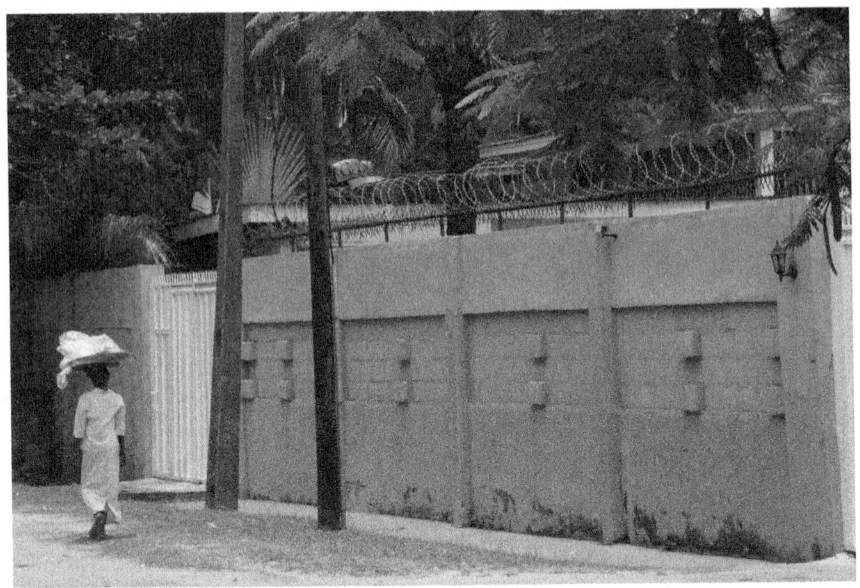

Figure 16.1. "On your life! We shop in air-conditioned stores!" Lagos, Nigeria. © Tejumola Olaniyan

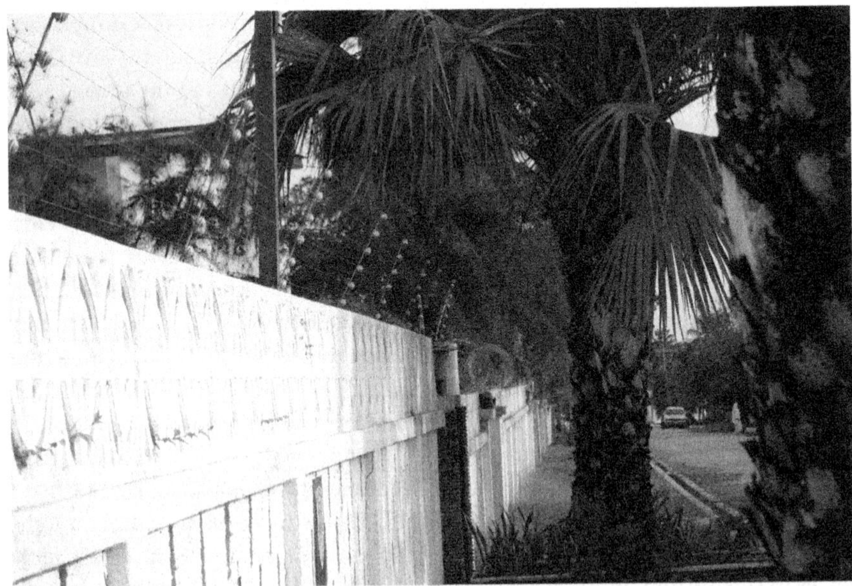

Figure 16.2. "Hear the standby generator? You mind electrocution?" Accra, Ghana. © Tejumola Olaniyan

Given the evident pervasiveness of the walled residence as a mode of life in urban Africa, it is surprising that it has not attracted much scholarly attention. To the field of African architecture scholarship, for instance, it would seem that the architecture worth studying is either traditional architecture, monuments of the postcolonial state such as museums, theaters, and so on, or arty experimental buildings or residences.[2] When residential housing in urban areas is discussed at all, it is most often about housing for the urban poor or the search for supposedly Africa-appropriate housing designs.[3] Sociologists and urban geographers, and a few cultural critics, have done much more in raising a host of issues of which garrison architecture is a small, but important part: urban crime, urban land use, gated communities, privatization of security, class segregation, wealth distribution, unemployment, policing, law and order, neighborhood associations, illegal street closures at night, nonstate spatial mechanisms, and so on.[4] Of recent, the distinguished Tanzanian-born British architect David Adjaye has been focusing on housing, but, of course, he is an architect and the emphasis of tantalizing titles such as Peter Allison's edited *David Adjaye: Houses* is still on arty and modernist designs.[5] The seven volumes in Adjaye's own massive *African Metropolitan Architecture* are incredibly useful in their photographs of houses and buildings in African cities, but their purpose is primarily visual documentary, and there are a score times more images than paragraphs of analyses in the volumes.[6]

I approach urban garrison architecture as an archive of knowledge and asking it what it can tell us about the nature and character of the state in postcolonial Africa. That question itself was catalyzed by my primary specialization, African literature, especially its constitutive world-famous, highly political character and relentless engagement with the postcolonial state. Portraying the increasingly sharper class distinctions in the postindependent nations also means portraying where and how the representatives of the different classes live and what that means for social, property, and power relations. To take a longer view is to see something even more interesting. Just compare Chinua Achebe's portrayals of African architecture at the turn of the twentieth century in his classic historical novels *Things Fall Apart* and *Arrow of God* with Chimamanda N. Adichie's portrayals for our own contemporary time in texts such *Purple Hibiscus* and *Half of a Yellow Sun*.[7] What one would get is a portable, suggestive look into the profound transformations in ways and modes of African living in the last one hundred-plus years—through the eyes of imaginative fiction, which not only complexly engages that reality but also offers suggestive understandings of it. Of course, studying urban garrison architecture has legitimacy all its own without reference to literary representations, but it is infinitely richer to draw from many sources—sociocultural forms and practices and disciplines—to understand the phenomenon.

For most African city residents today who may have bothered to give a thought at all to the fortresses of different kinds in which they live, garrison architecture is simply a response to the phenomenal increase in daring armed robberies in "recent times." No one worries exactly when the recent times began. Not that city residents should care too much about origins, for the safety and protection of life and property, which are said to be garrison architecture's main justifications, hold the status of philosophical good and are their own indubitable ends. But scholars need to produce deeper understanding. I suggest that urban garrison architecture emerged in part out of the conjunction of an expanding garish class inequality, the creation of a huge underclass in the sprawling ghettoes of the cities, and above all, the escalating ineffectiveness of the state in managing its exploding city population due to its weak and inadequate surveillance infrastructure and methods. The specific histories in particular countries may be different, but this is generally a post-1970s phenomenon in most African countries, even if the seeds of the explosion go further back. Garrison architecture—its incivility as a fortress right inside the city—it is clear, mirrors the wobbly and rudderless postcolonial state in Africa only too well, which itself began to unravel very shortly after independence.

I must say, though, that there is no need to overstate the rise of garrison architecture in postcolonial Africa, even if we could be excused for doing so. High-walled residences have been part of the landscape of African cities since the latter's emergence in antiquity, from Meroe in ancient Sudan to the Great Zimbabwe, just to mention two examples.[8] And for whatever central purpose or cluster of purposes such walls were built—ritual, ceremonial, refuge, commerce, industry—security was rarely outside the status of a constant. It was basic, primal; so it still is today. I want to make security, this constant, the link between then and now, even with the knowledge that security—its forms, processes, and meanings—changes over time and across space. The real task is in the more substantive differentiations to be made.

I have drawn a long line to the past, but I know that in precolonial Africa, from Harar in Ethiopia to Kano and Benin in Nigeria, we should be speaking, properly, of walled cities and palaces rather than walled residences of individuals or families, even if the latter may not be unheard of. Generally, precolonial high-walled residences were not the residences of wealthy persons but of this or that principality, king or emir. The catalyst for their construction was mostly the security of the chiefly person, and by metaphorical extension, the chiefly domain or kingdom. The structures protected individual lives and property, yes, but not as private selves and personal acquisitions but as core strands in the woven tapestry that secures and holds the community together. They embodied an investment of the collective—both implied and practically routinely affirmed—in their relative grandiosity in everyone's field of vision. Above all, the buildings were architecturally distinctive in conception and execution; in the plan, structure, location, as well as building materials, they were conceived more as monument than as general residence. That is why, very often, there was just only this one royal class act of its kind in town.[9]

We should be permitted, then, to see postcolonial garrison architecture as in a sense a democratization of the singular walled-up residence of old. But this is also saying that the postcolonial manifestation is in another category entirely. It belongs to an era of urbanization the like of which never existed before. The change is both quantitative and qualitative. In numbers, cities have become larger than ever. Very rare was the precolonial African city of two hundred, fifty thousand and above at any time in its existence before the twentieth century. Cairo, with over half a million people by 1900, was in a category all its own. At least from the seventeenth century, a population of five thousand was big and fifteen to thirty thousand, as we have in Segu and Timbuktu by the late eighteenth century, was really big, and rare. Special were the cases of Katsina, which approached nearly a hundred thousand at about the same time, and Ibadan, which was near a quarter of a million a century later. Compare all these to UN estimates for 2002 of over 235 African cities with a population of two hundred thousand or more, nearly a hundred of which are half a million and above. By 2016, the World Economic Forum had identified 528 African cities with a population of over two hundred, fifty thousand.[10] An "of course!" schematic way to interpret this development is to begin by agreeing that the steady rise in African population in general since 1900 means that the new bodies must be residing somewhere. Cities, as existing centers of attraction, were the main targets; citification, as the formation of more cities, was also a result. Having said all this, it is still important not to claim an automatic causal connection between higher population figures and runaway insecurity, the key justification for garrison architecture. The two are intimately linked, though.

As important as the quantitative dimension is the qualitative one: the characteristic dizzying diversity of postcolonial urban populations. Massed in the contemporary cities, metropoles, and conurbations is a population more diverse in every category—class, wealth, language, ethnicity, religion, age, profession/occupation, skill, status, goal and aspiration, worldview, allegiance—than ever before. And it is not just the sprawling categories of diversity to consider but also the hauntingly hierarchical relations between and among them. Such diversity is itself the result of profound transformations beginning markedly from the period I term the "age of the African masses"—the 1960s. Yes, this decade saw a dramatic rise in the number of political, regional, administrative, and commercial centers, but also a rise in mass education, mass information, mass transportation, and even mass health care. If we attach any positive valence to these at all, we would have to—even if grudgingly—acknowledge some of the good things the postcolonial African state has done since independence.

With the massed diversity in the cities also come new, different, and bigger challenges, not just in the management of population that is every state and every city authority's core task, but also in reimagining the very idea of authority itself. Conceptually, a city of any size could be difficult to manage and make lives insecure, leading to the necessity of residents to invent ways to protect themselves. Similarly, a large and diverse city need not automatically imply intractability in orderliness and policing, but there are certain and even linear connections between such size and diversity and the frequency of violations of whatever the reigning regime of the city's order is. So, yes, big precolonial African cities were diverse, but apart from the obvious point that they were far less so than cities of today, the critical fact is that their diversity was far easier to manage than today's. Take, for instance, the dominant pattern of spatial organization of the majority of precolonial African cities, governed as it was more by kinship and lineage structures and their hierarchies than by any preconceived abstract use of space. Space was not an empty lot occupied by anonymous entities. This is what the word "compound" tries to capture in describing the living pattern of many communities—a collection of houses, enclosed or open, in which nuclear and extended family members live. This arrangement obviously created and nourished bonds of kinship and is standardly given a positive valence in scholarship. That is not wrong, but the nourishment is also enforcement, and kinship bond itself is a vast and effective network of surveillance. The surveillance was productive and enabled order; it was able to do so particularly because it was (and still is) articulated in the psychologically stirring idiom of familial care. The spatial organization and the idiom of kinship care it engendered and was engendered by it were not closed to diversity—strangers, strange new things and ways. What they did well, in fact, was integrate and domesticate diversity, even if inchoately and incompletely. In the precolonial African city, the falcon heard and could loudly hear the falconer, by and large, to borrow a metaphor from the distinguished Irish poet William B. Yeats.

But we might say that the preceding narrative is of what we could call "autochthonous" or "aboriginal" cities as such, for want of a better term—that is, very old cities, whether primarily spiritual, political, or administrative, that evolved gradually over time with a more rather than less homogeneous population core, thereby firmly setting in place a specific cultural pattern of spatial arrangement that others coming later inevitably adapt to. We might then ask, what of defense cities that more often than not arose out of the hasty massing of very heterogeneous groups fleeing a region-wide war or catastrophe? This was particularly a major issue across much of Africa in the nineteenth century, from the Shaka wars in the south to the Fulani wars in the west. Ibadan in Nigeria is exemplary in this regard. It emerged in the late 1820s as a refuge from those fleeing the Fulani invasion of northern Oyo. Its hilly location made it most fitting for its defensive function.

The wars of the nineteenth century in the region pumped successive waves of refugees into the city, such that the population was nearly two hundred thousand by the 1890s, making Ibadan then the largest city in Africa south of the Sahara.[11] A roughly common language was shared in different dialects, but the population was far from homogeneous. In spite of that, the pattern of organization of space that evolved basically followed the pattern of kinship aggregations, but kinship by social relations—that is, social relations with this or that war leader or general or other significant powerful figure now replaced kinship by blood. In other words, a city founded on thoroughly secular social relations of affiliation borrowed a pattern of spatial organization that emerged in and is typical of contexts of sacred, blood-bonded relations of filiation that surrounded it. It was a grafting that resulted in reciprocal containment (the spatial arrangement and the operative kinship ideology), but unequally: what would have been the recalcitrant sprawl of the secular affiliative was, in effect, tamed by the sacred filiative and its typically affective idioms and protocols. The pattern of compounds of kins still survive in the older sections of the city today, though that would be virtually invisible to the outsider, given the lack of clear demarcations. This is perceptively captured in "Ibadan," a slightly idealized painting by Lekan Onabanjo of a lower-middle-class neighborhood, and "Rooftops of Ibadan, Nigeria," a 1951 photograph of the city by a British traveler (see figures 16.3 and 16.4).

Do not be deceived that the portrayed neighborhoods in both images look utterly unplanned; to invent a Yoruba proverb, every child knows its own mother's stall in the market. The economy of spatial organization represented here absolutely precludes the possibility of garrison architecture. It also shows that there is no social need for it.

Garrison architecture is simply nothing other than the product of a conception of space as empty and available for the inscription of standardized geometrical mappings for anonymous individuals who are also basically anonymous to one another. The dominant form if not the dominant aspiration everywhere in new developments since the 1970s seemed to be more or less rigidly intersecting straight streets carving up walled-up rigidly rectangular houses into blocks, even if "blocks" is not a commonly used term. I say "geometrical mappings" because one is almost always struck first by the shape and size and only secondarily by any curiosity about the occupants. This perception of a secondariness of human to property is apt; after all, the preeminent relational principle of the era and space of garrisoned homes is neither biological nor social kinship but private property—specifically of the most characteristically unruly kind. This is the reason the greatest enemy and nightmare of garrison architecture is none other than its identical twin, the slum. Kibera in Nairobi won the fiercely competitive lottery to be my example here (see figure 16.5).

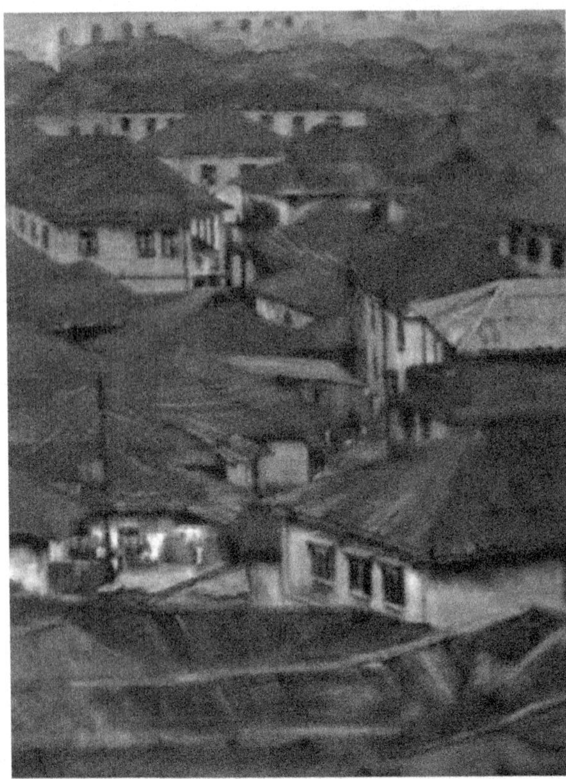

Figure 16.3. "Ibadan," by Lekan Onabanjo, circa 1980–1990s. © Lekan Onabanjo

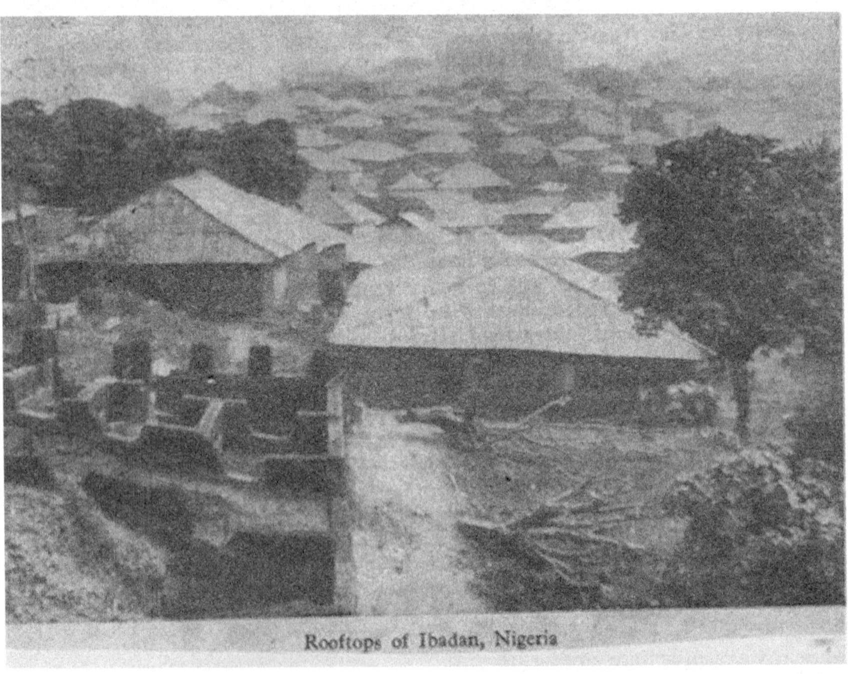

Figure 16.4. "Rooftops of Ibadan, Nigeria," 1951. © A Margaret Jefferies

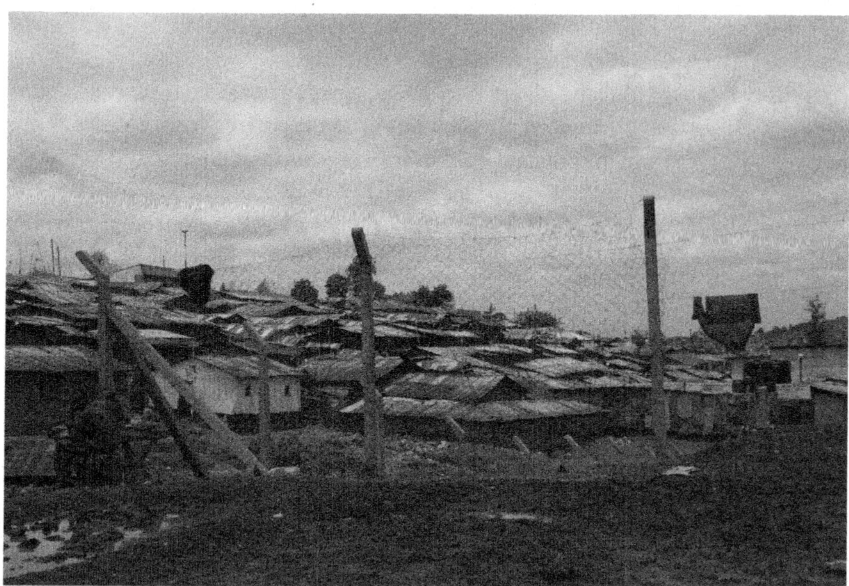

Figure 16.5. Kibera, the better part. Nairobi, Kenya. © Tejumola Olaniyan

Growth in private property went hand in hand with a whole array of other evolutions including in the structure of city authority, what counts as the law, how the law is to be enforced and by whom, the emergence of the single-family home and the distancing of the nuclear from the extended family, not to mention evolutions in psychological orientations occasioned by the new architectural and spatial arrangements. The heterogeneity of big postcolonial cities, anonymous relations, and protective high walls fit one another so well. To return to an image I invoked earlier, I would say that garrison architecture is the architecture par excellence of an age in which the falcon cannot hear the falconer.

I have named the central generative political economy of urban garrison architecture as "para-capitalism." It is related but parallel, a subsidiary to the dominant idea and practice of the thing it describes: abnormal, as in paranormal; functionally disordered, as in paramnesia. The nation, as substantive content, achievement, or aspiration, was a distinctive feature of neocolonialism; emptied or dispersed sovereignty is the handmaiden of para-capitalism. In the area of production, para-capitalism is basically and parasitically extractive and therefore not dependent on elaborate and functioning integrative infrastructure. Moreover, such production is subtended more by public funds than by the ingenuity of private enterprise such that the state, the government, is nothing but a maternity home for manufacturing millionaires, not through laws but through illegal private appropriation of public wealth—meaning that, in distribution of resources, para-capitalism is breathtakingly oligarchic.

"Lavish Life of Mugabe's Looter-in-Chief," reads a headline from the *Sunday Times* of December 21, 2008, written by Jon Swain reporting from Harare, Zimbabwe. The news, which was new only in its irony and not content, is that while "starving Zimbabweans face their bleakest Christmas ever, the head of the state bank put the last touches to his 47-bedroom palace."[12] The mansion also has "a glass swimming pool with underlights, a gym bigger than many good houses in the Zimbabwean capital, a mini-theatre and landscaped gardens." Gideon Gono, governor of the Reserve Bank of Zimbabwe, has, in truth, a civilized taste and excellent health habits.[13] Nobody knows the cost of the house except Gono himself, but that did not stop envious speculators and serious architects from citing millions of US dollars, more than enough to build and equip several primary schools. But the real and poignant news is that in spite of the typical security of the upscale suburb of Borrowdale where the mansion is located, and in spite of the security features houses there would typically have and which the mansion itself has, Gono, at completion time, was "not ready to move in just yet. Extra security sensors were recently installed on the outside perimeter and biometric iris recognition and finger print authentication systems were fitted in the interior, but he has yet to be convinced that it is entirely safe."[14] With an oligarchic mode of accumulation and distribution of social wealth, would the class of Gono ever be able to feel "entirely safe" in their urban garrisons?

In social reproduction, para-capitalism is characterized by the logic of reverse expectations: it is not just that there is growth without development, but also a progressive degradation rather than improvement in the quality of life for all, irrespective of class. Gono and his class may have all the money, but the para-capitalism they run will never free them from the uncalmable anxiety, not to mention the unachievable selfish goal, of being an "entirely safe" exploiter in a starving nation of the exploited.

Finally, and more immediate to my inquiry, para-capitalism is characterized by a systemic gulf between two things that are and should be closely related: security and surveillance. The para-capitalist state is incapable of *surveillance*, meaning the continuous, systematic, and need-not-be immediately goal-oriented observation and monitoring of the population. So, only the thematic and practice of *security*, which is the harried and goal-focused protection from immediate danger or injury—in all its (security) attendant rawness and violence—rule. In the absence of systematic surveillance, sorting of data, and noncrisis speculative protective action, the illusory and even delusional goal of every individual is an absolutely secure garrison for home. The postcolonial is part of the historical era of the "carceral," but its state management procedures belong to the spectacular crudity of the old age of the "scaffold."[15] This is the reason why, as we can see, not even the most sophisticated biometric iris recognition in the world could make Gono feel "entirely safe" in his garrison home. The postcolonial state in Africa, I declare, is a para-capitalist state.

Without question, the frame I have set up here is applicable to many postcolonial regions, and no one studying similar issues in Asia and Latin America, and some parts of Eastern Europe, for instance, would fail to find strong echoes of familiarity. In fact, even where the generative political economy is productive capitalist rather that para-capitalist, there are pockets of areas and neighborhoods to be found where, because of the extreme class disparities and the political power of the middle class to decide what it wants to be taxed for or not, garrison architecture reigns. Such is the case with the selected American suburbs studied by anthropologist Setha Low in *Behind the Gates: Life, Security, and the Pursuit of Happiness in Fortress America*.[16] What she could have made clearer are that (1) when all is said and done, that kind of fortress interpreted literally as wall is the exception rather than the rule in suburban America, and (2) the most muscular and most pervasive kind of garrison in America is not iron gates or walls but invisible bank accounts. America is a carceral society, distinguished by its systematic surveillance and ability to enforce some normality on a regime of unequal property relations with far less obvious violence. Consider Nigeria or South Africa as extreme opposite. Let us say you have a mere three-quarters of a million US dollars to spend on a house. The main features in the two posh residences, one in Lagos or Johannesburg—suburb or not—and the other in an American suburb, will be essentially the same; the immediately visible major difference will be that the one in Lagos or Johannesburg will be completely walled up and gated.

The impact of the garrison on the African creative mind has been enormous. Consider the rhetorical vigor and language-killing ellipses of this description by Nobel Laureate in Literature, Wole Soyinka in the preface to a play. The description is of 1970s Nigeria, but I take it as generic and continent-wide in application:

> *Opera Wonyosi* has been written at a high period of Nigeria's social decadence, the like of which will probably never again be experienced. The post civil-war years . . . has witnessed Nigeria's self-engorgement at the banquet of highway robberies, public executions, public floggings and other institutionalised sadisms, arsons, individual and mass megalomania, racketeering, hoarding, epidemic, road abuse and reckless slaughter, exhibitionism . . . callous and contemptuous ostentation, casual cruelties, wanton destruction, slummification, Nairamania and its attendant atavism (ritual murder for wealth); an orgy of physical filth . . . the near total collapse of human communication.[17]

It fits my purpose well that Soyinka began his open-ended laundry list with "highway robberies." What else can we expect from para-capitalism's skewed distribution mechanism if not an explosive rise in the ranks of those who insist

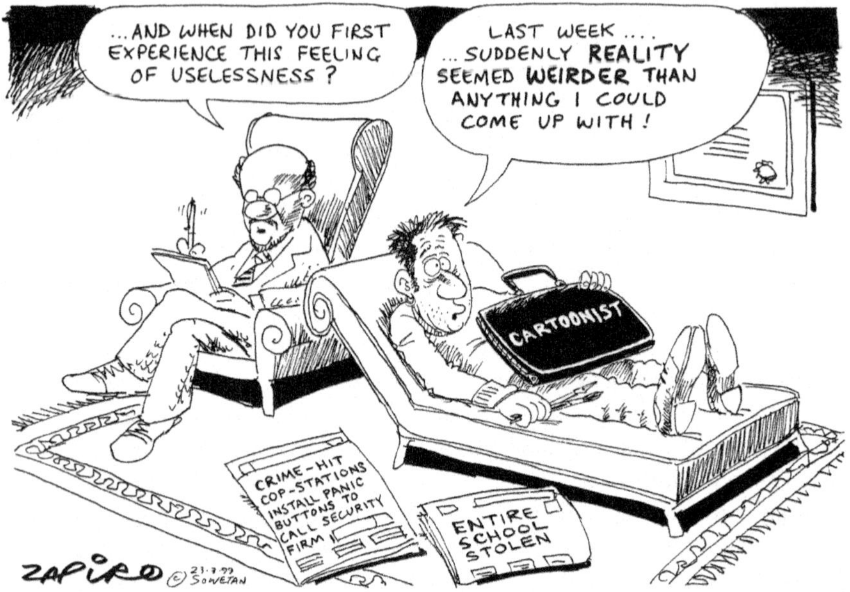

Figure 16.6. "Reality seemed weirder." *Sowetan*, January 23, 1999. © Zapiro

on forcefully sharing: armed robbers? Today, violent armed robbery is one of the central blights of postcolonial African cities. Even typically dauntless fictionalists are utterly defeated by reality; "stranger than fiction" is the new reality. "Reality seemed weirder" (figure 16.6) is the submission by Zapiro, the continent's leading cartoonist, in this editorial cartoon. The blight has transformed all work and leisure routines, making life unsafe, whether day or night. The many modern civil wars in the first half of the last century have served as important catalysts, making sophisticated firearms more widely accessible than at any time in the history of Africa.

The generic nature of the preceding narrative across much of Africa is best illustrated by considering South Africa, usually taken by scholars as different on so many matters. The trajectory of its case is merely longer, however, and not intrinsically different. The political economy and social engineering of an intensive colonial, racial capitalism that, from the first half of the twentieth century, forcefully proletarianized, disenfranchised, and ghettoized Africans, is a story more than less well known.[18] And what more poignant way to capture its familiar problematic than to invoke another distinguished African writer, Alan Paton (1903–1988)? In 1945 he published a short essay titled "Who Is Really to Blame for the Crime Wave in South Africa?"[19] He saw the crime wave then as unprecedented and suggested two ways of understanding it. The first is the usual breakdown of order typical of postwar societies everywhere—he's referencing World War II. He dismissed that out of hand and gave his preferred answer: "the disintegration of a native society beyond the safety point" by "our Western civilization."[20] This is truly suggestive, though Paton never specified what "the safety point" of "disintegration" the native society could take beyond which calamity resides. And does it mean that the "disintegration" of native society by "our Western civilization" was fine and could continue so long as it did not exceed "the safety point"?

To muddy his own interpretations further, Paton read the crime issue as one of civilizational differences between Africans and Europeans; the perpetrators are mostly African, after all. The "safety point" is determined by the white lawful authorities, and that point marks the limit of their capacity to handle the disintegration of the colonized society. Effectively, the disintegration can continue so long as the authorities are able to contain it so it does not lead to an unstoppable crime wave against white persons and property. The central effect of the disintegration, he said, is "moral and spiritual decay," hence so much crime and violation of the law. We may not agree with Paton's conceptual handle, but we certainly cannot fail to appreciate his keen sociological insights. "This decay of home life," he wrote, "was accelerated by overcrowding, the growth of slums, the increase of drinking, the lowness of wages; it decayed in the reserves, too, where men did not come back, and where women went away to look for them and often found someone else."[21] And the solution to the problem? "Moral and spiritual decay can be stopped only by moral and spiritual means—by education, by work, by opportunity, by creating conditions in which self-respect and decency and morality may grow again."[22] Ever the clear-eyed pragmatist, Paton suspected that even this, his oblique implication of apartheid's structural constraints—"education . . . work . . . opportunity"—would be too much for the majority of whites to swallow. So he thought of solutions "all may agree" on; with a few slight alterations, the solutions could have been offered by a conscientious official in today's Accra, Cairo, Nairobi, Lagos, Kampala, Harare, or Yaounde:

> more police, more non-European police, more pay for police, up-to-date equipment for police; the relatively swift and final segregation of dangerous offenders (in this regard the decision to refer most robbery cases to the Supreme Court is the utmost importance); greater precautions by householders; provisions of greater security by builders of houses.[23]

One cannot read Paton's essay today and not be struck anew by that altruistic hypocrisy of a classic, historically specific kind of South African white liberalism: a profound insight into the damages of apartheid on black South Africa, but also an inexhaustible capacity to find unending moral or pragmatic accommodations to that apartheid. In this sense, that liberalism's waterloo in 1948 was too long in coming. But the real significance of Paton's essay for me is that, with a fair degree of accuracy, we could name him as one of the earliest theorists of urban garrison architecture in Africa.

That was 1945. Fast-forward more than half a century later to 1998, to the worldwide headlines that explained "Why I'm Fleeing South Africa," by Anne Paton, Alan's widow. She was fleeing "because crime is rampaging through the land."[24] We can get a meaningful sense of what had happened in the intervening fifty-three years if we do a comparative literary study of metaphors. Her husband's choice, "wave," is almost wholly aesthetic, soothing even as it intimates danger. We know the ocean wave is dangerous, but there is also something beautiful and curious about it that makes one want to tarry a moment and see it. To hear "rampage," however, is to instantly dive for the bunker! Things have gotten infinitely more dangerous and more uncontrollable by the powers that be. Her views, otherwise, matched her husband's in the impeccable old mixture of acknowledgment of social inequities and, as solution, the invocation of morality—"hearts," "loving," "hating"—and tougher government maintenance of law and order: "The government needs to get its priorities right. We need a powerful, well-trained and well-equipped police force."[25] All of which gives a fresh new meaning to that phrase that Anne Paton knew too well, *Cry, the Beloved Country*, the title of her husband's most famous novel published in the same year as his essay.

I do not want to end this exploration on an elegiac note. Garrison architecture has assumed the status of a commonsense and has moved from the cities to even the villages. It is important to underscore how productive the cultural form has been. It has led to not just the explosion of security business services and the manufacturing of steel gates and doors but also the rise of cottage industries for the beautification of the garrison, such as artistic decoration of gates, whether metalwork or painting, painting on walls, and of horticulture. Figures 16.7–16.9 are examples of such productivity from Dar es Salaam and Lagos.

On the business of horticulture, I was thoroughly seduced by the young Kambili's description of her fortress house in Adichie's critically acclaimed novel, *Purple Hibiscus*:

> Our yard was wide enough to hold a hundred people dancing atilogu, spacious enough for each dancer to do the usual somersaults and land on the next dancer's shoulders. The compound walls, topped by coiled electric wires, were so high I could not see the cars driving by on our street. It was early rainy season, and the frangipani trees planted next to the walls already filled the yard with the sickly-sweet smell of their flowers. A row of purple bougainvillea, cut smooth and straight as a buffet table. . . .[26]

I salivated and swooned. But for the fact that I hate any "sickly-sweet smell," which the author insistently invoked again toward the end—this time upping the ante and using the puke word, "nauseated"—I could have taken this gated

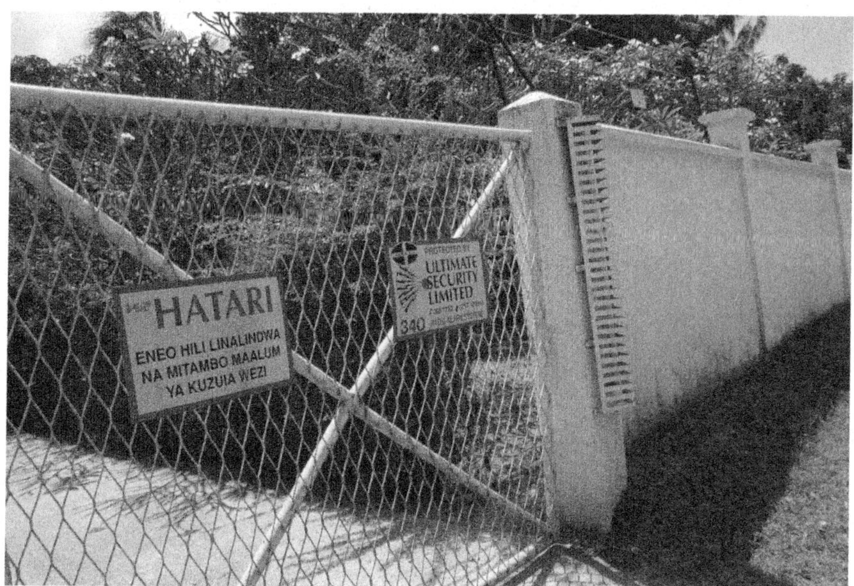

Figure 16.7. Security. It's ultimate but limited. Dar es Salaam, Tanzania. © Tejumola Olaniyan

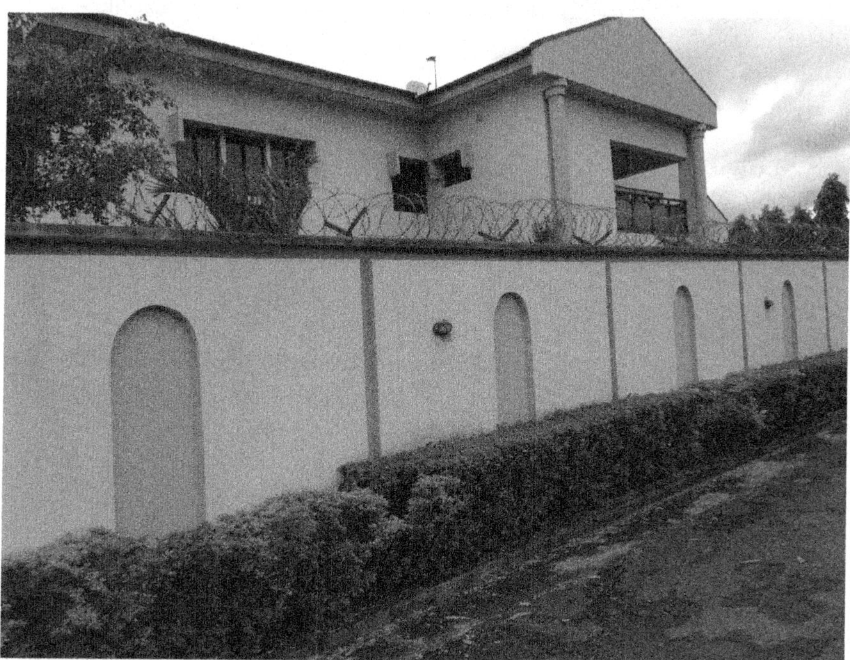

Figure 16.8. Leafy, smoothly horticultured, and safe. Lagos, Nigeria. © Tejumola Olaniyan

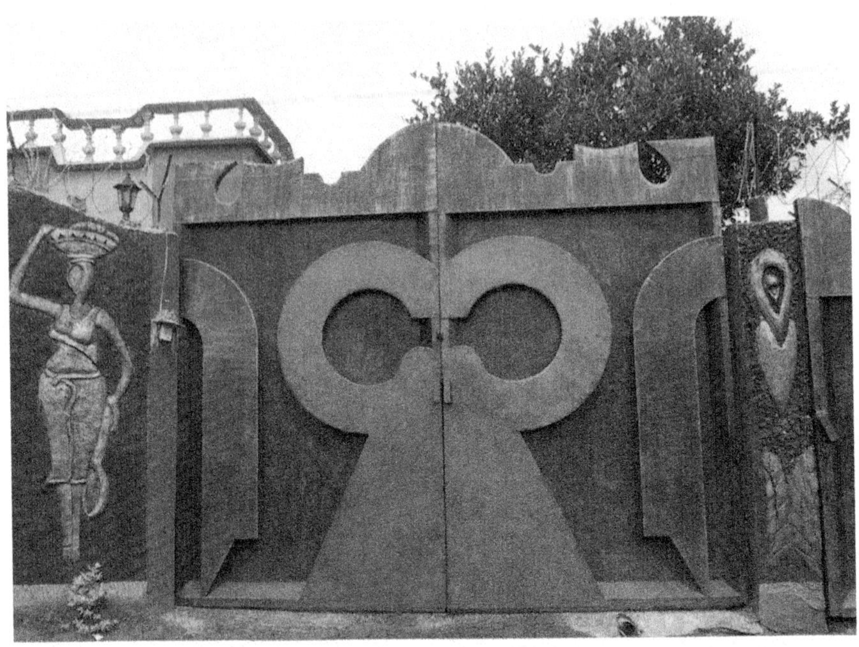

Figure 16.9. Security is *key*, and beautiful! Lagos, Nigeria. "Gates" series. © Nmadili N. Okwumabua

compound for a paradise.[27] So, I guess I must thank Adichie for so sweetly and doggedly puncturing any illusion I might have of a blissful, "entirely safe" garrisoned home amid the bountiful want of the majority in the postcolonial African city, no matter the bank-full of money I might, like Kambili's father, Eugene Achike—or Gono—have.

TEJUMOLA OLANIYAN is Louise Durham Mead Professor of English and African Cultural Studies at the University of Wisconsin, Madison. He is author of *Arrest the Music! Fela and His Rebel Art and Politics* and *Scars of Conquest.*

Notes

Regarding my title, I prefer "garrison architecture" over similar terms such as "fortress architecture" or "architecture of fear." The former has a too-old and too-affirmative resonance in art history, and the latter rushes too quickly to judgment in a moralistic way. "Garrison" has an unnerving edge that is so apt in its evocation of barracks, militarism, and authoritarianism that have marked the last half-century Africa in which garrison architecture became a common social practice and cultural form. This is an excerpt from a book in progress, *African Urban Garrison Architecture: Property, Armed Robbery, Para-capitalism.*

1. "Large Detached 2-Storey Family House," *Viviun*, http://www.viviun.com/AD-198064/ (accessed June 21, 2014).

2. See, for some examples, Nnamdi Elleh, *African Architecture: Evolution and Transformation* (New York: McGraw-Hill, 1997); Nnamdi Elleh, *Architecture and Power in Africa* (New York: Praeger, 2003); Janet Berry Hess, *Art and Architecture in Postcolonial Africa* (Jefferson, NC: McFarland, 2006); Udo Kulterman, *New Directions in African Architecture* (New York: G. Braziller, 1969); Suzanne Preston Blier, *The Anatomy of Architecture: Ontology and Metaphor in Batammaliba Architectural Expression* (Chicago: University of Chicago Press, 1987); Thorsten Deckler, Anne Graupner, and Henning Rasmuss, *Contemporary South African Architecture in a Landscape of Transition* (Lansdowne, South Africa: Double Storey Books, 2006); Anthony Folkers, *Modern Architecture in Africa* (Amsterdam: Sun Architecture, 2010); Andres Lepik, ed., *Afritecture: Building Social Change* (Berlin: Hatje Cantz, 2014); and Manuel Herz, ed., *African Modernism: The Architecture of Independence: Ghana, Senegal, Côte d'Ivoire, Kenya, Zambia* (Zurich: Park Books, 2015).

3. See Ambe J. Njoh, *Urban Planning, Housing and Spatial Structures in Sub-Saharan Africa: Nature, Impact and Development Implications of Exogenous Forces* (London: Ashgate, 1999); and Leah Libsekal, "Toponomic Urbanism: Bumbogo, Designing a Uniquely Rwandan Urban Morphology," *Another Africa*, August 12, 2012, http://www.anotherafrica.net/design/architecture/toponomic-urbanism-bumbogo-designing-a-uniquely-rwandan-urban-morphology.

4. See Tunde Agbola, *The Architecture of Fear: Urban Design and Construction Response to Urban Violence in Lagos, Nigeria* (Ibadan, Nigeria: IFRA, 1997); and Garth Meyers, *African Cities: Alternative Visions of Urban Theory and Practice* (London: Zed, 2011). See also Ato Quayson, *Oxford Street, Accra: City Life and the Itineraries of Transnationalism* (Durham, NC: Duke University Press, 2014).

5. Peter Allison, ed, *David Adjaye: Houses* (London: Thames and Hudson, 2006).

6. David Adjaye, *African Metropolitan Architecture* (New York: Rizzoli, 2011).

7. Chinua Achebe, *Things Fall Apart* (London: Heinemann, 1958); Chinua Achebe, *Arrow of God* (London: Heinemann, 1964); Chimamanda Ngozi Adichie, *Purple Hibiscus* (New York: Anchor, 2003); and Chimamanda Ngozi Adichie, *Half of a Yellow Sun* (New York: Anchor, 2007).

8. Richard W. Hull, *African Cities and Towns Before the European Conquest* (New York: Norton, 1976); Graham Connah, "African City Walls: A Neglected Source?" *African Urban Past*, ed. David M. Anderson and Richard Rathbone (London: James Currey, 2000), 36–51; D. James Tracy, *City Walls: The Urban Enceinte in Global Perspective* (Minneapolis: University of Minnesota Press, 2000).

9. The extreme vulgarization of this ideal for our modern times is the nearly twenty-three-million-dollar upgrade to the homestead of President Jacob Zuma of South Africa, at taxpayer expense. For more on "Nkandlagate," see "Report by the Minister of Police to Parliament on Security Upgrades at the Nkandla Private Residence of the President," *South African Government*, May 28, 2015, http://www.gov.za/speeches/report-minister-police-parliament-security-upgrades-nkandla-private-residence-president-28; and Phillip de Wet, "What Your Money Bought at Nkandla," *Mail & Guardian*, July 29, 2015, http://mg.co.za/article/2015-07-29-what-your-money-bought-at-nkandla.

10. See Hull, *African Cities*, xiii–xxi, 1–29; Rhett Butler, "Cities and Urban Areas in Africa with Population Over 100,000, Sorted by City Population," *Mongabay.com*, 2003, http://data.mongabay.com/igapo/Africa_cities.htm; David Kilcullen and Robert Muggah, "These Are

Africa's Fastest-growing Cities—And They'll Make or Break the Continent," *World Economic Forum*, May 4, 2016, https://www.weforum.org/agenda/2016/05/africa-biggest-cities-fragility/; and Mahmoud Yousry and Tarek A. Aboul Atta, "The Challenge of Urban Growth in Cairo," in *The Urban Challenge in Africa: Growth and Management of Its Large Cities*, ed. Carole Rakodi (New York: United Nations University Press, 1997), http://archive.unu.edu/unupress/unupbooks/uu26ue/uu26ue00.htm.

11. See J. F. A. Ajayi and R. Smith, *Yoruba Warfare in the Nineteenth Century*, 2nd ed. (Ibadan, Nigeria: Ibadan University Press, 1971).

12. Jon Swain, "Lavish Life of Mugabe's Looter-in-Chief," *Sunday Times*, December 21, 2008. http://www.thesundaytimes.co.uk/sto/news/world_news/article139112.ece.

13. Ibid.

14. Ibid.

15. Michel Foucault, *Discipline and Punish: The Birth of the Prison*, trans. Alan Sheridan (New York: Vintage Books, 1979).

16. Setha Low, *Behind the Gates: Life, Security, and the Pursuit of Happiness in Fortress America* (New York: Routledge, 2003).

17. Wole Soyinka, *Opera Wonyosi*, production script, 1977, typescript. When the play was subsequently published in 1981 in London by Rex Collings, the preface had given way to a polemical foreword directed at critics who challenged the play's unrelievingly somber vision of the postcolony. Wole Soyinka, *Opera Wonyosi* (London: Rex Collings, 1981).

18. Harold Wolpe, "Capitalism and Cheap Labour-power in South Africa: From Segregation to Apartheid," *Economy and Society* 1, no. 4 (1972): 424–456; Michael Burawoy, "The Capitalist State in South Africa: Marxist and Sociological Perspectives on Race and Class," *Political Power and Social Theory* 2 (1981): 279–335; Bernard M. Magubane, *The Political Economy of Race and Class in South Africa* (New York: Monthly Review, 1979); and Sampie Terreblanche, *A History of Inequality in South Africa 1652–2002* (Scottsville, South Africa: University of KwaZulu-Natal Press, 2002).

19. Alan Paton, "Who Is Really to Blame for the Crime Wave in South Africa," *The Forum* 8, no. 37 (1945): 7–8.

20. Quoted in "Cry the Beloved Country," *Cliffnotes.com*, https://www.cliffsnotes.com/literature/c/cry-the-beloved-country/critical-essays/alan-patons-who-is-really-to-blame-for-the-crime-wave-in-south-africa.

21. Ibid.

22. Ibid.

23. Ibid.

24. Anne Paton, "Why I'm Fleeing South Africa," *London Sunday Times*, November 29, 1998, *OurCivilization.com*, http://www.ourcivilisation.com/cry.htm.

25. Ibid.

26. Adichie, *Purple Hibiscus*, 9.

27. Ibid., 253. I also hate "vomits."

Index

CPSIA information can be obtained
at www.ICGtesting.com
Printed in the USA
BVOW06s1000041017
496726BV00017B/227/P

9 780253 029980